SOCIAL RESEARCH

strategy and tactics

SOCIAL RESEARCH

strategy and tactics

SOCIAL

Bernard S. Phillips
BOSTON UNIVERSITY

RESEARCH
strategy and tactics

SECOND EDITION

The Macmillan Company *New York*
Collier-Macmillan Limited   London

To those imaginative souls who are creating
the scientific methods of the future.

Preface to
the Second Edition

The past five years have witnessed a revolution in methodology, with many of the old certainties disappearing and few new ones to take their place. Not so long ago few researchers wondered about their impact on their subjects, the ideals of scientific objectivity and value neutrality were rarely questioned, social scientists hardly ever probed to uncover the assumptions on which their theories and methods rested, the utilization of more complex statistical tools was automatically equated with progress, ethical questions about the relationship between the social scientist and his granting agency were quite infrequent, and an examination of alternative futures via the medium of science fiction would have been viewed as a kind of mental aberration.

Viewing these changes in relation to their societal context, we see that the crumbling of methodological certainties is only part of a more general spectacle in which the key values of industrial society are being challenged. What people are questioning, among other things, is whether economic and technological progress also implies human development, or whether it is leading us toward destruction. Such questions have not come easily. It has taken depressions and wars, the exposure of racial injustice and dehumanizing poverty, the uncovering of alienation and mental illness, the poisoning of the physical environment and the threat of overpopulation, the discovery of the overpowering sickness within our educational institutions, and, in general, the sickness in society as a whole. Social scientists find themselves in the midst of accelerating problems which threaten man's development as well as his very existence.

The need for effective knowledge of human behavior is now more urgent than ever. The changes within social science in general and methodology in particular represent a response to this situation. Yet the results thus far produced by the sum of traditional and nontraditional social science can still, as of this writing, come under severe criticism. We agree with the following indictment:

> . . . Measured against the needs of the times there is nothing remotely resembling a science of man: there are only mountains of disciplinary journals, and hordes of busy specialists; what is their effectiveness in relation to the momentous problems of survival and human dignity in our time? To ask the question is already to answer it: taken separately, most of the disciplinary activity in the social sciences

represents trivial work. True, it is hard-working, certainly well-intentioned, at times deeply hopeful and anxious—but still somehow very much beside the point of the problems of man in contemporary society.[1]

How shall we make progress on this problem, attaining results that are significant with respect to both understanding and predicting of results that are also socially useful? I submit that the very way in which we have stated this question erects a barrier to solving the problem. In Western society we tend to be prisoners of the Aristotelian dichotomy, whether it be mind–body and good–evil, or truth–falsity, significant–insignificant, scientific–unscientific, quantitative–qualitative, objective–subjective, theory–method. By classifying ourselves in one category of a dichotomy we miss out on learning much about the value for us of the other category, adopt a rather static stance with respect to our own position as well as that of others, and fail to look for a path which could help us to develop beyond the partial truths contained in each of the categories.

This dichotomous orientation is an instance of a general approach to classification in which a set of supposedly distinct categories (for example, sociology, psychology, anthropology, political science, economics, history) are created. Such categories are far from useless. They help us to emphasize distinctions to which we would otherwise pay little attention. They are nominal scales and, as such, promote the organization of ideas. Yet they carry us only a limited distance, because they lack the power to integrate information that is characteristic of scales incorporating the ordinal, interval, and ratio properties of numbers.

Under certain conditions it would be unnecessary to go beyond a dichotomous or categorical approach. Suppose that phenomena are not in fact intertwined and interrelated, and that the universe is quite static. Then a series of mutually exclusive categories might indeed tell us a great deal about the world. But assume instead a universe of "open systems," with all phenomena interrelated and all systems in flux. Under such conditions it would be important to conceive of common dimensions along which the various categories lie so that we would be able to understand the significance of multiple categories applying to a given situation. We would want to move beyond simply categorical thinking in order to integrate the information presented by the multiple categories.

For this second edition of *Social Research* I emphasize the importance of moving beyond nominal scales, and I make the open-systems assumption explicitly, an assumption that was implicit in a good portion of the first edition. In that edition two guiding orientations were that theory constitutes the most important research tool available to the scientist and that research methods may be conceived of as strategies and tactics

---

[1] Ernest Becker, *The Structure of Evil: An Essay on the Unification of the Sciences of Man* (New York: Braziller, 1968), p. x.

adopted by a community of scientists. Such an emphasis on theory and on the community of scientists may be carried further by means of this open-systems assumption.

If we conceive of theory as an integration of ideas with ideas as well as of ideas with experiences, then theory becomes more meaningful and useful to the degree that it reaches out to a widening range of ideas and experiences. The open-systems orientation tends to point the investigator outward both in space and time. He must be sufficiently alert to multiple factors operating on the research situation, and he must acquaint himself with the time sequence involved. Although theory is an important scientific tool, not all scientific theories are equally useful. I submit that theory is implicit within methodology, and that, given the universe we live in, the kind of theory that provides the most useful basis for constructing methodology is theory consistent with the open-systems assumption.

Referring to the previous emphasis on the community of scientists, once again I believe that an explicit emphasis on an open-systems orientation carries the idea further. The idea of a community of scientists brings to bear the dynamic of social processes on the area of methodology, with methodology no longer standing apart from social science and providing the latter with its eternal verities. The processes of verification and discovery are social processes, in addition to whatever else they are, and by viewing them in this light we are able to bring to bear on them whatever knowledge the social sciences have thus far constructed.

Part One, "The Research Process," includes an expanded Chapter 1, in which methodology is related to a number of literatures (general systems theory, cybernetics, symbolic interactionism, game theory, the sociology of knowledge, the sociology of science, and social technology), a Chapter 2 which incorporates the paradigm with the other fundamental tools of inquiry, and a Chapter 3 which attempts to point the researcher in a direction enabling him to see far beyond where he presently is.

Part Two, "Data Collection," brings together the various categories that the researcher uses to describe what he is doing—experiment, survey, use of documents, observation, simulation—within a unitary framework where any mode of collecting data is seen as having both experimental and observational aspects. Special attention is paid to the phenomenon of investigator effect, with an attempt to explore its quite radical implications for methodology. The chapter on simulation is expanded so as to include a detailed example of computer simulation.

Part Three, "Measurement and Scaling," has been left largely unchanged aside from updating. At the time of the first edition developments in the direction of ratio scaling already had become apparent and were incorporated into the text. If my own opinion is taken as some evidence for a relative lack of rapid change in this aspect of methodology, perhaps this is an indication that certain other aspects of methodology, such as theory, must be carried further before much more can be done with measurement.

This represents a systems approach to the field of methodology, where changes in any one element of the system are dependent on changes in other elements.

Parts Four and Five, "Analysis of Data" and "Applications of Logic and Mathematics," carry forward the open-systems approach to the analysis of data and to model building. Accepting the importance of widely used models of investigating relationships among variables, the text also alerts the reader to a number of static implications and a lack of concern for context which these methods tend to incorporate. The open-systems assumption implies the universality of feedback relationships, whether direct or indirect. At the same time that we use tools which do not take this implication seriously, we might well be aware of their limitations and search for new modes of analysis.

One such mode is that which can be achieved with the aid of computer simulation. In the last section of the final chapter, I attempt to develop several parallel ways of structuring an open-systems approach (for example, a set of axioms, a piece of science fiction, an approach to computer simulation, a way of constructing reality). The discussion centers on a paradigm which, instead of closing off the development of theory within a fixed model, encourages the continual development of improved models.

I would like to acknowledge a widening number of individuals who have influenced my thinking, exemplified by those cited in the text. Special mention should be made of the work of Jay W. Forrester for its dynamic and systems-oriented approach to computer simulation and of Alfred Korzybski for his "head simulation" of a null-A (non-Aristotelian) world. Each of these individuals has in his own way suggested methodologies based on the open-systems assumption. My students at Boston University and at Florida State University also have helped me to step into a null-A world of methodology, most notably Bob Childs, Dave Dillon, Grace Garner, Jan Kreitzer, Bill Leong, Mike Masiello, Glenn Odenbrett, Bob Paul, Charlie Rose, Barry Shain, Christie Stiegman, Dave Stratman, and Matt Zelman.

B. S. P.

Preface to
the First Edition

There are two fundamental conceptions which form the basis for the ideas presented in this volume: that theory constitutes the most important research tool available to the scientist, and that research methods may be fruitfully conceived of as strategies and tactics adopted by a community of scientists.

It has long been acknowledged by behavioral scientists that theory and method should be integrally related, but efforts in this direction have been few. In this volume I try to contribute toward this end within the context of a presentation of the standard topics in a basic course on research methods. After a discussion of the elements of theory and a variety of research strategies, theory is utilized to explore the topics of data collection, measurement, the analysis of data, and the development of formal models. The approach taken is the use of theory as a tool for obtaining an understanding of the measurement situation itself as well as what goes on outside of it.

The conception of a community of scientists who are communicating with one another in an effort to explain and predict phenomena serves to provide a dynamic view of the research process. From this perspective the choices that each investigator makes may be evaluated in terms of how effectively they aid this community in reaching the goals of science. This principle will serve to liberate the investigator from undue reverence for any particular method. It will encourage him to make maximal use of his knowledge of the particular research situation facing him and to develop and rely on his own ideas.

I have developed one of the research illustrations in considerable detail and used it to help provide continuity throughout the volume. It is held up not as a model of ideal research procedure, but rather as a realistic picture of a series of choice situations in which the researcher finds himself, uncertain that his decisions will prove to be correct. Regardless of this lack of certainty, however, there exist various criteria for decision making which have served as useful guides for many researchers, and these are elaborated.

I have attempted to combine in this volume a treatment of both strategy and tactics. Broad orientations can be most effective when their detailed implications for research decisions are spelled out. Thus, for example, the special problems and techniques involved in experimentation, interviewing, observation, the use of documents, and simulation must be taken up, as well as some of the flavor and culture of methodology. Moreover, such information does not constitute mere elaboration. It is within the context of such particulars that the fundamental mechanisms of the research process are most clearly seen.

In Part One, "Theory and Method," a number of ideas selected from the philosophy of science are used to provide an introduction to the nature of theory and the dynamics of its construction. Part Two, "Data Collection," covers a wide range of quantitative and qualitative procedures. The aim of Part Three, "Measurement and Scaling," is to combine a portrayal of the axiomatic basis for measurement and scaling with descriptions of scaling procedures. The emphasis in Part Four, "Analysis of Data," is on integration of some core ideas from statistics within a more general analytical framework. Part Five, "Applications of Logic and Mathematics," is designed to introduce the reader to a field of growing importance in social science.

For their influence on the development of my ideas on the philosophy of science as well as the sociology of science, I owe a great intellectual debt to Abraham Kaplan, C. Wright Mills, Sidney Rome, Wesley Salmon, and Marx Wartofsky. My actual experiences in social research were made more meaningful to me in large measure as a result of my association with Kurt Back, Joel Montague, Edward Suchman, and Robin Williams. I would also like to acknowledge the aid which resulted from a critical reading of the first draft by Marx Wartofsky.

B. S. P.

CONTENTS

part one   **THE**
RESEARCH PROCESS

Sigmund Koch, in reviewing some of his findings based on a seven-volume study attempting to assess the facts, theories, and methods of psychology,[1] concludes

> . . . the massive 100-year effort to erect a discipline given to the positive study of man can hardly be counted a triumph. Here and there the effort has turned up a germane fact, or thrown off a spark of insight, but these victories have had an accidental relation to the programs believed to inspire them, and their sum total over time is heavily overbalanced by the pseudo-knowledge that has proliferated.[2]

According to Koch, a syndrome in modern scholarship that is in large measure responsible for this situation is "ameaningful thinking," involving a certain stance with respect to the scientific method: "Ameaningful thought or inquiry regards knowledge as the result of 'processing' rather than discovery. It presumes that knowledge is an almost automatic result of a gimmickry, an assembly line, a methodology."[3]

*   We agree with Koch's generally negative evaluation both of the knowledge that psychology has produced and the methods used to produce it, and we would extend this evaluation to the other behavioral sciences. As the basis for such an assessment we have in mind both the over-all failure of these sciences cumulatively to develop more comprehensive explanations and accurate predictions during the past century and the lack of development of incrementally*

---

[1] Sigmund Koch (ed.), *Psychology: A Study of a Science,* Vols. 1–7 (New York: McGraw-Hill, 1959).

[2] Sigmund Koch, "Psychology Cannot Be a Coherent Science," *Psychology Today,* **14** (1969), 64.

[3] Ibid.

more effective social technologies for dealing with important societal problems.

Yet if something is deeply, perhaps even desperately, wrong with the behavioral sciences, it remains to specify what that something is. In our view it is not an interest in a rigorous, quantitative science which seeks to obtain evidence for assessing conjectures and speculations. Nor is it a deep desire for a creative and humanistic science, one which encourages imaginative speculation and attempts to solve the larger problems of society. Rather, it is the lack of a broad, synthetic approach to the scientific method, one that is sufficiently inclusive to encompass the development of a rigorous and quantitative science that is also creative and humanistic.

In Part One we set forth a synthetic view of the research process. Its broad outline is sketched in Chapter 1, where we find ourselves drawing from a number of related literatures: general systems theory, cybernetics, symbolic interactionism, game theory, the sociology of knowledge, the sociology of science, and social technology. In Chapter 2 we describe the key elements used in the research process, including implicit as well as explicit factors. Chapter 3 treats the scientific method as a process encompassing discovery as well as justification, and human purposes along with particular techniques.

CHAPTER 1 A Frame of Reference Outlined and Illustrated

Every description of research methods, whether of a very specific technique or of a very general orientation to the scientific method, carries with it a theoretical approach to science and society. The choice of the methodologist is not whether to include or exclude this implicit theory but rather whether to leave his theoretical assumptions at the covert level or to attempt to bring them to the surface. We choose the latter alternative. Thus, our outline of a frame of reference will be both theoretical and methodological.

The research illustration (Section 1.2), chosen from our own work, reflects the type of investigation most prevalent in social science, the kind which focuses on justification or verification as distinct from discovery and applications. By evaluating this illustration (Section 1.3) from the perspective of our frame of reference, we hope to give the reader insight into the current situation of the social sciences as well as to chart the course that social science research appears to be taking.

1.1 OUTLINE OF THE FRAME OF REFERENCE

The scientific method is a triple synthesis: of concepts or ideas with other concepts or ideas, of ideas with experience, and of experience with experience. Science integrates the experience of one scientist with that of another by means of a symbolic process. Symbols are understood by scientists in a given discipline as having certain referents in experience; that is, ideas are linked to experience. Furthermore, these symbols are linked to one another in such forms as scientific theories or propositions, which are systematic unions of concepts with one another. Thus, through scientific communication one experience is linked to another via the indirect circuitry of symbols tied to experience as well as to one another.

Examining this triple synthesis from an evolutionary perspective, we may note the importance of symbolic abilities as a basis for the indirect circuitry described above. These abilities themselves constitute a highly developed means for an organism to alter itself on the basis of its experience. The plant, for example, also alters itself on the basis of experience whenever it directs its roots toward a source of water. However, the human's plasticity—especially that resulting from his great brain capacity—

far exceeds that of the plant, and the result is the human's far greater capacity and ability to adapt to or control his environment.

If we use this evolutionary perspective to extrapolate into the future, we might expect increasing ability to represent experience symbolically, to interrelate these symbolic representations, and thus to synthesize human experience. There appears to be no end point to such a continuing development. There are an infinite number of points in time corresponding to past experience and an infinite number corresponding to future experience, with science addressing itself to the task of integrating these experiences. Spatially, for any given point in time there are an infinite number of events occurring, and the exploration of their interrelationships is one of the tasks of science.

The preceding view of science and the scientific method derives in part from ideas associated with general systems theory, cybernetics, symbolic interactionism, game theory, the sociology of knowledge, the sociology of science, and social technology. Taken together, they reveal an information-flow approach to science. They also imply a future for science with infinite possibilities for further development, one based on an increasing unity among the various disciplines as well as a widening time perspective which also becomes more and more detailed. We shall proceed in this section to construct an outline of the research process by taking up relevant ideas from these seven literatures.

GENERAL SYSTEMS THEORY

A key concept from general systems theory[1] is that of "system." A system is simply a set or collection of elements or factors wherein certain relationships among the elements exist. Indeed, any collection of elements whatsoever may be treated as a system; for example, the birth of Alfred North Whitehead, today's rainfall in Peking, and the death of the sun. These elements are related in various ways; for example, all have to do with events in our own solar system, all are events not occurring during the first 4 billion years of the evolution of this solar system. Yet such systems are not utilized by scientists because they are not very useful to them. An apparently useful concept is that of the social system, where the elements may be defined, for example, as values, norms, and patterns of action. It seems useful to conceive of four general types of systems: physical, biological, personality, and social. The rainfall in Peking and the death of the sun are events within physical systems, whereas the birth of Alfred North Whitehead refers most directly to biological systems. White-

[1] The vast and growing systems literature, which extends into many disciplines, is exemplified by Walter Buckley (ed.), *Modern Systems Research for the Behavioral Scientist* (Chicago: Aldine, 1968); Ludwig von Bertalanffy, *General System Theory* (New York: Braziller, 1968); Walter Buckley, *Sociology and Modern Systems Theory* (Englewood Cliffs, N.J.: Prentice-Hall, 1967); and M. D. Mesarovic (ed.), *Views on a General Systems Theory* (New York: Wiley, 1964).

head's views on science constitute an aspect of his personality system, and those of his ideas that are widely shared among scientists constitute a part of the social system of science.[2]

The concept of system is useful to the scientist because it helps him to link together large numbers of factors in his efforts to explain phenomena. Rather than deal with separate or isolated factors, he can process a more manageable number of sets or systems of elements.

One type of system is the "open system," a system which is in continual transaction with its environment.[3] An open system, such as a group or a personality, changes its environment as a result of its behavior. In turn, the structure of the open system is changed as a result of environmental occurrences. If all personality and social systems are indeed open, then this implies continual change in these systems. When this concept of open system is applied to the social system of science or the personality system of the scientist, it supports our previously stated view of science as ever moving further outward toward a more inclusive integration of elements in space, that is, a widening synthesis of ideas and of experiences. This contrasts with a view of science and scientists as closed systems; that is, as systems that are eternal and unchanging, unaffected by their environments.

CYBERNETICS

From cybernetics[4]—the "science of communication and control" which has to do with the flow of information back and forth between a system and its environment—we draw the concept of ultrastability.[5] A system is ultrastable to the degree that it is able to alter its behavior on the basis of experience so as to correct for deviations from its goals, where goal is defined broadly enough to include the "goal" of the thermostat of staying within a given range of temperature or the "goal" of the automatic pilot to stay on a given course.

[2] For Whitehead's beliefs about science, which are similar to those within our own frame of reference, see his *Science and the Modern World* (New York: Mentor, 1948).

[3] There is a close relationship between this idea of a system's interchanges with its environment and exchange theory in sociology, anthropology, and economics. See, for example, Peter M. Blau, *Exchange and Power in Social Life* (New York: Wiley, 1964), and George C. Homans, *Social Behavior, Its Elementary Forms* (New York: Harcourt, 1961).

[4] The cybernetics literature overlaps with others, such as general systems theory, information theory, communication theory, and artificial intelligence. For classic statements of the nature of the field see Norbert Wiener, *The Human Use of Human Beings* (Garden City, N.Y.: Doubleday, 1954); Norbert Wiener, *Cybernetics* (Cambridge, Mass.: M.I.T. Press, 1965); and W. Ross Ashby, *An Introduction to Cybernetics* (New York: Wiley, 1963). A recent account of cybernetics along with some of its allied fields is contained in Jagjit Singh, *Great Ideas in Information Theory, Language and Cybernetics* (New York: Dover, 1966).

[5] For an illustration of how this concept may be used in political science, see Morton A. Kaplan, *Macropolitics: Selected Essays on the Philosophy and Science of Politics* (Chicago: Aldine, 1969).

From this perspective all systems—physical, biological, personality, social—have a certain degree of ultrastability. A rock and a chess-playing computer both are physical systems, with the computer having considerable ability and the rock having none to redirect its own behavior into more effective channels on the basis of experience, that is, to "learn" from its failures and successes. A human personality or social system has far more ultrastability than the most advanced computer yet developed. For one thing, computers are highly specialized mechanisms, designed to achieve a very narrow range of objectives. Also, the complex activities of a computer are fixed by its program, whereas human systems have the capacity to alter the "programs" they live by.[6]

A system can use its degree of ultrastability not only to adjust or adapt to its environment but also to change this environment. Rather than attain stability by circumscribing its deviations within a given range, it can attain a stability based on continuing change. This is like saying that change is the only constant. Whereas cybernetics has tended to concentrate on deviation-counteracting systems, such as thermostats and automatic pilots, we may refer to a "second cybernetics"[7] which focuses on deviation amplifications. Such amplifications may take various directions, some of which might be quite destructive (for example, a vicious circle of mutual distrust among nations leading to international conflict). The direction with which we are concerned is that of increasing ultrastability and thus increasing ability of a system to alter its environment. This direction is illustrated by the phenomenon of progressive evolution, defined by Herrick as "change in the direction of increase in the range, variety and efficiency of adjustment of the organism to its environment and environment to the use of the organism."[8] Thus, the series of mutations that produced increasing brain capacity in certain vertebrates built one upon the other: parents with a larger than average capacity, who were in the best position to proliferate, produced mutant children with still greater capacity; such children, in turn, were in the best position to multiply, and they, in turn, ultimately produced man, with his 10 billion nerve cells. And man has amply demonstrated his high degree of ultrastability through his transformations of his environment as well as his ability to adapt to a very wide variety of environments.

Our view of science is analogous to this description of progressive evo-

[6] Computer programs have been written which enable the computer to "learn" from its experiences, and alter its program to an extent as a result (for example, for playing chess). However, the original program must specify the ways in which learning is to take place, and these ways remain fixed.

[7] Magoroh Maruyama, "The Second Cybernetics: Deviation-Amplifying Mutual Causal Processes," *American Scientist,* **51** (1963), 164–79.

[8] C. Judson Herrick, *The Evolution of Human Nature* (Austin: University of Texas Press, 1956), p. 125. For a philosophical discussion of the significance of evolution see Pierre Teilhard de Chardin, *The Phenomenon of Man* (New York: Harper, 1961), and *The Future of Man* (New York: Harper, 1969).

lution: a deviation-amplifying process which moves in the direction of increasing ultrastability. Carrying forward the process of biological evolution, which yielded man's enormous brain capacity, and following the invention of oral and written languages, which improved man's information-processing abilities, the continuing development of science is yielding not only more information but also information about how to acquire information. This latter type of information might be called information about the scientific method. It was not readily available during man's early history; whatever information man had possessed about how to get more information generally was not made explicit, nor was it widely disseminated. As such information continues to develop, man increases his ability to accelerate the scientific revolution, just as capital investments lead to the expansion of productive capacity.

If increases in brain capacity were once indicative of a heightened potential for ultrastability, then the evolution of science has been serving to carry forward this potential into actuality. An increased amount of information flowing to and from the scientist yields improved ability to alter behavior and, consequently, greater effectiveness in adapting to or controlling the environment (that is, increased ultrastability). Let us now consider not simply an increasing total amount of information but also an increasing rate of acquiring information, through knowledge of effective scientific methods. Let us also consider not only information about how to acquire information but also information about how to acquire information about how to acquire information, that is, information about how to improve scientific methods. Investigators have barely touched on this level of information, yet it gives us perspective as to the future evolution of science. Furthermore, there appears to be no limit to the number of such levels. A physical analogy in the realm of mechanics would be that of increased distance, velocity, acceleration, rate of acceleration, and so on. If scientific methods proceed to the investigation of these various levels of information, we may expect an exponential increase in man's ability to synthesize or integrate his experiences in the future and, consequently, a similar increase in his ability to control his environment. Of course, the extinction of the dinosaurs and the current threats to man's continued existence should remind us that evolution need not be uniformly progressive, that detours may occupy thousands or millions of years. The problem of how to avoid such detours one day may be solved by science.

SYMBOLIC INTERACTIONISM

If general systems theory yields perspective on the spatial linkages or syntheses of science and if cybernetics has to do with the temporal dimension, symbolic interactionism yields insight into the symbolic tools which science uses to achieve its triple synthesis of ideas with ideas, ideas with experience, and experience with experience. This literature[9] teaches us that human experience comes to be mediated by a symbolic world and that it becomes impossible for the socialized individual to experience his environment or himself except through this world. For example, he attains a sense of identity through a symbolic construction in which he sees himself as an object with reference to the actions of others.

As for the specific ways in which this symbolic mediation takes place, we may begin by examining covert behavior. Only a portion of symbolic behavior is overt, such as speech and written communication, and it is such symbolic behavior with which we are most familiar. When we think of the scientific process, we tend to think of this type of behavior. Yet we need not lean on Freudian principles to realize that a great deal of symbolic activity goes on beneath the surface at various levels of consciousness (for example, our rather intangible thought processes).

We may distinguish between two types of covert behavior: covert review, or constructions of past events, and covert rehearsal,[10] or constructions of future occurrences. It is through these twin processes that humans are able to reach out from the instantaneous present and incorporate both past and future. The review process is evaluative, with a focus on the implications of past actions for goals or values. Within the scientific method this is analogous to the context of justification or verification, in which we examine the evidence that has been collected in order to determine to what degree it warrants certain conclusions. If our scientific goal is to explain a given phenomenon, then we evaluate certain past occurrences to determine what they contribute toward achieving this goal. As for the rehearsal process, that is analogous to the context of discovery within the scientific method. The procedure here is for the individual to assess the implications of a future course of action for his goals. Such an assessment, as in the case of covert review, need not take place at a very conscious level. These processes of covert review and rehearsal need not be

[9] For an introduction to this literature see, in addition to George Herbert Mead's *Mind, Self and Society* (Chicago: University of Chicago Press, 1934), Herbert Blumer, *Symbolic Interactionism* (Englewood Cliffs, N.J.: Prentice-Hall, 1969); Severyn Bruyn, *The Human Perspective in Sociology: The Methodology of Participant Observation* (Englewood Cliffs, N.J.: Prentice-Hall, 1966); T. T. Segerstedt, *The Nature of Social Reality* (Totowa, N.J.: Bedminster, 1966); and Arnold Rose (ed.), *Human Behavior and Social Processes: An Interactionist Approach* (Boston: Houghton Mifflin, 1962). An approach closely related to this literature which also takes very seriously symbolic behavior as well as the dynamic interaction between personality and social system is Erving Goffman's dramaturgical orientation, as illustrated by *Encounters* (Indianapolis: Bobbs-Merrill, 1966), *Stigma* (Englewood Cliffs, N.J.: Prentice-Hall, 1963), *Asylums* (Chicago: Aldine, 1962), and *The Presentation of Self in Everyday Life* (Garden City, N.Y.: Doubleday, 1959).

[10] We conceive of the process of covert review as paralleling that of covert rehearsal. The latter has been discussed by J. Edward Hulett, Jr., "A Symbolic Interactionist Model of Human Communication," *AV Communication Review,* **14** (1966), 5–33.

followed by action immediately. For example, a number of covert re-
hearsals may follow one another, with each having to do with a different
course of action or with a different way of assessing the implications of a
given course of action.

We tend to think of scientific activity as an overt process, yet the
scientist, as a human being, behaves in both covert and overt ways. His
covert behavior operates at various levels of consiousness and influences
both his own behavior and that of those whom he studies in many ways.
For example, the process of imagination generally is seen as an almost
unknowable domain, linked to covert processes deep within the scientist,
yet its importance for scientific discovery can scarcely be exaggerated.

Science has demonstrated the power of overt processes; by subjecting
experience to rational scrutiny and by constructing empirical tests of our
ideas, a great deal has been learned and many problems have been solved.
Yet the attention of science has yet to be sharply focused inward on the
covert processes of the scientist. What is involved is an extension of the
scientific process to include the process of sciencing itself. Such a science
of science includes covert behavior for two major reasons. The first we
have already outlined: an understanding of such behavior is intrinsic to
an understanding of the process of scientific discovery. The second has to
do with the process of justification or verification. Although widely
shared standards as to what constitutes evidence are developed for the
various scientific disciplines, these standards usually are not explicit. In
order to extend science so as to include justification we must become ex-
plicity aware of these standards so that we can monitor their effectiveness.
What is required is the treatment of such standards as so many hypotheses, themselves subject to the verification process on the basis of their
production of scientific understanding.

One lesson that science can learn from the phenomena of covert review
and covert rehearsal is the very short time span which may be involved.
The significance of this for science is based on the analogy between covert
review and verification, on the one hand, and between covert rehearsal
and discovery, on the other. During covert review the individual evaluates past behavior by invoking a series of standards based on his goals,
a process analogous to the subjection of data by the scientist to standards
for evidence based on such scientific goals as the quest for explanation.
Similarly, covert rehearsal represents a series of symbolic attempts to
discover solutions to problems, analogous to the scientific discovery of
improved explanations. To the extent that this analogy holds, what is
implied is the possibility of accelerating scientific justification and discovery.[11]

---

[11] The analogy between everyday and scientific behavior is drawn at length in George A.
Kelly, *A Theory of Personality* (New York: Norton, 1963).

GAME THEORY AND THE SOCIOLOGY OF KNOWLEDGE

If we conceive of a game[12] as being defined not by any particular goal, such as recreation, but rather by its incorporation of a system of rules which constrain the behavior of participants in certain directions, then the analogy between the game and everyday behavior comes to be salient. In ordinary life we also live in the context of systems of rules, or norms, which exert pressure for certain types of behavior. The rules of a game are more explicit than those of life, but that difference is one of degree. As a matter of fact, there are a great many unstated rules governing the behavior of game participants, rules corresponding to general societal norms for what constitutes appropriate behavior within such contexts; moreover, social scientists busy themselves making many of society's implicit rules more explicit.

But is it not true that games are simply games, and not the same as "real life"? Are they not artificial devices which can tell us very little about "actual" human behavior? These are the kinds of questions we shall take up in greater detail in Chapter 9, "Simulation." At this point we simply state that we do not accept the automatic validity of such arguments. The question of what is "real" and what is "unreal" or "artificial" stands back of all science and philosophy, and its complexities are manifold. Does man live an unreal or unnatural life when he constructs a loin cloth or a city? Is he less human when he is playing a game than when he is not? From our own perspective, anything that man does is real and is worthy of investigation, even the phenomenon of questioning whether certain human behaviors are real. The problem for the social scientist is to determine how the constellation of factors involved in any given situation operates so as to result in certain kinds of behavior as distinct from other kinds. If the given situation happens to be a game, the challenge for the social scientist is no less. Furthermore, success in understanding that context bodes well for understanding more everyday situations just because games are complex situations and not simply the formal or explicit rules which define the way the game is supposed to be played.

This analogy between the game and life implies a new framework for viewing social change. If life is a kind of game then we should be able to change the reality by changing the rules of the game. Indeed, this is exactly the perspective adopted recently by some students of the sociology of knowledge.[13] Such an approach does not do violence to the traditional

[12] The extensive literature on game theory is illustrated by John McDonald, *Strategy in Poker, Business and War* (New York: Norton, 1950): Anatol Rapoport, *The Essential Ideas of Two-Person Game Theory* (Ann Arbor: University of Michigan Press, 1966); and Anatol Rapoport and C. J. Orwant, *Prisoner's Dilemma: A Study in Conflict and Cooperation* (Ann Arbor: University of Michigan Press, 1965).

[13] For this social constructionist approach see Peter L. Berger and Thomas Luckmann, *The Social Construction of Reality* (Garden City, N.Y.: Doubleday, 1967); and Burkart Holzner,

approach in this field—as set forth by such men as Max Scheler, Karl Marx, and Karl Mannheim—that ideas are determined by social or environmental circumstances (for example, one's economic situation). Rather, the position of the new social constructionists completes the earlier point of view. Circumstances shape ideas, *and* ideas shape circumstances. Thus, the Hegelian tradition unites with the Marxian tradition. This pair of processes may be conceived of as occurring in a cyclical fashion: ideas shape circumstances, circumstances in turn shape ideas, ideas once again shape circumstances, and so on. Such a conception is based on viewing the ideas and the circumstances as open systems, each of which changes and is in turn changed by the other. Another way of stating this relationship is by the concept of feedback: ideas change circumstances, and then the informational repercussions of this change (feedback) returns to the initial ideas which, as a result, become transformed.

If we conceive of science as a game, then this metaphor would lead us to think of the rules of science as capable of change. Indeed, if we pay attention to the cybernetic concept of ultrastability, then the more open to change these rules are, the more science is in a position to change its environment. As a matter of fact, it is that very openness of science relative to other social systems which seems to have led to its environmental repercussions. Pursuing this line of thought further, we might inquire as to what there is about the game of science, in comparison to that of other social systems, which accounts for its high degree of ultrastability. The distinction between zero-sum and nonzero-sum games is useful in this context. A zero-sum game is illustrated by the typical parlor game in which one person's loss is another's gain. The total amount of reward (for example, the number of people who can win the game) remains fixed. The "game" of social stratification is also zero-sum: the number of positions at the top of a given hierarchy is limited and relatively fixed; the rise of some implies the descent of others. Science, however, tends to be more of a nonzero-sum game. If we focus on the reward of information as distinct from status or hierarchical position, then we shall discover the multiple-sum nature of science. If one scientist gains important new knowledge, and assuming that this knowledge is communicated widely, many scientists gain thereby. They improve their position vis-à-vis gaining additional information as a result of having received this communication. Moreover,

---

Reality Construction in Society (Cambridge, Mass.: Schenkman, 1968). This approach is closely related to earlier work in the sociology of knowledge, as illustrated by Karl Mannheim, *Ideology and Utopia* (New York: Harcourt, n.d.), and also to phenomenological sociology. The latter is illustrated by the classic work of Alfred Schutz, *Collected Papers, Volume I, The Problem of Social Reality* (The Hague: Martinus Nyhoff, 1967), and more recently by work in ethnomethodology, for example, Harold Garfinkel, *Studies in Ethnomethodology* (Englewood Cliffs, N.J.: Prentice-Hall, 1967); and Richard J. Hill and Kathleen S. Crittenden, *Proceedings of the Purdue Symposium on Ethnomethodology* (Lafayette, Ind.: Purdue Research Foundation, 1968).

the scientist who originally discovered and communicated this knowledge gains, and in ways in addition to fame or status. He is able to secure further testing of his ideas, and in addition he helps to bring others up to a level of knowledge where they are in a better position to make contributions to his own store of information.

It seems that there are two aspects of the game of science that are closely related to its high degree of ultrastability, with both related to the fact that science is a multiple-sum game with a focus on information. For one thing, ideally at least, all scientists stand to gain from the gain of any one, and vice versa. Thus, the multiple-sum game of science tends to open its doors wide to new information. Instead of posing a competitive threat, as it would in a zero-sum game, it tends to be welcomed. Second, information is the kind of goal which, potentially at least, is nonscarce or infinite in quantity, as we have argued in the preceding section on general systems theory. Thus, the scientific community can continue, without limit, to add to its store of information, thus changing itself and placing itself in an ever more favorable position to alter its environment. And as we have argued in the preceding section on symbolic interaction, such information can be applied to the process of obtaining information, and the result can be a continuing acceleration of the flow of information.

SOCIOLOGY OF SCIENCE

In the foregoing paragraphs we have been treating science not as a collection of wise rules which we must follow in order to achieve scientific salvation but as a social system.[14] As with any social system, only some of the rules are explicit, and all of them are in flux. As with any social system, there is in science a dynamic process of communication out of which norms, values, and patterns of action are developed and changed.

Certain covert aspects of science—sets of explicit assumptions within a given field—seem to form the basis for scientific revolutions. These paradigms,[15] such as the mechanistic assumptions of Newtonian physics, have both innovative and stultifying effects. On the one hand, they provide the researcher with a comprehensive theoretical framework as well

---

[14] This view of science is adopted by Norman W. Storer, *The Social System of Science* (New York: Holt, 1966), and by John Ziman, *Public Knowledge: The Social Dimension of Science* (Cambridge: Cambridge University Press, 1968). For a view of social science with particular emphasis on the sociology of knowledge see Gideon Sjoberg and Roger Nett, *A Methodology for Social Research* (New York: Harper, 1968); an approach within the framework of ethnomethodology is Aaron V. Cicourel, *Method and Measurement in Sociology* (New York: Free Press, 1964).

[15] Paradigms within science are discussed by Thomas S. Kuhn, *The Structure of Scientific Revolutions* (Chicago: University of Chicago Press, 1962), and by E. A. Burtt, *The Metaphysical Foundations of Modern Physical Science* (Garden City, N.Y.: Doubleday, n.d.).

as with ideas about effective research techniques. Thus, he can proceed to define specific research problems which carry forward the ideas within the paradigm. On the other hand, paradigms tend to persist long after they have exceeded their usefulness, slowing down the development of alternative paradigms. In addition, the scientist brought up within the tradition of a given paradigm does not learn to ask the very big questions, but rather learns to focus his attention on narrower issues.

These disadvantages could be lessened, and the advantages retained, to the degree that a paradigm is of such a nature that it focuses attention on itself. In this way it becomes overt and can be more readily modified on the basis of new evidence. We might view science as a whole as moving in the direction of this type of paradigm, where the covert and unquestioned assumptions of one era become the debatable hypotheses of another. For example, earlier assumptions within sociology that the investigator can learn to become ethically neutral as he proceeds with his research are just now being questioned seriously.

To the extent that science can question its own fundamental assumptions, it opens itself to basic internal changes. This illustrates the ability of a system to change its behavior or structure, which is the basis for achieving a high degree of ultrastability. From our preceding discussion of ultrastability in the section on cybernetics, we may note the association between such an ability and the ability of a system to adapt to or change its environment. Indeed, this latter ability of science is so well documented that the relevant question is not whether or not it exists but how it works. One path toward such an explanation is what might be called an information theory of power, and here we must consider science and technology together.

Science is structured around obtaining improved solutions for certain kinds of problems, such as those of explanation and prediction. It produces information, and this information becomes the basis for technological information, the kind of information essential for producing that which people value. Historically, the physical science revolution in western Europe became the basis for an industrial revolution which harnessed new sources of energy and put them to work in the production of unprecedented quantities of goods. Of course, factors other than that of scientific information were involved (for example, the values associated with Protestantism).

Students of science traditionally have distinguished sharply between science and technology, yet for the purpose of understanding the way in which science affects other social systems it may be useful to view them on the same continuum. Both science and technology are structured around developing information needed to solve various problems. As for the nature of these problems, science is concerned with the explanation of phenomena under controlled conditions, such as the velocity of a falling body in a vacuum. By excluding more complex situations scientists believe that they can obtain more solid evidence as to the dynamics of the phenomena on which they focus. Technologists begin, ideally, where scientists leave off. Accepting the findings of science, they proceed to examine less controlled and more complex situations, with a focus on the construction of valued objects. In the wind tunnel, for example, the aerodynamicist does not discover anew the laws of mechanics. Rather, he proceeds from them to the construction of airfoils and other objects which have the kinds of properties considered desirable by human beings, and he accomplishes this in an environment which simulates the complexities of the uncontrolled environment. Thus, we may conceive of a science–technology continuum; as we move toward the technology pole we encounter greater complexity or additional systems of factors that are operating.

Scientific information, then, can be converted into power to the degree that it can be technologized, that is, converted into phenomena or objects that are widely valued. We are assuming here that an exchange theory operates: if scientific information can provide what people value, then certain demands can be made in exchange for this information. Such a perspective is adopted, for example, in Galbraith's account of the growing power of the "scientific and educational estate."[16]

SOCIAL TECHNOLOGY

Examining more closely the science-technology continuum,[17] certain implications follow from our view of science and the scientist as open systems. Both are in continual transaction with society: they affect society and are affected by it. Neither science nor the scientist can be neutral, in the sense of avoiding such effects. The interviewer cannot hope to avoid influencing his interviewee in one manner or another. He may attempt to hide his own reactions to what his respondent says, but such a bland stance itself affects the respondent in certain ways. On the social system level, science has a powerful momentum which shapes society in certain ways. Some have argued that science moves society in humanistic directions—toward truth, independence, originality, dissent, freedom, and tolerance.[18] Others see science as pushing toward a bureaucratic, anti-

[16] John Kenneth Galbraith, *The New Industrial State* (Boston: Houghton Mifflin, 1967).

[17] For a profound examination of the philosophical basis for viewing technology—defined in terms of problem solving—as a part of science, see Leonard Goodwin, "The Historical–Philosophical Basis for Uniting Social Science with Social Problem-Solving," *Philosophy of Science,* **29** (1962), 377–92. Goodwin includes in his discussion ideas from Aristotle, Newton, Comte, Hegel, Marx, Heisenberg, Marcuse, and Mannheim.

[18] This is the thesis put forward by J. Bronowski, *Science and Human Values* (New York: Harper, 1965).

humanistic society.[19] Whatever is the case, it is difficult to maintain that science has a neutral effect on society.

If the scientist and science do affect their social milieu, then it behooves them to make an investigation of these effects as part of the scientific enterprise. If science cannot be neutral, then we must learn which alternatives for not being neutral exist. Are there, in particular, ways of not being neutral which advance the purposes of science more than others? And if there are such ways, how do they relate the nonscientific purposes of a given society (for example, the humanistic-individualistic tradition of Western society)?

We need not assume a zero-sum relationship between scientific values and societal values. It may be possible to organize scientific efforts so that they contribute both to the advancement of science and the solution of societal problems. Indeed, this is far more than just a possibility, because effective information can easily be a multiple-sum commodity: the communication of information can aid the recipient and also provide a test for the communicator. Furthermore, assuming that channels of communication remain open, there is increased likelihood that the recipient will be able to send more valuable information to the communicator as a result of what he has learned.

What is needed is not simply assumptions that a given approach to science is either zero-sum or multiple-sum, but also evidence as to what are its various repercussions for the solution of scientific and societal problems. In a general and abstract way, as science has proved its usefulness to society, society has in turn supported science more fully. But serious questions can be and have been raised as to the direction in which science is taking us. For example, a science geared to military objectives can produce a society which may be, in a very narrow sense, solving certain of its problems, but which in a wider sense may be moving toward decreasing ultrastability as the danger of mass annihilation increases. Thus, while solving some problems, science appears to be creating others.

It may be that the key problem in achieving a science that moves toward increasing ultrastability in the long run is that posed by the imbalance in the development of social science relative to physical science. In social science it appears that we have achieved neither the ability to monitor the positive and negative effects of science, or of other social systems, nor the ability to act effectively to achieve solutions when problems have been identified. Recently, attention has been turning to the monitoring problem as it exists on a broad societal scale, and attempts are being made to set up a series of "social indicators" which can help us

---

[19] Among the many who have taken this position, see Jacques Ellul, *The Technological Society* (New York: Vintage, 1964). Ellul does at least see some hope in the further development of the sciences of man.

with this task. As yet, very little progress has been made, but at least we have been made aware of the work that lies undone.[20]

Assuming that we become increasingly effective with respect to the monitoring problem, there is also the staggering task of devising effective social technologies. The power of social science can be brought to bear on this task to the extent that action programs are seen as field experiments, as distinct from simply one-shot attempts to solve problems. This requires of the social technologist familiarity with the literature of social science as well as an effort to derive from a given project whatever informational outputs can be obtained. In the field experiment the scientist-technologist has less control over the situation than he does in the laboratory, but he also is able to subject his scientific ideas to a more severe test as a result of these additional factors. By engaging in field experiments the social scientist is openly seeking to effect changes in society. This effect on society is something that always existed covertly. With an overt approach, however, it becomes possible to monitor these effects and then to alter them on the basis of political processes within society.

1.2 A RESEARCH ILLUSTRATION

For some years prior to the inauguration of this study of medical specialties in the fall of 1956, members of the American Public Health Association and officials in the U.S. Public Health Service had been concerned with recruiting medical students to a career in public health. It had been difficult to attract the more qualified medical students to available openings in public health. Although many explanations could be offered, none were supported by comprehensive and accurate facts about medical students in the United States. It was felt by individuals in the American Public Health Association who deal with problems of recruitment that solutions to these problems rested on the answer to the question, "What makes physicians choose or reject public health as a career?"

The decision was made to find the answer to this question by means of a thorough research study by social scientists. A research proposal was drafted, submitted to the National Institutes of Health, and subsequently approved. The study was to be national in scope, and the particular location selected for the project's headquarters was the School of Public Health of the University of North Carolina at Chapel Hill.

The professional staff who assembled for the initiation of the project in September, 1956, consisted of a career public health physician who served

---

[20] For an introduction to the literature on social indicators see Raymond A. Bauer (ed.), *Social Indicators* (Cambridge, Mass.: M.I.T. Press, 1966); Bertram M. Gross (ed.), *Social Intelligence for America's Future* (Boston: Allyn, 1969); and Bertram M. Gross, "The New Systems Budgeting," *Public Administration Review,* **29** (March–April, 1969).

as project director, a sociologist, a psychologist, and a statistician. During the ensuing five years a number of different studies were made, most of which had to do with either medical students or public health physicians. The present illustration is concerned with data collected during the first two years of the study, with the first year constituting phase one and the second year phase two.[21]

PHASE ONE

Definition of the Research Problem

Although the project started out purely as a service endeavor designed to aid in the recruitment of qualified medical students to public health, the goals set for the study were soon broadened. The social scientists who joined the project were, as a result of their own professional education, committed to exploring the possibilities for making a general contribution to knowledge. For example, information about the choice of public health by medical students was seen within the context of the general process of occupational choice. Research efforts were consequently expanded to include studying the process whereby medical students choose other medical fields, e.g., surgery, psychiatry, pathology.

This decision to investigate the process of choosing medical fields other than that of public health was based on the recognition of certain similarities in the sequence of events leading to the choice of any medical specialty. Because relatively few medical students are interested in public health as a career, definition of the problem in terms of public health alone would have made it extremely difficult to locate a sufficient number of individuals on which to base a thorough and comprehensive study. The broader definition allowed the investigators to bring a great deal of data to bear on the problems and made relevant the results of earlier studies of the process of occupational choice. In addition, any progress made would also represent a contribution to general knowledge of the dynamics of the choice process.

The task for the project staff came to be defined as one of obtaining sufficient knowledge of the choice process so that intelligent decisions might subsequently be made for dealing with the recruitment problem. This illustrates the role of the behavioral scientist in many different types of applied settings: rather than being asked to come up with specific recommendations for decisions, he is often asked simply to collect the information on which those decisions are to be based.

[21] For details on this study see Kurt W. Back et al., "Public Health as a Career of Medicine: Secondary Choice Within a Profession," *American Sociological Review*, **23** (1958), 533–41; and Bernard S. Phillips, "Expected Value Deprivation and Occupational Preference," *Sociometry*, **27** (1964), 151–60.

Data Collection

At the beginning of the study there was a considerable amount of groping for effective methods, concepts, and theories. Among the procedures tested was a series of interviews with teachers in medical school. This was followed by a series of questionnaires administered to small numbers of medical students. For example, some students were asked to write an "autobiography—from now to the future," the purpose of which was to obtain information on their aspirations and future plans. Included were such questions as, "How did you decide to study medicine?" "Do you usually plan, or do you act on the spur of the moment?"

Some students were presented with a series of ambiguous drawings and asked to imagine each one as some kind of situation and to describe how the situation came about, what was happening, and how it would probably turn out. This is a variant of the T.A.T., or Thematic Apperception Test, a test commonly used by clinical psychologists.

One of the standardized psychological inventories used was the Edwards Personal Preference Schedule, in which the student is asked to choose one statement from pairs of statements such as:

> A. I like to help my friends when they are in trouble.
> B. I like to do my best in whatever I undertake.

This schedule of 225 paired statements provides measures of such personality characteristics as achievement, deference, abasement, autonomy, dominance, aggression, and nurturance.

A different kind of research procedure involved an analysis of the abbreviated career descriptions found in the *Directory of Medical Specialists*. The backgrounds of specialists in public health were compared with those of specialists in internal medicine, surgery, pathology, and psychiatry. The purpose here was to unearth any differences existing between the career histories of public health physicians and physicians in other specialties.

One study involved a total of 253 students from the four classes of a Southern medical school. All the 300-odd medical students in the school were requested (but not required) to attend an assembly at which they were to fill out a questionnaire. One part of the questionnaire had to do with the social structure within the medical school. For example:

> A. Among the other medical students:
>   Whom do you like best?
>   To whom do you talk most about your plans for the future?
> B. Among the faculty:
>   Who is the best teacher?
>   To whom have you talked most about the future?

Measurement and Scaling

Another part of the questionnaire included this question, "With respect to the following fields of medicine, indicate in Column A what you would like *most* about working in that field and in Column B what you would like *least*." The eight medical fields listed were dermatology, general practice, internal medicine, pathology, psychiatry, public health, surgery, and teaching. This question was designed to determine what goals or values were important to medical students in their thinking about medical fields, and we may designate it as the *open-ended-values question.*

The following constitutes the question as well as a series of fairly typical responses:

With respect to the following fields of medicine, indicate in Column A what you would like *most* about working in that field and in Column B what you would like *least*.

	A Would Like Most	B Would Like Least
Dermatology	High income	It's difficult to cure patients
General practice	Being a family physician	Very hard work
Internal medicine	There would be interesting cases	Having the type of patient who is not very cooperative
Pathology	Doing research and the scientific status of the field	You don't deal with patients directly
Psychiatry	The chance to learn about people	Involves too much emotional strain
Public health	The working hours	Not being able to practice medicine
Surgery	I'd be able to use my hands	Mistakes could be fatal
Teaching	Research and learning experiences	Not having patients

The purpose of categorizing the approximately 4,000 responses (sixteen categories of responses for each of the 253 medical students involved) was to learn about the fundamental occupational goals of medical students. An open-ended question such as this allows the respondents latitude for indicating what is most important to them. The key problem was to reduce the variety of answers to a small number of categories which could provide a focus for later stages of the project. These categories would then constitute the basis for measuring occupational goals, with each category referring to a different goal. After reading a good many of the answers, investigators established a number of categories which seemed to distill most of the responses. Thus, for example, *closeness of relations with patients* summarizes the responses *being a family physician, you don't deal with patients directly,* and *not having patients.* When these categories had been compared with the data, and revisions and additions had been made, the result was a set of goals which were then utilized in subsequent phases of the project.

Analysis of Data

Much of the early work (for example, the open-ended-values question) proved to be suggestive in pointing the way to the development of more calculatedly structured instruments. Some of the methods tested, of course, were found to be inadequate. For example, the series of ambiguous drawings produced no clear-cut differentiation of responses between public health students and students not interested in that field. The Edwards Personal Preference Schedule, on the other hand, revealed that students not interested in public health had higher scores for achievement and aggression needs while public health students had higher scores for deference, abasement, and nurturance needs. (It was later decided, however, to exclude this instrument from the already long questionnaire because of the many questions involved.)

The analysis of data from the *Directory of Medical Specialists* proved to be revealing with respect to career patterns. Qualification as a specialist in a different field, which implies considerable experience in a second specialty and thus is infrequent, occurs most often among specialists in public health. These data, along with data on the ages of individuals in the different fields, provide some confirmation for the idea that physicians typically enter public health some years after graduation from medical school and after work in one or more other medical fields.

The analysis of social structure among the students in the Southern medical school revealed some evidence of influence of medical students upon one another's preferences for the various medical fields. (Data and conclusions on this aspect of the analysis are presented in Section 12.3 in the subsection "Social Relationships.")

PHASE TWO

Redefinition of the Research Problem

During the first phase the approach was quite eclectic—including personality characteristics, peer influence, faculty influence, the expectations and goals or values of the medical students, the concept of career as a sequence of occupational choices, the idea of degree of commitment to a choice, the notion of a "deviant" medical specialty, and the concept of optimum choice. The second phase focused on optimum or rational choice, as well as on the expectations and goals or values of the medical students. Although it was recognized that other factors were involved, the object was to see how far the more delimited framework could take the investigator.

This redefinition of the research problem enabled the researchers to formulate particular hypotheses, that is, tentative statements about relationships among phenomena. These hypotheses related the specialty choice of medical students, on the one hand, with certain of their values and expectations on the other. They emerged from the first phase of the study, in which a wide umbrella was provided for most of the important ideas about factors which affect the medical student's choice of specialty.

For example, many of the personality characteristics of medical students which seem to be involved in the choice process can be subsumed under their goals or values (for example, degree of interest in close relationships with patients, desire for a high income, interest in helping people). Much of peer influence and faculty influence can be conceived of as expectations which these individuals send out to a given medical student. Such expectations are then received by the student and play a large part in shaping the development of his own expectations about, for example, what the different specialties have to offer. Two basic hypotheses were involved:

1. The goals or values of medical students affect or are related to their choice of specialty.
2. The expectations medical students have about the opportunities for achieving desired goals (e.g., helping people, high income) affect or are related to their choice of specialty.

Neither of these hypotheses is a particularly startling one, but it should be borne in mind that the stuff of science often appears trivial. The scientist generally strives to discover the correct formulation, whether or not it is a new one.

The redefinition of the problem went one step further than the formulation of these two basic hypotheses. One important way in which research proceeds is to combine separate hypotheses about a given phenomenon in order to achieve a more comprehensive explanation and more accurate predictions. When this is done, we say that the researcher's formulation becomes more theoretical. Although the term *theory* has connotations of vagueness, impracticality, and uncertainty within the popular culture, it has different connotations for the scientist. To him it generally means a systematic formulation or set of statements about phenomena, a formulation which is quite explicit, one which can be tested directly or indirectly, and one which may provide a great deal of additional knowledge. Such knowledge may provide the basis for effective social technologies, and consequently may be extremely practical in the applied sense.

The combined formulation of the two hypotheses is quite simple. It is theorized that medical students are interested in a given specialty to the degree that their expected deprivation for entering that field is minimized. For example, one student may be very interested in close relationships with patients and another may not. Both will most likely have the same expectations about the field of pathology, that is, as offering little opportunity for close relationships. In such an event, the student who values close patient relationships would be seen as suffering expected deprivation with respect to pathology, but not the other student. Of course, many other goals or values than close patient relationships are involved, and expected deprivation, or more specifically, expected value deprivation, has to do with all of those that are relevant.

The concern with value deprivation and not value fulfillment during phase two was not the product of a conscious choice between the two. It grew out of a research context in which there was a great deal of interest in why almost all medical students did *not* choose public health as their specialty. Thus, the immediate problem at hand was to explain why students were avoiding public health, and the deprivation formulation seemed quite appropriate. We may speculate about whether a project oriented around a more popular field might have produced a gratification rather than a deprivation formulation.

Data Collection

Selection of appropriate instruments for data collection was an early and fundamental step in the research project, carrying heavy implications for the entire study. Early work on the study indicated that a number of different ways of looking at the process of occupational choice seemed potentially fruitful. It appeared to the investigators that a survey might be the best instrument for combining various approaches to the problem. One point in its favor was that the technology of probability sampling can be used quite readily within a survey research design. This meant that it would be possible to generalize the results of the study of a properly selected sample of medical students over all medical students in American society, with a limited and known degree of error. In other words, probability samples are representative of larger populations. This generalizability was important to the American Public Health Association, where the project was initiated, because recruitment of medical students to public health was conceived of as a national problem. Encouragement to use questionnaires was found in the fact that some of the most interesting results obtained from the first year's studies had come from questionnaire data. Self-administered questionnaires were favored over interviews because of the vast difference in costs, as well as because the investigators had already found that a complex questionnaire instrument could be handled by medical students with little difficulty.

Closely related to selection of the questionnaire survey as the primary instrument of data collection in the second phase of the project was the decision as to the most appropriate procedures for selecting the sample. Because generalizability of the results of the study to medical students throughout the continental United States was deemed important, some type of national probability sample was essential. But because any project is limited in its financial and human resources, only a limited number of medical schools could be involved. It was therefore decided to focus the entire resources of the project on a very few medical schools, and in this way achieve a study in depth. The outcome was the selection of eight medical schools under a random procedure that also assured geographic coverage of the United States and considerable variation among the schools in the fraction of graduates entering general practice. (This last safeguard seemed to be an objective way of assuring that schools of different quality and different patterns of specialty choice were covered.)

For collection of the data it was important to obtain the cooperation of all the eight medical schools selected. An immediate loss of even one eighth of the sample would make far more tenuous any generalization of results over medical students throughout the country. Efforts were therefore made to secure the support of a number of highly prestigeful medical organizations through the establishment of an advisory committee made up of their representatives. The director of the project (a physician) then visited the medical schools selected and arranged for special two- to three-hour sessions to be attended by the medical students in each. (Some schools formally required all students to attend the session; others put attendance on a voluntary basis.) The professional staff of the project subsequently supervised these sessions and also arranged for local interviewers to administer the questionnaire to as many as possible of those students who did not attend. The result was a questionnaire completion rate of 91 per cent for all schools, with a range for individual schools of 80 to 100 per cent and a total of 2,674 questionnaires completed.

Although the questionnaire included many different types of questions, those utilized in the second phase had to do with goals, expectations, and preferences or choices. This selective emphasis followed from the definition of the problem, which conceived preference for any medical specialization as a function of expected value deprivation. Because goals are difficult to measure, two different techniques were adopted. One is somewhat complex and is discussed in the ensuing subsection on measurement and scaling: the other is quite straightforward and is based on the *structured-values question,* which is presented in part on the following page.

It should be noted that this question permits the investigator to measure, within five approximate degrees of importance, each selected value or goal of a given individual.

Most people have some idea of what they would want in an ideal position, that is, if they could dream up a job which had all the elements they like. What importance would each of the following elements have in your ideal job? Put a check in Column A, B, C, D, or E.

	A Indis- pensable	B Extremely Important	C Very Important	D Fairly Important	E Little or No Impor- tance (or Would Rather Not Have)
In my ideal job I would like an opportunity for:					
A. Developing warm personal relationships with patients	____	____	____	____	____
B. Being virtually certain that my specific medical actions will lead to the desired results	____	____	____	____	____
C. Having prestige among my colleagues in the medical profession	____	____	____	____	____
D. Being in a position to make a contribution to knowledge	____	____	____	____	____
E. Having the chance to help people	____	____	____	____	____

To measure expectations for the achievement of various goals within the different medical fields, the following *expectations question* was utilized:

In which of these six fields of medicine in the columns below do you think you have the greatest chance to obtain each of the following things? In which field next? In which field would you have the least chance? Rank the following fields from 1 to 6 according to how they provide opportunities for

	A General Practice	B Internal Medicine	C Pathol- ogy	D Psychi- atry	E Public Health	F Surgery
A. Developing warm personal relationships with patients	_____	_____	_____	_____	_____	_____
B. Being virtually certain that your specific medical actions will lead to the desired results	_____	_____	_____	_____	_____	_____
C. Having prestige among your colleagues in the medical profession	_____	_____	_____	_____	_____	_____
D. Being in a position to make a contribution to knowledge	_____	_____	_____	_____	_____	_____
E. Having the chance to help people	_____	_____	_____	_____	_____	_____

When data from this question are combined with the data from the structured-values question, measures of "expected value deprivation" may be obtained, a procedure to be discussed under "Analysis of Data."

Finally, a *preference-ranking question* elicited ratings of students' interest in a number of medical fields:[22]

How would you rank the following fields of medicine according to your interest in working in them? (1 for the specialty you would be most interested in, 2 for the next, 3 to 6 the ones you are least interested in working in.)

General practice	Psychiatry
Internal medicine	Public health
Pathology	Surgery

[22] The preference-ranking question actually called for students to rank dermatology and obstetrics–gynecology in addition to the other six fields. However, because the expectations question deals with only the six medical fields, no analysis was made with respect to preference for dermatology and obstetrics.

This rating constituted the effect which the investigator was attempting to explain. The tools for its explanation had to do with the concepts of goals and expectations.

Measurement and Scaling

Of the questionnaire's two techniques for measuring goals, the more elaborate was the *careers-value question.* Careers of four physicians representing different medical fields were described, and students were asked to react to each aspect of the different careers. In the following illustration of a surgical career, students were asked to underline those sentences referring to something they like, to cross out those sentences referring to something disliked, and to make no mark where they had no definite feeling one way or the other.

CAREER B

During your internship and residency you realized, far more concretely than you had before, that a high level of manual dexterity was necessary for the field of your choice. Why was this so important? The answer was obvious. In major operations, a slight mistake might prove fatal to the patient. However, the majority of operations were purely routine matters, with similar techniques used over and over again. Still, the emotional pressures involved were often extremely great.

After completing your residency, you took further work in a special field within your specialty. You then set up practice in the city of Wake, which has a population of 1 million. In the ensuing years you have come to depend on the referrals of others for much of your practice.

The service you give to your patients, the degree to which you are able to help, is great. The changes for the better which you see are often quite striking. And, of course, the esteem you command among laymen in general is very high.

Your working week comes to about fifty hours. Some of your time is spent in getting out numerous hospital reports. Occasionally, some emergency work at unexpected hours is necessary. The work usually involves a great deal of physical exertion, so much so that you are often completely exhausted. In addition, your work is often emotionally taxing. Your yearly income fifteen years after your M.D. degree comes to $25,000.

You have felt, with respect to therapy, that the accumulated knowledge which could be brought to bear on your patients' illnesses has been great. Results have usually been immediate and definite rather than drawn out and vague.

There were several reasons for using a question of this design. One was that students found it to be rather interesting, and it broke the monotony of filling out a very long questionnaire. The more interest a question has to the respondent, the less likelihood there is that he will rapidly fill in any kind of answer simply to finish the task. Another reason was the hope that the concreteness of the descriptions of the different possible goals would be more meaningful to the student than the structured-values question. Also, the careers-value question can distinguish among those goals that are salient to the respondent—those that he either underlines or crosses out—and those that are not. In the structured-values question, on the other hand, respondents are required to take a position even if they do not feel strongly about it one way or the other. Finally, the question brings several different measures to bear on each goal in a way which neither bores the respondent nor questions his honesty.

It is the fact that several different items are used to measure the same goal that enables the investigator to formulate a scale for each goal which combines scores on different but related items and yields a single over-all score for each goal. Almost all the scales consist of three or four items, with each item appearing in a different career description. Thus, for example, *closeness of patient relationships* is represented in three separate career descriptions, as follows:

1. During your years of practice, you have developed close and long-standing relationships with many of your patients.
2. In the years you have been practicing, you have come to know almost all your patients and their families intimately.
3. Your contact with individual patients has been limited because in much of your work you do not deal directly with them.

Individuals who underlined the first two sentences and crossed out the third were given a score of 3, indicating the highest degree of interest in close relations with patients. Conversely, individuals who did not mark any of the sentences were scored 1, the lowest degree of interest. Individuals who either underlined one of the first two sentences or crossed out the third were scored 2, indicating a limited degree of interest, and those who indicated their interest in two of the three sentences were also scored 2.[23] There were almost no responses indicating dislike for close relationships with patients. Thus the scoring procedure combines the data for the three different items into a single scale based on all of them.

Analysis of Data

The problem selected for analysis was to try to explain and predict the students' preferences for the different medical fields. These preferences

---

[23] These two different response patterns were lumped together so that the total number of categories would be three. This is the same as the number of categories which was obtainable in the expectations question. With respect to the expectations question, it should be noted that there seem to be six possible ranks which may be accorded to any given field as to the opportunities for a given value: 1, 2, 3, 4, 5, and 6. Actually, much of this detail was lost in the processing of the questionnaires in an effort to save time and cut costs. Thus, the available information on which the study is based has to do with whether the rank is 1, 6, or somewhere between 2 and 5 inclusive.

were expressed in responses to the *preference-ranking question,* in which students were asked to rank six different fields of medicine according to their interest in them. Although it would be useful to be able to under-stand and predict effectively a student's exact rankings, such a goal is too lofty for present knowledge in this area to fulfill. The tactics adopted in-volved the classification of each ranking as "favorable" or "unfavorable," depending on whether the rank was 1–3 or 4–6, respectively.

The analysis centered on trying to understand why students rated a given field favorably or unfavorably, and the two concepts utilized were values and expectations. Because the two values questions produced con-sistent results, it is enough here to present the analysis of data from the careers-value question. A rating of 3, for example, indicated the highest degree of interest in close relationships with patients, whereas a 1 indi-cated the least degree of interest in this goal. This same type of scoring was used for nine other values: opportunities for learning, research, in-volvement with complex problems, utilizing abilities, helping people, prestige among colleagues, high income, hours which are not extremely long, and work without great physical exertion. Students received ratings of 3, 2, or 1 on each of them, depending on their degree of interest in each.

With respect to expectations for achieving various goals in the different medical fields, the data were obtained from the expectations question. Students were asked to rank six fields of medicine on each of a number of values. Thus, for example, if value is placed on the chances for developing warm personal relationships with patients, general practice might be ranked first, and pathology might be ranked last. The scoring procedures on the careers-value question and on the expectations question were de-signed to have the same range: 1 to 3. Thus, a score of 3 indicates the greatest chance for achieving a given value, whereas a score of 1 indicates the least chance. Those fields seen by a given student as offering neither greatest nor least chances for achieving a given goal received a score of 2.

It would have been possible to conduct the analysis by separately ex-amining the relationship between occupational values and occupational preferences, and between expectations and preferences. As a strategy for research this did not seem to lead to advancement of knowledge on the subject, because other studies had already indicated that values and ex-pectations are factors involved in the occupational choice process. By putting the concepts of values and expectation together in a specific way, however, one can glimpse the beginnings of a theory which might add to our knowledge of the process.

The specific way of putting these two concepts together was to measure the gap between what the student wanted in a career (his values) and what he expected would be the opportunities for achieving these goals in a given career (his expectations). This gap would be his expected value dep-rivation for a given field. Thus, for example, Table 1-1 illustrates the sit-uation of a student who is very interested in research (value score of 3)

TABLE 1–1

Partial Profile of a Student's Scores for Pathology and General Practice

Values	Value Scores (V)	Pathology Expectations (EP)	Pathology Deprivation (V — EP)	General Practice Expectations (EG)	General Practice Deprivation (V — EG)
Research	3	3	3 — 3 = 0	1	3 — 1 = 2
Close patient relationships	1	1	1 — 1 = 0	3	1 — 3 → 0
Expected value deprivation:			0		2

and who is uninterested in close patient relationships (value score of 1). His expected value deprivation for pathology, where he perceives maximal opportunities for research, is 0. However, he perceives general practice as offering minimal opportunities for research, and his expected value deprivation for general practice is 2. The negative score (1 — 3) is not summed; rather it is treated as 0 (1 — 3 → 0) because it represents a situation where the student is only minimally interested in a goal he perceives as easily attainable. Presumably, if goals are not important to an individual, possibilities for their achievement in a given field would neither increase nor decrease his interest in that field.[24] It should be noted that Table 1-1 presents only a partial profile for a student: scores are presented for only two of the ten values analyzed, and expectations and deprivations are listed for only two of the six medical fields under consideration. In addition to research and close patient relationships, these values were actually taken into account: learning, involvement with complex problems, utilizing abilities, helping people, prestige among colleagues, high income, hours not extremely long, and work without great physical exertion.

In Table 1-2 the expected-value-deprivation score for a given field is arrived at by summing the positive deprivations for all ten values. Each student is given six such total expected-value-deprivation scores, one for each of the medical fields. These scores are then ranked for each individual, with the smallest total expected value deprivation being accorded a rank of 1, and the largest 6. To the extent that the theory under consideration is a good one, those students with the least expected value deprivation (the smallest expected-value-deprivation ranks) for a given field would actually rate that field favorably in answer to the preference-ranking question. On the other hand, those students with the largest expected

[24] This assumption is challenged in a later formulation by the author which is presented in Section 17.3.

TABLE 1-2

Profile of a Student's Total Deprivation Scores, and the Deprivation Ranks Assigned to Them for Six Medical Fields

Total Depriva-vation	General Practice	Internal Medicine	Surgery	Psychi-atry	Pathol-ogy	Public Health
Score (Ten values)	2	3	6	7	9	12
Deprivation ranks	1	2	3	4	5	6

value deprivation (the largest expected-value-deprivation ranks) for a given field would be expected to rate that field unfavorably.

Table 1-3 summarizes the basic theoretical finding of the study. The central hypothesis is that medical fields are preferred to the degree that their expected value deprivation is minimized. The left-hand entry under "Deprivation Ranks," for example, indicates that, of those individuals (1,213) who are given an expected-value-deprivation rank of 1 for any of the six medical fields, 86 per cent rate that field favorably. The right-hand entry under "Deprivation Ranks" signifies that 17 per cent of those individuals (1,844) who receive a deprivation rank of 6 for a given field actually rate that field favorably. Thus, if we know that a student receives a deprivation rank of 1 or 6 for a given medical field, we are able to predict successfully whether or not he would actually rate that field favorably a high proportion of the time. These results provide confirmation for the central hypothesis of the study wherein the gap between goals and expectations for fulfilling them is viewed as an important factor in the processes leading to preferences among medical fields.

Theory involves putting together separate ideas or hypotheses in a sys-

TABLE 1-3

Expected-Value-Deprivation Ranks Assigned to Medical Students and Per Cent of Students Who Actually Rate Fields Favorably

	Deprivation Ranks*					
	1	2	3	4	5	6
Percentage who give favorable ratings	86	71	60	44	37	17
Percentage who give unfavorable ratings	14	29	40	56	63	83
Total	100	100	100	100	100	100

* Tied ranks are omitted from this table. Consequently percentages are not based on the total sample of 2,674 but totals which are over 1,200 for each of the six ranks.

tematic way, and this often results in the putting together of many scattered bits of data. The resulting chore of data processing can be immense, and this was true of the present study. For each respondent, approximately thirty items of information were utilized to secure ratings on the ten values in the careers-value question, or an average of three items for each value. With respect to the expectations question, each student ranked the six medical fields on each of the ten values, constituting a total of sixty rankings in all. If we add to this the student's ranking of his actual interest in the six fields, we have a grand total of almost 100 items per respondent, or approximately 250,000 separate scores for a sample of size 2,674.

Theory refers to a set of related statements or hypotheses about a given phenomenon. To the extent that the relationships among these statements are explicit it is possible to state theory in the language of mathematics. Such a procedure is usually a valuable one, because it serves to make the theory more systematic than previously and to provide more specific predictions.

The difference between a more and a less explicit theory may be illustrated. We may start with the general idea that factors A and B, when both operate together, cause a change in C. This becomes more explicitly stated when we say that factor A produces the same degree of change in C as does B, and that factors A and B have no effect on one another. Explicitness might be increased still further by stating that the change in C is directly proportional to the change in A or B.

With respect to the present formulation we may distinguish between the mathematical statement which combines the concepts of values and expectations into that of expected value deprivation (EVD), on the one hand, and the mathematical statement which states the relationship between EVD and interest in a given medical specialty, on the other. Both types of statment are important for most mathematical formulations. In this instance, the first ties together in a highly explicit fashion those factors that are conceived of as having an important impact on the student's preferences among specialties. The second mathematical statement, which relates EVD to interest in a given specialty, is crucial in that it makes use of the theory for purposes of explaining and predicting preferences for the specialties.

More specifically, the first mathematical statement is based on a conception of expected value deprivation, that is, the gap between the student's interest in certain goals and his expectations as to the opportunities for achieving them. In particular, the expected value deprivation (EVD) of a given individual for a given medical field is the summation (Σ) of the difference between his value scores (V_i) and his expectations for fulfilling the corresponding values (E_i) over the set of ten values. Thus:

$$EVD = \Sigma(V_i - E_i) \qquad \text{where } V_i - E_i \text{ is positive}$$

In this formulation it is important to note that only those difference scores which are positive (that is, where value scores are greater than their corresponding expectation scores) enter into the summation. In these situations something is desired but is conceived of as relatively unavailable, and this seems to be the kind of context in which it is most meaningful to speak of expected value deprivation. Where something is not desired but is available, for example, the concept of expected value deprivation does not seem appropriate. Thus, where $V_i - E_i$ is negative or 0, nothing is contributed to expected value deprivation.

As for the second mathematical statement, it is based on the idea that the greater the individual's expected value deprivation for a given field, the greater is the likelihood that he will not prefer that field over others. This may be stated symbolically as follows:

$$\text{EVD}_{f, s} = k \cdot p(\text{unfavorable rating})_{f, s}$$

This reads "The expected value deprivation for a given field (f) by a given student (s) is equal to a constant (k) times the probability of an unfavorable rating of the field by the student." More succinctly, degree of expected value deprivation is directly proportional to the probability of an unfavorable rating.

Such mathematical formulations as this are most useful when they can be tested by actual data. From Table 1-3, we have these data:

	Deprivation Ranks					
	1	2	3	4	5	6
Percentage who give unfavorable ratings	14	29	40	56	63	83

If a student's EVD for a given field is higher than for all other fields, he will receive a deprivation rank of 6 for that field. If, on the other hand, his EVD for a field is lower than that for other fields, his deprivation rank will be 1. From these data we can indeed see that the greater the individual's EVD for a given field (relative to other fields), the greater is the likelihood that he will rate that field unfavorably. Only 14 per cent of students who had a minimum of expected value deprivation for a given field rated that field unfavorably, whereas 83 per cent of those having a maximum of EVD for a field rated it unfavorably. The degree of EVD is in fact related to the per cent rating a field unfavorably, and this per cent can in turn be interpreted as the probability that a given individual will rate a field unfavorably. Further support for a mathematical formulation can be seen in the fact that the percentages increase in approximately equal amounts for each change in the deprivation rank. This is an indication that the relationship between deprivation rank and the percentage of students giving unfavorable ratings is one of direct proportionality.

1.3 A CRITIQUE OF THE ILLUSTRATION

Let us now examine the preceding research illustration from the perspective of the frame of reference presented in Section 1.1. We shall construct this critique around the literatures which constitute the frame of reference: general systems theory, cybernetics, symbolic interactionism, game theory, sociology of science, and social technology.

GENERAL SYSTEMS THEORY

The concept of science and the scientist as open systems is illustrated by the changes in research procedure and ideas from one phase to the next. Starting with a focus on the problem of recruitment to public health, the project broadened into an investigation of the general process of occupational choice. Methodologically, the research moved from a literature review and informal interviews with informed individuals, through a preliminary questionnaire with open-ended questions and a sociometric study in one medical school, to a more structured and focused study of students in eight medical schools. Yet at the same time the study also illustrates limitations to the utilization of this open-systems concept. For one thing little attention was paid directly to measuring the effect of those who administered the questionnaire on the responses obtained, although indirect measures were obtained. Also, if science and the scientist are viewed as continually changing and changed by their environment, then it follows that we must also view the environment (for example, the medical students studied) as open systems. But the students in the study were treated as relatively static entities. Their goals, beliefs, and specialty preferences were measured at a given point in time and then interrelated, but the crucial problem of how their goals and beliefs got to be what they were at that point, that is, what causes them to change, was not asked. For example, to what degree was goal commitment based on the student's self-assessment of his own abilities, taking into account his medical successes and failures?

CYBERNETICS

Once again the study proves to be a mixed bag. On the positive side, it proved to be possible to bring together a large number of factors, pulled together under the concept of expected value deprivation, and use them as a partial explanation of preference for medical fields. One way of telling just how close the relationship is between expected value deprivation and medical preference is to examine the percentage spread in Table 1-4: from 86 per cent of those with very low expected value deprivation for a given field who rated that field favorably to 17 per cent of those with very high expected value deprivation for a given field who rated that field favorably, or a spread of 69 per cent. This is an exceptionally wide spread, as social science studies go, indicating definite progress with regard to the problem of specialty choice and, more generally, occupational choice. We might also note that the theoretical framework provided a means for the processing of very large amounts of information in an orderly and rapid fashion, bringing all of this information to bear on the central hypothesis.

On the negative side it might be argued that the study merely retested a central idea—that humans are oriented to the achievement of goals—without adding anything in the way of new information or, for that matter, increased ultrastability for science. After all, have not hundreds of studies in a great many different contexts demonstrated the same kind of thing? And even if a wide spread of percentages was achieved, how can that help us to affect the dynamic process of occupational choice (for example, to correct misperceptions about a field)? If this cannot be done, it may be argued, then we have not constructed a genuine advance in our understanding of the occupational choice process. These arguments have considerable merit. We can point to very few studies in social science which represent important advances in our store of information and can provide the basis for a considerable improvement in our problem-solving ability, whether of the problem of explanation and prediction or that of building effective social technologies.

SYMBOLIC INTERACTIONISM

This study incorporates an overt reconstruction of covert symbolic processes. The concept of expected value deprivation organizes and inter-relates a large number of other concepts: those relating to a number of the individual's goals and those involving expectations as to the probability of achieving a given goal in a given field. We cannot be sure that the processes of covert review and covert rehearsal are indeed operating according to the same formula. What we do know is that the results of the investigation indicate a high probability that some functional equivalent of the calculation of this formula takes place within the individual.

GAME THEORY AND THE SOCIOLOGY OF KNOWLEDGE

Much of game theory is based on the assumption of goal orientation in the individual (for example, that the individual assigns different degrees of utility to different alternatives). By testing how far such a utility orientation can carry us in the explanation of occupational choice, the study makes good use of a cultural tenet of game theory. Furthermore, the careers-value questions, with their career descriptions, utilized other aspects of the same idea. The researcher who sets up a game frequently does so in order to involve his subjects in a series of actions, as distinct from merely verbal responses. In this way they may not have the time or inclination to consider consciously what answer the interviewer is most interested in getting. The career-value questions achieved this at least to some extent; respondents were required to react to each sentence, out of a long series of sentences. Also, these questions constructed hypothetical situations much in the manner that games constitute hypothetical environments.

Despite this, the key idea of the game as a tool for the social construction of reality was lacking. The situations described in the career-value question do not quite substitute for the actual playing of games. These questions were not used experimentally but, rather, as supplementary tests for measuring values. They were conceived of as relatively passive instruments, as distinct from active tools for constructing a new symbolic environment in order to test the repercussions of such a construction.

SOCIOLOGY OF SCIENCE

The study illustrates the implicit acceptance of the methodological paradigm that justification or verification is the crucial task of social research. By so doing, it exemplifies both the advantages and the limitations of this paradigm. The study does indeed add a considerable degree of evidence on the potential of a goal-fulfillment approach for explaining occupational choice and, to a degree, human choices of any type whatsoever. Such evidence was achieved by building on general ideas and detailed procedures related to the justificatory or verificational paradigm. Yet at the same time the study contributes little to our understanding of the discovery process or of the technological or applied problems in the field of occupational choice. This was due to an implicit acceptance of a paradigm for social research which relegated such concerns to a low order of priority.

SOCIAL TECHNOLOGY

On the face of it, the study appears to be a genuine marriage of scientific and technological interests: the basic problem of occupational choice and the applied problem of motivating medical students to enter the field of public health. We might even grant that some progress was made in each of these areas. A theoretical framework of wide scope was set forth, a methodology for testing it was developed, and evidence of progress in predicting occupational preferences was set forth. All of this provided at least a generalized store of information which could easily prove quite useful in approaching the problem of recruitment of students into public health. For example, descriptions of the negative stereotypes of public health were constructed.

Yet at a deeper level the basic research and the technological progress were limited. From this relatively static study little can be learned about the dynamics of the socialization of medical students as they move through the occupational choice process. Moreover, technological concerns were so narrowly conceived that broader technological issues, which could have shed light on the narrower one, were ignored. For example, what would happen to public health if it devised a more effective recruitment process on the basis of this study, drawing the best students away from other fields? Might not that stimulate professors from these fields to counterattack, perhaps creating even more unfavorable stereotypes about the nature of public health, and thus hurting public health's recruitment program?

A concern with the status of public health vis-à-vis other fields, and with the relative effectiveness of various fields in recruiting excellent students, is a zero-sum approach. It is conceivable that a broader technological orientation might have pointed up a more feasible path toward an upgrading of public health, one not based on competitive recruitment policies. For example, we might conceive of health as on a continuum, with medical practice having traditionally focused on the negative end as distinct from the center or positive end. Public health traditionally has had a good deal to do with both research and social science knowledge as a way of enlarging on physiological knowledge of health and illness. A multiple-sum path for public health could be a combined emphasis on physiological and behavioral science factors as a key to moving individuals toward positive health. From this perspective progress in public health would also constitute progress in other medical fields, and vice versa; effective research on positive health could open up new opportunities for all the medical fields.

It is also possible to examine the social significance of this type of study within a much broader framework. Even granting that it might have pointed in this multiple-sum direction, what assumptions about the structure of society does such a direction imply, and what is the significance of alternate structures for human development generally? Are we to assume that we are to move toward positive health within the framework of a bureaucratic society, and if so, how far is it possible to go toward positive health within such a framework? Or are there any other structures of society that are more conducive to the continuing development of positive health? If so, what does any given study of medical education contribute toward our understanding of how to take steps in such a direction?

EXERCISES

1. Examine a paper you have written for another course. Look for the implicit theoretical assumptions that you have made. In what ways do they differ from the frame of reference presented in Section 1.1, and in what ways do they agree with it?

2. In a small group where you are discussing a problem of mutual interest, such as plans for your research projects, make periodic assessments of each individual's implicit theoretical assumptions. For example, to what degree do you see your personality as fixed or changing, to what degree do you adopt a zero-sum view of situations? Now attempt overtly to alter your theoretical assumptions so that they are more in accord with those of the framework presented in Section 1.1. What specific implications does this alteration have for the projects?

3. Construct a frame of reference for dealing with the problem-solving process, basing it on your own personal experiences in attempting to solve major and mundane problems. How does your own model compare with the research model presented in Section 1.1?

4. Review the most fundamental ideas presented in several of your social science courses. Now attempt to develop a broad theoretical framework which succeeds in integrating as many of these ideas as possible.

5. With respect to question 2 above, develop criteria for monitoring the impact of your altered theoretical assumptions. For example, attempt to measure changes in your problem-solving ability, in your level of aspiration, or in your rate of learning.

ANNOTATED REFERENCES

BECKER, ERNEST. *The Structure of Evil: An Essay on the Unification of the Sciences of Man.* New York: George Braziller, Inc., 1968. This theoretical synthesis can complement the broad frame of reference sketched in Section 1.1. Becker's special focus is on the kind of synthesis which can be the basis for human progress and which is no less scientific as a result. His principle of self-esteem maintenance recalls much of the tradition of symbolic interactionism and, more generally, the Western humanistic tradition.

BERGER, PETER L., and THOMAS LUCKMANN. *The Social Construction of Reality: A Treatise in the Sociology of Knowledge.* Garden City, N.Y.: Doubleday & Company, Inc., 1967. The authors state that "the sociology of knowledge must concern itself with everything that passes for 'knowledge' in society"; with this broad perspective, they attempt to show how reality is socially constructed. The result is a dynamic framework in which the development and communication of "knowledge," very broadly defined, becomes a vital basis for understanding human behavior.

MILLS, C. WRIGHT. *The Sociological Imagination.* New York: Grove Press, Inc., 1961. Decrying the specialization of his day, and it is our day as well, into separate camps of theoreticians and methodologists, and castigating the bureaucratic ethos of the research institute and the large project, Mills argues that each sociologist should be his own theorist and his own methodologist. In an appendix. "On Intellectual Craftsmanship," he portrays for the researcher an alternative to the bureaucratic ethos.

CHAPTER 2 **Elements of Inquiry**

2.1 THE LANGUAGE OF SCIENCE

Four elements of scientific inquiry are paradigms, concepts, propositions, and theories.[1] Paradigms are sets of assumptions, implicit or explicit, about phenomena; concepts are ways of perceiving phenomena; propositions are statements about the nature of phenomena; and theories are systems of propositions. The four together may be viewed as constituting the language of science.

We may gain insight into the language of science by examining its relation to the synthetic functions of science, that is, its integration of experience with experience via the synthesis of ideas with ideas and ideas with experience. These latter syntheses imply movement back and forth between an abstract and a concrete level of analysis. To examine such movement it is useful to conceive of a ladder of abstraction, with a series of levels instead of simply two. The continuum or dimension along which these levels occur (degree of abstraction) is what enables the scientist to escape narrow boundaries in space and time and yet attain concrete meaning.

LADDER OF ABSTRACTION

Figure 2-1 presents a "ladder of abstraction" for concepts.[2] As the concepts become more abstract, they acquire wider scope and apply to more

---

[1] For the student who wishes to enlarge on the treatment of the language of science in this chapter, a comprehensive discussion may be found in Abraham Kaplan, *The Conduct of Inquiry* (San Francisco: Chandler, 1964). Relevant collections of papers include May Brodbeck (ed.), *Readings in the Philosophy of the Social Sciences* (New York: Macmillan, 1968); Llewellyn Gross (ed.), *Sociological Theory: Inquiries and Paradigms* (New York: Harper, 1967), and *Symposium on Sociological Theory* (New York: Harper, 1959); Gordon J. Direnzo (ed.), *Concepts, Theory, and Explanation in the Behavioral Sciences* (New York: Random House, 1966); David Braybrooke (ed.), *Philosophical Problems of the Social Sciences* (New York: Macmillan, 1965); and Maurice Natanson (ed.), *Philosophy of the Social Sciences* (New York: Random House, 1963). For an approach which delves into the history of methodology, philosophy, and psychology and which represents a broad and open-ended approach to the language of science, see Joseph F. Rychlak, *A Philosophy of Science for Personality Theory* (Boston: Houghton Mifflin, 1968).

[2] This idea of drawing a ladder of abstraction is based on S. I. Hayakawa, *Language in Thought and Action* (New York: Harcourt, 1949), p. 169.

and more phenomena. Scientific concepts, such as the *choice behavior of human beings,* constitute abstractions which are selective and which have a degree of scope. They enable the scientist to communicate about the environment, but they have a special, related function for science: they constitute the elements utilized in statements designed to explore the very nature of the environment.

The concepts in Figure 2-1 ascend in level of abstraction from *John Smith's answer to a question about his preferences among occupations* to *the choice behavior of human beings.* The less abstract the concept, the closer it lies to actual measurement procedures. More abstract concepts, however, such as *the choice behavior of human beings,* can also be measured.

FIGURE 2-1 A Ladder of Abstraction for Concepts

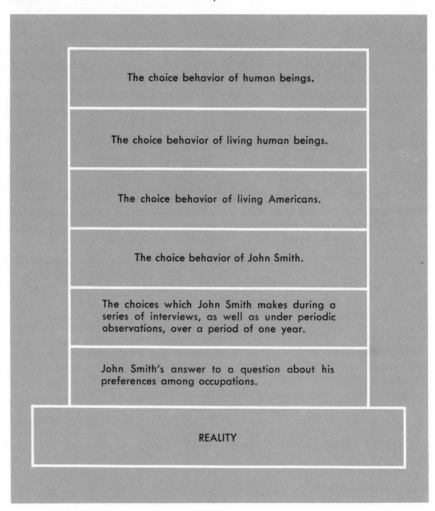

The choice behavior of human beings.

The choice behavior of living human beings.

The choice behavior of living Americans.

The choice behavior of John Smith.

The choices which John Smith makes during a series of interviews, as well as under periodic observations, over a period of one year.

John Smith's answer to a question about his preferences among occupations.

REALITY

But because of their very wide scope, only a small proportion of the total number of situations to which they apply can be investigated by the scientist. This is the price exacted for such scope, but the return may be great. The concept of choice behavior may become an element of a highly effective theory for explaining and predicting human choices. If indeed it does, this will constitute a very important return, because the availability of such a general theory in the social sciences would be analogous to important breakthroughs in the physical sciences.

It is one thing to put together sense data in a certain way so as to come up with the concept of *chair*. It is quite another to state *John Smith pushed the chair and it fell on its side*. Here one is not merely adopting a particular convention for viewing phenomena, but utilizing several such conventions to describe something that is happening. Concepts enable one to make such statements, but they are not statements in themselves. Thus, a concept is neither true nor false, for it is only a designation or naming of sense data, such as the name *John Smith*. The statements made by utilizing concepts, however, can be tested. Although scientists do not accept the idea that any test can ascertain the nature of reality, sufficient evidence may be obtained to make such statements highly credible.

Figure 2-2 presents a ladder of abstraction for propositions and theories. Like the ladder for concepts, its lower rungs deal only with a very limited range of situations. The statements rise in level of abstraction from attempts to explain and predict John Smith's preferences among medical fields to attempts to explain and predict the choice behavior of human beings, with the choice behavior of human beings covering much more territory. Such a formulation selects very little from the ongoing phenomena to which it refers, and, by this token, is highly abstract; its scope, however, is so wide that it can be applied to much of the phenomena with which behavioral scientists are concerned.

It should be noted that the statements at the lowest two rungs of the ladder in Figure 2-2 are sets of two propositions that are not put together in any systematic way. The two factors of *values* and *expectations as to the opportunities for fulfilling them in the various fields* are cited as affecting *preferences among medical fields*. Just how these factors affect such preferences is left unspecified. The other rungs of the ladder, however, fill in these gaps by predicting that the alternative chosen is the one with the lowest expected value deprivation. Such statements might be called theories, for they put together several propositions in a systematic way.

SINGLE-LEVEL ABSTRACTION

Single-level abstraction in ordinary speech or writing may result in the stringing together of vague generalities (the top of the ladder) or in the dull and disconnected exposition of highly specific reports (the bottom of

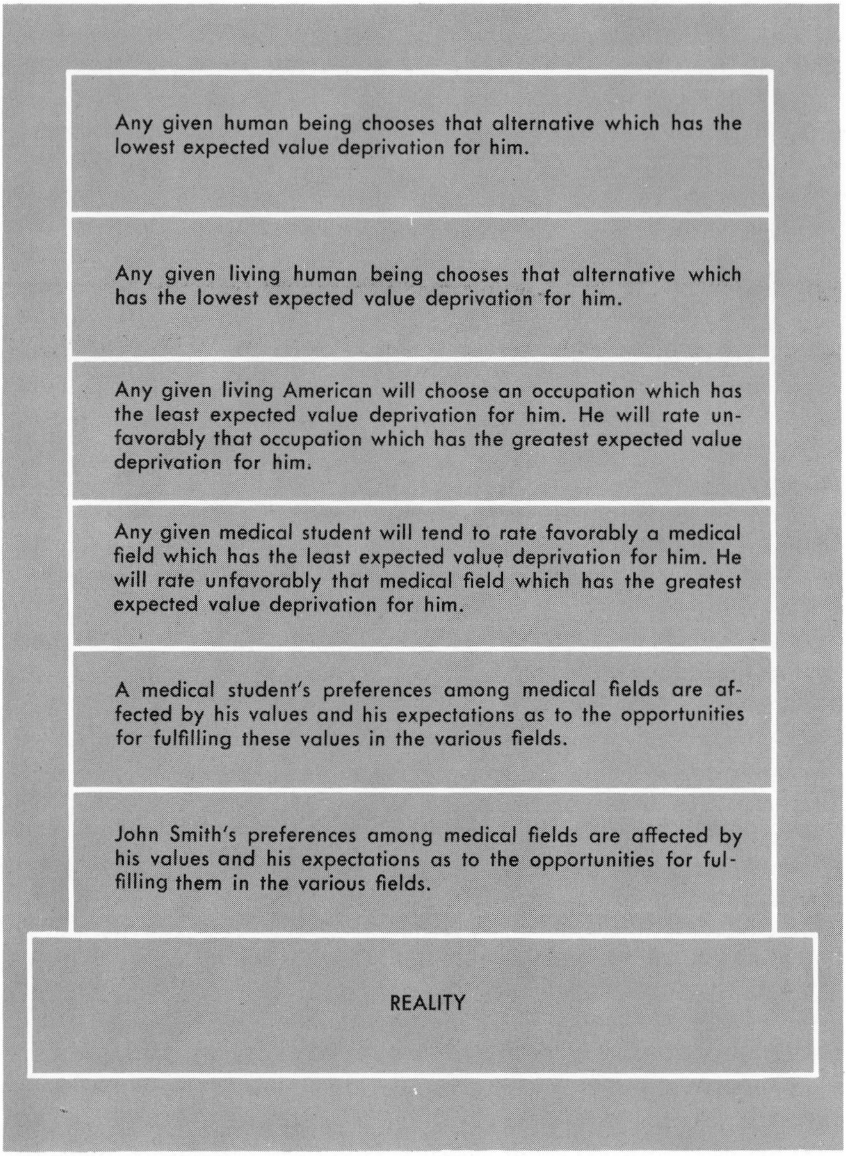

Any given human being chooses that alternative which has the lowest expected value deprivation for him.

Any given living human being chooses that alternative which has the lowest expected value deprivation for him.

Any given living American will choose an occupation which has the least expected value deprivation for him. He will rate unfavorably that occupation which has the greatest expected value deprivation for him.

Any given medical student will tend to rate favorably a medical field which has the least expected value deprivation for him. He will rate unfavorably that medical field which has the greatest expected value deprivation for him.

A medical student's preferences among medical fields are affected by his values and his expectations as to the opportunities for fulfilling these values in the various fields.

John Smith's preferences among medical fields are affected by his values and his expectations as to the opportunities for fulfilling them in the various fields.

REALITY

FIGURE 2-2 A Ladder of Abstraction for Propositions and Theories

the ladder). Such procedures also have their effects on the scientific process, and some of these are discussed by C. Wright Mills:

> The basic cause of grand theory is the initial choice of a level of thinking so general that its practitioners cannot logically get down to observation. They

never, as grand theorists, get down from the higher generalities to problems in their historical and structural contexts. This absence of a firm sense of genuine problems, in turn, makes for the unreality so noticeable in their pages. One resulting characteristic is a seemingly arbitrary and certainly endless elaboration of distinctions, which neither enlarge our understanding nor make our experience more sensible.[3]

In addition to taking to task "grand theory," which remains at the top of the ladder of abstraction, Mills also denounces "abstracted empiricism," where, by staying as close as possible to the bottom of the ladder, both rigor and triviality are simultaneously achieved.

Mills' highly individualistic conception of research strategy reveals his alarm over the "bureaucratization" of research. He wanted every social scientist to be his own theorist and his own methodologist, with the aim of moving investigations back and forth between the formulation and the testing of theory. If a particular scientist specializes in theory and neglects verification, or vice versa, scientific progress may be endangered if other scientists are not interested in complementing his work. Although such complementing may take place in the case of the most well-known scholars, it occurs all too infrequently as a rule. Thus, the strategy of specialization in theory or empiricism denounced by Mills may in fact militate against cumulative growth in behavioral science.

IMPLICIT IDEAS

The Western world tends to polarize or dichotomize a great many concepts, and its view of science does not escape this tradition. Scientific ideas, in addition to being seen as perfectly rational, are also generally viewed as explicit. The scientist supposedly verbalizes and records all the essential ideas related to his research. The layman, by contrast, is prone to superstition and obedience to authority and is full of rationalizations, projections, and other assorted Freudian defense mechanisms.

The view we put forward differs from this one. Not only is the layman an incipient scientist, as a being who attempts to solve problems with the aid of conceptual abstractions, but the scientist (as well as the layman) is prone to just about all the nonrational types of behavior known to man. Among these is the failure to be aware of implicit assumptions and, consequently, the isolation of such assumptions from the verification process. Thus, the explicit language of science refers to only a portion of the ideas involved in the research process. Some of the most fundamental ones, the paradigms out of which spring the explicit theories under examination, go largely unrecognized.

[3] C. Wright Mills, *The Sociological Imagination* (New York: Grove, 1961), p. 33.

2.2   PARADIGMS

Behind every idea are assumptions, most of which are unstated, which give the idea direction and meaning. For example, sociologists assume that human life on the planet Earth in the twentieth century is important enough to be worth studying. They also assume, along with most other behavioral scientists, that humans are goal-oriented creatures, that is, they seek to achieve goals. Survey researchers assume that verbal data are important keys to human behavior. These and other social scientists generally assume that a scientific approach to human behavior is both possible and desirable.

A paradigm is a set of assumptions, both stated and unstated, which provides the basis on which scientific ideas rest.[4] It is perhaps impossible to bare the entire paradigm behind a given idea. We might think of the process of unearthing a paradigm as a progressive one: one assumption suggests another which, in turn, suggests others. Let us explore a portion of the paradigm behind the medical student study for illustrative purposes.

1. *Goal orientation.* If expected value deprivation is used as a basis for understanding choice of medical field, this implies an assumption that medical students are oriented to avoiding goal deprivation or to attaining goal fulfillment. Such an assumption of goal orientation, common to most work in the behavioral sciences, is rarely stated explicitly. As a result of recent work in cybernetics,[5] the concept of goal has come to be defined broadly enough so that it can be applied to many nonliving systems. For example, the "goal" of a thermostat can be said to be that of keeping a given environment within a given temperature range. Regardless of whether a goal is determined from within or programmed from without, the behavior of any system in attempting to achieve its goals is analogous to that of any other system. Thus, the assumption of goal orientation is proving to be valuable for studying a very wide range of phenomena.

2. *Orientation to social stasis vs. social change.* Implicit within the questionnaire was the view that the problem of recruiting excellent medical students to public health is one of perception and motivation: if they could only learn to see through the haze of stereotypes about public

---

[4] For a discussion of the paradigms that have been dominant in the different areas of the development of physical science, and of their positive and negative contributions to this development, see Thomas S. Kuhn, *The Structure of Scientific Revolutions* (Chicago: University of Chicago Press, 1962). For a more comprehensive and detailed approach to the fundamental paradigms of Western intellectual history see Stephen C. Pepper, *World Hypotheses* (Berkeley: University of California Press, 1961).

[5] See, for example, the six articles in Part V, "Cybernetics: Purpose, Self-regulation, and Self-direction," in Walter Buckley (ed.), *Modern Systems Research for the Behavioral Scientist* (Chicago: Aldine, 1968).

health, they would become motivated to enter the field. Yet it is entirely possible that the field itself must be restructured if students are to be attracted to it. It is even conceivable that major changes in culture and society are a necessary prerequisite for the field to become attractive. For example, we may question whether a society emphasizing wealth and status can produce a sufficient proportion of individuals motivated to enter salaried positions and take over the status of government bureaucrats (which tends to be lower than that of self-employed professionals).

3. *Investigator effect.* Despite efforts to develop several different measurements for the most important concepts, despite care in not over-generalizing from the results of the study, and despite the result that the study was in large measure successful in corroborating and extending certain basic social science ideas, the ways in which researchers affected the responses of students were almost completely untapped. This was because of an implicit assumption that if the investigator attempts to minimize investigator effect, it is unnecessary for him to do anything more about this problem. Yet an effective case can be made—for this or almost any other survey—that despite ordinary precautions, investigator effect may be large enough to invalidate findings. Thus, the implicit assumption in the medical student study about the relative unimportance of investigator effect may have produced conditions which invalidate the conclusions of the study.

4. *Individual stasis.* The medical student study did not follow up the the students to determine the relationship between the students' stated preferences and the fields they actually entered after completing their medical education. Implicitly, there is an assumption here that the student's preference while pursuing his studies is an indicator of his subsequent choice. Yet this will be true only to the extent that the perceptual, motivational, and situational factors lying behind the student's preference remain relatively constant over an extended period of time.

5. *Zero-sum.* The preferences of a given individual student were viewed as mutually exclusive: his preference for one field would preclude his going into any other field. Also, if his expected value deprivation for a given field were very high, this militated against a high expected deprivation for other fields. All of this implies a view of a student as having a fixed maximum amount of affect, with portions of this affect being apportioned to different fields and with this resulting in different relative preferences. Of course, there are alternative ways of viewing occupational choices (for example, that of the individual successively entering different occupations and continually learning to build up greater affect in each occupation he enters as a result of his experience in previous occupations). Such a view may not be so foreign to the field of public health, which constitutes a second occupation for a substantial proportion of doctors.

By these examples of implicit assumptions in social science research we do not mean to imply either the inherent inferiority of social science when compared to physical science or the hopelessness of the scientific enterprise. The Newtonian mechanistic paradigm and many others have dominated the history of the physical sciences, with their positive as well as negative effects on scientific progress. Furthermore, it is not the paradigm itself which is harmful, but the failure to convert implicit paradigms into explicit ones. Without such conversions, the paradigm remains untouched and untouchable, outside of the realm of scientific investigation. It takes on the status of unquestioned dogma.

It is only when we recognize that paradigms lie behind every scientific idea that we can begin to unearth their nature. Without such recognition, it is all too easy for the scientist to deceive himself into thinking that he is proceeding in a perfectly rational and open-minded way, with no hidden assumptions whatsoever. Yet it is the nature of any human being, whether he calls himself a scientist or uses some other designation, to be conscious of only a proportion of his ideas and motives. Furthermore, it is the nature of human language to be replete with vagueness and emotional overtones. Finally, it is the nature of deduction to proceed from certain premises, whether stated or unstated. Given this combination, we might do well to turn our attention away from the hopeless task of eliminating implicit assumptions and toward the fruitful task of learning the nature of our assumptions with a view toward subjecting them to empirical testing.

The current emphasis on the uncovering of paradigms is, in many ways, in the tradition of Freudian thought. Whatever else Freud believed, he focused attention on the submerged portion of the iceberg of the personality, and his therapeutic efforts were in the direction of raising that portion to full view. We need not of course take an optimistic view about our ability to uncover deeply hidden paradigms or deeply repressed desires. An alternative view is illustrated by the following:

> Freud's legacy is a fundamental mistrust of the intellectual attitude: he unmasked the aesthetic attitude as nonsensical, the moral and religious as illusory, and proceeded to debunk all intellectual utterances as the distorted products of 'hidden' fantasies, derived from the repressed sex and aggressive instincts in their various stages of development. Yet, somewhere in the distant future, Freud hoped, scientists would discover something about the reality of the world through which men could increase their power and according to which they could regulate their lives. With the fragmentation of the world into warring universes of discourse, however, we have lost the last illusion which Freud still left us.[6]

However, we may also view these warring universes of discourse as a symptom of the search for a universe of discourse which can release man's potential, and perhaps such warring can accomplish this through uncovering the unquestioned assumptions which lock man or the scientist into

---

[6] Gunter W. Remmling, *Road to Suspicion* (New York: Meredith, 1967), p. 210.

a narrow and unproductive way of life. Remmling's view is valuable insofar as it alerts us to the enormous obstacles in the path of the goldfish that is attempting to discover the water all around it, but all is lost if this leads the goldfish to define the situation as an impossible one.

2.3 CONCEPTS

CLARITY AND SCOPE

Concepts are abstractions used by the scientist as building blocks for the development of propositions and theories which explain and predict phenomena. They are unitary and thus are not the same as relationships between phenomena. For example, the behavioral scientist ordinarily would not speak of "the process of occupational choice" as a concept, but would refer to "choice" and "values" as concepts.

A concept represents a selection of certain phenomena that are grouped or classified together. Such a selection is neither true nor false; rather, it is judged in terms of its utility for the advancement of scientific knowledge. Its degree of freedom from vagueness and ambiguity—that is, how precisely it specifies or connotes a particular set of phenomena (its determinacy) and how uniform its usage is for all users of the language (its uniformity of usage)—will also affect its value for the communicative process.

Clarity is greatly affected by whether or not the terms used to designate the concept are part of the lay vocabulary. If they are, as is usually the case with concepts in behavioral science, the meanings of the terms as used in everyday speech may obscure the meaning which the scientist is attempting to convey. For example, one definition of the concept *role* by behavioral scientists is *a pattern of behavior associated with a distinctive social position*. In the lay vocabulary, the term *social position* connotes the place of individuals in a social-prestige hierarchy. In the vocabulary of behavioral science, *social position* usually means a social category such as father, wife, engineer, and so on.

Lack of clarity may lead to statements which seem to provide explanations but which in fact do not. The following paragraph was constructed to illustrate this point.

Psychopathic personality has been defined in many different ways. One example makes reference to the characteristic of emotional abnormality without the break from reality which characterizes psychotics. Another refers to the lack of a fully developed conscience. A third definition refers directly to antisocial acts and criminal behavior. We will accept this latter definition. We come now to one of the basic questions which the student of human behavior is called upon to answer: What are the causes of crime? Although these are many, one of the most important ones has to do with the personality structure of the individual. As we all know, crime is by definition a violation of the code of society, and it is the psychopathic personality, unchecked by a socially developed conscience, which feels no compunctions about violating social norms. *Thus, a partial explanation for the occurrence of crime is that it is in large measure a product of the psychopathic personality.*

Psychopathic personality, defined as *antisocial acts and criminal behavior* in the first part of the paragraph, is used in the sentence at the end of the paragraph as a partial explanation for the occurrence of crime. This amounts to saying that criminal behavior is one of the causes of criminal behavior. An unwary reader, however, may read the term *psychopathic personality* to mean something different from its definition in terms of criminal behavior. Because he adds meanings to the term other than those implied by the author, the reasoning does not appear to him to be circular.

A critical approach to concepts and definitions is consonant with the tradition of scientific skepticism. Three different kinds of criteria for judgment are scope, clarity, and systematic import. Scope refers to the inclusiveness of the class of situations to which the concept applies (concepts at the higher rungs of the ladder of abstraction have greater scope than those at the lower rungs); clarity, to the concept's potential for moving down the ladder of abstraction to an objective determination or measurement; and systematic import, to the degree to which the concept is incorporated in propositions and theories. Both the scope of the propositions and their degree of clarity affect systematic import.

One chapter in a leading textbook used in introductory sociology introduces these terms: *self, socialization, instinct, symbolic interaction, unconscious socialization, I, me, id, ego, superego, looking-glass self, ideal self, inner controls, static adaptation, dynamic adaptation, adequate ego, identification, inadequate ego, significant others, natural sign, nonverbal communication, generalized other, other-directed, inner-directed, anticipatory socialization, resocialization, basic personality, national character,* and *Oedipus complex.* These concepts all have considerable scope because they can apply to human situations anywhere and any time. Some of them (for example, *nonverbal communication*) have more scope than others (for example, *anticipatory socialization*). Whereas the former concept can be applied to almost all situations in which social interaction is taking place, the latter refers primarily to those situations in which the individual's actions help him to prepare for a future change in role.

Clarity has to do with the degree to which the concept implies a chain of lower-level abstractions. For example, the concepts *God, ultimate good,* and *beautiful* mean very different things to different individuals. It is difficult for each to move down the ladder of abstraction to instances in which the phenomenon does and does not occur. Of course, no concept means exactly the same thing to different individuals, and a certain amount of vagueness may even be useful, for it leaves the concept open to many applications. Thus, for example, *social interaction* may be defined as *the process in which one person's behavior affects another person's behavior.* But, in a sense, every person's behavior is affected, however slightly or indirectly, by the behavior of every other person. Should we then limit *interaction* to face-to-face situations? This would exclude the interaction between an author and a reader or between the proponents of an ideology and the masses of followers. Thus, sometimes it would be useful to investigate social interactions that are not face to face. It might even be useful to study indirect interaction through a number of intermediaries. The vagueness of the concept *interaction,* as defined above, provides a "tent" within which all of these investigations may take place.

SYSTEMATIC IMPORT

In addition to the criteria of scope and clarity for the evaluation of concepts we have that of systematic import. In the following passage this criterion is pitted against that of formulating precise "operational definitions," with the latter being closely related to the criterion of clarity.

> In the contemporary methodological literature of psychology and the social sciences, the need for "operational definitions" is often emphasized to the neglect of the requirement of systematic import, and occasionally the impression is given that the most promising way of furthering the growth of sociology as a scientific discipline is to create a large supply of "operationally defined" terms of high determinacy and uniformity of usage, leaving it to subsequent research to discover whether these terms lend themselves to the formulation of fruitful theoretical principles. But concept formation in science cannot be separated from theoretical considerations.[7]

In this view, concepts should not be treated separately from the propositions and theories of which they are a part. If concepts are to be evaluated in terms of their contribution to explanation and prediction, then their role as elements of existing propositions and theories (the major tools for explanation and prediction)—their systematic import— must be taken into account.

This criterion is certainly not an infallible guide to the evaluation of a given concept. New concepts, for example, may have very little systematic import and still ultimately achieve a great deal. Heavy reliance on systematic import would yield a very conservative research strategy; neglect of systematic import would result in a failure to learn from previous research. If there are few verified propositions with wide scope in a given field and, as appears to be the case in behavioral science, few sys-

[7] Carl G. Hempel, *Fundamentals of Concept Formation in Empirical Science* (Chicago: University of Chicago Press, 1952), p. 47.

tems of such propositions, then it is very difficult to reach any agreement as to which concepts have systematic import and which do not. In this situation almost all concepts have very little systematic import, and their value lies primarily in their potential for the development of systematic import. When objective criteria, such as systematic import, cannot readily be applied, the way is then open for less pragmatic criteria—such as the authority of the person using the concept, the status of the journal in which the publication appears, the nonsystematic linking of the concept with others in vogue, the degree to which the concept involves words or grammatical constructions uncommon in the lay vocabulary, the mere assertion that the concept is an important one, and so on.

The extent to which scientists may be guided by these less pragmatic criteria has been demonstrated by a tongue-in-cheek article designed to evaluate the effect of these criteria. One excerpt, in which a theory of "deumbilification" is presented, reads as follows:

> This constant contact [between fetus and umbilical cord] builds up expectations, through conditioning, of further contact. When the fetus loses the umbilical cord, an awareness of its absence is manifest. So far as is known, after parturition, in all societies and peoples the umbilical cord is removed from the newborn, either by cutting, biting, or letting it atrophy, as it does, naturally. It *is a normal course for the newborn, among all peoples, to be deumbilificated.* The absence of the umbilical cord, and the memory traces associated with it, are the underlying reasons for the insecurity manifest in man.[8]

Borgatta uses all possible ploys, and then some, to push the concept of deumbilification: its extensive scope is emphasized, the work of well-known sociologists is footnoted, new terms are introduced (*deumbilification, mammary envy, Lenny complex, person-group, reference-person theory, no-person group, ascetophysician*), numerous words are underlined, well-known theories and methods are constantly evoked, unusual grammatical constructions and phraseology are employed, and a generally pretentious tone is adopted. The result was that many professional social scientists took the article seriously and at face value. This, perhaps, should serve to emphasize the value of scientific skepticism as well as the fact that many scientists are not well versed in utilizing scientific skepticism.

EXTREME OPERATIONISM AND OPERATIONISM

Behavioral scientists vary in the degree to which they emphasize the clarity of a given concept and the ease of developing objective measures on the basis of that concept. The tendency of some behavioral scientists to view clarity and ease of objective measurement as the most important

---

[8] Edgar F. Borgatta, "Sidesteps Toward a Nonspecial Theory," *Psychological Review,* **61** (1954), 345–46.

criteria for concept formation may be referred to as the *strategy of extreme operationism*. Under this approach, a concept such as *goal* might not pass muster because, regardless of its relatively high degree of systematic import, it is more difficult to measure than many others. Another kind of concept which would be rejected is exemplified by Max Weber's ideal types:

> An ideal-type is formed by the one-sided accentuation of one or more points of view and by the synthesis of a great many diffuse, discrete, more or less present and occasionally absent *concrete individual* phenomena, which are arranged according to those one-sidedly emphasized viewpoints into a unified analytical construct. In its conceptual purity, the mental construct cannot be found empirically anywhere in reality. It is a utopia.[9]

The purpose of setting up ideal types is to help the investigator develop concepts which may prove to have systematic import. Thus, for example, one ideal type might be the "urban personality," conceived of as having all of the characteristics associated with cosmopolitanism, urbanity, and sophistication, and none of the characteristics conflicting with these. Although such personalities do not actually exist, this conception enables the scientist to talk about the various degrees of "urbanity." He can then treat degree of urbanity as a variable and proceed to relate it to other variables, thus testing propositions and theories.

The ideal type is an example of a concept referring to phenomena which are not directly observable. The word *construct* is often used to denote such phenomena. Historically, many constructs (such as *perfect vacuum*) have been used quite successfully by physical scientists. The lack of direct observability of the phenomena specified has been justified by the fact that they are often to be found in systems of propositions in which many of the concepts involved refer to observable phenomena. This gives indirect confirmation to those that do not.

In its extreme form, the operationist position is that the concept has no meaning apart from the specific operations used to measure the phenomena to which it refers. Thus, for example, the only meaning of the concept *intelligence* is provided by describing the operations used to measure intelligence—or "intelligence is whatever is measured by an intelligence test."

Operationism performs a valuable service by calling attention to the importance of clarity, precision, and operational definitions. More generally, operationist thought emphasizes the importance of moving down the ladder of abstraction. But without such concepts as *intelligence,* the investigator has no guide to the direction of future research. Unless the

[9] Max Weber, "Objectivity in Social Science and Social Policy," in Edward A. Shils and Henry A. Finch (trans. and ed.), *The Methodology of the Social Sciences* (New York: Free Press, 1949), p. 90.

investigator is guided by the abstract concept *intelligence,* he has no criterion by which to assess and improve the intelligence test he has constructed. The extreme operationist viewpoint loses sight of the fact that clarity and precision are means to achieve the goals of explanation and prediction. Viewed as ends in themselves, they can easily result in the sacrifice of potentially fruitful concepts because of measurement difficulties.

A further difficulty is that concepts or abstractions are necessarily used by the most rigorous operationists. Even statements about measurement operations are abstractions. For example, a description of the operations involved in a given intelligence test cannot completely avoid conceptualization and abstraction. Because no two phenomena are ever exactly alike and all objects undergo change, a test situation is never exactly repeatable. Thus, the operationist must resort to whatever it is that many different test situations involving a given intelligence test have in common. If this kind of abstraction is justified, the rigorous stance of the operationist becomes less formidable, for higher levels of abstraction differ only in degree.

The deficiencies of extreme operationism do not detract from the importance of a more balanced operationist approach, which emphasizes the importance of specific measurement procedures or operations in order to test propositions but also allows for the importance of concepts and abstractions. In this broad sense, most scientists, if they are at all concerned with testing propositions and theories, are operationists.

2.4 PROPOSITIONS

THE NATURE OF PROPOSITIONS

Propositions are statements about the nature of reality and thus can be judged in terms of truth and falsity, provided they refer to observable phenomena. Hypotheses are propositions formulated for empirical testing. Laws are propositions which have very wide scope and which have received a high degree of confirmation.

Propositions in sociology and psychology generally involve a statement of the relationship between two or more concepts. For example, propositions would more often be of the type *Exposure to the mass media of communication is a factor in the development of the urban personality* than of the type *More than half of the population of the United States reads less than one book per year.* Both are propositions in that they are statements about the nature of reality and may be tested, but the first relates two factors to one another whereas the second deals with the distribution of only one factor. In addition, the first implies a concern with a cause-and-effect relationship, which is a dominant concern among behavioral scientists.

The term *theorem* is used in a manner roughly synonymous to that of *proposition*. The concept of *theorem* derives from the literature of mathematics and logic, and it has a formalistic connotation. Thus, we would expect to be able to derive, by deductive logic, any given theorem from a specified set of axioms or postulates, as in Euclidean geometry.

TESTABILITY

Analogous to the criteria of clarity, scope, and systematic import (for concepts) are those of testability, scope, and the effectiveness of explanations and predictions (for propositions). Propositions are testable if it is possible (in principle) to obtain data which can be used as evidence for acceptance or rejection. Because what is or is not considered as evidence is determined by the community of scientists, what is viewed as not testable at one time may become testable at another.

An example of a proposition which currently is generally considered to be untestable is *Democracy is the best form of government.* Although there would be great difficulty involved in clarifying and measuring *democracy,* the central problem lies in the concept of *best,* for "one man's meat may be another man's poison." *Best* is so vague and ambiguous that a scientist would not be able to devise a measurement procedure which would be generally accepted within the community of scientists. However, the proposition might be converted into a testable statement if it is revised to *Democracy is the best form of government for maximizing citizens' participation in the decisions which affect their behavior.* Here the concept *best* is qualified; it refers to maximizing the political participation of individuals. It would be possible to devise a generally accepted procedure for measuring political participation, a relatively clear and unambiguous concept.

VARIABLES AND HYPOTHESES

A variable is a concept which takes on two or more degrees or values. Thus the concept *chair* is not a variable, but the concept *weight of chair* is. *Chair* does not imply a multiplicity of values, for it makes no specification as to what characteristic is being referred to (for example, *color, weight, height,* and so on). Once such a characteristic is specified, one can talk about the different colors, heights, and weights that are possible. *Sex* takes on the values of *male* and *female* and thus may be called a variable, along with most of the concepts used by social scientists.

Concepts which do not directly imply a multiplicity of values can usually be converted into variables by focusing on a particular property or characteristic. Thus, *ego* can be converted into *ego strength,* and socialization may be converted into *rapidity of socialization* or *degree of socialization,* and so on.

Hypotheses have been called "questions put to nature" and are fundamental tools in scientific research. They may be divided into descriptive and relational types. In descriptive hypotheses, the question asked deals with the distribution or occurrence of a given variable, with no attempt to explore the relationships among variables. If we seek to determine whether or not the number of individuals over sixty-five in a given community exceeds a certain percentage, we are dealing with a descriptive hypothesis. A relational hypothesis, on the other hand, might be the statement *Age is inversely related to mental health.* The question here is whether or not the mental health of older individuals tends to be poorer than that of younger individuals.

Social scientists use relational hypotheses almost to the exclusion of descriptive hypotheses. Description is generally not preceded by the statement or formal testing of any particular hypothesis; it is often viewed as a means for obtaining ideas about the interrelationships among phenomena, which, in turn, are used in setting up relational hypotheses. Relational hypotheses are used by the behavioral scientist as aids in obtaining evidence on cause-and-effect relationships.

Another important tool of the social scientist is the distinction between independent variables (the presumed cause) and dependent variables (the presumed effect). The independent variable is presumed to be antecedent to, or simultaneous with, the dependent variable. In the relational hypothesis on age and mental health cited earlier, age is presumed to be a causal factor affecting mental health. Thus, *age* would be called the independent variable; *mental health,* the dependent variable.

Although in this example the investigator has no choice but to consider age as the independent variable (the state of one's mental health cannot be conceived of as affecting his chronological age), the behavioral scientist often does have a choice. Consider the variables *decision on whether or not to move from a rural to an urban community* and *exposure to the mass media of communication.* One hypothesis which could be posed is *A greater proportion of those who are exposed to the mass media decide to move than of those who are not.* In this case *exposure* is treated as the independent variable, and *the decision to move* is treated as the dependent variable. But the investigator might be more interested in the reverse hypothesis: *The decision to move induces individuals to expose themselves to the mass media.* Here, *the decision to move* is treated as independent; *exposure,* as dependent. Because the investigator is free to pose different types of questions, a given variable may be treated as dependent or independent, or both.

RELATIONSHIPS AMONG VARIABLES: EXISTENCE, DEGREE, AND TYPE

One can test the hypothesis *Age is directly related to mental illness* and, on the basis of the results, decide whether or not such a relationship exists. We may then say that we have evidence that there is a higher probability for older people to be mentally ill than for younger people. Efforts to establish the *existence* of relationships constitute a large proportion of the research of social scientists. When we know that a relationship between age and mental illness, for example, exists, this does not of course enable us to predict accurately whether a person of a given age will or will not be mentally ill. But it is quite valuable as a step in the direction of obtaining a thorough understanding of the causes of mental illness. To capitalize on such findings it is usually necessary to do much additional research designed to locate other variables related to mental illness and to develop gradually a theory which can account for all of these relationships.

Such a theory might enable the researcher to go beyond a simple statement which specifies that a relationship exists between a given variable and the probability of mental illness. For example, he might be able to state how close this association is. If a close relationship between age and the probability of mental illness were established, he would be able to state that the greater the age of an individual, the higher the probability of his being mentally ill. This indicates that the probability of mental illness consistently increases with increasing age, a finding that considerably augments the simple statement that a relationship exists between these two variables. For example, there might be a good deal of variation in the probability of mental illness for the different age groupings below the age of forty, and there might similarly be great variation among age groupings forty years of age and over. In this situation we would still be able to say that a relationship exists between age and the probability of mental illness, provided that the forty-and-over group as a whole included a larger proportion of mentally ill individuals than the under-forty group. However, we would not be able to say that there is a high degree of relationship between age and the probability of mental illness, because the increase in the proportion of mentally ill individuals with increasing age would not be a consistent one.

Although it is not generally too difficult to obtain evidence indicating that various relationships exist, it is quite another matter to locate variables which have a high degree of interrelationship. Thus far efforts by social scientists to do so have met with limited success, although there are a substantial number of exceptions. The trend seems to be one of increasing concern on the part of social scientists with unearthing those relationships which are close ones.

When a close association is found between two variables we are still generally not able to predict the value of one variable accurately on the basis of the other. For example, the proportion of mentally ill individuals may increase consistently with increasing age, but the degree of such increases may vary greatly from one age group to the next. The rate may increase by one tenth from age fifty to age fifty-five, by one third from fifty-five to sixty, and by one half from sixty to sixty-five.

The ability to predict is a most difficult attainment for the social scientist. Here, as in the case of efforts to find close associations, a theory of considerable scope that is based on a large number of confirming specific findings is called for. In advance of considerable supporting evidence, efforts to state relationships mathematically are premature, because such statements are broad in scope and obviously are ineffective unless the predictions they imply can reasonably be expected to be confirmed.

Such a mathematical statement might be illustrated within the context of the present example. Suppose we knew, for example, that the relationship between age and the probability of mental illness is one of direct proportionality. In other words, suppose we had data to show that the probability of mental illness increases in approximately equal steps with each increase in age. Such a relationship would be expressed symbolically in the same way as was the expression for the relationship between EVD and the probability of an unfavorable rating on p. 32:

$$\text{Age}_i = k \cdot p \text{ (mental illness)}_i$$

This reads, "The age of a given individual (i) is equal to a constant (k) times the probability of mental illness on the part of the given individual." In this way, the relationship of direct proportionality is expressed symbolically. Such formulas can be used to predict the actual probability of mental illness for an individual of a given age, provided k is known.

Of course, the preceding relationship is only a hypothetical one. Even if evidence in support of it were collected, it would still be necessary to determine a figure or value for the constant k, one which would hold generally and not be limited to just a few highly specific situations. It seems likely, also, that mathematical statements which can effectively predict mental illness will be more complicated than the one above and will include at least several factors, as distinct from simply that of age. A good deal remains to be done before relationships of this type, or other mathematical formulations, are uncovered and are widely tested. Efforts to develop and test mathematical formulations in social science have increased very rapidly within the last decade, and we can look to an even more rapid increase in the future as a result of the widespread availability of computers for processing mathematical formulations.

2.5 THEORIES

SOME CONFLICTING CONCEPTIONS OF THEORY

Theories, as well as propositions, can be evaluated in terms of their testability, scope, and capacity to explain and predict. Zetterberg has distinguished three older conceptions associated by sociologists with the term *theory: sociological classics, sociological criticism,* and *sociological taxonomy.* The first denotes the important works of early sociologists which provided the basis for a great deal of the work that followed; the second traces the relationships and continuities among sociological ideas from an historical perspective; the third refers to an orderly arrangement of sociological ideas into neat categories.[10]

Zetterberg's own use of the term *theory*—as a set of systematically interrelated propositions—corresponds to that generally occurring in the physical sciences, in the philosophy of science, and (to a lesser extent) in the social sciences.

It is important to understand that theory is here conceived as to a degree specifying relationships among propositions. Any theory may then be evaluated with respect to the magnitude of this degree as well as in terms of testability, scope, and capacity to explain and predict.[11] By avoiding an all-or-none evaluation of theory we are able to give due recognition to the many formulations within social science which are not highly systematic but which nevertheless represent important contributions. Such an approach is constructive in that it does not limit use of this highly prestigious word to only a very few formulations, with the implication that the remaining ones are worthless.

Figure 2-3 illustrates the interrelationship among propositions and theories. Each of the three propositions may be tested separately. In the case of the first proposition, for example, medical students interested in close patient relationships also tend to be more interested in general practice. In the case of the second proposition, those who assess public health as providing little in the way of opportunities for a high income tend to be less favorably disposed toward that field. In the third proposition there is indirect evidence that social relationships among students lead to a degree of agreement among them as to preferences for the various medical fields.

Theory 2 incorporates Propositions 1 and 2, although it is certainly not the only theory which can perform this function. Proposition 3, which deals with social relationships, is not directly incorporated in Theory 2; however, it may be conceived of as being indirectly involved, for social relationships may be conceived of as leading to the development of values and expectations.

Because Theory 2 is only one of many possible theories based on Propositions 1, 2, and 3 which could be constructed, proving the truth of these propositions does not automatically prove the truth of Theory 2. What proving the truth of the propositions would show is that one of a class of

[10] Hans L. Zetterberg, *On Theory and Verification in Sociology* (Totowa, N.J.: Bedminster Press, 1963), pp. 4–5.

[11] It should be noted that a common conception of theory among philosophers of science specifies that the propositions involved be *laws* (or propositions with universal scope). Such a conception seems unduly restrictive in the context of behavioral science.

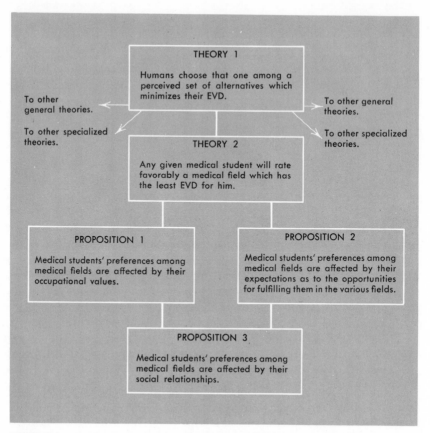

FIGURE 2-3 An Example of the Interrelationship Among Propositions and Theories

theories consistent with these propositions is true, and we would know that Theory 2 is a member of that class. However, if, for example, Proposition 1 is proved to be false, then we could be confident that Theory 2 is false, because Proposition 1 represents an integral component of this theory. Much scientific research is directed toward disproof in this manner rather than toward direct attempts at proof. For example, much of the technology for the statistical testing of hypotheses, a topic to be discussed in Chapters 14 and 15, is directed toward the disproof, rather than the proof, of hypotheses.

Theory 1 is far more general than Theory 2. Evidence for Theory 2, as well as for other theories of choice applicable to special situations, may be used as evidence for Theory 1. This is indicated in Figure 2-3 by the arrows leading from Theory 1 "to other specialized theories." Thus, for example, specialized theories that are similar to Theory 2 may be developed for the choice of a house, a community, a mate, a physician, and so on. Also, Theory 1 may be related to other general theories (as indicated by the arrows in Figure 2-3); for example, a theory focusing on the interrelationships among groups.

We might say that Theory 1 has much greater scope than Theory 2. Moreover, Theory 1 is partially tested by testing Theory 2. Of course the greater the scope of theory, the greater becomes the difficulty of testing more than a minute proportion of the instances to which it applies. This is yet another reason for the conclusion that, although evidence can be brought to bear in support of a theory, a theory with wide scope can never be definitely confirmed. Although the scientist can only demonstrate the credibility of a theory, he can nevertheless proceed to utilize it for purposes of explanation and prediction. Each such use also functions to provide additional evidence for the theory.

THE SPATIAL NETWORK ANALOGY

Very often explanations of abstract entities can be facilitated by means of analogies or models. Carl Hempel uses this approach when he discusses theory:

> A scientific theory might therefore be likened to a complex spatial network: its terms are represented by the knots, while the threads connecting the latter correspond, in part, to the fundamental and derivative hypotheses included in the theory. The whole system floats, as it were, above the plane of observation and is anchored to it by rules of interpretation. These might be viewed as strings which are not part of the network but link certain points of the latter with specific places in the plane of observation.[12]

Pursuing this analogy further, we might distinguish between preliminary theory and more advanced theory. In the former case, the "knots" (or concepts) will be rather large, and the "strings" tying them to the plane of observation will be correspondingly thick, corresponding to the vagueness and diffuseness of the concepts and the lack of precision of the operational definitions. Thus, for example, the concept of *social class* is often conceptually defined in such a way that it includes aspects of *social interaction, norms,* and *values.* Also, the different operational definitions or measurements of *social class* vary with respect to one another.

In this preliminary theory, the strings which tie the concepts together are also quite thick, corresponding to the lack of clear specification of the types of interrelationships involved. Furthermore, the number of these threads is minimal, for most propositions are separate and distinct. Another way of saying this is that the concepts within the theory have very little systematic import.

More advanced theory might be represented by rather small knots, with

---

[12] Hempel, op. cit., p. 36.

thin strings tying the concepts to the plane of observation, and a large number of strings providing connections among the concepts. This corresponds to more precise conceptualization, greater agreement among the various indexes of a given concept, specification of the types of relationships among the concepts, and a fairly systematic integration of all of the concepts and propositions.

Numerous remedies have been proposed for developing sociological theory from the preliminary to the advanced state (see Chapter 3). One point of view is that the concepts of sociology are vague and overlapping, and that there is little agreement on the usage of terms. The remedy proposed is that all concepts should be very precise so that particular measurements or operational definitions are implied, and that sociologists should attempt to achieve a greater degree of agreement on usages. An opposing view is that the systematic import of concepts is the only significant factor and that an adequate theory which incorporates concepts necessarily precedes conceptual clarity and precise operational definitions. For instance, the concept of *temperature* in physics was clarified only after a theory was developed in which temperature was understood to be a function of the velocity of molecules. Within this context, the many overlapping and vague definitions in sociology are seen as symptoms rather than causes of the "diseased" state of sociological theory.

As for how sociologists and other social scientists can move rapidly toward advanced theory, this is the fundamental problem of scientific creativity and discovery, a problem which has rarely been approached by scientists in a systematic way. Yet if the social scientist takes his discipline at all seriously, he will tend to conclude that there is no bar to the attainment of this kind of knowledge. We shall take up the process of scientific discovery as well as its complement, the context of justification, in Chapter 3.

MODELS

Because of our conception of theory as referring to propositions that are interrelated to a degree, it becomes useful to differentiate those theories which are highly systematic from those which are less so. As for the meaning of systematic, we have reference to the powerful tools of mathematical and logical analysis which can interrelate vast varieties of phenomena. When such tools can be employed, the theory involved must be fairly systematic. We may refer to such theories as models.

Of the various types of models, we wish to distinguish between those which are relatively static and those which are relatively dynamic. For example, our model of the choice process of medical students is relatively static, because the flow of time is not taken very seriously. Students are seen as making a single choice which, they expect, will yield certain satisfactions. This contrasts with a more dynamic framework where, as distinct from a single decision, we might analyze the flow of decisions over a specified unit of time. In such a dynamic formulation, moreover, the different aspects of the model may be conceived of as occurring in sequential fashion and taking up finite amounts of time. Such a model, as applied to the preferences of medical students, might focus on the student's series of occupational choices, the flow of rewards and information related to this series, and the implications of these flows for the student's subsequent series of choices. Thus, initial choices directing a student toward a career in cardiovascular surgery might expose him to a series of disappointments about his own abilities which, in turn, might lower his level of aspiration for such a career, shifting him to a different career line. Such a change might build up over a very long period, or it might build up quite rapidly, but in any case a finite time period is a factor necessary for its occurrence.

EXERCISES

1. Explore the relationship between scientific language and everyday language. What does this suggest concerning the view of man's everyday behavior as analogous to the behavior of the scientist?

2. If there are assumptions behind any scientific idea, there are also general assumptions behind any specific set of assumptions. What are some of the general assumptions behind the implicit assumptions relating to the medical student study discussed in Section 2.2? How are these assumptions related to the model of the scientific method treated in Chapter 1?

3. Taking into account the purposes and nature of the scientific method, what is the advantage of working with variables as distinct from concepts that are not treated as variables?

4. On the basis of your social science knowledge, state a proposition in mathematical form. What kind of data would provide evidence against the truth of your proposition?

5. State a social science theory. What are its component propositions, and how are they interrelated?

ANNOTATED REFERENCES

KUHN, THOMAS S. *The Structure of Scientific Revolutions.* Chicago: University of Chicago Press, 1962. The work of the individual scientist may be better understood by paying attention to the paradigm within which he is operating. Such a focus alerts us to the dominant traditions and schools of thought in any given era; we must come to take seriously science as a social system. If we can come to understand the ways in which such paradigms encourage and inhibit scientific discovery, then we will have traveled a good distance on the road to a science of scientific discovery.

OFSHE, RICHARD (ed.). *The Sociology of the Possible.* Englewood Cliffs, N.J.: Prentice-Hall, Inc., 1970. If the goldfish is to learn about the water around it, it must somehow conceive of a world quite different from the one in which it lives and, in this way, discover its own unquestioned assumptions. This is a potential function which imaginative literature, such as this collection of social science fiction, has for us goldfish. The nineteen chapters include selections from *Walden Two, Brave New World, The City and the Stars, Erewhon, Utopia Minus X, The Republic, Utopia,* and *Looking Backward.*

RYCHLAK, JOSEPH F. *A Philosophy of Science for Personality Theory.* Boston: Houghton Mifflin Company, 1968. Rychlak contrasts the dialectical tradition (idealism, subjective, emphasis on theory, ethics of freedom, philosophy and art, applied, armchair thinking) with the demonstrative tradition (realism, objective, emphasis on method, ethics of control, science and engineering, basic, gadgeteers). He advocates the utilization of both approaches, but he sees in modern psychology an overemphasis on the latter.

CHAPTER 3 The Process of Inquiry

3.1 GOALS OF BEHAVIORAL SCIENCE

Paradigms, concepts, propositions, and theories provide the structure or content of a science, but these ideas are developed and tested by individuals who have certain goals and certain investigative strategies and tactics. It is the live, dynamic process of investigation which must be understood if one is to achieve any adequate comprehension of science. In looking at science as a process carried forward by individuals, our major point of reference will be the goals that scientists as a group are trying to achieve.

Some of these goals may be inferred from our discussion of the language of science. *Paradigms* were defined as *sets of assumptions which provide the basis for scientific ideas; concepts* as *abstractions which are used by the scientist for the development of propositions which explain and predict phenomena; propositions* as *statements about the nature of reality;* and *theory* as *a set of propositions which are systematically interrelated.* Propositions and theory are concerned with the processes of prediction and explanation, two fundamental scientific goals. Paradigms alert us to be wary about the ways in which we achieve such explanations and predictions (for example, we should become aware of our implicit assumptions). Concepts are important tools for the development of propositions, theories, and paradigms. In the following paragraphs we shall explore the nature of the scientific goals of prediction and explanation.

PREDICTION

Scientists are interested in prediction in order to be able to cope effectively with their environment. Precise predictions constitute one of the most impressive achievements of the scientist. The astronomer has been able to predict accurately the positions of the planets in our solar system many years ahead of time. The physicist's knowledge of the relationship between distance fallen and time in free fall of a body in a vacuum can be used together with other physical laws to predict the trajectory of a missile. There are limits to the accuracy of these predictions, however. Fundamentally, there is no guarantee that the scientist's predictions will actually come to pass. In addition, available measuring instruments limit the accuracy of predictions. Furthermore, many aspects of the physical world have not yet yielded to precise predictions (a classic example is the weather). When we move from the macroscopic to the microscopic world, our capacity for prediction is drastically reduced.

It is possible to predict accurately certain aspects of human behavior; if it were not possible, life as we know it could not continue for very long. Who would dare to drive a car if he did not have confidence in the prediction that there is very little chance that one of the hundreds of thousands of drivers he will meet during his lifetime will deliberately seek to collide with him head on? We can also expect, with a high degree of confidence, that our close friends will not betray us, that our currency can be exchanged for goods and services, that we will be taxed periodically, and so on.

In addition to the regularities that are obvious to most individuals, social scientists have unearthed many regularities that are or once were not so obvious. There are, for example, the uniform patterns of behavior, attitudes, values, and social interaction exhibited by the members of a given social class, a given family, or a given society.[1]

As in the case of the physical scientists, all predictions by social scientists are fundamentally uncertain and limited in accuracy. If we think of predictions in terms of probability rather than certainty, it would be correct to say that predictions in the social sciences generally have a lower probability of success than those in the physical sciences. We can predict, for example, that contact between a majority-group member and a minority-group member will tend to reduce the degree of prejudice of the former with respect to the latter. But such a "tendency" prediction will prove to be correct little more than 50 per cent of the time, for many other factors that affect the reduction of prejudice are not taken into account. Some of these are the relative social statuses of the two individuals, the normative expectations of the majority-group member's "significant others," the degree to which the minority-group member does in fact illustrate the negative stereotypes of his group, whether the contact situation is socially defined as intimate or impersonal, and the frequency and duration of the contact.

One of the reasons why the difference in predictive capacity between the physical and social sciences is so keenly felt is that the physical sciences have constructed a highly successful technology that is almost universally regarded as having contributed enormously to man's welfare. The lack of a comparable technology in the social sciences is appallingly obvious, whether it be in the field of intergroup relations, international politics, crime and delinquency, mental illness, self-realization and crea-

[1] See Bernard Berelson and Gary A. Steiner, *Human Behavior: An Inventory of Scientific Findings* (New York: Harcourt, 1965).

tivity, family relationships, distribution of goods and services, or organization and control of power.

There have, of course, been many efforts to achieve the kinds of predictions on which such a technology might be based. For example, a study of information, collected by penal institutions in New Zealand formed the basis for Albert Morris' attempt to develop an instrument which would be used to predict which individuals would escape from these institutions.[2] (The method he used follows the general pattern of that used by the Gluecks.[3]) After investigating a number of factors that might differentiate between absconders, he selected six factors that seemed to so differentiate most effectively: age, marital status, present offense, previous offenses, present sentence, and total number of previous escapes. A total score for a given individual was then computed on the basis of these factors.

These total scores were then compared with the records of past escapes. This is not prediction as the word is ordinarily understood, for such a comparison merely indicates how well the total scores could have predicted escapes if they had been collected *before* the escapes. Nevertheless, such information is quite valuable for the development of effective predictions of future events. The results of these comparisons were twofold: (1) with respect to those individuals who actually did escape, 88 per cent received total scores indicating a high escape risk; and (2) in spite of this accuracy, so many individuals received total scores indicating a high escape risk who actually did not escape that such scores would have been ineffective as a prediction of escape tendencies. In other words, the scores would have provided excellent predictions for the small number of individuals who actually did escape. But so many other individuals who subsequently did not escape received the same total scores that the total mixture of scores indicating future escapes would have been quite inaccurate. As a matter of fact, only 8 per cent of all those individuals for whom escapes were predicted actually did abscond, whereas 92 per cent did not. (The latter might be called the "false positives," for erroneous predictions of escapes would be involved.)

Predictions often must be quite accurate to be of genuine utility. The study of absconders provides an example of the development of a rather good index for discriminating between absconders and nonabsconders, but is was not sufficiently selective for the demands of the practical situation. In general, it is extremely difficult to predict occurrences that are relatively rare.

This example illustrates the difficulties involved in efforts at prediction. Although it is not always necessary for predictions to achieve a high de-

[2]Albert Morris, *Absconders from Penal Institutions* (Wellington, New Zealand: Department of Justice, 1961).

[3]Sheldon Glueck and Eleanor Glueck, *Predicting Delinquency and Crime* (Cambridge, Mass.: Harvard University Press, 1959).

gree of accuracy in order to have general utility, greater accuracy than has yet been generally achieved is necessary for the development of significant technologies for dealing with most human problems. The path to more accurate predications seems to lie in the further development of theories out of which more accurate predictors may be put together. At least this seems to have been the process in the physical sciences. Predictive indexes that are not solidly based on theory tend to be limited in scope. They may seem to be accurate in reference to the specific groups on the basis of which they were constructed, but this accuracy tends to decrease when these indexes are applied to slightly different groups or situations. A well-developed theory, however, is sufficiently comprehensive and systematic to account for changes in any factors that are relevant to the prediction at issue.

This relationship between theory and prediction suggests a distinction between prediction and prophecy. Scientific predictions are based on propositions of the form, "If A occurs, then X will occur." Although predictions are conditional statements, prophecies are not; they are of the form, "X will occur." Prophecies thus are not scientific in the sense that they do not derive from propositions or theory.

Sometimes it is a useful task for the social scientist to attempt to convert prophecies about human behavior into predictions. For example, individuals who are unusually perceptive about themselves or others may be able to make accurate prophecies about certain events. However, if the factual basis for such effective prophecies is considered, then the prophecies can be converted into predictions. Here, the propositions on which such predictions could be based would combine the factual basis for the prophecy *If* A *occurs* with the prophecy X *will occur.* When the two are combined, we have a prediction *If* A *occurs,* X *will occur.*

EXPLANATION

In lay language, the term *explanation* need have little reference to the scientific process, as when one *explains* the reasons for his actions. The scientist, however, does not consider this an explanation for the actions in question unless there is acceptable evidence for it. The individual's own explanation is quite fallible. For example, he may be unaware of the true reasons for his actions, or he may desire to emphasize those reasons which are most socially acceptable and omit those which are not.

In its scientific usage, explanation is similar to prediction in that both are tied to propositions and theories. To the extent that there is evidence for propositions and theories, they can be and are used by scientists for explanations as well as predictions.

Scientific explanations usually describe the relationship between one or more causes and one or more effects. They are made on the basis of a degree of evidence for this relationship. For example, an individual may explain his vote for a given candidate on the basis of the candidate's qualifications for office. Assuming that the scientist has facts to the contrary, such a lay explanation will not be acceptable as a scientific one. For example, the social scientist may, from interviewing the individual, have good reason to believe that his interest in lower taxes is the crucial factor influencing his vote. The scientific explanation would consequently emphasize this factor, although it would be omitted from the lay explanation.

In discussing these two senses of *explanation*, Kaplan distinguishes between what he calls act meaning (the interpretation made by the individual himself) and action meaning (that made by the scientist).[4] A confusion between these two has sometimes been made by sociologists who have emphasized the concept of *verstehen* (understanding). The process of *verstehen* constitutes an attempt by the investigator to explain the acts of another by imagining himself to be in that person's situation and then introspecting as to the reasons involved. Thus, the investigator confuses his own act meanings in the hypothetical situation with action meaning. The basis for such an inference is that human beings share many experiences and have the capacity to "empathize." However valuable such inferences may be as hypotheses, they may or may not be correct in reference to the actual act meanings of the individual under observation. Furthermore, however valuable they may be as data from which to infer action meaning, these inferences must be combined with additional facts and theories before an adequate scientific explanation of the behavior can be formulated.

Just as predictions may vary in their accuracy, so is it true that explanations may vary in their completeness. The aforementioned voter's interest in lower taxes may be only one among a number of factors affecting his vote. This range of variation for both predictions and explanations is understandable when we take into account the fact that they both rest on scientific propositions and theories. Propositions and theories vary greatly in their scope; thus they may specify very few or very many of the relevant factors involved in a given situation.

Even if all of the relevant factors are included in the theory, their interrelationships might not be described very precisely by the theory. For example, the theory might include a proposition that there *exists* a relationship between the goals of voters (including interest in lower taxes) and their political preferences, but it might go no further than that. It might not specify the *type* of relationship between these goals and political preferences. If such were true, predictions based on this theory could not be highly accurate, nor could explanations be complete.

---

[4] Abraham Kaplan, *The Conduct of Inquiry* (San Francisco: Chandler, 1964), p. 359.

Is it possible to have explanation without also being able to predict, or to have predictions without also being able to provide explanations? No, if both are understood to be matters of degree and to rest on propositions and theories. Thus, a very incomplete explanation might be based on a proposition of quite limited scope; a prediction based on the same proposition could be developed, although it might be a highly inaccurate one. In the same way, the propositions or theory on which a given prediction is based could be utilized to develop an explanation.

The relationship between explanation and prediction can easily be confused if we do not conceive of them as matters of degree. For example, it might be maintained that we understand and can explain the effect of the various forces that act on a falling leaf without being able to predict its resting place. As a matter of fact, we *are* able to make a prediction about its resting place, although this prediction will be a probability statement rather than one which is completely specific as to exact place. In addition, although our understanding and explanation of the forces operating on the leaf is great, it is limited. If the theory on which such explanations are based improves, we might in fact be able to make a far more accurate prediction about where the leaf will come to rest.

Explanations tell us why things happen either by focusing on the phenomena to provide greater detail or by placing the phenomena within a larger framework. In order to explain why a light bulb emits light when a switch is turned on, we may refer to a sequence of detailed events, such as the completion of an electric circuit, the difference in potential between the two wires connected to the socket, the flow of electrons through the circuit, the resistance of the filament to the flow of electrons, and so on. We may also place the occurrence within a larger framework by referring to the expectation of the individual who turns on the switch that it will be followed by the emission of light from the bulb, the desire of this individual to read a textbook, his desire to complete an assignment for a course, his interest in learning as well as in obtaining an adequate grade, and so on. The explanation may be thought of either with reference to Events *A, B, C, D, E,* . . . , occurring between *X,* a switch being turned on, and *Y,* a bulb emitting light, or with reference to the Events *M, N, O, P, Q,* . . . , prior to *X.* (Further discussion of sequences of events within the causal process is presented in Section 16.1.)

Explanations are selective in that only some phenomena are included: those which are believed to be relevant. To the extent that the explanation depends on well-developed scientific theories about the motion of electrons, say, or the decisions of human beings, the patterns of events selected as relevant constitute deductions from propositions. Thus, for example, there is a general proposition that a potential difference is necessary in order for electrons to flow in an electrical circuit, or there is a general proposition that motives or goals are instrumental in producing action in human beings. These explanations are generally considered to be more dependable than explanations not supported by such theories, because the former are backed up by masses of evidence relating to many different types of phenomena.

Like prediction, explanation can serve both technological and scientific functions. Even if it is generally not possible for the social scientist to make very accurate predictions about human behavior, he can at least provide explanations of varying scope and validity which can be used to help develop techniques for dealing with many problems and to provide direction for scientific investigation. The scientist should therefore be wary of explanations which, instead, tend to close the door on further research. (For example, the postulation of "instinct" as an explanation of many different kinds of behavior tended to discourage the search for non-biological factors.)

Explanation is also pursued by the scientific community for its own sake, and this seems to be one of the most important factors motivating scientists generally. Numerous scientific investigations take place which appear to offer no immediate or long-range benefits to society other than the acquisition of knowledge. Many laymen find such a motive hard to understand, especially in a society such as that of the United States, with its emphasis on practical applications. Of course, the history of science is full of examples of research which appeared that way originally but which ultimately had enormous technological repercussions.

Functionalism represents an approach to providing explanations of social systems and human behavior which, together with the technique of *verstehen,* aids in the development of hypotheses. A functional explanation devotes attention to the needs or requirements of a given system and consequently directs the investigator toward observing phenomena he might ordinarily overlook. As in the case of the *verstehen* technique, however, evidence is needed before much credence can be given to any functional explanation; categorical statements about the "functional prerequisites" or the "functional necessities" of a given system do not have any special immunity from the testing process.

3.2 CONTEXTS OF DISCOVERY AND JUSTIFICATION

One distinction that will aid us in viewing science as a process is that between the *context of discovery* and the *context of justification.* When we view inquiry within the context of discovery we are concerned with the strategy and tactics leading to the development of ideas that may result in scientific progress. Ideas may or may not bear fruit, and it is within the context of justification that evidence is presented and decisions about the worth of ideas are made.

RELATIONSHIP

The two contexts are closely interrelated. The ultimate test of strategies for the context of discovery, as well as for ideas developed within that context, is provided in the context of justification. The results of tests within the context of justification suggest the directions for future inquiry. Evidence may be provided which indicates not only that the ideas are worthwhile and should be followed up but also what kinds of new data are most urgently needed. If the evidence indicates that the ideas are incorrect, the investigator is directed toward new efforts within the context of discovery.

Unless the investigator recognizes this interdependence, he may attempt to evaluate strategies for the context of discovery on a basis other than the evidence for or against them presented in the context of justification. This is especially true in a situation where there is little evidence available as to the merits and demerits of every research technique for a given situation. This seems to be the situation in behavioral science: the tools are available for evaluating the various strategies of discovery, but thus far very little of such evaluation has taken place. This, of course, encourages the evaluation of strategies of discovery on other grounds (for example, the prestige of their proponents). (Additional discussion of various strategies of research will be presented in Section 3.4.)

DISCOVERY

One of the ideas used by scientists within the context of discovery is that of cause and effect. Many scientists do not like to state their propositions in these terms because science is not in a position either to prove that such relationships exist or to prove that any given relationship is one of cause and effect. But these scientists generally continue to think in terms of cause and effect. Is it wise for them to give up this idea because of its uncertain status? Max Planck answers this question as follows:

> The law of causality is neither true nor false. It is, rather, a signpost—and, in my opinion, our most valuable signpost—to help us find our bearings in a bewildering maze of occurrences, and to show us the direction in which scientific research must advance in order to achieve fertile results. The law of causality, which immediately impresses the awakening soul of the child and plants the untiring question *Why?* into his mouth, remains a lifelong companion of the scientist and confronts him incessantly with new problems.[5]

A distinction for understanding the context of discovery is that between

[5] Max Planck, "The Concept of Causality in Physics," in Phillip P. Wiener (ed.), *Readings in the Philosophy of Science* (New York: Scribner, 1953), p. 87.

"logic in use" and "reconstructed logic."[6] The methods actually used by the scientist in investigating phenomena are illustrations of logic in use; the rules, procedures, or methods of research that are systematized and codified are examples of reconstructed logic. The distinction is between what the scientist actually does, which has a "logic" of its own, and idealizations of scientific practice.

This book, for example, constitutes a reconstructed logic, whereas the author's actual behavior in performing research constitutes a logic in use. The two may differ to a greater or lesser extent. The researcher's actual behavior very often departs from his ideas on the way research should be conducted, and he may be aware of such departures only to a limited degree. His reconstructed logic might call for trying out a wide range of methods, but his present skills and the exigencies of time may prevent him from doing so.

It may occur that a given logic in use is superior to the most prestigeful reconstructed logic available. In such situations it is usually necessary for such a logic in use to be codified and expressed as a new reconstructed logic if it is to gain widespread acceptance. Such acceptance may be difficult to obtain in spite of the availability of evidence in its favor. This is because the prestigeful reconstructed logic may be treated as self-justifying, rather than as in need of evaluation within the context of justification. However, the history of science seems to show that in time the evidence for a given reconstructed logic makes its weight felt.

It is when the proponent of a given reconstructed logic acts as an "umpire"[7] in the game of scientific discovery and rules out all reconstructed logics which do not conform to his own that potentially lines of investigation may be blocked. This approach on the part of leading scientists may lead the practicing scientist to distrust his own ideas about research methods and thus fail to develop and test them. Instead of feeling a sense of freedom and autonomy for constructing the most appropriate research techniques to fit a given situation, he may feel a sense of impotence in in the face of established ideas. In psychology, for example, certain kinds of highly controlled experiments are revered while less controlled "field experiments" are often disparaged. In sociology, the large probability sample survey is often valued for its own sake, whereas the small non-probability sample survey is lightly regarded. In anthropology, very detailed interviews repeated over long periods of time are regarded by many as the *sine qua non* of research methods.

If it is important for the researcher to feel free to develop his own logic in use, no matter how unconventional it might be, it is at least as important for him to learn how to develop a highly effective logic in use. Un-

[6] Kaplan, op. cit., pp. 3–11.
[7] Ibid., p. 25.

fortunately, there exists almost no systematic knowledge about an effective logic in use within the context of discovery.[8] Indeed, the whole subject of the process of creation, innovation, or discovery has been all but ignored by the social sciences.

If we assume an important relationship between scientific discovery and the emergence of new concepts, then this statement by Schon about the latter is relevant here:

> In spite of the abundance of the literature and the innumerable contributions that have been made, theories on the subject fall into one of two categories: either they make the process mysterious, and therefore intrinsically unexplainable; or they regard novelty as illusory and, therefore, requiring no explanation. . . .
>
> ...The difficulty comes in large part from our inclination, with things and thoughts alike, to take an after-the-fact view. . . [which] has tended to keep from investigation a kind of process which is central to this subject matter: the process of metaphor or, as I will call it, the displacement of concepts.[9]

This idea about the importance of metaphor is, at this stage, no more than a promising lead, yet it does at least provide one direction for further inquiry. If it is true that our thinking process is to a great extent guided by metaphors, then an ability to direct this process consciously might prove to be exceedingly useful.[10]

JUSTIFICATION

The context of justification provides the scientist with bench marks which enable him to assess whether his efforts have produced results of some worth. The ability to achieve accurate prediction is perhaps the

[8] Of course there does exist a literature on the subject of discovery, but somehow this literature skirts an investigation of the basic processes involved in discovery. For example, Karl R. Popper's *The Logic of Scientific Discovery* (New York: Harper, 1965) emphasizes the importance of constructing hypotheses, but it provides little information on how to construct them; Barney G. Glaser and Anselm L. Strauss in their *The Discovery of Grounded Theory* (Chicago: Aldine, 1967) talk about the importance of discovery and provide some guidance but do not produce a systematic formulation; and Brewster Ghiselin's compilation of autobiographical statements (including Einstein, Van Gogh, Jung, A. E. Housman, Yeats, Henry James, Henry Miller, Thomas Wolfe, Henry Moore, and D. H. Lawrence) in his *The Creative Process* (New York: Mentor, n.d.) incorporates many interesting insights but does not build up to any general conclusion. There are also the many more extended autobiographical accounts, such as James D. Watson's *The Double Helix* (New York: Atheneum, 1968), which have the advantages as well as the disadvantages of the Ghiselin collection.

[9] Donald A. Schon, *Invention and the Evolution of Ideas* (London: Tavistock Publications, Social Science Paperbacks, 1967).

[10] Many others have discussed the role of metaphor in the discovery process. See, for example Mary B. Hesse, *Models and Analogies in Science* (Notre Dame, Ind.: University of Notre Dame Press, 1966); Scott Greer, *The Logic of Social Inquiry* (Chicago: Aldine, 1969); Max Black, *Models and Metaphors* (Ithaca, N.Y.: Cornell University Press, 1962), and Norwood R. Hanson, *Patterns of Discovery* (Cambridge: Cambridge University Press, 1958).

bench mark most widely accepted by the physical science community. In the behavioral sciences, however, other criteria of assessment have been adopted. The behavioral scientist tends to assess on the basis of whether or not relationships are found to *exist* as distinct from the *degree* or *type* of relationship.[11]

We might inquire as to the scientific basis for setting up given evaluative criteria within the context of justification and, in so doing, explore the paradigm relating to this context. For the physical scientist, predictions tend to be seen as forming part of the total picture, instead of being considered alone, and as leading to greater scope. The ability to achieve accurate predictions of widening scope is itself tied to the construction of increasingly effective models or systematic theories representing the scientist's attempt to synthesize experiences by synthesizing ideas with ideas and ideas with experience. Thus, prediction is related to the synthetic nature of the scientific method itself, with mathematics providing a highly effective tool for achieving such integration. Predictions are important insofar as they encourage the cumulative development of science in this direction; consequently, they are tied to theories of ever-widening scope.

As for behavioral science, the prevailing view is quite similar: if we establish the existence of relationships, this will lead to a building up of increasingly accurate knowledge about more and more phenomena. Yet there is a crucial difference between this argument and that of the physical scientist: it is quite rare to be able to achieve accurate predictions of wide scope without basing them on models, whereas models are not easily derived from the location of existing relationships. Thus, success in the context of justification is tied, for the physical scientist, to successful theory building; this is not the case for behavioral science. As a result, the behavioral scientist is able to evaluate his research as being quite worthwhile without achieving important theoretical progress. His view that somehow his efforts will build on the work of many others may not be a realistic one if there is no systematic theoretical framework to which they are all tied. For example, each of a large number of researches may be concerned with the relationship among a small set of concepts. However, accurate prediction may depend on taking into account simultaneously a large number of concepts, and thus the different studies need not build on one another.

To use the language employed in Chapter 1, the "indicators" of behavioral science progress may not be appropriate to the task of effectively assessing behavioral science progress. One way to determine how appropriate they are is to fall back on other indicators which would tend to follow along with scientific progress. Thus, for example, the physical

---

[11] See Section 2.3 for a discussion of the distinctions among existence, degree, and type of relationship. We shall take up statistical criteria for determining whether or not relationships exist in Chapters 14 and 15.

scientist can point to a vast variety of technological achievements along-side of his predictive abilities, with technological achievement viewed as an indirect indicator of scientific development. Social technology, by contrast, seems to be almost completely ineffective in the face of the vast problems of modern societies.

This analysis does not imply that efforts at establishing the existence of relationships be abandoned in favor of attempts to specify types of relationships. But it does imply that a shift toward emphasizing the latter may be called for at the present time. It is not possible to determine in advance whether such a change in strategy will prove to be fruitful. All we can say is that such an approach has been highly effective in the physical sciences, and that the present-day strategy that tends to predominate may no longer be justified in view of its scientific and technological accomplishments.

3.3 THE HUMAN EQUATION: A DIALOGUE

Discussions about the problems and prospects of behavioral science frequently stop at a relatively superficial level, with dogmatic attack followed by dogmatic defense, as distinct from the unearthing of implicit assumptions behind the positions verbally expressed. In this section we have selected a number of fundamental questions about behavioral science, and we explore them by means of hypothetical dialogues. Our aim is not to convince readers that they must renew their faith in the future of behavioral science and suppress all doubts. Rather, it is to aid them in bringing to the surface their own paradigms with respect to the nature of behavioral science.

FREE WILL

    A: Human beings are not governed by scientific laws, because they have free will. They are not physical objects or automata but are free to choose among various courses of action.

    B: The automobile driver may subjectively feel that he is "free" to crash into other cars, but we can predict that he will not ordinarily attempt to do so; we can also formulate laws based on such regular patterns of behavior. To generalize that "normative pressures will be effective in inducing behavioral conformity depending on the severity of the sanctions involved" is not to deny that individuals who are conforming subjectively feel that they have a choice in the matter. Even the freest of choices seem to have causes, but this is not to say that they are "governed" by outside forces which the individual is powerless to control. Theories of choice emphasize internal forces, such as values and expectations, leaving room for external forces as well.

    A: But if we assume that all behavior is caused, then the internal forces within the individual which lead him to choose one alternative over another are themselves caused, and those causes themselves are caused, and so on. In this way we move back in time to a series of initial conditions which have caused everything subsequent in time. According to this line of reasoning, the individual's behavior is simply a product of this set of initial causes, and he has no freedom of action. But we know that we do indeed have freedom of action, and so the entire argument that all human behavior can be explained by causes falls through.

B: The individual's behavior is indeed a product of series of causes which have preceded it, but this does not imply that he has no freedom of action. The individual can and does change his environment, depending on his nature as well as the nature of his environment. His ability to change his environment—in a sense, his freedom—may be viewed as a matter of degree, depending on his knowledge of how to capture the forces within himself and his environment. It is behavioral science knowledge, moreover, which can point the individual in this direction. Thus, far from the situation where attention to behavioral science opposes the idea that man has free will, the development of behavioral science may progressively give man more and more of such freedom.

COMPLEXITY AND CHANGE

A: Human behavior is too complex and changeable for a genuine science ever to emerge. Every individual is unique; people behave differently in different historical periods; and anthropologists have demonstrated the wide range of behavior among cultures. The most that we can hope to do is to try to understand individuals in a given society during a limited period of time.

B: It has often occurred within the history of science that, prior to the formulation of scientific explanations, phenomena have appeared to be immensely complicated. For example, at one time it must have seemed preposterous that one law might account for the velocity of *any* freely falling object, including apples of all shapes, sizes, and colors; pears; people; chairs; and so on. The fact that there are some differences in behavior among different societies and historical epochs does not deny the possibility that there are some (or many) similarities. As a matter of fact, the supposed differences may not refer to laws of human behavior but, rather, to constants or parameters similar to g in Galileo's law for freely falling bodies: $s = \frac{1}{2}gt^2$, in which g (the gravitational constant) takes on different values at different latitudes, although the same law holds at all latitudes.

A: Granting the *possibility* that behavioral science may one day learn how to deal with complex and changing events, this seems to be very unlikely in the next several generations. The order of complexity of the phenomena described by $s = \frac{1}{2}gt^2$ is incomparably less than that involved in the simplest movements by even the simplest kinds of living systems. With respect to most human behavior the complex feedback processes and the large number of systems involved are such as to defy mathematical solutions.

B: On the contrary, new computer technologies for the study of complex and changing systems enable the investigator without any mathematical background to go far beyond even the most sophisticated mathematics in the analysis of complex systems. Some of these techniques are such as to lead to the cumulative development of successively more adequate models for studying such systems. At the present time there is a lag between the existence of such technologies and their widespread diffusion.

BIAS

A: Human beings cannot possibly study other human beings without bias. The student of human behavior cannot but have a vital interest in the kinds of conclusions he reaches, and this prevents him from seeing and analyzing phenomena objectively. Furthermore, his biases also operate in the selection of problems for study.

B: It is true that behavioral scientists are human beings and that their behavior is therefore guided by their own values, but this is true of all scientists. Among the values of the social scientist, however, is that of scientific objectivity, and he generally makes every effort to limit the effect of his own values on his presentation of the data and his assessment of the evidence. A still more effective check on bias in the behavioral sciences is the fact that studies are replicated and data are interpreted by different social scientists who have different values and who provide checks and balances against bias. As for bias in the selection of a problem (as distinct from bias in its analysis), both behavioral scientists and physical scientists are in this regard influenced by their own values. But in this case, too, the values of both may be oriented to the selection of those problems which offer possibilities for the greatest advances in scientific knowledge. Even when problems are selected on the basis of other values, the collection and analysis of the data may still be highly objective.

A: Although the scientific ideal sounds fine, what happens in practice is very far from this ideal. Even with the best of intentions as to minimizing bias, the behavioral scientist, in common with all other human beings, is very much a product both of his covert ideas and values and of environmental forces. If he is an academician, then he may be more concerned with frequent publication than with developing and communicating ideas of genuine worth. Whatever his position, the implications of his research for his own status will tend to be quite important. He will tend to apply for those research grants which are most readily available rather than those which offer the greatest scientific promise. Pure scientific objectivity is impossible for human beings who lack complete knowledge of themselves and who exist in an environment which values things other than pure scientific objectivity.

B: I agree with everything you say. You are right to get down to the reality of scientific research rather than to talk in terms of ideals alone. Yet once we do face up to the various forces operating within the research situation other than that of advancing scientific knowledge, something can be done about them. These forces themselves can become objects of research, and the ways in which they affect research outcomes can be charted. This is not simply a question of the researcher openly revealing his biases. It involves his doing research on his biases and the ways in which they influence his investigations and conclusions. Another way of doing something about bias is to adopt the criterion of accurate prediction within the context of justification. Then, in spite of whatever biases may exist, the investigator gets little credit for his work unless he is able to achieve such prediction. If, then, bias is sufficiently severe to result in the neglect of important factors, accurate predictions will not be achieved.

EFFECTS OF PREDICTIONS

A: Predictions about human behavior may not hold because the individuals involved may become aware of these predictions and alter their behavior accordingly.

B: The interference of the observer with the phenomena under observation is common to all the sciences. Current techniques of data collection seek to minimize this influence. More fundamental, however, is the fact that the law governing the velocity of a freely falling body is not invalidated if the predictions based on it do not hold true as a result of someone's altering the velocity by shooting at the object. What is required, and what is certainly possible, is that additional laws be developed about the ways in which individuals alter their behavior when they have knowledge of the predictions of the social scientist.

A: Once again your answer is framed on the basis of what is possible more than the existing situation, on the ideal more than the reality. Generally we can make use of laws describing the motion of physical objects without changing the ways in which those laws operate. However, this is not generally true for behavioral science. And it is not enough to dream about how, someday, we will learn to predict the ways in which predictions alter human behavior. If we cannot do this now, then our predictions of human behavior have limited worth from a practical point of view.

B: And once again I agree with what you say. Let us accept your idea that behavioral science predictions presently have little practical worth because of this and other problems. Now, where do we go from there? Do we simply give up, or should we seek to learn about the ways in which predictions of human behavior tend to alter the nature of the behavior being predicted? Logically, there appears to be nothing which would stand in the way of our being able to do so. What matters, of course, is not merely the existence of this logical possibility but whether or not such research gets under way.

TRIVIALITY IN BEHAVIORAL SCIENCE

A: Behavioral science has yielded very little knowledge about human behavior and seems to consist mainly of trivial statements that are quite obvious to most observant individuals. It is not a science; rather it is an exercise in proving the obvious.

B: What may be "obvious" to one individual may not be to another. An inventory of many of the findings of social science will reveal to the skeptic that a great many of them were previously not "obvious" to him. As for triviality, social scientists generally grant the insufficiencies in their propositions, theories, explanations, and predictions, but we might just as well ridicule the field of meteorology because of the inaccuracy of weather forecasts. A more responsible role for the critic is that of working toward the creation of conditions that will encourage the field to develop more rapidly.

A: After all is said and done in defense of the worth of behavioral science, the fact remains that, in terms of such criteria as accuracy of prediction or effectiveness of social technology, behavioral science is very far behind physical science. Comparing behavioral science with meteorology, talking about logical possibilities, and advising faith in the future of behavioral science do not create less trivial results.

B: What might help quite quickly is the adoption of criteria in the context of justification which give weight to less trivial research; for example, model building of very wide scope. What is also needed is more faith in the possibilities of behavioral science, faith largely destroyed by failures thus far. Skepticism is fine if it influences the investigator to be suspicious of dogmatism, but it can be destructive if it is not followed by efforts to improve what has been criticized.

IMMORALITY

A: A science of human behavior will never develop because it is immoral and society will resist it. Human beings are not ciphers or equations and it is inhuman to treat them in this manner. Progress in social science will mean that human beings can be manipulated, and this will set the stage for the most complete totalitarianism man has ever known. Furthermore, it would be immoral to experiment on human beings.

B: Knowledge is power, and power may be used for good as well as for evil. Manipulation may be one result, but a fuller development of man's creative capacities might well be another. Social science offers the hope of freeing man from ignorance. In questions of morality, more than one value is usually involved, and if harm can come from experimentation on human beings, good may also come of it.

A: A platitude about the two-edge sword of science does not really speak to the issues of the day. The fact is that behavioral science has been captured by those organizations which have the funds to finance research. Far from furthering the good of humanity, and I grant that this is a logical possibility, behavioral science has functioned to strengthen bureaucracy and reduce the autonomy of individuals.

B: Naming an enemy does not necessarily solve problems. Are the people running the big bad bureaucracies actually the enemy, or is a bigger enemy the failure on the part of critics and proponents of behavioral science alike to learn how to develop and apply the kind of knowledge about human behavior which will produce human development? By turning away from the scientific method we abandon what may be our most powerful tool for achieving this end.

PREDICTION

A: The astronomer can predict the position of a given planet years from now, but how can anyone hope to predict where a given person will be in several years? So many accidents occur which completely change the direction of human lives. For example, if I hadn't happened to fall down and land in the hospital, I would have been on that plane that was lost over the Atlantic.

B: Long-range prediction is not the distinguishing characteristic of a science; it can be achieved where the phenomena are relatively isolated from outside influence and some closure has been achieved. The physicist cannot accurately predict where a falling leaf will be blown by the wind, but because we have evidence for laws such as the relationship between time of free fall and distance fallen *in a vacuum,* we evaluate physics as an effective science. In the same way behavioral science has uncovered many relationships among phenomena which can be used to explain at least partially the behavior of a given individual and actually to predict his behavior, although with a substantially lower probability of success than that achieved in many (but not all) branches of physics. The time may come when many now supposedly "accidental" phenomena will be explained and predicted.

A: A difference in degree may be the difference between an ineffective science and an effective one. What good does it do to know that behavioral scientists can predict with an accuracy greater than chance if such predictions are so inaccurate that they are useless for all practical purposes? Partial explanations are not enough. Behavioral science should either produce something of genuine value for society or else confess its inabilities so that some other approach can be adopted to achieve the desired result.

B: Accepting your argument as valid, the problem seems to boil down not to how to achieve long-range prediction, but how to achieve the kind of prediction which could provide the basis for effective social technologies. An analogy might help here. Physical science constructed the kind of knowledge which led not to our ability to predict the position and velocity of the elementary particles over long periods of time, but to our ability to create the kinds of conditions necessary for releasing enormous amounts of atomic energy and harnessing this energy for both destructive and useful purposes. The same kind of thing occurred in the earlier prenuclear era; we developed the ability to release energy from natural resources, such as coal, oil, and water, and to transform this energy into different kinds of energy for use in a variety of situations. We might look to behavioral science to achieve the same kind of result but to channel it into constructive paths as a result of learning from the mistakes of the past, to teach us about the kinds of social and cultural conditions which would result in the release of what may prove to be an enormous or unlimited potential energy for human development.

3.4 VALUES AND THE SCIENTIST

Behavioral scientists differ on what they believe constitute the most effective approaches to research. Choices have to be made because resources for research are limited, and the problem for the scientist is to make the most effective choices. Unfortunately, research on the research process itself has been limited, and information about what have been successful strategies is primarily of a qualitative nature. Moreover, because the degree of success achieved by the social sciences is limited, objective evaluations of strategies are sparse.

SELECTION OF PROBLEMS FOR INVESTIGATION

Although behavioral scientists generally agree that scientific investigation of human behavior is both possible and desirable, a specific question which seems to be the subject of much controversy concerns the selection of problems for investigation: whether or not problems that are defined as important in terms of their implications for human welfare are also important problems for scientific study.

In his presidential address to the American Sociological Association in 1949, Talcott Parsons advanced the following point of view:

> It is not a question of *whether* we try to live up to our social responsibilities, but of *how*. If we should put the overwhelming bulk of our resources, especially of trained talent, into immediately practical problems, it would do some good—but I have no doubt that it would have to be at the expense of our greater usefulness to society in the future. For it is only by systematic work on problems where the probable scientific significance has priority over any immediate possibility of application that the greatest and most rapid scientific advance can be made.[12]

Behavioral scientists have had much experience with the shortsightedness of many individuals who control research funds. The conflict for funds between "basic" and "applied" research is not limited to the social sciences, as any chemist who has been prevented from following a scientifically promising lead because of its limited remunerative potentiality will readily declare. Parsons' position states the importance of "scientific" definitions of problems over definitions which focus on immediate practical problems.

C. Wright Mills takes the following stance in viewing the selection of problems:

> . . . whether he is aware of it or not, anyone who spends his life studying society and publishing the results is acting morally and usually politically as well. The question is whether he faces this condition and makes up his own mind, or whether he conceals it from himself and from others and drifts morally. Many— I should say most—social scientists in America today are easily or uneasily liberal.

[12] Talcott Parsons, "The Prospects of Sociological Theory," *American Sociological Review,* **15** (1950), 15.

They conform to the prevailing fear of any passionate commitment. This, and not "scientific objectivity," is what is really wanted by such men when they complain about "making value judgments."[13]

Mills' argument is that social scientists often use scientific objectivity as an excuse for an uncritical acceptance of the framework of society and that, as a result, they spend their intellectual force on "the details of small-scale milieu" instead of concentrating on the large problems of society.

It seems that the debate has pointed up a central question: Which strategies for the selection of problems can maximize the advancement of scientific knowledge as well as the solution of important human problems? Parsons' position stresses the importance of allowing latitude for the investigator to define problems in terms of their "scientific" significance. Mills maintains that ethical neutrality in the selection of problems is a fiction and that those who profess it tend to take the safe road of avoiding a certain class of those scientific problems, the conclusions for which may imply fundamental criticism of societal institutions.

The debate seems to focus on the relative merits of two different reconstructed logics for the context of discovery: ethical neutrality in the selection of problems, and the selection of problems which are politically and historically "important." But like any reconstructed logic of discovery, these are tentative hypotheses about the fruitfulness of certain procedures for the selection of problems. The ultimate test of any logic-in-use is not its conformity with some previously successful reconstructed logic but, rather, its achievement of accurate predictions and substantiated explanations of considerable scope.

The fundamental problem seems to be that neither of these two reconstructed logics has as yet yielded important results; we have neither effective behavioral science predictions nor effective social technologies. The presumed conflict between them does not appear to be the product of logical contradictions. If we had achieved accurate predictive models, then we could learn how to apply them to solving important societal problems. Moreover, if we had developed genuinely effective social technologies, then it is reasonable to believe that they would have been developed on the basis of systematic theory, just as engineering technologies have been dependent on physical science theory.

Alternatives to these two reconstructed logics exist. For example, we might define one in which it is generally important to make *both* scientific progress and technological progress, with the assumption that each type of advance supports the other. One advantage which such a reconstructed logic may have is the setting up of a higher level of aspiration for the

[13] C. Wright Mills, *The Sociological Imagination* (New York: Grove, 1961), p. 79.

scientist and the technologist: the former's ideas would have to be good enough to work in uncontrolled situations, whereas the latter's would be evaluated in part on the basis of their general contribution to knowledge. Such an increase in level of aspiration may be valuable at the present stage of development of behavioral science, with its emphasis on existence rather than type of relationship within the context of justification.

A second advantage might be to improve communication between scientists and technologists, with the presumption that the ideas of one may aid the work of the other. A third might be improved societal support both for science and for social technology. The scientist's activities tend to be encouraged by society to the extent that there is recognition that his work contributes, directly or indirectly, to the solution of societal problems, and such a reconstructed logic would point up such contributions. As for the social technologist (for example, the teacher), his work could come to be defined as incorporating the component of scientific creativity, an occurrence which would tend to be accompanied by appropriate material and nonmaterial rewards.

THE QUANTITATIVE–QUALITATIVE AXIS

Some social scientists prefer highly quantitative and precise techniques, and there are those who prefer to stay as close as possible to "realistic" situations and conduct research along qualitative lines. There are preferences for quantitative or qualitative studies, laboratory or field experiments, unstructured, semistructured, or structured interviews and observation schedules, and so on. These differences occur within each of the social sciences, but entire disciplines also tend to be located on the quantitative–qualitative axis. Psychology, for example, is generally closer to the quantitative pole than sociology, but sociology is generally closer to it than anthropology. In psychology, operationist thought has had the greatest influence and the laboratory experiment is quite popular. In sociology, the most frequent mode of investigation is the survey, and a variety of quantitative design and analysis techniques have been developed. Anthropologists also rely heavily on interviews, but their techniques tend to be less structured and they often devote a great deal of time and attention to securing the kind of details which help to provide the full context of the phenomena under investigation.

Some of the differences within a given field are as great as differences between fields. The clinical psychologist learns to have an appreciation for objective measurement, but his orientation tends to be far more qualitative and contextual than that of the experimental psychologist. The qualitative sociologist may adopt a method of participant observation with the aim of understanding a given system as a functioning unit; the survey-research analyst, on the other hand, operates with a set of dependent and independent variables by means of quantitative analytic techniques and is also concerned with the construction of objective scales of measurement. Within anthropology there is a vast gap between those who are oriented to obtaining thorough descriptions of a given culture and those who utilize a combination of unstructured interviewing techniques and highly structured survey techniques.

The behavioral scientist who is oriented to qualitative studies may argue that the realism of the natural social world is lost when phenomena are forced into a quantitative mold, and that techniques of analysis which focus on a limited set of "variables" play havoc with the total context of the situation under study. The quantitative social scientist might answer by maintaining that it is the controlled situation, such as the laboratory experiment, which provides the best opportunity for getting beneath surface phenomena to the vital factors and processes that are often hidden in natural situations. He might also refer to the improved techniques now available, such as multivariate statistical procedures and electronic computer techniques, which make it possible for the scientist to take into account large numbers of variables at one time and thus deal with the context of a situation in an objective manner.

There is a parallel between the controversy over scientific neutrality versus societal problem solving and that between the quantitative and the qualitative approach. In the case of the latter as well as the former each alternative has demonstrated severe limitations, and a third alternative may be in order. Quantitative methods in behavioral science have pointed toward locating relationships which exist as distinct from locating types of relationships, whereas the qualitative approach has not generally succeeded in unearthing a sufficient number of the causal factors operating in those situations studied so as to yield thorough understanding of them. A possible alternative is the kind of approach which captures the best of both the qualitative and the quantitative orientations, an approach which is yet to be developed for behavioral science. Yet the theoretical and methodological tools for beginning to construct it seem to be at hand: theories which locate many of the relatively intangible, qualitative dimensions that are crucial for understanding human behavior; computer technology for putting together a very large number of factors in order to reconstruct the context of a situation; and models which can yield predictions.

AN OPEN-SYSTEMS APPROACH

A large literature is developing which documents many of the ways in which the values of the investigator affect the research process,[14] a topic

[14] See, for example, Gideon Sjoberg (ed.), *Ethics, Politics, and Social Research* (Cambridge, Mass.: Schenkman, 1967); Ralph L. Beals, *Politics of Social Research* (Chicago: Aldine, 1969); William R. Nelson, *The Politics of Science* (New York: Oxford University Press, 1968); and Irving L. Horowitz, *Professing Sociology* (Chicago: Aldine, 1968).

that we shall take up more thoroughly in Section 4.4. However, illustrations are insufficient for informing the social scientist of procedures which will enable him to take into account these effects in a systematic matter. One approach to the problem is that taken by Meehan, who advocates a "system paradigm" for explanation as distinct from a "deductive paradigm."[15] The latter, which is the one typically used, attaches no weight to the purposes for which explanations are sought or the manner in which they are used. As a result, it tends to produce a single-factor standard for explanation and eliminates the possibility of grading explanations in accordance with their degree of usefulness.

Meehan differentiates between the two paradigms with the following example:

> . . . According to those who accept the deductive paradigm, the question, "Why is that swan white?" can be answered, in Europe, by referring to the "established empirical generalization" which states that "All European swans are white," and to the rules of formal logic. . . . Anyone using the system paradigm would first of all want to know, "What is your purpose in asking?" Because the deductive paradigm avoids the question, the explanations it provides may tell us nothing that is in any sense useful, except to keep small children from asking further questions.[16]

If we think in terms of an "open-systems paradigm," we can obtain perspective on the deficiencies of the deductive paradigm. If all phenomena are interrelated, in accordance with the open-systems approach, then the researcher must choose among the vast number of events in the universe in responding to any "Why?" question. If the purpose of the questioner is unclear, that is, if the researcher has little explicit knowledge of what use will be made of the answer to this question, then he has little conscious guidance for selecting a limited set of phenomena in responding to this question. In such a situation he will tend to be guided by implicit criteria for selection, and these may not be very useful. With a clear purpose, the investigator not only has guidance initially, he also has guidance throughout the research process. Each time he selects phenomena for a given explanation he can test them as to the degree to which they enable him to achieve his purposes, and his subsequent selection of phenomena can take advantage of whatever he has learned in his initial selection. What we are suggesting here is that the values of the investigator need not be viewed as an obstacle to the research process, as something to be controlled or eliminated. Rather, they may play a very positive role, indeed, an essential one. Of course if this is to occur we need to focus a considerable proportion of our research efforts on the investigator.

[15] Eugene J. Meehan, *Explanation in Social Science: A System Paradigm* (Homewood, Ill.: Dorsey, 1968).

[16] Ibid., pp. 28–29.

EXERCISES

1. Compare the predictions and explanations of the scientist with those developed in everyday life. What are the similarities? What are the differences?

2. Develop a strategy of research for learning how to achieve discoveries in behavioral science. What approach would you be taking within the context of justification?

3. What is one argument you have heard about the problems and prospects of behavioral science that was not discussed in the dialogues on the human equation? Develop a dialogue for it analogous to those in the text.

4. Construct two paradigms relating to the dialogues on the human equation, one for individual A and one for B. How do these paradigms relate to the model of the research process presented in Chapter 1?

5. What do you consider to be the best over-all strategy for research in the behavioral sciences at the present time? What implications does this strategy have for specific projects which should or should not be undertaken?

ANNOTATED REFERENCES

BOGUSLAW, ROBERT. *The New Utopians.* Englewood Cliffs, N.J.: Prentice-Hall, Inc., 1965. The new utopians include systems engineers, computer manufacturers, operations researchers, data-processing specialists, and systems designers. These individuals, as distinct from the social scientists, do not live in an observer culture. Rather, they are intimately associated with the forces that are shaping, for good or evil, postindustrial society.

BRONOWSKI, J. *Science and Human Values.* New York: Harper & Row, Publishers, 1965. Too often we tend to ignore the humanistic aspects of the scientific tradition. Bronowski reminds us of the power of science as a force for independence, originality, free inquiry, free thought, free speech, and tolerance. By exploring the nature of the scientific society we can gain insight into a type of society that is quite unique in human experience.

SCHON, DONALD A. *Invention and the Evolution of Ideas.* London: Tavistock Publications, Social Science Paperbacks, 1967. If this book constitutes any evidence, then surely we are moving toward a union of art and science. Schon examines the role of metaphor in the process of discovering concepts, a process that is related to the more general one of scientific discovery. In so doing he points a direction for exploring a process about which we know virtually nothing.

part two DATA COLLECTION

It is indeed unfortunate that there exists in social science a rather wide gap between theory and research or, more exactly, between conscious theory and research. For all research techniques, whether they have to do with methods of data collection, scaling procedures, or techniques for the analysis of data, imply some kind of theoretical framework. It is perhaps the duty of the researcher to unearth his implicit framework and come to terms with it on a conscious level. In the ensuing chapters in Part Two we have attempted to set the stage for this kind of approach in order to move toward a closer relationship between theory and method. In perspective, it must be admitted that we have only scratched the surface.

Chapter 4 sets forth a framework within which all the techniques of data collection are seen as incorporating both experimental and observational aspects and as varying in their relative emphasis on each component. Chapters 5 through 9 take up five methods of data collection: experiments, interviews (and questionnaires), observation, the use of documents, and simulation. We have attempted throughout to achieve a wedding between the quantitative and the qualitative orientations, with the marriage being performed by a theoretical approach. The union is not an easy one to achieve and, as in the case of the relationship between theory and method, it will take prodigious efforts on the part of a great many researchers to attain a lasting one. We are dealing here with two cultures which have kept themselves apart for a long time. A great many bridges must be built before we can expect to achieve even a passable level of communication.

CHAPTER 4 Principles of Data Collection

4.1 OVERVIEW

In seeking perspectives concerning the process of collecting data, we shall begin with an analysis of the relations among the various methods and a discussion of temporal sequences within the research process.

RELATIONS AMONG METHODS

We might divide the methods of data collection under two general headings, those which emphasize observation (very broadly defined) and those which emphasize experimentation. Under the former heading we place the interview or questionnaire survey, the analysis of documents, and observation. Under the latter we classify the experiment and simulation.

The observational study attempts to examine phenomena in such a way that the investigative process does not affect or alter the phenomena under examination. The experiment, by contrast, focuses on the introduction of certain "treatments" to a given situation which are deliberately designed to alter the nature of the situation, and the experimenter attempts to understand the processes of change in the situation which results.

Yet despite this difference between these two methods of data collection, it is only one of degree. The observational study cannot examine phenomena without altering their nature or without injecting the ideas of the investigator into the interpretation of the results. Thus, we find that all observational studies are to an extent experimental in the sense that they alter the phenomena under investigation. The changes are not deliberate, but they are real nevertheless. What is required to convert them into partial experiments is a careful study of the nature of the factors that are introduced by the investigator and of the ways in which these factors alter the situation.

Similarly, experimental studies are in part observational. In one type of design, for example—the before and after study—observations are taken both prior to and following the experimental treatment. A key assumption made for the before and the after parts of the experiment is similar to an assumption in the observational study: that the phenomena observed are not affected by the observational process. Of course, in the more complex experimental designs where several control groups are involved, data are collected which provide evidence for or against this assumption. Nevertheless, the similarity between the observational parts of the experiment and of the observational study persists.

If all methods of investigation to a degree incorporate both observational and experimental aspects, then a recognition of this situation could constitute a prelude to the extraction of both types of data from any given study. Thus, in the observational study the researcher would make the preparations necessary to take full advantage of whatever changes he produces within the research setting, that is, he would assess the nature of the changes and the process producing them. In the experimental study he would draw inferences, after locating those changes for which his experiment was responsible, about what the research situation would have been like had he not interfered with it, and he would then use these inferences as observational data.

TEMPORAL SEQUENCES

When research is reported it generally follows a seemingly logical and rational sequence, but this apparent sequence is far more logical than the one which actually occurs. In other words. the reconstructed logic of a given study generally differs substantially from the logic in use. The most important ideas shaping or emerging from a study may be in large part the result of a long night of insomnia or a very long traffic stoplight. There may be an apparently insane sequence of frenzied ideas and compromises, incredibly stupid mistakes and brilliant insights, long periods of boredom and repetitive tasks, administrative headaches, and irrelevant business to attend to.

A major problem for the researcher which partially explains this difference between logic in use and reconstructed logic is that presently we possess no effective reconstructed logic for the process of scientific discovery. Thus, every researcher is on his own to a great extent in dealing with the problem of how to make discoveries. In this situation it is easy to slip into the fallacy of believing that if the research process proceeds in a highly formalized way with a number of neat sequential stages, then this will produce important discoveries. This approach mistakes the symptom for the underlying cause. If we were using an effective logic of discovery, then in all probability we would follow a series of well-organized procedures. However, by devising organized procedures, there is no guarantee that an effective logic of discovery will be incorporated into these procedures.

In spite of the general state of disorganization of the research process, a state which frequently provides a shattering experience for the novice researcher, we may distinguish a temporal movement from (1) the theoretical definition of a problem, to (2) the research design and collection of data which test the theoretical ideas, to (3) the redefinition of the problem, to (4) the subjecting of the reformulation to empirical test, and so on. This movement follows our definition of the scientific method as a synthesis of ideas with ideas (theory) and a synthesis of ideas with experience (empirical testing) which together produce an integration of experience.

This view of the research process points up the importance of flexibility and cumulative effort. A rigid research plan would not allow successive redefinitions of the problem; thus the investigator would not be able to correct for his initial mistakes as he went along. Drawing an analogy between scientific research and everyday human problem solving, this would be similar to an individual who was open to learning for only short periods of time after long periods of rigidly following his preconceptions.

As for cumulation, successive revisions can take into account the data collected at earlier stages and point more successfully to the kinds of data that are most vitally needed. In this way each research project becomes in a sense a series of projects, with each building on the results of the preceding ones. All too often—given the state of project financing, the rewards for various types of research, and the difficulties of scientific communication—projects are not designed to succeed one another. Thus, whatever cumulation that results must occur largely within a given project.

4.2 DEFINITION OF THE PROBLEM

When the scientist speaks of "defining a problem," he usually means utilizing the best ideas he has in order to decide on the goals of his inquiry. When he speaks of "research design," he is usually talking about the general blueprint for achieving these goals. Problem definition is nothing less than the application of a theoretical framework to the particular questions at hand. Thus, for example, the investigator might emerge with a series of hypotheses which bear on the questions he is dealing with, based on available theory, available knowledge of the research situation, and his own ideas about theory and how to apply it.

The medical student study outlined in Chapter 1 may be used to illustrate problem definition. Actually, the problem was defined and redefined many times, with the following constituting some of the major stages of problem definition as well as important factors which led to each such definition:

1. Initially, the problem was defined by those individuals submitting the grant proposal, none of whom were on the staff of the project when it actually began. This early definition emphasized the difficulty of recruit-

ing qualified physicians for public health positions, with its consequent repercussions on the field of public health. The proposal called for a definitive national study in order to determine what factors were producing this situation and how best to cope with it. Studies of medical students as well as other studies were envisaged, although only the medical student studies will be discussed here.

This problem definition emphasized the need for the development of a social technology, that is, a mechanism that would help to solve recruitment problems in the field of public health. There was little emphasis on social science theory or its needs as distinct from the needed social technology. Social science was regarded as a valuable resource which, through the use of its investigative techniques, hopefully would come up with answers to the recruitment problem. Thus, social science was viewed as a methodological tool more than as a body of theory.

2. During the initial stage of the project the problem definition stated in the grant proposal was altered. In order to understand what occurred it is first necessary to realize that funding agencies generally allow a great deal of latitude for the redefinition of problems originally stated in grant proposals. They recognize that such flexibility allows investigators to make use of knowledge obtained during early stages of the research and thus leads to more effective investigations.

The major change was a broadening of the study, from a sole concern with the mechanism whereby students choose or do not choose public health as a career, to a concern with the general process of specialty choice. The source of this change was a conception of social science different (stemming primarily from the staff psychologist and sociologist) from that of an investigative tool. Granted that social science has produced many tools for data collection and analysis, perhaps the heart of social science consists of its theories and propositions. In particular, theories having to do with occupational choice were not generally limited to specific fields such as that of public health. In order to apply these theories, all of which seemed to be in a very early stage of development, it was seen that a wider range of data than would be provided by a sole concern with public health was called for. Without such broader testing of the theories, the investigators could have far less confidence in their applicability to processes involved in the choice of public health.

Although the changed definition of the problem resulted from a desire to obtain improved conditions for the development of a social technology, at the same time it enabled the investigators to satisfy some of the needs of social science itself. The testing of occupational choice theories within the medical student context may lead to a better understanding of the choice of public health, but it also may lead to the further development of these theories in particular and social science in general. Here was a situation, certainly not an atypical one, where there was little conflict between basic science goals and technological ones.

3. The development of a particular theory of occupational choice, based on the expected value deprivation of medical students for the different fields, was part of a redefinition of the problem. Within the preliminary studies many different variables were found to be related to specialty preferences. The next stage was conceived as one in which as many of these variables as possible would be gathered together so as to provide a thorough explanation of the choice process. It was also felt that the best way of combining the variables would be within the framework of a systematic theory. Concern with theory was related both to the desire to make an important contribution to social science and to the interest in developing the most effective instrument possible on which social technologies could be built. The formulation was put into mathematical terms, because it was felt that this would at least point the study in the direction of accurate prediction.

4. The fact that the data seemed to lend great support to the mathematical formulation based on expected value deprivation encourages further research on this formulation or modifications of it. The data are not viewed as definitively establishing the theory, but rather as pointing up the possibility that this or a similar theory might be valid.

4.3   RESEARCH DESIGN

PROBLEM AND DESIGN

The research design constitutes the blueprint for the collection, measurement, and analysis of data. It aids the scientist in the allocation of his limited resources by posing crucial choices: Is the blueprint to include experiments, interviews, observation, the analysis of records, simulation, or some combination of these? Are the methods of data collection and the research situation to be highly structured? Is an intensive study of a small sample more effective than a less intensive study of a large sample? Should the analysis be primarily quantitative or qualitative?

The attempt to formulate a research design very early in the development of the investigation can aid the scientist in achieving a more focused approach. In moving from problem definition to research design, the implications of the general research goals must be outlined in order to make decisions on specific procedures. The development of a research design, however, does not necessaryily move the researcher toward more highly structured techniques. The question of structure is a separate one which may be evaluated in terms of its potential contribution to the solution of the problem.

Unfortunately, the scientist sometimes discovers at the completion of a project that, although the results are quite interesting, they do not really answer the questions originally posed. Often the fault lies in a definition of the problem so vague that it provides little guidance in the construction of the research design.

What the investigator sometimes does in order to make the problem definition more explicit is to make up hypothetical data which might result from a given problem definition and research design. He then examines these data to determine whether or not they provide answers to the problem in which he is genuinely interested. If not, he proceeds to redefine the problem and alter the research design accordingly.

It seems useful to define the problem before considering questions of research design. By allowing design considerations to influence problem definition, the researcher tends to limit his choice to those problems about which objective data can be most readily obtained. In some cases, problems of great importance might be ignored because of measurement difficulties. Of course, there are many practical considerations in each research project, but if these subsequently modify the definition of the problem, at least the scientist is fully aware of what he is sacrificing.

SAMPLING

The scientist works toward the development of propositions and theories that have the widest possible scope, but he can only obtain a limited number of observations. Thus, in order to secure the best possible test for his theory, he must choose these observations wisely. He must decide (1) what kinds of observations to make, and (2) how many observations to make.

One of the most powerful ideas the investigator has to work with is that of *probability sampling*, a topic which will be treated more fully in Section 15.1. By selecting his observations in accordance with the principles of probability sampling, the investigator is greatly aided in obtaining a set of observations (sample) that is *representative* of the much larger set of observations to which his theory has applicability. The saving is immense. For example, a probability sample of only a few thousand Americans can provide an accurate basis for uncovering the opinions of the entire population.

Probability sampling refers to a particular method of selecting a sample or a subset of units from a population or larger set. Each unit or element of the population has a known probability of being included in the sample. Although individual human beings frequently constitute these units, they may be any entity in which the investigator is interested (for example, families, organizations, communities, societies, time periods, pages of a newspaper, and so on).

One common type of probability sampling is simple random sampling, in which each unit or subset of units within the population has an equal chance of being included in the sample. If, for example, numbered pieces of paper in a hat correspond to the population, then a simple random sample might be approximated by mixing up these pieces extremely well and then having a blindfolded individual select the sample.[1]

The method of sample selection constitutes evidence within the context of justification. Probability samples help the investigator to validate his propositions widely and thus to assess their scope. They possess the particular advantage of aiding the investigator to generalize, with a known degree of error, findings based on his sample data to the population from which the sample was drawn. As the size of the probability sample increases, this degree of error shrinks rapidly.

Decisions on the size and type of sample must take into account several factors. One of these is the practical consideration that research resources are limited. Although the investigator might decide that he would like to be able to estimate the characteristics of the population to within 1 per cent of their actual occurrence, he may not be able to afford a sample large enough to yield this degree of accuracy. Another factor is the degree of heterogeneity of the entities selected for investigation. The chemist may not have to worry very much about variations in the chemical properties of a given element or compound from one sample to another, but human beings from different cultures or subcultures differ very markedly. An unanswered question is whether this difference constitutes a variation in the basic mechanisms of human behavior or merely in its outward manifestations.

In coming to a decision, the investigator would do well to be guided very closely by his definition of the problem. It might, for example, be very tempting to expend research resources on securing an excellent probability sample of the entire population of individuals in the United States. Such an expenditure would be great because of the high cost of obtaining probability samples. But if the definition of the problem emphasizes the context of discovery, a superior strategy for a given problem might be to secure detailed data on a nonprobability sample. The money saved by using such a sample might well be employed in other phases of the investigation. By the same token, a detailed case study of one medical school may be more suggestive than a less detailed study of all the medical schools in the United States. One strategy adopted by some researchers is to make use of large probability samples only at the point at which propositions of considerable merit have been developed and are ready for wider testing. The argument supporting this point of view is that it is not

[1] More convient for the researcher is the table of random numbers. Many statistics textbooks contain such tables. For large tables, see The Rand Corporation, *A Million Random Digits with 100,000 Normal Deviates* (New York: Free Press, 1955). A table issued to researchers free of charge is the Interstate Commerce Commission's *Table of 105,000 Random Decimal Digits,* Statement 4914, File No. 261–A–1 (Washington, D.C.: Bureau of Transport Economics and Statistics 51494).

important to be able to say something that is true for the entire population of a given society, if that something is a trivial statement which adds little to our ability to explain and predict human behavior.

4.4 INVESTIGATOR EFFECT

The Heisenberg principle of indeterminacy illustrates the effect of the investigator on the phenomena under investigation in quantum physics. The process of observation necessitates the bombardment of the observed particles with photons of light, thus changing their position and velocity. The position and velocity of the particles prior to such bombardment thus remains unknown.

The situation is not quite the same in the observation of human behavior, for the social scientist can hide behind one-way mirrors for some situations, or he may enter certain situations as a participant and disguise the fact that he is an observer. Even in these instances, however, there is interaction between observer and observed, for the phenomena observed affect observers differently, and scientists may try to read into their observations some degree of agreement with their colleagues.

Most research situations in the social sciences are not of the one-way-mirror type. The interviewer or experimenter or observer brings his own set of constraints which apply to the individuals under observation. Very little is known about the nature of these constraints, for some of them are extremely subtle. A middle-class interviewer of a working-class respondent may have a carefully developed technique for asking questions and reacting to answers that does not in the least betray his own values and expectations. Yet the fact that he is a middle-class interviewer can hardly be hidden from most respondents, who would be alert to such cues as type of dress, manner of speech, and the very fact that interviewing is not a working-class occupation. If, to avoid some of these constraints, interviewers of working-class individuals were selected from among working-class applicants, a somewhat different set of constraints would emerge. Some feelings might more readily be divulged to a social equal; others (for example, any ideas which might be interpreted as pro-middle-class or anti-working-class) would be more carefully hidden under these circumstances.

Because the observer can control his interaction with the observed only to a limited extent, it behooves him to take those measurements which will enable him to correct for the interaction. For example, the middle-class interviewer might ask the respondent what he thinks the interviewer's expectations are. Efforts to develop objective observational techniques, and the replication of observations by other social scientists, achieve some degree of control with respect to the effect of the observed on the observer.

As for the effect of the observer on the observed, what seems to be needed is the collection of data on this effect as well as the other phenomena in which the investigator is interested. The fact that the respondent's behavior will be influenced by the observer is a research problem in and of itself. Explanations of such effects both add to our over-all knowledge of human behavior and contribute to our ability to correct for this interaction in research situations.

It is easy enough of course to outline a general remedy; the difficulty lies in devising the specifics. What kind of theory, for example, is broad enough to encompass the complex interaction process between investigator and subject? And what specific techniques can be used to gain information about this process?

To illustrate the magnitude of the problem, let us take a large interview survey as an illustration. Not only is there the interaction between the interviewer and the interviewee, but there is also that among interviewers as well as that between the field director and the interviewers. Let us also bear in mind that, despite a common training experience in preparing for the survey, each interviewer is a unique individual. Trite as this may sound, it implies that he or she will be oriented in certain ways and that this will be revealed to the interviewee in one way or another. Add to this situation the uniqueness of each interviewee, with his own preconceptions about the interview situation and reactions to it, and we have a great variety of interview situations.

What is required is research on what is going on in each of the interview situations, guided by theory that is broad enough to encompass the complexities involved, and guided by methodology that is sufficiently well developed to make such a research effort feasible. What is almost universally done, by contrast, is almost nothing along these lines, partly because the theory and methodology to support such a research effort are lacking. Rarely is any data about the interview situation collected, with the implication that no special correction need be applied to an interview schedule in order to take that situation into account. Yet we know full well that such corrections often are vital. Overwhelming evidence about the magnitude of investigator effect is accumulating for the experiment.[2] We can infer that this magnitude should be multiplied several times for the interview survey, where the opportunities for investigator effect are increased by extensive interaction between interviewer and interviewee.

Given our ignorance about investigator effect, it may well be that a great many of the conclusions of social science are erroneous. This may not be the case, but without focusing on this problem there is little way of

[2] See, for example, Robert Rosenthal, *Experimenter Effects in Behavioral Research* (New York: Appleton, 1966); Neil Friedman, *The Social Nature of Psychological Research* (New York: Basic Books, 1967); and James A. Wiggins, "Hypothesis Validity and Experimental Laboratory Methods," in Hubert M. Blalock and Ann B. Blalock (eds.) *Methodology in Social Research* (New York: McGraw-Hill, 1968), Chap. 10.

telling just what the actual situation is. It is easy enough to imagine situations where social scientists expect to obtain certain findings, where they transmit these expectations to the interviewers, whether nonverbally or by implication from the wording of the question, where these expectations are then transmitted to the interviewees, and where the interviewees tend to conform (to a greater or lesser extent) to what is expected of them.

We do not mean to imply that nothing at all is known about investigator effect. Indeed, within the last five years this problem has come into prominence in the methodological literature. Yet the studies of this phenomenon provide us with illustrations more than with a theory and methodology for dealing with it.

Progress in understanding investigator effect should have important implications for a general understanding of human behavior. Such progress may be described as learning about the properties of the lens we use to observe behavior: in what ways does it distort what we are looking at, and how can we correct for these distortions? In addition, when we learn about these distortions we are also learning about the distortions of ordinary individuals in their everyday interactions.

4.5 DEGREE OF STRUCTURE

THE UNEASY COMPROMISE

In most of the behavioral sciences there seems to exist an uneasy compromise between those who conceive of research as a highly structured, objective, quantitative, and rigorous affair and those who are more qualitatively oriented and less concerned with rigorous proof. Claims of superiority are made by advocates of both methods, but trivial or fruitful results may be the outcome of either.

The controversy seems to be one aspect of the division between the "two cultures," the sciences and the humanities. Some historians, for example, treat their discipline as one of the humanities, whereas others place it among the sciences. Some economists rely heavily on Aristotelian logic as well as introspection, whereas others are the model builders, econometricians, and reconstructionists. Some psychologists would exclude introspection on the part of the investigator and others would regard introspective data as admissible.

Within sociology the controversy is best viewed in historical perspective. Hinkle and Hinkle[3] discuss the early period of American sociology (1905–1918) as one characterized by social reformism, faith in progressive social change, a belief in the existence of natural laws governing human

[3] Roscoe C. Hinkle, Jr., and Gisela J. Hinkle, *The Development of Modern Sociology* (Garden City, N.Y.: Doubleday, 1954).

behavior, and the general quest to make sociology scientific. An important controversy centered around William I. Thomas' and Florian Znaniecki's *The Polish Peasant in Europe and America,* which made extensive use of personal documents, such as letters and autobiographies, in order to present a series of detailed "life-histories" or case studies. Many sociologists felt this method provided an excellent opportunity to convey a thorough account of all phases of life, and, in particular, man's inner mental life. A number of quantitative or statistically oriented sociologists attacked the method on the grounds that the citation of examples does not constitute scientific proof and that the method is highly subjective, especially because the investigator can select life histories to suit his own purposes.

This controversy within sociology has been resolved to some extent, with most sociologists agreeing that both case studies and statistics can contribute to the scientific process. The advantages of case studies lie not so much in the context of justification as in the context of discovery. Quantitative studies are considered especially important in the context of justification. Actually, the compromise is an uneasy one. The controversy between the quantitatively oriented, who believe in highly structured techniques, and the qualitatively oriented, who believe in less structured techniques, does not generally manifest itself by way of formal or informal debate; rather, it is evidenced by research methods used. Actually this is far more consequential than mere debate, for what sociologists do usually matters more than what they say.

LEVELS OF ABSTRACTION

Both less-structured and more-structured methods seem to have played important roles in the history of the sciences generally. Within one general pattern of research, investigation may move back and forth between the two. In the medical student study, for example, the first phase was largely exploratory in nature and the second phase was fairly structured. This movement between methods of data collection is analogous to the movement of investigators up and down the ladder of abstraction in order to develop systematic theory and validate it.

Abstraction is, by definition, a selection of only some elements from among the large set of elements under observation. When the survey researcher, for example, asks an individual to react in one of several possible ways to a given hypothetical situation, he is limiting his focus to the very few characteristics which he includes in the hypothetical situation and the very few response categories. This abstraction process is utilized by all investigators to some degree, because the very language in which we think forces us to select some phenomena over others and to pattern them in certain ways. Thus the contrast is drawn between *more-structured* and *less-structured* methods, and not between structured and unstructured methods. There does remain a difference in degree of abstraction, however. In the more-structured approach the investigator comes to the data-collection situation with consciously formulated ideas which may then be tested and further developed. In the less-structured approach the researcher often uses the research situation as a means of focusing his initial ideas, which may be vague and not consciously formulated.

To the degree that the compromise between the two methods is an uneasy one, investigators will experience difficulty in moving back and forth between them. To rely on structured methods exclusively is to close down many avenues which might have been used for the best possible development of a theory. A dependence on less-structured methods may mean failure to test the theory adequately.

One advantage that highly structured methods have within the context of justification is that the procedures of observation involved are relatively explicit and repeatable by different observers. In addition, where observational procedures are explicit it is less difficult for the investigator to measure the impact of such procedures on the individuals under observation. Where less-structured observational procedures are concerned, similar measurements pose greater problems.

The debate between proponents of more- and of less-structured methods is a species of the more general one between advocates of quantitative and of qualitative research. The participant observer may feel, for example, that the only way to discover the essence of the social system under investigation is actually to watch it work over a long period of time, avoiding preconceived notions or structured techniques of measurement. The experimenter may feel that the reality is effectively hidden by the many extraneous, phenotypical, or surface phenomena found in field situations, and that the best way to uncover the genotypes is to create a situation which abstracts them from the surface phenomena and enables the investigator to perform definitive tests on them.

Neither method, however, represents a sure path to success; each has certain weaknesses. The reality can never be seen directly, but the scientist's best method for arriving at a close approximation of it is to utilize the kinds of techniques of investigation *at some point* which will enable his results to be checked by others. The failure of a participant observer to reach this point results in little confidence on the part of the scientific community that he has actually collected evidence within the context of justification. The higher level of abstraction of the experimenter can be extremely effective when it is coupled with important concepts and fruitful theory. When, on the other hand, this method of investigation leads him to select only those concepts and theories that can be rigorously quantified and tested, the results yielded may be quite true but also quite trivial. Furthermore, both the more- and the less-structured methods may rest on implicit paradigms which do violence to consciously accepted knowledge.

EXERCISES

1. Select any observational study with which you are familiar and show how you might convert it into a partial experiment by assessing the processes involved in the investigator effect which occurs.

2. Select any experimental study with which you are familiar. How would you convert it into a series of experiments, each of which is based on the knowledge derived from the preceding ones?

3. Develop a detailed research design for the study of investigator effect in the context of an experimental study.

4. Present pros and cons with respect to the argument that most existing behavioral science knowledge is suspect because of lack of adequate attention to investigator effect.

5. Do you believe that it is more likely for implicit (versus explicit) paradigms to be present in less-structured (versus more-structured) techniques? Why?

ANNOTATED REFERENCES

PERLS, FREDERICK S. *In and Out the Garbage Pail.* Lafayette, Calif.: Real People's Press, 1969. This unusual autobiography by the originator of Gestalt therapy is a mosaic of poetry, art, speculation, theory, humor, and many other things. Most important for present purposes, it illustrates a kind of awareness of circumstances, an ability to look at self from a variety of perspectives, which would be invaluable for an investigator concerned about assessing his impact on those he is studying.

ROSENTHAL, ROBERT. *Experimenter Effects in Behavioral Research.* New York: Appleton-Century-Crofts, Inc., 1966. The author has contributed a great number of studies on the effects of the experimenter on his subjects and, in so doing, has helped to focus attention on a very serious problem in experimental, as well as other, data collection. If we take this problem to heart, then it becomes essential for us to reformulate many of the traditional ideas about the nature of the scientific method in the behavioral sciences.

SJOBERG, GIDEON, and ROGER NETT. *A Methodology for Social Research.* New York: Harper & Row, Publishers, 1968. This book represents a perspective on data collection, and other aspects of research, that is based on the sociology of knowledge. The authors are concerned with examining the impact of the researcher upon each step of the research process. Thus, for example, the researcher's ethical stance is viewed as an integral feature of the research design.

CHAPTER 5 **The Experiment**

5.1 INTRODUCTION

The experiment, a method for the collection and analysis of data, has contributed so vastly to developments in the physical and biological sciences that it is widely thought of as the foundation for the scientific method. Within the social sciences it has been utilized chiefly by psychologists, but there are indications that it is coming into more widespread use within sociology and other social sciences.

In common with other methods for collecting and analyzing data, the experiment is designed to aid in the development and testing of propositions and theories. Most of these have to do directly or indirectly with cause-and-effect relationships, and thus it is the task of the researcher to collect the kind of data which provides evidence for the existence of such relationships. There are various types of evidence that can be advanced for or against the existence of a given causal relationship. A number of these were categorized by John Stuart Mill as the *method of agreement,* the *method of difference,* the *method of concomitant variation*, and the *method of residues.* Although Mill called these the experimental methods, one or more of them are actually utilized in modern form in all scientific methods for the collection and analysis of data. After a discussion of Mill's methods, we shall be in a position to understand the nature of the experiment as distinguished from other methods.

5.2 MILL'S EXPERIMENTAL METHODS

METHOD OF AGREEMENT

Mill describes the method of agreement as follows: "If two or more instances of the phenomenon under investigation have only one circumstance in common, the circumstance in which alone all the instances agree is the cause of the given phenomenon."[1]

---

[1] Quoted in Morris R. Cohen and Ernest Nagel, *An Introduction to Logic and the Scientific Method* (New York: Harcourt, 1934), p. 251. From John Stuart Mill, *A System of Logic,* Vol. I (New York: Harper, 1891).

Let us suppose that the phenomenon under investigation is the plan of parents to send their children to college. Let us also assume that the only circumstance which a number of parents planning to send their children to college have in common is the fact that they saw a film that stressed the importance of a college education. Then, according to the method of agreement, we may infer that exposure to the film caused the parents to plan to send their children to college.

There are a number of things wrong with this argument. First, it is difficult to imagine a situation in which individuals have only one thing in common. The fact that they all are human beings, speak English, live on the planet Earth, or live in the twentieth century would constitute other characteristics in common. Is it possible to find a situation in which individuals have only one thing in common? Second, a causal statement cannot be proved with any certainty if it is a statement about reality. We may obtain evidence for a given cause-and-effect relationship, but we cannot say definitively that any given factor is the cause of any other factor.

In spite of these inadequacies, however, the method of agreement can be a valuable tool in the analysis of cause-and-effect relationships, for it can be used as a mechanism for obtaining evidence about such a relationship.

For example, what is commonly called the *descriptive study* follows the rationale of the method of agreement. Whatever the investigator wishes to describe corresponds to the "phenomenon under investigation" (for example, medical students who are interested in public health as a career). He may then attempt to describe the characteristics that a number of medical students with this interest ("two or more instances of the phenomenon") have in common. The approach need not be to accept as evidence situations in which they have only one factor in common, for this will never occur. Thus, for example, these students, aside from job security, might be found to be very interested in helping people. The investigator does not then infer that these goals alone cause the students to be interested in public health; rather, he may treat such data as partial evidence for the existence of a cause-and-effect relationship. Of course, he may discover that no such relationship actually exists.

METHOD OF DIFFERENCE

The method of difference is stated in this manner: "If an instance in which the phenomenon under investigation occurs, and an instance in which it does not occur, have every circumstance in common save one, that one occurring in the former, the circumstances in which alone the two instances differ is the effect, or the cause, or an indispensable part of the cause, of the phenomenon."[2]

---

[2] Cohen and Nagel, op. cit., p. 256.

Suppose that the plan of parents to send their children to college is the phenomenon under investigation (as in the above example). We may then compare a group of parents exposed to the film on the importance of college with one that is not (a circumstance the two groups do not have in common). Let us assume that the only difference between these groups is whether or not they were exposed to the film. Then, according to the method of difference, the decision to send children to college is either a cause or an effect of seeing the film. Because the decision is made subsequent to the showing of the film, the conclusion (following Mill) is that the decision is the effect of seeing the film. As in the method of agreement, there are shortcomings to the reasoning involved here: the "proof" of the existence of a cause-and-effect relationship lies in limited empirical data, and it is difficult or impossible to locate phenomena that have one and only one difference other than that under investigation.

METHOD OF CONCOMITANT VARIATIONS

Mill's method of concomitant variations is stated in this way: "Whatever phenomenon varies in any manner, whenever another phenomenon varies in some particular manner, is either a cause or an effect of that phenomenon, or is connected with it through some fact of causation."[3]

One advantage of this method is that it moves the focus of an investigation from qualitative hypotheses about the existence of relationships to quantitative hypotheses about the degree of relationships.

In an experimental context, we might be concerned about the relationship between the number of minutes of exposure to the film and the degree to which parents changed their attitudes on the importance of a college education. Thus, a number of different groups could be set up with each one representing a different degree of exposure to filmed material. The investigation would seek to determine whether the greater the time of exposure of a given group to the film, the greater the change in parental attitudes. If this were true, then according to Mill's formulation, exposure and attitude change would be causally related. The shortcoming in this reasoning lies, as in his other methods, in the lack of certainty of such a "proof." Although it does provide some evidence, any such association may be pure coincidence.

METHOD OF RESIDUES

Mill's method of residues is stated as follows: "Subduct from any phenomenon such part as is known by previous inductions to be the effect of certain antecedents, and the residue of the phenomenon is the effect of the remaining antecedents."[4]

[3] Ibid., pp. 261–262.
[4] Ibid., p. 264.

Using the example of the film on college once more, let us assume that we have two groups of parents who differ only with respect to whether or not they were exposed to the film. Let us also assume that, during the course of the experiment, both groups happened to read news stories about the greater earning capacities of college graduates. Finally, let us assume that both groups became more positive to a certain extent about college for their children as a result of the news stories, although this change is mixed with the effects of the film for the exposed group. Then, according to the method of residues, we are in a position to calculate the effect of the film on the group exposed to it.

This is accomplished by conceiving of the total change in the exposed group (T) as being made up of two parts: that which results from having read the news stories (N) and that resulting from exposure to the film (F). We can measure the change in the unexposed group which resulted from the news stories, and since this group has been equated with the exposed group, we may assume that this change corresponds to N for the exposed group. We can also measure the total change in the exposed group (T). In order to calculate the effect of the film, then, we perform the following subtraction:

$$F = T - N$$

As we shall see in Section 5.4, "interaction effects" may lead to a much more complicated situation than Mill formulated, although his procedure would be accurate in many situations.

5.3 THE NATURE OF THE EXPERIMENT

The nature of the experiment can be most clearly seen by examining the illustration used for Mill's method of difference. One group of parents was exposed to the film whereas the other was not, and the change in the college plans of the exposed group (assuming that the unexposed group experienced no change) was then attributed to their exposure. A typical characteristic of the experiment has to do with whether or not the investigator can *assign* the presumed causal or independent variable (exposure or lack of exposure) to the different groups. In this example such assignment does in fact take place, with one group being shown the film and the other group not seeing it. The investigator thus plays a very active role in the experiment, manipulating the experimental conditions in a certain way.

Although variables such as exposure to a film can be easily manipulated, this is not the case for such variables as age and sex. The investigator cannot *assign* age or sex to any group. Thus, when such variables are conceived of as causal or independent, other techniques of investigation than that of the experiment are generally used. The exception to this rule occurs where the investigator constructs a concept which, in fact, can be assigned, that is cognate to the nonmanipulable one. For example, an investigator interested in the impact of age on certain factors might be able to study this indirectly by manipulating an individual's "subjective age" (that is, how old the individual feels as distinct from how old he is chronologically).

Although investigators assign the experimental conditions in almost all experiments in order to achieve a high degree of control over various types of error, this is not the defining characteristic of the experiment. What is crucial is (1) that there be a focus on some change which occurs, whether introduced by the experimenter or by environmental circumstances, and (2) that the investigator be able either to achieve a high degree of control over the experimental situation or to understand it well enough that he can make allowances for relevant factors in the situation.

The laboratory experiment generally fulfills these requirements fairly well, but we should bear in mind that this fulfillment is a matter of degree. For any given laboratory experiment the change can be small or large, and the investigator is able to gather only a certain amount of data bearing on the processes producing the change. Even in a supposedly highly controlled experiment, there will be great gaps in knowledge of many kinds of factors (for example, those having to do with experimenter effect).

We might conceive of the "natural experiment" (where the treatments are introduced by forces outside of the control of the experimenter) as also fulfilling the requirements (of knowledge of relevant factors and of a focus on some change that is introduced) to a degree. Take the Great Depression in the United States, for example. To study this phenomenon as a natural experiment requires thoroughgoing attention to the locating of those factors producing the change, to the change itself, and to those factors resulting from the change. Potential natural experiments resulting in changes of lesser magnitude are occurring all the time. What is required to convert them into natural experiments is this kind of thoroughgoing research.

RANDOMIZATION

One of the most important controls involved in experimental procedures is the technique of randomization. Randomization has to do with the process by which subjects (or whatever other units are being investigated) are assigned to the various experimental procedures. Let us assume we are testing the effectiveness of a given communication in changing the values of the subjects. The classical experimental design provides for an *experimental group,* which is subjected to one treatment (in this case, exposure to the communication), and a *control group,* which is not.

Randomization, in this context, is a procedure for assigning available subjects to the experimental and control groups in such a way that the two groups will be quite similar. It is important to achieve this similarity, for then differential changes in the values of subjects in the two groups may be more readily associated with the different treatments involved, rather than with the pre-existing differences between the two groups. A procedure that might be used in this context is the assignment of a random sample of subjects participating in the experiment to the experimental group and a random sample of the same size to the control group. In this manner each of the two groups becomes a random sample of the initial pool of available subjects, for each subject in the pool had an equal chance of being placed in either group. Thus each of the two groups can be treated as being representative (within an estimated degree of error) of the initial pool of subjects, and consequently the two groups will tend to be quite similar because "things equal to the same thing are equal to each other."

The significance of the randomization procedure is far-reaching, for it achieves a matching of the two groups on *all* variables, with an estimated degree of error. This degree of error can be reduced by increasing the size of the experimental and control groups. (Of course, no matter how large the groups are, there is always a finite probability that the groups will differ by a given degree.)

Of course, it is not possible to achieve randomization in the natural experiment, because it is not the experimenter who assigns treatments, but outside forces. Thus, the natural experiment generally achieves less control over relevant factors operating in the experimental situation. Yet we should bear in mind that there is no such thing as perfect control when randomization procedures are used. It is also quite possible that an experimenter who uses randomization has so little knowledge of the forces operating in the experimental situation that he is able to learn much less than if he initiated a well-conceived natural experiment.

FREQUENCY DISTRIBUTION AND PRECISION CONTROL

Randomization procedures may be contrasted with matching procedures, which attempt to equate the groups only on a limited number of variables. One type of matching procedure commonly used is *frequency-distribution control,* which involves equating the experimental and the control groups on whatever variables are deemed to be important (for example, those factors that might influence the effectiveness of the given communication in changing the subjects' values). If frequency-distribution control is achieved with respect to sex, for example, then both groups will contain the same proportion of each sex. Only a limited number of factors can be subjected to such control, however, and each of them must be identifiable and measurable. Randomization, on the other hand, achieves control (within an estimated degree of error) over factors that have not yet been discovered.

Precision control is another matching technique that involves pairing individuals on the basis of several factors and then placing one member of each pair in the experimental group and the other in the control group. The advantage of this technique over frequency-distribution control is the matching of the joint distribution of several factors, rather than of the distribution of single factors. Thus, frequency-distribution control based on sex and social class alone might lead to a much higher proportion of middle-class males in the experimental group than in the control group. With precision control, however, the two groups would contain the same proportion of middle-class males. Precision control has a disadvantage, however. Because it is difficult to achieve this kind of pairing, a large proportion of potential subjects from the initial pool will remain unpaired and consequently will not be utilized in the experiment. This loss of cases will be especially great if the attempt is made to achieve precision control on more than a very few factors.

Important differences among precision control, frequency-distribution control, and randomization procedures are illustrated in Table 5-1. Let us assume that we are investigating the effect of a lecture on attitudes about the desirability of having female candidates for the presidency, and that we proceed by lecturing to an experimental group and not lecturing to a control group. Given this problem, it would seem to be desirable to control both on sex and on social class, because we know from prior research that each of these variables is quite relevant to such attitudes.

When we control on variables within this context we attempt to make sure that the experimental group and the control group are as close to identical as possible with respect to the distribution of such variables. In this way, whatever influence such variables have on the experiment will make its impact felt within the control group as well as the experimental group and the experimenter will thus be able to account for it.

In comparing the result of precision control and frequency-distribution control techniques on the data, we can see from Table 5-1 that both techniques have two end results in common: (1) they both yield an experimental group with thirty males, thirty females, twenty middle-class individuals, and forty working-class individuals; and (2) they both yield a control group with thirty males, thirty females, twenty middle-class individuals, and forty working-class individuals. Thus, seemingly both techniques are equally effective in constructing an experimental group that has the same distribution with respect to these two variables as the control group.

TABLE 5–1

A Comparison of Precision Control, Frequency-Distribution Control, and Randomization
Procedures for Hypothetical Data on 120 Subjects

Control Procedure		Experimental Group (N = 60)		Control Group (N = 60)	
		Males	Females		Males	Females
Precision control	Middle-class	10	10	Middle-class	10	10
	Working-class	20	20	Working-class	20	20
		Males	Females		Males	Females
Frequency-distribution control	Middle-class	5	15	Middle-class	15	5
	Working-class	25	15	Working-class	15	25
		Males	Females		Males	Females
Randomization	Middle-class	12	8	Middle-class	8	12
	Working-class	18	22	Working-class	22	18

But we can see that there are also differences resulting from these two techniques, and these may be summarized as follows:

1. Precision control produces ten middle-class males in both the experimental and the control group, whereas frequency-distribution control produces five middle-class males in the experimental group and fifteen middle-class males in the control group.
2. Precision control produces ten middle-class females in the two groups, whereas frequency-distribution control yields fifteen in the experimental group and five in the control group.
3. Precision control yields twenty working-class males and twenty working-class females in each of the two groups. Frequency-distribution control produces twenty-five working-class males and fifteen working-class females in the experimental group, and fifteen working-class females and twenty-five working-class males in the control group.

The difference between experimental and control groups produced by frequency-distribution control techniques (as distinct from precision control) may or may not "contaminate" the factor of hearing or not hearing the lecture on female candidates for the presidency. The point is that the experimenter cannot have confidence that *any* difference between the experimental and the control group will have no effect on his interpretation of the experimental data. Any difference serves to change the pure situation in which the *only* factor available for him to attribute any difference between these two groups at the close of the experiment is whether or not a group heard the lecture.

From Table 5-1 alone it would seem that randomization is superior to frequency-distribution control but inferior to precision control. This is because there is some variation, as between the experimental and control group, on the proportion of middle-class males, middle-class females, working-class males, and working-class females. Such variation is less than that occurring as a result of frequency-distribution control but greater than that for precision control. Actually, there are several other characteristics not shown in Table 5-1 that make randomization generally superior to precision control:

1. Precision control can only be exercised on a very few variables that are related to whatever is randomized. Thus, for example, if subjects are assigned at random to the experimental group and the control group, then all variables having to do with individual differences are controlled. The degree of control is not perfect, as can be seen from the example, but it increases as the size of the groups increase.
2. Randomization procedures utilize all the subjects from the initial pool available for the experiment, but many cases are lost with precision control, with the number lost increasing as each additional variable is controlled. This is especially serious in the situation where the initial pool of subjects is representative of some larger population. As cases are lost from this pool it becomes less and less representative of the population, and the experimenter is no longer able to generalize the results of his experiment to the population with any degree of confidence.

Frequency-distribution control or precision-control techniques can be combined with randomization procedures. Such a combination might be advantageous when the experimental and control groups are fairly small and one or more factors were known to exert an important influence on the phenomena under investigation. The advantage here is that randomization would serve to control all variables relating to individual differences (if subjects were randomized) that were not controlled by frequency-distribution or precision-control procedures.

Randomization and the procedures of frequency and precision control are ways of preventing the interference of extraneous factors. We need not think of them only in the context of the assignment of subjects to experimental and control groups, for we can also utilize these procedures in the actual setting up of the experimental- and control-group *situations* in such a way that they are as nearly equivalent as possible. It should be borne in mind that thus far all of our examples have had to do with randomization procedures as applied to subjects. They have wider implications, however.

The experimenter, for example, will generally attempt to match the two groups on the various aspects of the physical situation under which the experiment takes place. If this matching is achieved by utilizing the same room for both groups, thus leading to a difference in the time of day at which the data are collected, he might decide to control the time factor by a randomization procedure: he might use two experimental and two control groups, with one experimental group randomly selected for an early time on one day and one control group randomly selected for an early time on another day.

Thus, the experimenter tries to equate the experimental- and control-group situations by matching and randomization so as to avoid error in drawing conclusions about the relationship between the independent and the dependent variable. Without such matching, the experimenter might conclude that his different treatments of the experimental and control groups led to an observed difference in their behavior, when actually the observed difference arose from a difference in the situations (for example, time of day).

There are other procedures for achieving control. Where differences between experimental and control groups cannot be eliminated, it is often possible to take them into account through analytical procedures. One such technique is that of "controlling on a third variable," a procedure to be discussed in Chapter 16.

THEORY

Perhaps more than any other method of data collection, the experiment epitomizes the most highly effective methodological procedures, for is it not true that the powerful physical sciences utilized this procedure more than any other method of collecting data? In this context it is tempting to believe that if one goes through the mechanics of a relatively sophisticated experimental design, valuable data will emerge. As for theory, it becomes difficult to discern how it is important, because the mechanics of experimental design do not seem to require any special consideration of theory. Theory deals with the quality of the experiment, the content as distinct from the form.

We might draw an analogy between experimental design and the "design" or plan for taking courses in a university in order to matriculate. If we focus on form, there are rather definite procedures for both, whether they involve setting up control groups or taking various sequences of courses in order to satisfy requirements. What is irrelevant with respect to achieving a college degree is which course from among the available possibilities the student takes. If some courses are poorly taught and others well taught, if some are more appropriate than others for a specific student, this is not directly relevant to the accumulation of the correct number of credits for the fulfillment of college requirements. Similarly, one can seek to perform a rigorous and sophisticated experiment, going through all the appropriate procedures, and yet miss doing an important experiment, just as the student who is only concerned with satisfying requirements may fail to secure an education.

Accepting the importance of theory for the experiment, how can we build the content of a design into one of high quality where the results will be fruitful for the further development of understanding? Unfortunately, behavioral scientists as yet have done almost no research which can be brought to bear on this question. However, there are some general guidelines that are relevant both to this context of discovery and to the context of justification.

What appears to be required is the kind of theory which provides a very comprehensive framework for the experiment and which is put together in a systematic fashion. Such a framework could be broad enough to bear on the processes involved in the generation of experimenter effect, and systematic enough to correct for whatever effects are involved. It could be inclusive enough not only to achieve more satisfactory control over the experimental situation but also to take advantage of what goes on in this situation. Narrow theory would set up blinders to anything not directly related to the initial definition of the problem. A broader theory could, thus, convert the process by which investigator effect is generated into an important finding within the study, to be placed alongside those findings which were the chief focus of the study. Of course, along with such a broad theoretical framework would have to go carefully designed methodological procedures for applying it to the research situation. Furthermore, we need not wait for perfection with respect to theory or method; we can move by way of successive approximation, developing more comprehensive and systematic theories on which to base more effective methodology, which in turn can serve as the base for improved theories, and so on.

5.4 EXPERIMENTAL DESIGN

THE CLASSICAL DESIGN

In order to understand the process of experimentation, it is most helpful to examine various sources of error as well as the way in which control groups work toward the elimination of these errors. The general function of the control group in the classical design is to create a situation as nearly equivalent to the experimental-group situation as possible. In this way, any resulting differences between the two groups may be attributed to the different treatments accorded to the two groups by the experimenter. A good deal of error often stems from the fact that it is not possible to set up groups that "have every circumstance in common" except the one under investigation (as in the method of difference). The experimenter has to settle for less, and one procedure is to utilize randomization and matching techniques to come as close to the ideal as possible.

Assuming that the two groups are essentially equivalent, we may proceed to trace the impact of a variety of factors on the two groups. It would be useful to view this experiment, which may be called the *before–after experiment with one control group,* with reference to a series of stages. These may be presented schematically as follows:

Stages	Experimental Group	Control Group
1. Selection of subjects: matching and/or randomization	Yes	Yes
2. Experimental conditions: matching and/or randomization	Yes	Yes
3. "Before" measurement (pretest)	Yes	Yes
4. Exposure to test stimuli	Yes	No
5. "After" measurement (posttest)	Yes	Yes

We have already discussed the way in which matching and randomization techniques operate to increase the similarity of the two groups. This is vital, for if the two groups differ on any factor related to the variables under investigation, erroneous conclusions may easily be drawn. *Experimental conditions* refer to all the stimuli having to do with the experiment once the subjects have been selected and prior to the "before" measurement (the physical conditions involved in the experiment) and any interaction between experimenter and subjects.

In this case, the "before" measurement constitutes an index of the initial attitudes of the parents on the subject of sending their children to college. The test stimuli would then be the film that is subsequently shown to the experimental group and withheld from the control group. The "after" measurement is an index of the subsequent attitudes of parents on the importance of a college education for their children. The difference between the "before" and "after" measurements constitutes the change in attitude. When the change for the control group is subtracted from that for the experimental group, we have a measure of the effect of the film itself. The rationale here stems directly from the method of residues.

The method of residues constitutes a procedure for taking into account those factors other than the test stimuli that affect the dependent variable. These may be divided somewhat arbitrarily into three groups: *internal factors,* or those originating in the subjects themselves; *experi-*

menter factors, or those originating in the stimuli sent out by the experimenter; and *external factors,* or those originating outside the experimental situation.

An example of an internal factor might be a maturational process within the individual. This factor might be especially relevant if the experiment were conducted over a long period of time. If there were no control group, a change in the experimental group might appear to arise from the test factor, whereas it might actually be a result of maturational processes. Here we see the value of the control group. This error is avoided by utilizing the method of residues and subtracting the change in the control group from that in the experimental group.

The "before" measure may alert the subject to the desire of the experimenter to influence his attitude with respect to a college education for his children, an experimenter factor. The subject may react to this positively or negatively. If, for example, he tries to give responses in the posttest which he thinks are very socially acceptable to the experimenter, he will then exhibit what appears to be a change in attitude as a result of seeing the film. But if a pretest and posttest measurement of a control group are taken, this error in interpretation can be eliminated.

A potential source of external factors is magnified when the experiment takes place over a long period of time. Occurrences reported in the mass media of communication having to do with the importance of a college education may change the attitudes of subjects between the pretest and the posttest. This change might be erroneously ascribed to the efficiency of the test factor unless a control group were subjected to the same external factors. Any influence from external sources may be canceled by the method of residues (that is, by subtracting the change in the control group from that in the experimental group).

SOLOMON'S TWO-CONTROL-GROUP DESIGN

Solomon has developed extensions of the classical design that involve more than one control group.[5] One of these calls for one experimental group and two control groups.

The advantage of this design becomes evident in situations where the "before" measurement is expected to interact with the test stimuli. For example, let us assume that the "before" measurement on plans to send one's children to college only partially sensitizes the subject to the purposes of the experiment, and that the same is true of exposure to the film. When the subject experiences both the "before" measurement and the test stimuli, he may be able to "put two and two together." If this realization of the purposes of the experiment significantly affects his behavior

---

[5] R. L. Solomon, "Extension of Control Group Design," *Psychological Bulletin,* **46** (1949), 137–50.

on the "after" measurement, we have what is known as an *interaction effect*. In this situation the combined effect of the "before" measurement and the test stimuli is out of proportion to the separate effects of these two factors. The Solomon design for a *before–after experiment with two control groups* is aimed at providing both an estimate of the magnitude of any such interaction and an estimate of the effect of the test stimuli alone.

Stages	Experimental Group	Control Group 1	Control Group 2
1. Selection of subjects: matching and/or randomization	Yes	Yes	Yes
2. Experimental conditions: matching and/or randomization	Yes	Yes	Yes
3. "Before" measurement (pretest)	Yes	Yes	No
4. Exposure to test stimuli	Yes	No	Yes
5. "After" measurement (posttest)	Yes	Yes	Yes
Difference	D	D'	D''

In this design the experimental group and one control group are treated as they would be in any study with only one control group. The second control group is given no pretest. However, we may estimate this group's initial attitudes about sending one's children to college by averaging the "before" measurements of the experimental group and the first control group. This procedure is justified because the three groups have been selected by randomization, and thus they may be expected to vary on any factor only to a limited degree. Consequently, a difference D'' between these estimated pretest scores and posttest scores for the second control group may be obtained. Because there is no possibility that D'' reflects the effect of a pretest or of interaction between a pretest and test stimuli (no pretest was involved), we may attribute D'' to the influence of the test stimuli alone.

The difference D' between the pretest and posttest scores for the first control group may be attributed to the influence of the pretest alone, for the lack of exposure to test stimuli precludes the influence or interactional effects of these stimuli. The difference D between pretest and posttest scores for the experimental group, which experiences both a pretest and exposure to test stimuli, constitutes a measure of the influence of the pretest, the test stimuli, and the interaction between the two.

If the experimenter's interest is not limited to investigating the effects of the test stimuli, he will want to examine the process whereby the pretest measure has an impact on the subjects, by itself or in interaction with the test stimuli. In this context the mechanisms involved in the data-collection procedure are viewed as data about human behavior, not simply as tools for testing other ideas. Already D' constitutes a measure of the influence of the pretest alone, and it remains to estimate the magnitude of the interaction. Solomon provides a formula for estimating interaction (I):

$$I = D - (D' + D'')$$

This follows the method of residues, for we subtract the effects of the pretest and the test stimuli from D (the measure of the effects of these two factors plus that of interaction) to obtain a measure of interaction alone. Armed with estimates of the influence of the pretest and that of interaction, we may then proceed to investigate the source of these two effects.

The Solomon technique might be illustrated by hypothetical data on this example:

Measurements	Experimental Group	Control Group 1	Control Group 2
Before measurement (% with college plans)	20	20	(20)
After measurement (% with college plans)	90	30	30
	$D = 90 - 20$	$D' = 30 - 20$	$D'' = 30 - 20$
	$= 70$	$= 10$	$= 10$

Here the percentage of parents with college plans for their children changes greatly within the experimental group, from 20 per cent to 90 per cent. This difference D results from the impact of the before measurement, the exposure to the film, and the interaction between the two. For Control Group 1, the 10 per cent change D' results only from the before measurement. For Control Group 2 the 10 per cent change D'' results only from exposure to the film (because no before measurement is taken). Interaction between the before measurement and exposure to the film is calculated as follows:

$$I = D - (D' + D'') = 70 - (10 + 10) = 50$$

Here it can be seen that there is a large interaction effect in addition to the separate effects of the before measurement and exposures to the film.

BEFORE–AFTER EXPERIMENT WITH NO CONTROL GROUP

We have already discussed before–after designs that involve one or more control groups. It is also possible to conduct an experiment with no control group at all. Such an experiment would be schematized as follows:

Stages	Experimental Group
1. Selection of subjects: matching and/or randomization	Yes
2. Experimental conditions: matching and/or randomization	Yes
3. "Before" measurement (pretest)	Yes
4. Exposure to test stimuli	Yes
5. "After" measurement (posttest)	Yes

This design illustrates the fact that control can be achieved in various ways. Group members, as well as the experimental conditions, are "matched to themselves": that is, they serve as their own controls. This is accomplished by comparing a given group's performance, at the beginning of the experiment, with its own performance at the close of the experiment. The difference between the pretest and the posttest is used as an estimate of the influence of the test stimuli. Such a design may result in accurate conclusions if there is reason to believe that the external factors, experimenter factors, and internal factors exert little or no influence on the performance of subjects and that there is no significant interaction between the pretest and the test simuli. Whenever such influences are present, and no control groups are employed to take them into account, their effects may erroneously be attributed to the test stimuli.

AFTER–ONLY EXPERIMENT WITH ONE CONTROL GROUP

The after–only experiment with one control group is described as follows:

Stages	Experimental Group	Control Group
1. Selection of subjects: matching and/or randomization	Yes	Yes
2. Experimental conditions: matching and/or randomization	Yes	Yes
3. "Before" measurement (pretest)	No	No
4. Exposure to test stimuli	Yes	No
5. "After" measurement (posttest)	Yes	Yes

This design achieves control over factors not controlled by the before–

after experiment with no control groups. The existence of a control group helps the experimenter to avoid attributing the influence of external factors, experimenter factors, and internal factors to the test stimuli. Furthermore, with no pretest given to the control group, there can be no interaction between the pretest and the test stimuli. This method, however, possesses certain drawbacks. Without a "before" measure, it is difficult to establish the degree of change in the subjects. In addition, the uncovering and testing of the function that describes the type of relationship involved becomes even more arduous. Of course, the before–after experiment provides no guarantees that such functions will be uncovered and tested. Nevertheless, it at least provides data describing the degree to which each individual changes, and this kind of information is needed to test predictions of change on an individual basis.

RANDOMIZED-GROUPS DESIGN

The four experimental designs thus far discussed all involve only one experimental group. As a result the inferences that can be drawn from their test-stimuli data have been limited. With respect to the dependent variable (for example, change in plans about sending one's children to college) the three before–after experiments all provide specific quantitative data as to the magnitude of change. However, these designs, and the fourth as well, only provide for the testing of the relative effects of absence and presence of the test stimuli. Whereas this measurement incorporates the method of difference insofar as the independent or test variable is concerned, it does not incorporate the method of concomitant variations between the independent and dependent variables. It is thus limited in the data it provides for an analysis of the degree of relationship. This limitation can be avoided by setting up a series of experimental groups that vary in magnitude with respect to the independent variable.

One of the most popular of such designs is the randomized-groups design, which involves the random assignment of subjects to each of the experimental groups as well as to the control group (if one is included). A randomized-groups design for two experimental groups and one control group follows:

Stages	Experimental Group 1	Experimental Group 2	Control Group
1. Selection of subjects: randomization	Yes	Yes	Yes
2. Experimental conditions: matching and/or randomization	Yes	Yes	Yes
3. "Before" measurement (pretest)	Yes	Yes	Yes
4. Exposure to test stimuli	Yes	Yes	No
5. "After" measurement (posttest)	Yes	Yes	Yes

The test stimuli may be a film of a certain length, and the length of the film may be varied between the first and second experimental groups. Data may then be analyzed by comparing the change resulting in the first and second experimental groups with that exhibited in the control group. In this manner the effects of different degrees of exposure to the film may be compared.

FACTORIAL DESIGN

Thus far the discussion of experimental design has been limited to the consideration of only one independent variable in each experiment. The factorial design has two or more independent variables, and each is varied in two or more ways. Each combination of the variables is incorporated as a separate experimental condition. Suppose that one of the independent variables is the length of the film, with one condition being one hour and the other one-half hour. A second independent variable might be the major emphasis of the film as to the significant reason for going to college, with one emphasis being vocational and the other humanistic. The factorial design for this experiment is as follows:

Stages	Experimental Group 1	Experimental Group 2	Experimental Group 3	Experimental Group 4
1. Selection of subjects by matching and/or randomization	Yes	Yes	Yes	Yes
2. Experimental conditions: matching and/or randomization	Yes	Yes	Yes	Yes
3. "Before" measurement (pretest)	Yes	Yes	Yes	Yes
4. Exposure to test stimuli	Yes: one-hour film; vocational emphasis	Yes: one-hour film; humanistic emphasis	Yes: half-hour film; vocational emphasis	Yes: half-hour film; humanistic emphasis
5. "After" measurement (posttest)	Yes	Yes	Yes	Yes

By taking the average change between pretest and posttest for the first and third experimental groups and comparing it with the average change for the second and fourth experimental groups, we may assess the relative effectiveness of the vocational and the humanistic emphasis. And if we compare the average change for the first and second groups with that for the third and fourth groups, then we can also assess the relative effectiveness of a one-hour film and a half-hour film.

One advantage of the factorial design is that the investigator can combine several different hypotheses within the same experiment and can also test for interaction between the two independent variables. The concept of interaction in this context is the same as in the context of the before–after experiment with two control groups (when interaction between the pretest and the test stimuli was discussed).

LATIN-SQUARE DESIGN

The Latin-square design may be used in situations where it is desirable and possible to expose each subject to a number of different sets of test stimuli. In all the designs discussed so far, the subjects were exposed to only one "treatment" or set of test stimuli. A major advantage of the Latin-square approach is the economy involved, for the total number of available subjects is used for each treatment, rather than being divided into smaller groups, with the increase in variation between the groups resulting from this reduced size. The Latin-square design constitutes a way of controlling the effect on the subjects of the order in which they are exposed to the different experimental treatments or conditions.

The Latin square itself is a table of R rows and r columns, with each of the cells formed containing a letter. The letters are assigned in such a way that each letter appears only once in each row and each column. The following is an example of a 5×5 Latin square:

B	E	D	C	A
C	A	B	E	D
D	B	C	A	E
E	C	A	D	B
A	D	E	B	C

Each of the letters $A, B, C, D,$ and E represents a different experimental condition, and each row corresponds to a different subject. Thus, the square pictured above has to do with five individuals, each of whom is subjected to five different experimental conditions. In this way, equal numbers of subjects are introduced to a given treatment as the first in the series, the second, the third, the fourth, and the fifth. Thus, the effectiveness of any given treatment may be calculated by averaging its impact over the five different orders of occurrence.

5.5   THE FIELD EXPERIMENT

As in other methods of data collection, there is a continuum on the degree of closure achieved or the degree to which variables other than those being investigated are controlled in the experiment. The terms *laboratory experiment* and *field experiment* are used to designate the opposing poles of the continuum. Both approaches represent attempts to understand reality, but the strategies differ.

Because the laboratory experiment often has a high degree of control, the stage is set for the objective verification of whatever ideas are under investigation. If these ideas are fruitful, then a great deal of understanding can be achieved which can then be applied to the investigation of more complex situations which are closer to the field-experiment end of the continuum. The field experiment tends to incorporate fewer controls and to achieve less closure: as a result, objective verification suffers. Like other less-structured techniques, however, it tends to be highly suggestive within the context of discovery.

Holmberg's "participant intervention" in the hacienda Vicos, located in Peru and rented by Cornell University, provides an interesting example of a field experiment.[6] Over a period of years a wide variety of innovations was introduced which resulted in the transformation of a traditional hacienda system into a new system of community organization based on shared interests and local control. Significant changes also occurred in many other areas, such as income, education, production, and health facilities.

One important advantage of this research-and-development approach to the experiment is the immediate and comprehensive feedback of information on the effectiveness of interventions. This does not have the same significance in the context of justification as does the feedback resulting from an analysis of data and a testing of hypotheses in a laboratory experiment. But the opportunities afforded within the context of discovery for the reformulation and continual development and improvement of ideas are great. If one of the functions of research is to point the investigator toward the next research questions to be asked, then participant intervention seems to offer some unusual advantages in this area.

Of course, it is only to the extent that controls can be developed within the field situation that relatively definite answers to these questions can be obtained. In such situations all the sources of error previously discussed—internal, external and experimenter factors, as well as various kinds of interactions—tend to be magnified. If one is dealing with clusters

---

[6] Allan R. Holmberg, "The Research-and-Development Approach to Change: Participant Intervention in the Field," in Richard N. Adams and Jack J. Preiss (eds.), *Human Organization Research* (Homewood, Ill.: Dorsey 1960), pp. 76–89.

of variables at a time, and if the unit is one culture or society rather than a number of subjects, it becomes difficult to provide objective evidence for hypotheses about the relationships among variables.

Perhaps these and related problems made it difficult for the Cornell investigators, as well as other field experimenters, to generate the kind of evidence in the context of justification which could be impressive to quantitatively oriented researchers. Let us assume that this study achieved very significant changes in various social systems. Despite this, however, we know very little about the processes which produced these changes.

The problem that Holmberg and his colleagues faced was more complicated than that of hitting on the correct experimental design or procedure for measurement or analysis of data. Recalling our discussion of theory, what is required in addition to experimental technique is comprehensive and systematic theory. Achieving control over error provides no guarantee that one is able to explain adequately what occurs during the experiment. All that this accomplishes is an avoidance of certain types of misinterpretations, but correct interpretations are another matter. Experimental design is valuable primarily in the context of justification, where the investigator has developed effective theory and wishes to validate it. As for the discovery of such theory, the experiment provides little direction to this end.

Yet the field experiment points in certain directions which might be suggestive in the context of discovery. For one thing, it generally takes place over a relatively long period of time compared with that of the laboratory experiment. Within the context of justification this creates difficulties in knowing which of the many factors involved within the time period were most important in producing whatever changes occurred. However, an extended period gives the investigator a greater chance to build up to the creation of major changes. When such changes have been produced, one can then proceed with sophisticated experimental designs (with the aid of theory) to determine the sequence of factors which produced the changes.

A second direction is related to the first. On the basis of information feedback from the initial experimental effort it is possible to alter the succeeding efforts so as to take advantage of this information. In this way it is possible for the experimenter to accumulate knowledge and effectiveness in problem solving within a single experiment. Laboratory experiments tend to be so definitely structured initially as to allow no such changes in direction. As a result, whatever the investigator learns must await a new experiment before it can be utilized. Of course, it is possible to modify experimental designs so as to emphasize cumulation within the experiment. New technologies for the rapid analysis of data, such as "on-line" computers which produce information within the time constraints of the ongoing experiment, facilitate this approach.

EXERCISES

1. Explore the paradigm dealing with cause and effect behind Mill's methods of agreement, difference, concomitant variation, and residues.

2. Natural experiments are quite rare in the literature on experiments. Assuming that they are an important type of investigation, what do you think might be done to make them more popular?

3. For any experiment you are familiar with, attempt to expand its theoretical framework and also deal with this framework as systematically as possible. Now reinterpret what occurred during the experiment, as reported by the experimenter, in the light of this new framework, with a focus on locating paths for improving the experiment.

4. For any one of the experimental designs discussed outline a number of limitations of the design within the context of justification.

5. What is the relationship between the field experiment and the natural experiment? Discuss differences and similarities.

ANNOTATED REFERENCES

AMERICAN BEHAVIORAL SCIENTIST, **8**, 7 (1965). This issue is devoted to the Cornell field experiment in Vicos. To the extent that the experiment proved to be successful in yielding community development, it becomes important to learn more about the reasons for the successes. It is hoped that such knowledge can prove to be useful for field experiments on a smaller scale as well as a larger one.

JOUVENEL, BERTRAND DE. *The Art of Conjecture.* New York: Basic Books, Inc., 1967. It is all too easy, as we are enmeshed in the discussion of experimental procedure, to forget that (1) experiments are frequently dependent for their success on the incorporation of ideas based on leaps of the imagination, and (2) natural experiments can provide an important complement to field and laboratory experiments. De Jouvenal proposes the institutionalization within society of a "surmising forum" to provide general predictions, via the pooling of specialized knowledge, of the future of society. We might view this as a proposal for a continuing series of natural experiments where the definition of possible futures would serve to alter the present.

ROSS, JOHN, and PERRY SMITH. "Orthodox Experimental Designs," in Hubert M. Blalock and Ann B. Blalock (eds.), *Methodology in Social Research.* New York: McGraw-Hill Book Company, 1968. Chapter 9. This fifty-seven-page discussion of the experiment focuses on (1) types of variables associated with the experiment, (2) unobtrusive measurements and treatments, (3) pitfalls of the experiment, (4) ability to generalize from the conclusions, (5) simple experimental designs, and (6) classic designs developed in agriculture, genetics, and biology.

CHAPTER 6 Interviews, Questionnaires, and Surveys

6.1 EXPERIMENTS AND SURVEYS

The concept of *survey* in ordinary usage often carries the connotations of public-opinion polls on political views or consumer attitudes. Within the context of scientific research, the survey constitutes a method of data collection that utilizes interview or questionnaire techniques for recording the verbal behavior of respondents. It is limited neither to opinions or attitudes nor to the sheer description of percentages of individuals who have given characteristics. Instead, it constitutes an effective tool for getting at cause-and-effect relationships.

One important distinction between the survey and the experiment is that the former does not center around an analysis of the effects of certain test stimuli on the individual but focuses on the reconstruction of processes that occurred prior to the investigation. This difference gives survey techniques both potential advantages and disadvantages. On the positive side, the investigator can cover a wide range of phenomena and is not limited to analyzing the effects of a few test stimuli; the potential richness of survey data is often illustrated by the contributions of investigators who have analyzed data that have been collected by others for completely different purposes. Thus, survey data can be used to put together a great deal of the information about an individual's values, expectations, and social relationships needed to investigate his behavior. Another advantage of the survey not intrinsic to the method is the relative ease with which the investigator can obtain the cooperation of a probability sample of individuals from some defined population.

The experiment is almost invariably conceived of as a laboratory experiment, but it is entirely feasible to utilize "interviewers" or "experimenters" to perform their experiments in the context of an interview situation. This might involve a randomization procedure that would result in some respondents being presented with some stimuli and other respondents being exposed to different experiences. The major limitation here has to do with the type of stimuli that could be effectively presented within an interview situation.

An important disadvantage of the survey technique is its lesser degree of control over the data-collection situation and the resultant greater possibility for factors that are unknown to the investigator to interfere with the results. One aspect of control within the experiment has to do with the time sequence involved in the "before" measure, the introduction of test stimuli, and the "after" measure. Because it is the experimenter himself who introduces or assigns these factors, he has no difficulty in inferring whether a change in attitude came before or after the test stimuli. Another important aspect of experimental control has to do with the processes of randomization and the existence of one or more control groups. The survey researcher cannot similarly deal with internal, experimenter, and external sources of error, although he does have some useful techniques for handling them. Thus, he can make his statements about relationships among variables with a lesser degree of confidence. With his lesser degree of control, it is more likely that the relationships he uncovers will result from chance.

One argument often used against the survey method is that verbal behavior is quite unreliable, for individuals tend to say what they think is socially acceptable. This is a real problem for survey research, but it does not seem to be insuperable. The same kind of problem also occurs in the context of the experiment. If individuals can give socially acceptable verbal responses, they can also attempt to act in accordance with what they believe to be the experimenter's expectations. Another argument against the survey is that the individual's responses about his own behavior are limited by his insight. This is true, but scientists in any field usually do not expect easy answers to difficult questions. Act meanings (that is, the individual's own definition of the situation) are in themselves important. It is too much to expect to obtain action meanings (that is, scientific explanations) from the respondent himself. Also, nonverbal behavior does not automatically provide us with action meanings.

An argument often used by sociologists against the experiment is that it is conducted in "artificial" laboratory situations, and that consequently the results obtained cannot be generalized to more complex situations. The implication is that the survey researcher deals more directly with "real" behavior by conducting his investigations in a more everyday setting. One flaw in this argument is that there are such things as field experiments which can be performed within the context of the interview situation. It is, however, such prejudicial attitudes against the experiment that prevent the further development of the field experiment. The argument also rests on a rather naïve assumption that "reality" is relatively close to the surface and is to be apprehended by avoiding abstraction and dealing with phenomena as they occur in everyday settings. A reverse argument may be equally well defended; namely, that so-called artificial laboratory situations are in fact closer to reality than more everyday settings, for the higher level of abstraction involved aids in eliminating many extraneous factors that would otherwise obscure the situation.

The point here is not that one method is generally superior to the other, but that each has certain strengths and certain weaknesses, and much can be done to repair the weaknesses and extend the strengths of both. For example, references have been made to the possibilities of incorporating a fuller range of data about the subjects within the experiment as well as experimenting within the interview situation.

The data emerging from the experimental designs presented in Chapter 5 are generally analyzed according to groups rather than individuals. Thus, the average change in attitude for the experimental group is compared with that for the control group, or the change in one experimental group is compared with that for others. Within these research contexts, only a small amount of information about the characteristics of each individual is brought to bear on an anlysis of his behavior within the experiment . Such information may be quite useful if it can be theoretically organized. In fact, if it is true that the behavior of the individual is in large measure a function of his own goals and expectations, then it may be necessary to obtain this kind of information from the individuals involved in the experiment in order to understand what is going on.

Many psychologists might have reservations about performing experiments outside a laboratory situation. Two crucial factors involved in the experiment, however, seem to be the high degree of control involved and the focus of the experiment on the effects of stimuli introduced by the experimenter. Both factors can be produced within the context of interviews. It is easy enough to randomize respondents so that equated groups of respondents are subjected to different kinds of interview experiences. The more crucial question is whether the interviewer can present stimuli. the effects of which deserve to be the focus of the investigation. If this is the case, then other problems, such as that of problem controlling the uniformity of the stimuli presented by interviewers, would not generally serve to invalidate such an approach.

In a comparison of data obtained from surveys and experiments, Hovland has found marked differences in the picture of the effects of mass media obtained from each.[1] However, his interpretation reveals that the seeming divergence can be accounted for on the basis of different theoretical approaches as well as differences in the type of communicator, audience, and issue utilized. He concludes that a genuine understanding of the effects of communications on attitudes requires both survey and experimental methodologies, reasoning as follows:

> there appear to be certain inherent limitations of each method which must be understood by the researcher if he is not to be blinded by his preoccupation with one or the other type of design. Integration of the two methodologies will require on the part of the experimentalist an awareness of the narrowness of the laboratory in interpreting the larger and more comprehensive effects of communication.

[1] Carl I. Hovland, "Reconciling Conflicting Results Derived from Experimental and Survey Studies of Attitude Change," *American Psychologist,* **14** (1959), 8–17.

It will require on the part of the survey researcher a great awareness of the limitations of the correlational method as a basis for establishing causal relationships.[2]

6.2 INTERVIEWER AND RESPONDENT

In the interview, as well as in the experiment, the investigator should be aware of the interaction between researchers and subjects.[3] It is difficult to predict the effects of any type of interaction unless one knows a good deal about the values and expectations of the participants. When such knowledge is available, it can be used to interpret and assess the information obtained in the interview. It is also possible to use the interview situation itself as data, for an understanding of the dynamics involved may lead toward a wider understanding of social interaction as a whole.

At the present stage of social science, very little is known about interview and questionnaire situations. Some individuals feel that the degree of knowledge needed to effectively control what goes on in these situations will never become available, and that questionnaire construction as well as interview technique will always be something of an art. More optimistic social scientists point toward the progress already made and look forward to further revealing studies on the interviewer–respondent situation.

STANDARDIZED, SEMISTANDARDIZED, AND UNSTANDARDIZED INTERVIEWS

Any consideration of the interview situation must take into account the different types of interviews. These may be classified into three broad groups: the standardized interview, the unstandardized interview, and the semistandardized interview. In the standardized interview, the interviewer is held to the specific wording in the interview question schedule; he is not free to adapt his questions to the specific situation, to change the order of topics, or to ask other questions. In the unstandardized interview, the interviewer is free to develop each situation in whatever ways he deems most appropriate for the purposes at hand. In the semistandardized interview, the interviewer may have to ask a number of specific major questions, but he may be free to probe beyond the answers to these questions.

One way of understanding the relative utility of each type of interview

[2] Ibid., p. 14.

[3] The communicative process which takes place between interviewer and subject is explored in Raymond L. Gorden, *Interviewing: Strategy, Techniques and Tactics* (Homewood, Ill.: Dorsey, 1969); Stephen A. Richardson et al., *Interviewing: Its Forms and Functions* (New York: Basic Books, 1965); and Herbert Hyman, *Interviewing in Social Research* (Chicago: University of Chicago Press, 1954). For a collection of three articles on interviewer–respondent interaction, see Norman K. Denzin (ed.), *Sociological Methods: A Sourcebook* (Chicago: Aldine, 1970), Part V, "The Sociological Interview: Problems and Strategies."

is to examine its contributions in the context of justification and in the context of discovery. The standardized interview seems to have certain advantages in the context of justification that arise from the relative uniformity in the behavior of the interviewer and the resulting ease with which other investigators can duplicate these interview situations. The argument for this approach is that it is necessary to know what stimuli produced the verbal behavior recorded if one is to develop an understanding of relationships among phenomena that can then be replicated by other scientists.

The unstandardized interview seems to have advantages within the context of discovery. A skilled interviewer who is quite familiar with the broad purposes of the study may be stimulated by the answers of the respondent to develop new ideas about the phenomena under investigation. If he is not confined by the limits of a standardized interview, he will be able to explore any such ideas fully and thus go considerably beyond the original formulation of the problem. In addition, he might find it necessary to change his general line of questioning if important results are not forthcoming. In the unstandardized interview, the interviewer can be quite flexible in adapting his approach to whatever appears to be most fruitful for a given respondent. For example, a standardized question might not be fully understood by respondents from different social classes, and the interviewer can strive to alter the wording of the questions so as to achieve some equivalence in meaning for different kinds of respondents.

Of course, each type of interview can contribute both within the context of justification and within the context of discovery. New ideas may arise from an analysis of standardized interviews. And it is also possible to develop quantitative analyses of the materials from unstandardized interviews and to test various kinds of hypotheses. The semistandardized interview appears to combine some of the advantages and the disadvantages of each of the other types.

THE FOCUSED INTERVIEW

Merton and Kendall have developed what they call a *focused interview,*[4] which is an example of the semistandardized interview. The wording of questions is not specified. There is, however, a definite focus on the effects of a given phenomenon experienced by the respondent. The interviewer comes to the interview situation with a list of topics based on his previous definition of the problem and understanding of the phenomenon under investigation. His knowledge of the content of the phenomenon enables him to distinguish between the stimuli to which the respondent

[4] Robert K. Merton and Patricia L. Kendall, "The Focused Interview," *American Journal of Sociology,* **51** (1946), 541–57; Merton et al., *The Focused Interview* (New York: Free Press, 1956).

was exposed and those which he actually received. It also allows him to direct his questioning so as to discover the kinds of perceptual distortions which resulted, as well as some of the factors which influenced degree of distortion. This type of interview, with its focus on some change which has occurred, is closely related to, and merges into, the natural experiment, depending in part on how thorough an analysis of the change the investigator is able to develop.

There is a close relationship between the focused interview, the historian's oral history, and the writer's journalistic novel. These latter two forms divide into nonfiction and fiction, but they too are dependent on detailed interviews focused on phenomena experienced by the respondents or informants. For example, Studs Terkel's *Hard Times: An Oral History of the Great Depression*[5] includes 162 different points of view about the Depression from people who lived through it. The focus here is not on an event of quite short duration, as in the focused interview, but rather on a process that stretched over many years.

THE NONDIRECTIVE INTERVIEW

The *nondirective interview* is unstandardized. Here the interviewer avoids channeling the interview in certain directions.[6] Instead, he attempts to develop a very permissive atmosphere in which the respondent will feel perfectly free to express his feelings without fear of disapproval. Of course, even the highly skilled nondirective interviewer does influence the respondent in various ways, but the purpose of the nondirective interview is to minimize this influence.

SOCIAL DESIRABILITY

The various types of interviews differ considerably from one another. One common characteristic, however, is the influence of the interviewer and the interview situation on the respondent. If we assume that the respondent's behavior is a product of his values and expectations, then it follows that his expectations will vary with the interview situation.

Edwards has studied what he calls *the social-desirability variable* as it affects responses to questionnaires.[7] Personality-trait items were rated by

[5] (New York: Pantheon, 1970.) For a study which is not focused on any particular event but which develops a more thorough analysis of behavior by concentrating on one family, see Oscar Lewis, *The Children of Sanchez* (New York: Random House, 1961). Lewis' approach has much in common with the life history method of study, once more popular in sociology than it is today. This latter method focuses on reconstructing the subjective reactions to a range of events by an individual or group; see, for example, Denzin, op. cit., Part X, "The Life History Method."

[6] C. R. Rogers, "The Nondirective Method as a Technique for Social Research," *American Journal of Sociology,* **50** (1945), 279–83.

[7] Allen L. Edwards, "The Relationship Between the Judged Desirability of a Trait and the Probability That the Trait Will Be Endorsed," *Journal of Applied Psychology,* **37** (1953), 90–93.

respondents who were asked "to judge the traits in terms of whether you consider them desirable or undesirable in others." A different group of individuals was then asked to indicate whether the items were characteristic of themselves. A close relationship was found between the social desirability of a given item and the probability of its appearance among the self-ratings.

If the findings in the Edwards study hold for interview situations as well, then much the interviewee says may be strongly influenced by his conception of the social desirability of saying it. The degree to which this occurs should vary from one interviewee to the next, and from one topic to the next. This variation would be related to the importance of this goal of appearing in a socially desirable light on the part of a given interviewee on a given topic.

ABILITY AND WILLINGNESS OF RESPONDENTS

There is always the possibility, of course, that those personality traits that are most socially desirable are also the ones that are most widely distributed. If, however, this is assumed not to be the case, there seem to be two possible explanations. First, it may be that respondents see themselves differently from the way others see them, in which case they are not deliberately exaggerating or distorting the truth, but, rather, lack insight into implications of their own behavior as it appears to others. Or it may be that respondents try to present a more favorable image of themselves, in which case they are consciously attempting to exaggerate or distort the truth.

Although Edwards' study focused on questionnaire situations, it also has implications for interview studies. Any investigator must ponder a general question: How is one to take into account respondents' unknowing perceptual or conceptual distortions as well as their conscious attempts at exaggeration, distortion, or falsehood? These are the two difficulties most often cited in discussions of the limitations of the interview technique. Although it has been suggested that the investigator focus a portion of the research effort on an assessment of the degree to which these factors operate, there remains the problem of identifying and developing those interview techniques that will help to minimize their effects.

The focused interview seems to possess particular advantages in revealing conceptual distortion and lack of insight. Because knowledge of the situation under investigation obtained independently of the interviewee is available to the interviewer, he can detect not only the nature of the distortion but also its degree and its possible sources. The nondirective interview is designed to produce the permissive atmosphere that will minimize any motive on the part of the respondent deliberately to distort the truth. It is difficult, however, to determine how successful the technique is for a given respondent unless specific means are devised to check for truth or falsity. On this point, research on the interview situation itself can provide important information. To what degree, for example, is a given answer on the part of the respondent socially desirable in terms of his own value system? To what degree does the respondent bring other values to the interview situation which have to do, for example, with the importance of his telling the truth for the advancement of scientific knowledge?

The kind and degree of distortion which respondents introduce consciously and unconsciously are significant for interview situations in general. An individual who is not aware that his statements represent a distortion of phenomena as seen through the eyes of others is providing valuable data on his own definition of the situation, for unless we understand the respondent's way of looking at things, we will not be able to understand his behavior. A view of the phenomena through the eyes of respondents will provide the investigator with data that can be used, as in the focused interview, to identify the mechanism producing this distortion.

Conscious or deliberate distortion is another matter entirely, and a great deal of interviewing technique centers on creating the kind of atmosphere that will minimize the respondent's need to distort. Interviewers are generally instructed to be very careful about expressing approval or disapproval of statements made by the respondent, and to develop noncommittal gestures and verbal responses when the respondent indicates a desire for some reaction. These techniques are a cardinal principle of the nondirective interview, but they are also generally stressed for almost all interview situations. Nevertheless, the interviewer must tread a fine line: if he is overly demonstrative, the respondent may look to him for approval or disapproval; but if he is too reserved, his degree of interaction with the respondent will be so minimal that the respondent may not be motivated to do his best.

One possible solution to this problem is for the interviewer not to try to minimize his interaction with the respondent, because interviewer behavior constitutes one of the most important rewards for the respondent in the interview situation. At the same time, however, the interviewer might maintain a permissive atmosphere and avoid any evaluative gestures or comments (for example, a look of surprise in reaction to the respondent's answer, a "yes" or "I agree" spoken after the respondent gives an opinion). The tendency of respondents to distort may also be reduced if the interviewer shows by word and manner that he takes the interview very seriously and that the information being obtained from the respondent is vitally important to the study and, perhaps, to the progress of science. This technique may serve to counterbalance whatever reasons exist for distortions.

We should bear in mind the limitations of any advice to the interviewer on how to act. An analogy might be drawn between this and advice on child-rearing to parents or on techniques of intercourse to lovers; it is not easy and most likely not desirable for the individual to attempt to mask his own personality and go through the motions of following certain rules which may conflict with deep-seated emotions. If this is attempted, then more harm than good can emerge, with the interviewer (or parent or lover) conveying an aura of hypocrisy and feeling most uncomfortable. Our discussion of investigator effect in Chapter 4 is relevant here. To the degree that the interviewer is aware of his own personality system and the directions in which he tends to influence respondents, he can take this into account in his report. In this way it becomes unnecessary for him to attempt to put on a mask, which probably could not hide his personality anyway. Of course, it is possible for genuine learning and personality change (of the type that would make it easier for interviewees to respond about their fundamental beliefs) on the part of the interviewer to occur.

THE INITIAL CONTACT

These techniques for minimizing distortion also can be used during the initial contact between interviewer and respondent when the immediate task of the interviewer is to secure the cooperation of the respondent in undertaking the interview. Novice interviewers sometimes feel uncomfortable unless they have memorized an approach they think will be effective. This technique, however, is too inflexible to take into account and use to advantage the variations in each contact situation. Still worse, few individuals have the ability to make memorized material spontaneous. As in the interview situation itself, the task of the interviewer during the initial contact with the respondent is to convey the importance of the study and some of the more immediate rewards that would result from cooperation. These rewards involve the respondent's interest in being interviewed, an interest greatly affected by the manner and personality of the interviewer. Of course, some individuals simply do not care very much with whom they talk as long as they get a chance to talk, but most people would rather talk with someone who seems personable and interesting.

Another important technique that can be effective in the contact situation involves the structuring of the request for the interview. For example, if the interviewer asks, "Do you have any time now for me to interview you?" he will more likely receive a no than if he says, "If you can possibly help us out in this research project, I'd like to ask you some questions now or at another time." The first approach intimates that the respondent is being asked to give up something, namely, his time. If the respondent's attention is focused on this value when he is asked to make his decision, he may tend to overlook the rewards involved in the interview. The second approach intimates that positive values will result from permitting the interview to take place, progress in scientific research and the personal appreciation of the interviewer. The two approaches differ in another respect: The first emphasizes the respondent's decision as to whether or not to permit the interview to take place at all, whereas the second implies that the respondent may choose only the time when he is to allow the interviewer to ask some questions. Some interviewers have been highly successful in obtaining interviews by structuring a choice between the alternatives of being interviewed "now" or "later this week." By setting up different kinds of choices, the different approaches also structure the ease with which the respondent may decline to be interviewed. Respondents seem to find it more difficult to refuse to allow interviewers to ask them questions than to decide that they do not have time to be interviewed. Indeed the plea of "lack of time" constitutes a convenient excuse for terminating the contact gracefully.

These interviewing techniques may appear to be quite manipulative. The question may be posed, "What right does the interviewer have to structure a situation for the interviewee so as to make it more likely that the latter will give up valuable time to answer a bunch of questions which will do him no good?" This query is a version of the dialogue in Section 3.3 on the presumed immorality of behavioral science. What is involved here is a choice which, like all choices, has important ethical implications. To structure the initial contact so as to increase the possibility of obtaining an interview is one alternative, and to structure it so as to make a refusal likely is another. If the study is quite trivial, then it would be difficult to defend the morality of imposing on the respondent's—or, indeed, the interviewer's—time. Equally, if the study is of general significance, it would be difficult to defend the morality of techniques which would tend to prevent data from being collected.

THE RECORDING OF DATA

Thus far the discussion has emphasized the ways in which the interviewer affects the respondent. Interaction, however, implies a two-way flow, and therefore it is important to consider the impact of the respondent on the interviewer. This impact has already been referred to in the discussion of the advantages of the nonstandardized interview, in which the interviewer is given considerable latitude to design questions on the basis of the respondent's statements. One of the problems involved in securing accurate data in any interview situation has to do with whether or not the interviewer actually perceives and records the statements made by the respondent. For example, the interviewer may develop initial expectations about respondents' behavior on the basis of their answers to the preliminary questions, as well as through observation. This "set" can then operate to prevent the interviewer from correctly perceiving an answer that conflicts with these expectations. A technique that can effectively eliminate this difficulty is the mechanical recording of the interview. Such an approach serves to prevent not only interviewer distortion but also substantial loss in the amount of the interview content.

The question as to how data might best be recorded by the interviewer deserves attention. Mechanical recording can have a good deal of importance because it reproduces the emphasis, intonation, pitch, and pauses of the respondent as well as the entire content of the interview, including the verbal stimuli introduced by the interviewer. If it is true that the respondent's verbal behavior is in large measure a product of the particular interview situation, then a mechanical recording can help to provide an accurate understanding of this situation. Furthermore, the detail such a recording furnishes about the respondent has great potential value in determining how the respondent defines the situation. It may be argued that note taking is a more "natural" procedure, but this may merely result from the fact that very few studies have ever been based on mechanical recording. The impact of this technical equipment on the spontaneity and veracity of the respondent can be determined only by research. Experience has already shown that the introduction of recording equipment can result in very few refusals. The technique of introducing such equipment would, of course, affect the refusal rate, and the situation might be appropriately structured using the strategy suggested for the initial contact between interviewer and respondent: the respondent might be asked to suggest the best place for the recording equipment rather than being asked whether a recording may be made. Ethical considerations are definitely involved in the researcher's choice of strategy. However, whatever the interviewer says constitutes one kind of structuring of the situation. Thus, the ethical issue is not whether structuring in itself is evil, because it can hardly be avoided; rather, the question is what kind of structuring. What are the implications for the values held by the interviewer and the respondent of a given kind of structuring?

6.3 SURVEY ADMINISTRATION

Interviewing is often thought of as taking place within the context of large and well-financed surveys with large numbers of interviewers and research analysts. This is not necessarily the case. The interview may also be found within the context of experiments. In that situation, there may be one interviewer and one respondent, or there may be many of each. The respondents selected may or may not represent a probability sample of some given population. The data may be analyzed by electronic computers or by hand. The choices made depend on the goals to be achieved —the ends to which the interview is a means. When the context of discovery is more important than the context of justification, for example, a large probability sample may possess no special advantages over a small nonprobability sample. An arbitrary number of interviews or some particular approach to sampling becomes necessary when the survey is viewed as an end in itself. This attitude militates against the utilization of the small nonprobability survey when, in fact, it might be the most appropriate tool for a variety of research situations.

The large survey, especially when it is based on a probability sample, possesses important advantages within the context of justification, but it also gives rise to various difficulties. Not the least of these difficulties is caused by the many administrative problems involved. Although there are survey organizations of different types that specialize in this kind of research and retain a staff of interviewers and analysts, most survey research is performed on an ad hoc basis. It is difficult to develop a sampling design for a large study; to hire, train, and supervise a large number of interviewers; to supervise the processing and analysis of data; to deal with staff members who are aware of the short-term nature of their positions; and to coordinate all these activities within a specific time schedule. Therefore, it is not surprising that those researchers who are responsible for directing a large survey project often spend more time on administrative duties than on activities more closely related to their technical competence.

The selection, training, and supervision of interviewers is a crucial aspect of survey research, The difference between the performance of poorly motivated and badly trained interviewers and that of a well-motivated and well-trained staff affects the quality of the data obtained. Poise, a degree of maturity, and intelligence on the part of the interviewer are valuable both in establishing personal contact (in order to gain the cooperation of the respondent) and in maintaining this kind of contact during the interview (in order to keep the respondent motivated to provide a good interview). Intelligence and adaptability are important during the training process. One of the most important aspects of this process is the effective communication of the nature and importance of the study, for the interviewer in turn must be capable of communicating this information to potential respondents if he is to win their cooperation. Because many of the problems interviewers experience occur during their first few interviews, it would seem advisable to continue training sessions while interviewing is in progress. Careful analysis of initial interviews will provide feedback information and reveal any tendency on the part of new interviewers to make up data out of whole cloth. (Such cheating is quite possible in a poorly supervised study, and a given interviewer may happily proceed to "interview" as many as thirty or forty "respondents" in this manner.) One effective supervisory procedure is to inform interviewers that their work will be periodically checked through contact with the respondents, and then to perform such checks by telephone, by letter, or in person.

Despite the seeming efficiency of large survey organizations with well-trained staffs of interviewers and professional personnel, there is a lack of effective knowledge for this and other methods of data collection, whether attempted by a large staff or an individual researcher. We should not forget how little is presently known about the processes producing interviewer effect or about many other processes in the interview situation. Under these circumstances any assumptions about the high degree of effectiveness of existing survey technologies will serve to make existing inadequacies more rigid and direct attention away from the vital research tasks. Not only has behavioral science not yet constructed the kind of knowledge which can provide the basis for solving important societal problems, but its knowledge is not as yet a sufficient basis for effective survey technologies.

As a matter of fact, we might go further and state that there is evidence from the literature on bureaucracy that in situations that are similar, from an organizational point of view, to that of the interviewer in the survey organization or large project, performance can be extremely poor. Roth elaborates on this point as follows:

> A hired hand is a person who feels that he has no stake in the research that he is working on. . . . .
> I am convinced that research tasks carried out by hired hands are characterized, not rarely or occasionally, but *typically*, by restricted production, failure to carry out portions of the task, avoidance of the more unpleasant or difficult aspects of the research, and outright cheating. The results of research done in part or wholly by hired hands should be viewed as a dubious source for information. . . .[8]

According to Roth, the hired-hand mentality can be developed by supervisors who do not elicit the creative talents of employees and who ignore their suggestions and efforts at active participation.

6.4 CONSTRUCTION OF QUESTIONNAIRES AND INTERVIEW SCHEDULES[9]

OPEN AND FIXED-ALTERNATIVE QUESTIONS

We may broadly distinguish between *open* or *open-ended* questions and *closed* or *fixed-alternative* questions. The open or open-ended question does not provide a list of alternative answers; for example,

---

[8] Julius Roth, "Hired Hand Research," *American Sociologist,* **1** (1966), 195.

[9] For a detailed treatment of this topic see A. N. Oppenheim, *Questionnaire Design and Attitude Measurement* (New York: Basic Books, 1966).

Why did you choose medicine as a career?
What do you like most about surgery?
How do you feel about America's system of higher education?
How would you react if you were proctoring an examination and saw a close friend of yours cheating?

The closed or fixed-alternatives question, on the other hand, limits the respondent to a choice among specific alternatives; for example,

What importance would an opportunity for developing warm personal relationships with patients have for you in your ideal job?

indispensable_____   extremely important_____   very important_____   fairly important_____
little or no importance (or would rather not have)_____

Each type of question has its advantages. The open question, because it puts very few words in the mouth of the respondent, is more effective in revealing his own definition of the situation, whatever it is. The closed question is, in this respect, analogous to the "leading questions" that are not permissible in most aspects of courtroom procedure. If the respondent does not understand the question or if he grossly misunderstands, this too will be revealed in his answers to open questions. In addition, the phrasing of the open question is closer to that used in ordinary conversation and, as a result, may encourage spontaneity on the part of respondent as well as reinforce his motivation to communicate effectively and thoroughly. The respondent may react negatively to fixed-alternative questions because he is not able to give highly individualized answers: he may even feel that such procedures are inaccurate and thus come to question the value of the interview.

On the other hand, the fixed-alternative or closed question produces greater uniformity among respondents along the specific dimensions in which the investigator is interested. Consequently, it aids greatly within the context of justification in that the investigator is assured that he will be able to obtain relatively complete information from his entire sample about the specific phenomena with which he is concerned. Many answers to open questions are not useful in testing specific hypotheses because they constitute responses along many different dimensions. For example, one student might answer the question about why he chose medicine as a career by referring to his own goals; another, by referring to his expectations about the favorable characteristics of the field; another, by discussing the unfavorable characteristics of other fields; and still another, by referring to individuals who have influenced him in this direction. Although this variety of answers is quite valuable within the context of discovery, it makes the testing of specific hypotheses difficult. There is also a practical consideration attached to the use of closed questions: the costs and time involved in processing the answers tend to be much less than those in the case of open questions. The problem for the researcher is to create the best possible instrument for data collection while taking into account his limitations with respect to resources.

THE "WHY?" QUESTION AND REASON ANALYSIS

The "Why?" question, a type of open question, has been the subject of particular attention on the part of some social scientists, and a suggested procedure for asking and analyzing such questions is called *reason analysis*.[10] The approach involves a careful assessment, through pretesting or preliminary interviews, of the range of possible reasons that might be given in response to a particular "Why?" question. For example, the interviewer might isolate four different kinds of reasons for choosing a medical career. During the actual interviewing, he might follow the general "Why?" question by a series of questions designed to explore whichever of these four dimensions are omitted by the respondent. In addition, the interviewer might attempt to describe the choices through time and differentiate specific decisions from more general ones. Finally, he would attempt to put together all the pieces of information in an outline of the dynamic relationships among all these factors.

Reason analysis provides an illustration of what is known as the "funnel" technique in questionnaire- and interview-schedule design. Many studies include a range of questions, some open and some closed, and the investigator must decide on an ordering of the various questions. The funnel technique specifies initial questions which are open and subsequent questions which are more specific and are generally of the closed variety. Reason analysis may begin with the general "Why?" question and then proceed to the more specific aspects of the choice process. The advantage of this technique is that it permits an analysis of the respondent's spontaneous frame of reference while assuring that data will be collected from each respondent on each of the desired topics.

SOME TACTICS

In the construction of questionnaires and interview schedules it is of course important that the verbal stimuli presented by the interviewer or questionnaire be as clear as possible. There is always a degree of vagueness attached to language, but it is important that the researcher try to minimize vagueness and ambiguity. Unless this is done, respondents are, in effect, being presented with varying and uncontrolled stimuli and the

[10] The initiation of these ideas is credited to Paul F. Lazarsfeld. For a discussion, see Hans Zeisel, *Say It with Figures* (New York: Harper, 1957), pp. 131–74.

significance of their responses would consequently be difficult to assess. The investigator can promote clarity by avoiding long questions and words with double meanings; specifying the time, place, and context the respondent is being asked to assume; prefacing unfamiliar or unusually complicated questions with an explanatory paragraph or an illustration; and asking questions in terms of the respondent's own immediate and recent experience rather than in generalities.[11]

An additional approach is to accept the vagueness in language, as well as its differential meanings for different respondents, and focus on learning about the meanings various terms have for a given respondent. This is analogous to a concern for the nature of interviewer effect in a given situation as distinct from the hopeless effort to eliminate this effect.

Although it is very important for the interviewer to create the kind of atmosphere that motivates the respondent to be as candid as possible, it is also important for him to phrase his questions in such a way as to encourage veracity. This is of special importance when an interview deals with sensitive topics, that is, where a given answer has a very high or very low degree of social desirability. Among the guidelines developed for interviewers are the following:

1. Indicate that other people have what might ordinarily be considered to be a socially undesirable attitude or characteristic (for example, "Most people have thought about suicide at one time or another").
2. Attempt to achieve some balance of social desirability among choices (for example, "Some political leaders believe . . . while other political leaders believe . . .").
3. Structure the question in such a way that the respondent is assumed to possess the socially undesirable characteristic, thus placing on him the burden of denial. (For example, "How much are your monthly payments?" might be preferable to "Have you purchased anything on the installment plan during the last two years?")
4. Substitute euphemisms for more value-loaded language. (For example, *training methods* might be superior to *methods of discipline* in discussing child-rearing.) And, in general, try to avoid words which convey a high degree of social desirability or undesirability.
5. If it is desired that the respondent express criticism of something, first provide him with an opportunity for voicing praise so that he will not feel that he is being unfair.
6. Structure the question in such a way that the respondent will be able to admit gracefully that he is not familiar with something or that he has not yet formed a particular expectation. (For example, "Do you

---

[11] These suggestions are taken from Eleanor E. Maccoby and Nathan Maccoby, "The Interview: A Tool of Social Science," in Gardner Lindzey (ed.), *Handbook of Social Psychology*, Vol. I (Cambridge, Mass.: Addison-Wesley, 1954), p. 456.

have any feelings about how X should behave?" might be preferable to "How do you feel that X should behave?") The funnel technique provides an additional mechanism for achieving this effect.[12]

We must note that these rough guidelines do not substitute for a genuine understanding of the dynamics of a given interview situation. For example, the balanced approach implied by these guidelines might work very well with most interviewees. However, it might not work with a minority who tend to confine themselves to bland statements unless they are provoked into taking a position by one-sided questions. Of course, such one-sidedness will affect different rsepondents in different ways. Thus, we should not assume that a balanced approach is the perfect solution. What researchers require is what they do not possess: a theory that is sufficiently broad and predictive to enable them to assess each interview situation separately and interpret responses on the basis of the dynamics of that situation.

QUESTION ORDER

Within the questionnaire or interview situation the researcher or interviewer emits a series of stimuli, many of which are in the form of questions of one type or another. The guidelines used for determining question order are based on the possible effects a given stimulus might have on subsequent ones. Some of the rules of thumb in general use are the following:

1. On a given topic, general questions should usually precede specific ones. This advice is in accord with the funnel technique, in which initial questions are open and subsequent questions are closed. If, for example, a respondent were queried on whether A constituted one of the reasons for his political preference prior to being asked what his reasons are, he might be tempted to include A among his reasons in response to the more general question.
2. The entire sequence of questions should follow some logical order, so that the respondent is not called upon to make abrupt transitions and so that the sequence aids him in answering the questions. A common logical order is the time sequence, with the respondent being asked about the past, the present, and the future in that order. Another procedure is to move from the more specific or familiar to the more abstract or unfamiliar.
3. Some questions are of such a nature that they might exert an important effect on all subsequent questions. For a given study, questions about income or religion might so antagonize the respondent that the

12 This list is based on ideas presented in ibid., p. 457.

remainder of his responses would be greatly affected. Sometimes a question that reveals the guiding purpose of the study can affect subsequent answers. An example of this is provided by the medical student study. Care was taken to avoid asking more questions about public health than about other medical fields until the very last part of the questionnaire. This procedure of deferring such questions for as long as possible is the one generally adopted.

QUESTIONNAIRE AND INTERVIEW COMPARED

The most obvious practical difference between the questionnaire and the interview survey is cost. Within the medical student study this was the most important consideration governing the choice of a questionnaire instrument over the interview schedule, although other factors were involved. A related factor was the considerable time required to obtain a very large number of interviews. If more immediate results are desired, then a special staff of interviewers must be trained. This poses problems in itself, because it is very easy to lose most of the advantages of interview procedure if the interviewers are not highly trained and motivated.

The decision to utilize questionnaires in the national study was based on a trial run or pretest in one medical school. It was found that at least there seemed to be little difficulty in communicating effectively to the students via this medium. The questionnaire approach offered the possibility of avoiding the differences in approach so difficult to control as between one interviewer and another. Finally, because the questionnaire would be administered by the staff in group sessions, it was felt that ambiguities could be explained to students who had questions.

Some of the advantages of the interview over the questionnaire are implied in the foregoing. Where respondents are not literate and cannot handle complex questions (if they are called for), the questionnaire would fail in its purpose. The factor of lack of motivation to respond also frequently militates against use of the questionnaire, because it is the direct contact with an interviewer that provides many of the rewards involved in responding, as well as much of the pressure to respond. Questionnaires, especially if they are mailed, usually have a smaller percentage of returns than interviews.

The interview is also a much more flexible instrument than the questionnaire, depending, of course, on the skill of the interviewer. The interviewer has the opportunity to explain to the respondent any ambiguities that emerge. In addition, depending on the type of interview involved, he may be able to explore in depth any given area of the study. He may emerge from the interview with important ideas that might lead to corrective changes in many of the propositions involved in the study.

6.5   PROJECTIVE TECHNIQUES AND OTHER INDIRECT METHODS

These techniques for dealing with sensitive or value-loaded topics serve to aid in creating the kind of situation in which the respondent will feel free to admit to having socially undesirable ideas or characteristics. A variety of indirect methods of questioning has been developed for the purpose of eliciting detailed information on sensitive topics, and such methods may also be used to obtain data about which the respondent himself may not be aware. Thus, indirect methods are directed at overcoming two of the major difficulties involved in the interview process—the willingness and the ability of respondents to provide information.

If the object of the interview is to get the respondent to admit socially undesirable characteristics, the rationale for indirect methods is quite straightforward. Although the interviewer can painstakingly try to create the kind of situation that will motivate the respondent to be candid, in some situations such motivation may be insufficient to elicit certain responses. This may occur, for example, in a situation where the respondent is questioned about aspects of his own behavior that would generally be considered highly undesirable. By employing an indirect method, however, the respondent is no longer motivated to conceal information because he is not made aware that it reveals behavior he considers to be socially undesirable. Indirect techniques represent an attempt to penetrate the awareness or conscious world of the respondent, to increase his ability to provide certain kinds of data (as distinct from his willingness to do so). Implied in such efforts is the assumption that factors beyond the awareness of individuals may have important effects on their behavior. These factors may include values or goals that conflict with the individual's own view of himself.

Projective techniques are data-collection methods that involve the presentation of relatively unstructured stimuli to the respondent. It is assumed that, because the stimuli are unstructured, the respondent will be required to organize or structure them and will, in the process, reveal important aspects of his own personality and behavior. Although these techniques were originally utilized in clinical situations, they are presently being applied in more general social science research. The Rorschach Test is an example of a projective test that has been widely used in clinical settings. Subjects are presented with a series of cards, each of which has a different picture of an ink blot, and are asked, "What might this be?" Another example of a commonly used projective technique is the Thematic Apperception Test, in which the respondent is asked to tell a story about each of a series of pictures. The ink blots and pictures constitute the relatively unstructured stimuli, and the respondent's answers to the questions represent his structuring of the stimuli and thus (it is hoped) reveal personal characteristics that would not be easily ascertainable by means of more direct questioning.

Projective techniques vary in the degree to which the stimuli are unstructured. The Sentence Completion Test is generally more structured than either the Rorschach Test or the Thematic Apperception Test. In this approach the respondent is asked to complete a series of sentences (for example, "My favorite————"; "John's father made him————"). Because the stimuli consist of words rather than ink blots or pictures, the investigator can focus attention on a much greater range of phenomena. For example, if he is interested in the values of the respondent, sentences such as those given as samples may help him to uncover them. The items can vary from those which assume that the respondent will project his own characteristics ("A young person doesn't like to be told _____") to those which are more direct ("My favorite _____"). The purposes of the more direct questions are more obvious to the respondent, but they depend less on the assumption of projection.

Another type of projective technique has to do with asking the respondent to play one or more roles. This technique is called *psychodrama* if he plays himself, *sociodrama* if he acts out the roles of others. Here the respondent is removed from the paper-and-pencil situation, and has relatively little time to prepare an answer he thinks would have social desirability. If the interviewer himself adopts a role which complements that adopted by the respondent, he has the opportunity of subjecting the rsependent to sequences of stimuli and to investigating the dynamics of his behavior.

One of the difficulties involved in the use of projective techniques is the problem of developing reliable methods for analyzing the data produced. *Indirect methods,* which are more structured and which consequently tend to have a higher degree of reliability, have been reviewed by Campbell.[13] In the error-choice method,[14] for example, respondents are asked to choose among different possible answers to a factual question (such as "What is the salary of the average psychiatrist?"). All the answers provided are incorrect, and the direction of the error a respondent makes is used as a measure of his values, attitudes, or expectations. Another relatively structured indirect test is the information test, which is based on the premise that the amount and kind of information an individual possesses about a given subject are related to his values and expectations.

[13] D. T. Campbell, "The Indirect Assessment of Social Attitudes," *Psychological Bulletin,* **47** (1950), 15–38.

[14] K. R. Hammond, "Measuring Attitudes by Error-Choice, and Indirect Method," *Journal of Abnormal and Social Psychology,* **32** (1948), 38–48.

Consequently, information questions may be utilized as indirect measures of these dimensions.[15]

Questions have been raised as to the validity of the various indirect tests (that is, the degree to which they actually succeed in measuring those characteristics of the individual that are not easily measurable by more direct methods). Campbell states that the literature is almost devoid of evidence indicating that indirect questions provide more valid data than information produced by direct questions.[16] Knowledge of the interview situation, however, seems to indicate that the respondent's lack of insight or his interest in going along with what is socially desirable can seriously jeopardize the quality of interview data. Thus, although indirect tests generally have not yet proved their reliability and validity, the issue is by no means closed. Furthermore, there is no reason why reliable and valid indirect techniques cannot be developed. (Criteria used for establishing reliability and validity will be discussed in Chapter 10.)

Indirect methods of investigation, whatever their failings, are designed to remedy serious deficiencies in the direct techniques. If projective methods are as yet ineffective, then this should serve notice on students of human behavior not to abandon efforts to develop them but rather that some remedies for these deficiencies are urgently required.

EXERCISES

1. Construct three short interview schedules which center on attitudes about some controversial topic. Word the questions in such a way that one is very biased in one direction, one is relatively balanced, and one is very biased in the other direction. Now conduct one interview with each schedule using a different respondent for each interview. After each of these standardized interviews, initiate an unstandardized or semistandardized one in which you attempt to assess the impact of the question wording on the respondent. What are your conclusions?

2. Design a series of training sessions for interviewers which focus on their gaining insight into the ways in which, on the basis of their own personalities, they will tend to affect respondents.

3. Develop an indirect test of a concept you are interested in. Use it along with a parallel direct test on several respondents and assess its advantages and disadvantages on this basis.

---

[15] This indirect method is discussed by T. M. Newcomb, "The Influence of Attitude Climate Upon Some Determinants of Information," *Journal of Abnormal and Social Psychology,* **42** (1946), 291–302.

[16] Campbell, op. cit., p. 30.

ANNOTATED REFERENCES

GORDEN, RAYMOND L. *Interviewing: Strategy, Techniques, and Tactics.* Homewood, Ill.: Dorsey Press, 1969. One strength of this book is that it provides a framework, along with a good deal of both information and problems, within which the researcher may work toward the improvement of his interviewing skills. Some examples of specific topics are silence as a technique ("I'm too busy now!" "I don't want to be on tape!" "I don't remember, I don't know!"), dealing with falsification, and doing the interview for self-improvement.

TERKEL, STUDS. *Hard Times: An Oral History of the Great Depression.* New York: Pantheon Books, Inc., 1970. The oral history has much in common with the focused-interview technique, the life history, the natural experiment, the journalistic novel, and *cinéma vérité.* The tape recorder and the movie camera are being employed in the recurring search for realism. With even such simple technologies the researcher's ability to explore human behavior is vastly improved, yet this ability still remains dependent on the theory which enables him to select from the phenomena that surround him. Because of the great variation in the types of individuals interviewed and because of the large number of interviews, this book is particularly useful for illustrative purposes.

WILENSKY, HAROLD L. *Organizational Intelligence.* New York: Basic Books, Inc., 1967. Knowledge shapes policy, but in our hierarchical and specialized organizations failures at coordinating information necessary to achieve the solution of problems tend to be both frequent and serious. Wilensky addresses himself to the processes which produce such failures, processes which occur in the research organization as well as other kinds of organizations.

CHAPTER 7 **Use of Documents**

7.1 INTRODUCTION

Documents will here refer to any written materials that may be used as a source of information about human behavior. Although written materials are involved in experiments, surveys, and observational studies at one stage or another, attention will be focused on those materials the recording of which has not been the result of any special effort on the part of the investigator. This includes, for example, population censuses, previous surveys by social scientists, health statistics, economic statistics, records of voluntary organizations, court records, documents collected by social agencies, school records, documents collected by personnel departments in industry, legal papers, newspaper and magazine reports, radio and television tapes, motion picture scenarios and play scripts, fiction, songs, poetry, folklore, laws and regulations, editorials, speeches, letters to the editor, pamphlets, essays, treatises by social scientists (including histories, biographies, articles in professional journals, monographs, textbooks), autobiographies, diaries, personal letters, notebooks, and memoranda.

7.2 THE HISTORIAN'S APPROACH TO DOCUMENTS

THE ESTABLISHMENT OF CREDIBILITY

Historians have developed various procedures for the analysis of documents. One of the problems has involved the development of procedures for assessing the validity of truth of the written materials contained in documents. These efforts may roughly be divided into techniques of external criticism and those of internal criticism. External criticism has to do with procedures for distinguishing between a hoax or misrepresentation and a genuine document, whereas internal criticism is aimed at establishing the degree to which a particular document is credible. Although the ultimate concern is with truth, or what actually happened in history, the historian more realistically attempts to establish credibility, that is, statements about events that are "as close to what actually happened as we can learn from a critical examination of the best available sources."[1]

Four tests historians have developed within the context of internal criticism are the following:

1. Was the ultimate source of the detail (the primary witness) *able* to tell the truth?
2. Was the primary witness *willing* to tell the truth?
3. Is the primary witness *accurately reported* with regard to the detail under examination?
4. Is there any *external corroboration* of the detail under examination?[2]

It should be noted that the tests of ability and willingness to tell the truth refer to those factors that constitute difficulties in the interview situation. A respondent may not have sufficient insight into his own behavior or the behavior of others to be able to provide certain types of information, or he may provide distorted information in an effort to achieve social desirability. In addition, witnesses may be too remote from the event in question or may be incompetent observers or may have paid little attention to the event, and consequently they may not have the ability to provide credible statements. Their willingness to tell the truth may be reduced if they are interested parties to the conclusions, or if what they say will please or displease others, or if laws or conventions (for example, libel laws) require them to depart from strict veracity. The third test has to do with secondary evidence. If statements by a primary witness are unavailable, then statements by secondary witnesses constitute evidence that must, of course, be evaluated for its accuracy. The fourth test follows the general rule of historians to accept only "facts" that rest upon the independent testimony of two or more witnesses, and thus the historian looks for corroboration of a given statement.

THE HISTORIAN AND THE SOCIOLOGIST

Although there are similarities between the techniques of sociologists and historians for assessing documentary data, there are differences in emphasis. The sociologist tends to be more concerned with analyzing statements in order to use them to develop and test propositions that will explain and predict human behavior in general, whereas the historian often is interested in obtaining a set of credible statements about particular historical occurrences. Actually, these approaches are not so far apart as they may appear, for many historians are interested in going beyond

[1] Louis Gottschalk, Clyde Kluckhohn, and Robert Angell, *The Use of Personal Documents in History, Anthropology and Sociology,* Bulletin no. 53 (New York: Social Science Research Council, 1945), p. 35.
[2] Ibid., p. 38.

the particulars to general propositions, and they attempt to make use of available knowledge from other social sciences.

As a result of these differences in orientation, documents that illustrate the application of the first test (that is, ability to tell the truth) provide important data in their own right for the sociologist. The historian who is concerned with establishing credible statements about historical events may discard statements that reveal an inability to tell the truth. Yet the sociologist tends to be quite interested in such statements, because they reveal the individual's personal definition of the situation and are consequently invaluable in arriving at an explanation of his behavior. For example, the following is used to illustrate situations that are conducive to lack of credibility from the point of view of the historian:

> Expectation or anticipation frequently leads a witness astray. Those who count on revolutionaries to be bloodthirsty and conservatives to be gentlemanly, those who expect the young to be irreverent and the old to be crabbed, those who know Germans to be ruthless and Englishmen to lack humor usually find bloodthirsty revolutionaries and gentlemanly conservatives, irreverent youth and crabbed old age, ruthless Germans and humorless Englishmen.[3]

These very expectations, which may lead to statements lacking in credibility, constitute important aspects of the individual's definition of the situation.

Survey researchers and social scientists concerned with the analysis of documents would do well to pay attention to the advice of the historian concerning the test that has to do with the willingness of the witness to tell the truth. In addition to the analysis of willingness, the sociologist is often in the position of securing external corroboration (the fourth test of the historian) from the statements of other individuals or on the basis of his own observations. Thus, for example, the technique of the focused interview prescribes that the interviewer himself be familiar with the phenomena under discussion. The historian's technique of not relying on statements unless they are based on the independent testimony of two or more witnesses seems quite sensible on the basis of what we know of human behavior.

In the process of collecting his own documents by means of interview surveys, the sociologist is in an advantageous situation for obtaining such corroboration. The fact is, however, that procedures such as the focused interview or the interviewing of several respondents within a given family or group on the same subject are not frequently employed. To the extent that the social scientist attempts to analyze the factors leading to veracity on the part of the respondents, and to the extent that he attempts to achieve corroboration, the charge sometimes made—that there is no way

[3] Ibid., p. 42.

of being able to tell whether statements by respondents are valid—may be effectively answered.

7.3 THE SOCIOLOGIST'S APPROACH TO PERSONAL DOCUMENTS

All documents are personal in the sense that they are produced by human beings and reveal something about human behavior. Some, however—such as autobiographies, diaries, and personal letters and memoranda—tend to reveal more of the personality and behavior of those who have written them, and the term *personal document* has these connotations.

The controversy over the methods used by Thomas and Znaniecki, in *The Polish Peasant in Europe and America,* and the resulting uneasy compromise have previously been discussed in Section 4.5. The general result seems to be that sociologists tend to pay less attention to personal documents than they once did. One of these has to do with the difficulty of saying very much within the context of justification on the basis of the analysis of a single case.

The importance of personal documents within the context of discovery, however, should not be neglected. Although it is conceivable that a given diary may have been written with the intent to deceive the future reader, the chances are that most such documents are not. The situation in which the individual writes a diary seems to be one in which factors conducive to willingness to tell the truth tend to be stronger than they are in most interview situations, where the social-desirability variable may operate effectively.

The argument that it is difficult to provide much evidence for general propositions about human behavior when only a single individual is involved is only partially true. Much depends on what is defined as the unit of analysis. If the unit is the over-all personality of the individual, the investigator focuses on this either as an independent or a dependent variable, and then there will in fact be only one case, with its resulting limitations. If, however, the investigator is analyzing the effects of a series of experimentally induced changes in the individual's values or expectations on a series of choices the individual makes, then the research no longer involves a single case.

Although sociologists tend to worry about the single case where the personal documents of individuals are involved, there is much less tendency to be concerned over the limitations of a single case where the focus is on a given social system. Where only one unit is involved, whether it be a given individual or a given social system, what can be said within the context of justification becomes quite limited. For, in effect, the single case gives us merely a "proof" by example, and proof by example (according to an old Jewish proverb) is no proof at all. Different investigators can easily select examples to "prove" opposite hypotheses, and this fact gave rise to much of the controversy that raged over *The Polish Peasant in Europe and America*. The ways out of this difficulty are several, as in the situation with respect to the analysis of personal documents. One of them is to utilize these data only within the context of discovery and not attempt to say anything within the context of justification. Another is to define the units of investigation so that, in spite of the existence of only one case at one level of analysis, a number of cases exists at other levels. A third way out of the difficulty is to collect more cases or instances, and this may be done with respect to personal documents or social systems.

These may not actually be ways out of the existing aversion to using personal documents if the implicit assumptions behind the controversy are not strictly methodological. As a matter of fact, it seems likely that this aversion in large measure stems from the association between personal documents and clinical psychology, thus defining such research outside of the realm of sociology. If this is true, then what is required is nothing less than a redefinition of sociological interests so as to make use of data on personality dynamics.

7.4 STATISTICAL DOCUMENTS

SOME STANDARD SOURCES

Sociologists are well aware of the potential import of such data as census statistics, partly owing to Durkheim's classic study of suicide.[4] Durkheim used several kinds of documents and, in spite of the unreliability and general inadequacy of many of them, succeeded in putting forward and testing propositions that are still deemed to be of considerable importance. The modern social scientist has at his disposal far more reliable documents on many more aspects of human behavior.

The United States government, for example, periodically collects a great deal of statistical information. Among these data there are the periodic censuses of agriculture, business and industry, foreign trade, governments, and the decennial censuses of population and housing. Summaries of much of this information are contained in the annual *Statistical Abstract of the United States* and in *Historical Statistics of the United States* (Colonial Period to 1957). In addition, the U.S. Bureau of the Census publishes the *Current Population Survey,* based on a sample of about 35,000 households and issued a number of times a year. (Special tabulations are usually provided by the Bureau to researchers at cost.) Among the many other governmental publications of interest to social scientists are the *Monthly Labor Review* (U.S. Bureau of Labor Statistics) and the

---

[4] Emile Durkheim, *Suicide,* translated by George Simpson (New York: Free Press, 1951).

National Health Survey and the monthly *Indicators* (U.S. Department of Health, Education, and Welfare).

CENSUS TRACT DATA

These publications have in common the aggregation of data about large numbers of individuals and the description of these aggregates by means of such statistics as frequencies, percentages, averages, and ratios. The types of aggregates depend on the purposes of the investigation. One unit of analysis that has proved to be of special importance to the sociologist is the census tract, or small area within a particular city or metropolitan area. Such data can provide numerous indications as to the social climate and style of life within a given area. To illustrate the kinds of data available and some of the differences that may occur between census tracts, let us compare a number of facts about two specific tracts in the city of Cambridge. Cambridge is part of the Boston metropolitan area, one of the standard metropolitan areas in the United States.[5] Both tracts are approximately equal in population.

Characteristics of the Population	Tract MC-7	Tract MC-21
Population 1960	3,305	3,450
Population 1950	3,055	3,985
Percentage of change	8.2	13.4
Male population	1,623	1,388
Nonwhite population	84	53
Total foreign stock	1,737	1,272
Median school years completed for those twenty-five or over	9.1	16 +
Median family income	$5,042	$8,080
Age and Economic Characteristics		
Persons under five	395	168
Persons sixty-five and over	358	677
Persons twenty-one and over	1,947	2,894
Professional, technical, managerial, officials, and proprietors	81	1,136
Clerical and sales	240	435
Craftsmen, foremen	159	38
Operatives	488	51
Private household, service, laborers	204	178

[5] These data are adapted from summary tables, based on the 1960 Census of Population, compiled by the Research Division of the United Community Services of Metropolitan Boston.

Information such as the above might be of considerable value for the researcher who is doing a community study of Cambridge. For example, it would generally be of considerable aid in locating groups and areas he wishes to study. Rather than relying on less objective data, such as the rough estimates of city officials or private organizations, he can turn to such census tract data.

These data also have their limitations for such purposes. The census is a decennial one, and many characteristics of the population can change within a short time. Also, a given tract is far from homogeneous. For example, individuals with a very high or a very low income may be clustered within certain sections of a given tract. The investigator cannot assume that, if he selects a small sample of individuals from a tract where the average income is high, he will emerge with a high average income for his sample.

Another important limitation is that census tract information is incomplete for certain purposes. For example, no data on religion are presently available, although it is possible to obtain rough estimates about the distribution of the religious groupings from other characteristics (for example, race and ethnic background).

The researcher might also utilize such data to determine the social class composition of a given tract. We see, for example, that Tract MC-21 has a median family income of $8,080, that the median number of school years complete for individuals twenty-five or over is over sixteen, and that there are 1,136 individuals whose occupations carry the highest social status (professional, technical, managerial, and so on). Tract MC-7, by contrast, has a median family income of $5,042, a schooling median of 9.1 years, and only eighty-one individuals in the occupational grouping of highest status. The two tracts vary only slightly in total population and only somewhat in the number of individuals in the age bracket twenty-one to sixty-five, so that the difference in the number of individuals in high-status occupations cannot be accounted for by the difference in the number of employed individuals between the tracts. This assessment of the differences between the tracts in social-class composition is in accord with other facts about the tracts (for example, MC-21 is adjacent to Harvard University and borders the Charles River and MC-7 has, by contrast, numerous commercial establishments).

Many different types of studies can be done with census tract data:

1. They can be combined with questionnaire or interview data to provide objective information about the social milieu of the respondent. The major problem here is that the census tract is not a homogeneous unit, so that his actual social milieu (for example, the social class and ethnic background of his neighbors) may vary considerably from the average for his tract.

2. One can investigate the extent to which various characteristics are associated with one another. Thus, for example, we see a direct relationship between median number of years of schooling and median family income for tracts MC-7 and MC-21: in MC-7 both of these are relatively low, whereas in MC-21 both are relatively high. Data from a large number of tracts may be examined in this way to see whether the relationship holds (existence of the relationship), how close it is (degree of relationship), and whether or not it can be accurately predicted. Such investigations may be directed by hypotheses and theories just as are studies utilizing other types of data.

3. These data are valuable for studies of social change. We see from the preceding data that MC-7 had a population of 3,055 in 1950 and a population of 3,305 in 1960—a gain of 8.2 per cent. MC-21 moved from 3,985 to 3,450—a loss of 13.4 per cent. Many factors can account for such change (for example, outward migration, inward migration, rezoning, and urban renewal), and the analysis of census tract data should be supplemented by other studies for best results.

From another perspective, the utilization of census data offers a valuable opportunity, namely, the chance to integrate data on physical systems with data on behavioral systems. Perhaps one of the greatest tragedies in the history of the behavioral sciences, analogous to the mind–body dichotomy and the split between biology and the behavioral sciences, is the isolation of these fields from knowledge of nonliving systems. It is easy to recognize at a verbal level that human behavior is deeply affected by environmental surroundings, yet the thrust of behavioral science has been to ignore this insight. For example, the physical structures created in densely populated environments, granting that their creation is a product of a variety of social systems, have impacts of their own on the flow of information among human beings. These impacts may well be different from what occurs in sparsely populated areas where the man-created physical environment does not resemble that in denser areas. Census data is too rough to do more than point in such directions, but such pointing itself can be quite valuable in leading us to take the next steps.

7.5 PRIOR SOCIAL SCIENCE RESEARCH

Social scientists have been doing research on human behavior for many years. For example, the amount of survey data collected on a wide range of topics is vast.

One of the important advantages of survey techniques is the variety of data that can be collected and brought to bear on many different research questions. Because the analysis of a given survey can take many different directions and much time is involved in thoroughly exploring any one of these, any given investigator usually explores only a few of these directions. Thus vast amounts of data are analyzed only to a very limited extent, and they constitute an important set of documents for further analysis.

These data are located at universities and other research institutions as well as in a number of survey archives developed only within the past decade.[6] The major archives within the United States are located in Ann Arbor, Berkeley, New Haven, and Williamstown. The Roper Public Opinion Research Center at Williams College, for example, is the repository for data collected by over forty research organizations, including the National Opinion Research Center (University of Chicago); the Bureau of Applied Social Research (Columbia University); the Office of Public Opinion Research (Princeton University); the American Institute of Public Opinion (Gallup Poll); Crossley, Inc.; the Opinion Research Corporation; Alfred Politz Research, Inc.; The Psychological Corporation of New York; Elmo Roper and Associates; Market Research Africa, Ltd.; Australian Public Opinion Polls; Institut Français d'Opinion Publique; Nederlandse Stichting Voor Statistiek; Istituto Italiano dell'Opinione; Società Italiana per le Ricerche di Mercato; Swedish Institute of Public Opinion Research, Ltd.; and the Canadian Institute of Public Opinion.

In seeking to analyze such data, the investigator is, of course, limited to the items that were incorporated in the original interview schedules and questionnaires. If, however, he is willing to settle for items that were designed for other purposes but that are nevertheless adequate for his own, he may find it possible to test and further develop his hypotheses and theory within the context of an enormous range of data. Such data record responses made by human beings to questions put to them by other human beings. If a theory is truly general in scope, it should be able to explain a good deal of such data, provided that adequate measures for the crucial variables can be adapted from the original items. Each survey might be considered to be a puzzle, the pieces of which are items used in the survey. If the pieces are, in fact, available, and if we know how to put them together, we will be able to assemble the puzzle and see the picture it forms.

One approach which may be adopted by an investigator in the analysis of available data is to work with the original data, perhaps testing new relationships on the basis of different hypotheses and theories. Such data need not be limited to those emanating from interview or questionnaire surveys. The historian and political scientist, for example, usually work

---

[6] For a description of this development see David Nasatir, "Social Science Data Libraries," *American Sociologist,* **2** (1967), 207–212.

with many other types of documents. One codification of documents on a wide range of cultures is The Human Relations Area Files, which is of special interest to researchers interested in cross-cultural comparisons.[7]

One way of analyzing such data that has been developed quite recently is that of computer simulation, a topic to be taken up in Chapters 9 and 17. Generally, the following stages are involved:

1. The development of a theoretical framework which is comprehensive enough to bear directly on the available data.
2. The construction of a mathematical or logical model based on the theoretical framework as it applies to the specific data available.
3. The utilization of the model in a computer simulation in order to generate data which are then compared to the available data from actual phenomena, with the subsequent revision of the model.

Time series data obtained from "panel studies"[8] (comparable data collected at a series of time intervals) is the most valuable type for this kind of approach. Here a model developed to work adequately over one time interval can be tested and improved by using it on subsequent intervals. However, the approach can also be used on data collected at a single point in time, provided that the investigator is willing to risk inferences that rest on shakier ground. Indeed, if a theoretical framework were sufficiently comprehensive, it might become the basis for models that could simulate data in many kinds of surveys.

EXERCISES

1. If the sociologist can learn from the historian's experience with the analysis of documents, it may also be true that such historical analysis can profit from sociological theory and methodology. Give some illustrations to show how this might be so.
2. Critically examine survey research procedures that are generally used in the light of the historian's criteria for establishing credibility.
3. Accepting the idea at the end of 'Section 7.3—that a redefinition of sociological interests pertaining to personality dynamics may be necessary if sociologists are to become interested in personal documents—what

---

[7] New techniques for the analysis of large amounts of data via computer technology are being constructed. See, for example, Phillip J. Stone et al., *The General Inquirer: A Computer Approach to Content Analysis* (Cambridge, Mass.: M.I.T. Press, 1966).

[8] For a collection of articles on the analysis of change see Paul F. Lazarsfeld and Morris Rosenberg (eds.), *The Language of Social Research* (New York: Free Press, 1955), Section III, "The Analysis of Change Through Time."

kind of redefinition would you propose? How would you justify it as good sociology?

4. Examine two census tracts from data on a metropolitan area in the 1970 census which contrast markedly with respect to family income. Do the other variables relate to one another in the same way or in different ways, as do the variables in tracts MC-7 and MC-21?

5. Locate some data collected by behavioral scientists by going to original source materials such as questionnaires and codebooks. Develop an original plan for the analysis of a portion of these data to provide evidence with respect to your own definition of a problem that the data bear on.

ANNOTATED REFERENCES

GOTTSCHALK, LOUIS. *Understanding History*. New York: Alfred A. Knopf, Inc., 1969. The bulk of this book is about methods of historical research. It includes such topics as imagination in historiography, the "human" and the "personal" document, tests of authenticity, sciences auxiliary to history, nature of historical fact, ability to tell the truth, willingness to tell the truth, and corroboration.

HOYLE, FRED. *The Black Cloud*. New York: Signet Books, 1959. One rather important kind of document, from the standpoint of attempting to understand the nature of society, is imaginative literature as illustrated by the science fiction story. In this book Hoyle applies implicitly a theory of power and social change which emphasizes the importance of information and communication. Further, he gives us a glimpse of one possible future for human societies by describing the genesis of an intelligence vastly greater than man's. The serious analysis of this kind of document for research purposes can prove to be highly suggestive.

WEBB, EUGENE J., et al. *Unobtrusive Measures: Nonreactive Research in the Social Sciences*. Chicago: Rand McNally, 1966. If investigators have important and often unknown effects on those whom they study, then it may be effective strategy for them to seek the kinds of methods which tend to minimize such effects. This book devotes three chapters to the analysis of physical and archival data and includes, in addition, discussions of observational techniques.

CHAPTER 8 **Observation**

8.1 INTRODUCTION

THE NATURE OF OBSERVATION

Observational methods of data collection are techniques for gathering information without direct questioning on the part of the investigator. They may involve one or more of his senses, and methods developed thus far center on his ability to see and hear.

Although it is possible to consider these methods separately, they are very often used in combination with others. The interviewer, for example, may be required to make observational ratings on the characteristics of a respondent or his environment. If the interview is not a standardized one, his observations of the respondent's behavior aid him in formulating questions and in interpreting the significance of the respondent's answers. Communication seems to proceed at a nonverbal as well as a verbal level, and the interviewer who is alert to nonverbal cues and adept at interpreting their significance may emerge with a far greater knowledge of the respondent than one who pays attention to verbal responses alone. Many psychoanalysts stress nonverbal communication as a means of detecting phenomena that the respondent might either be unable or unwilling to import. Observation of such behavior constitutes an indirect data-collection method, similar to projective tests and other indirect methods.

RELATIONSHIP TO OTHER METHODS

Each data-collection method is admittedly limited and imperfect, and it is often a combination of several methods that gives rise to a more complete understanding of the phenomena under investigation. Such a combination of approaches is illustrated in anthropology. Under ideal conditions the anthropologist learns to include an analysis of available data about the society he plans to study before collecting new data. The period during which he lives with the people he studies affords opportunities for making use of a wide range of observational and interview procedures. In recent years some anthropologists have become interested in adding to their repertoire the survey techniques popular among sociologists.[1]

Such a combination of research approaches has proved to be of considerable value in other social sciences as well. For example, the sociologist who intends to conduct a survey of a given population is usually well advised to begin by thoroughly familiarizing himself with the research setting. In addition to a search of available published and unpublished materials, much can be learned by observational techniques. These may be highly informal ones as well as procedures that are carefully codified and structured. What he learns as a result of them may frequently be difficult for him to verbalize. Nevertheless, such observation has often been found to be highly productive both in the development of theory which applies to the setting and in the construction of interview schedules and other research tools which prove to be effective.

Useful within the context of the interview, observational techniques also constitute an important aspect of experimental procedure. For example, the pretest and posttest of the before-and-after experiment may be based on the observation of behavior rather than on paper-and-pencil tests or interviews. As in the survey, careful observation of subjects in experimental situations may provide insight into the limitations of the experimental procedure as well as ideas for future study. Guthrie, discussing learning theory, emphasizes the importance of observing very fine details in experimental and other situations:

> When Skinner records how many times a rat presses a bar, he is counting "environmental events," or the effect of the rat's movements on the environment. But Guthrie argues that the rat could have achieved the change in the environment by use of his paw, his snout, his ear, or one of many other "movements." That is, calling the response a "bar press" or an "ice-cream getting" covers up the important event, that is, whether the response was "pawing at the bar," "a snout-press," "an ice-cream snatch," or "an ice-cream run."[2]

8.2 OBSERVATION AND VALUES

ABILITY AND WILLINGNESS RECONSIDERED

In discussions of the relationship between the interviewer and the respondent in Chapters 6 and 7, it was pointed out that two factors that

---

[1] For an analysis of the way in which participant observation and survey data can complement one another, see Arthur J. Vidich and Gilbert Shapiro, "A Comparison of Participant Observation and Survey Data," *American Sociological Review*, **20** (1955), 28–33.

[2] William W. Lambert, "Stimulus-Response Contiguity and Reinforcement Theory in Social Psychology," in Gardner Lindzey (ed.), *Handbook of Social Psychology* (Cambridge, Mass.: Addison-Wesley, 1954), p. 74.

affect the quality of data secured are the ability and the willingness of the respondent to give truthful answers to questions asked. For example, he may not possess an awareness of his own values or goals, or he may deliberately seek to avoid placing himself in an unfavorable light. It will now be useful to re-examine this distinction with the object of providing a more thorough treatment of some of the subtleties involved in order to better depict the place of observational procedures within the research enterprise. We shall limit this analysis to the problem of obtaining data on the values or goals of the individual, although the discussion should have broader relevance.

What is central here is the definition of *goal*. By conceiving of goals as ends of which the individual is not necessarily aware, we imply that there may be a wide divergence between those goals he thinks he has and those he actually does. In other words, his self-image with respect to goals may be far from congruent with reality.

This distinction between the statements of the individual and the reality may be seen within the context of act meaning and action meaning. With respect to an individual's goals, act meaning refers to the individual's own conception of them, whereas action meaning refers to those goals for the existence of which there is scientific evidence. The collection of such evidence is, of course, a very difficult problem.

In this light, we may distinguish between the goals that actually serve to direct the individual's behavior and the individual's self-image or expectations as to the nature of his goals. The ability of the individual to respond truthfully about his goals is manifested by the congruence between these two factors. This is not necessarily identical with the ability to see oneself as others see one, because others might be wrong according to the standards of scientific evidence.

The willingness of the individual to respond "truthfully" may refer either to the "truth" as the individual believes it to be or the truth as the scientist believes it to be, and thus there is definite ambiguity in the phrase. When the individual is unwilling to tell the truth, his reference is to the truth as he believes it to be, because he is generally unaware of the other truth. It may even occur that the individual, in his efforts to hide or distort the truth as he sees it, ends up by revealing the truth as seen by the scientist. We may wonder here whether to say that the individual is lying or telling the truth, but the appearance of such ambiguities in ordinary parlance is not unusual.

RELEVANCE FOR OBSERVATIONAL PROCEDURES

The role of the researcher would indeed be a simple one if observational techniques automatically yielded the truth about the nature of the individual's values (as distinct from the act meanings of the individual as yielded by interview procedure). Some critics of the interview technique naïvely assume that reality is far more easily discovered when the investigator turns his attention from words to deeds. If this were indeed the case, then we should have learned a great deal more from the results of such procedures than we actually have.

The researcher does not, of course, have to decide between interview and observational procedures, because both can easily be combined. In fact, the preceding discussion seems to imply that the two may produce complementary data. Interview data yield information pertaining to those goals of which the individual is aware. The situation might be such that the individual will faithfully convey to the interviewer a detailed picture of such conscious goals. Or the individual might to a greater or lesser degree distort this picture, usually in favor of an image more socially acceptable.

Observational data are generally less subject to the conscious desire of the individual to present a false image of himself, although this depends on the period and type of observation. When observation occurs over a long period of time, and in instances where the individual is unaware that he is being observed for scientific purposes, the observed individual is less likely to be able to maintain such a pose successfully.

But is it true, therefore, that observational data reflect accurately the individual's conscious goals? Not necessarily, because such conscious goals may markedly diverge from the goals that actually operate to direct the individual's behavior. Observational procedures are quite useful in helping the investigator locate and obtain evidence for goals of which the individual is not aware but which nevertheless guide his behavior. The individual may be successful in hiding from his own awareness those goals he would consciously label as repugnant, but the careful observer should be able to identify such goals.

Does this mean, then, that observational data are to be relied on for the measurement of covert goals, whereas interview data yield conscious goals? Not at all. Interviewing is generally superior for specifying overt goals in a situation where the respondent has no reason to distort the image he projects. In cases where he attempts distortion it is quite useful for the researcher to be able to fall back on observational data, preferably collected over a period of time, since it is difficult for the individual to maintain such conscious distortions consistently in a series of situations.

As for the measurement of covert goals, information about overt goals derived from interview data may provide a valuable supplement to observational data. The individual may convey in the interview situation a picture of himself as perfectly honorable, good, self-sacrificing, and so on, and he may actually believe this to be the case. Knowledge of this self-image, false as it may be, can be a valuable clue to uncovering covert goals. The investigator can then search for the covert reasons or goals that impel the individual to maintain such a picture of himself. He may find that the individual's desire to maintain such a picture of himself in fact covertly affects much of his behavior, and that he will go to almost any lengths (unrealized) to avoid facing himself.

8.3 SELECTION OF PHENOMENA FOR OBSERVATION

If the detailed movements of the organism are important to an understanding of its behavior, the problem of selecting phenomena for observation becomes very real. If we are investigating interaction between two individuals, do we observe the exact sequence of physical movements made by each, the physiological changes each undergoes during the process, the words spoken and other sounds made by each (taking note of emphasis, intonation, pitch, and pauses), the physical environment and how it relates to the interaction, or a combination of all these? If an investigator wanted to observe any of these factors, he would have to define carefully what it is that he is observing as well as develop specific indexes or measures. If he is interested in "physical movements," he must specify what constitutes a separate and distinct movement, for a good deal of behavior appears to be relatively continuous. He might decide to take sound movies of the interaction, but although this would enable him to collect much of the data he wants, the problem of processing it would have to be faced eventually. One of the crucial problems confronting anthropologists has been that of effectively coping with the mountains of data collected during field work. This problem is certainly not unique to observational data-collection methods, for surveys and other types of data collection can be equally prolific.

It is important to understand that the problem here is not merely one of selecting from masses of data or quantities of discrete phenomena the items of greatest import. Phenomena are not discrete entities; rather, it is the observer who categorizes them on the basis of a variety of concepts and frames of reference which enable him to organize the incoherent jumble of the real world. Once phenomena are so categorized according to a particular set of orientations, the result may be perfectly useless in achieving an understanding of what has occurred. It will be recalled that a given concept may or may not have clarity, wide scope, and systematic import; without these characteristics it is difficult indeed to develop a theory that can effectively explain and predict. The problem of selecting phenomena for observation seems, then, to be intricately linked with the problem of conceptualization. If we are conducting observations on choice of speciality in a medical school, for example, our ideas about which factors affect those in which we are interested, and how they all operate together, will serve to focus our attention on certain phenomena.

Because the observer is bombarded by a vast amount and variety of stimuli, he must choose among them.

8.4 LESS-STRUCTURED AND MORE-STRUCTURED TECHNIQUES

It may be argued that it is poor strategy to attempt to collect data by committing oneself to a particular set of concepts and a theory and thus neglecting what may prove to be the most important phenomena in the situation. This argument is often used in defense of less-structured observational techniques. It is also frequently used in promoting the field experiment over the laboratory experiment or the unstandardized interview over the standardized one.

Needless to say, less-structured techniques have an important place among observational procedures, especially within the context of discovery. Another argument in their behalf is that they bring the investigator in closer touch with reality. This argument seems to be based on the kind of distrust of abstractions that characterizes extreme operationists. According to this approach, it is not permissible to create observational situations that are in themselves abstractions from naturalistic phenomena.

This argument, however, may be refuted. In the first place, the observer in a naturalistic setting does not necessarily come face to face with reality. Whether or not he is conscious of observing within the context of a particular set of concepts and propositions, he is nevertheless doing just that. Just as the extreme operationist deals with an abstraction whenever he talks about any given operational definition, the observer views phenomena through the particular abstractions that constitute his language and ideas as to their interrelationship. Thus, although the naturalistic situation does constitute reality, what the observer sees is a particular selection of phenomena constructed out of the reality.

The second argument promotes the utility of dealing with naturalistic observational settings as distinct from highly structured ones. But because both will be viewed through the abstract concepts of the observer and because neither is more real than the other in the sense that it can be viewed without any abstractions, a decision on the utility of investigating one type of setting rather than the other would seem to be to put the cart before the horse. Both types of settings provide opportunities for developing and testing propositions and theories, and it is in terms of these opportunities that each must be evaluated. It would seem that studies in both kinds of situations have contributed to the development of the behavioral sciences. What do seem relatively sterile are those studies in naturalistic settings where little attempt is made to improve on the common-sense conceptualizations and theories about human behavior that most individuals utilize. A conscious attempt to avoid dealing with such abstractions merely results in the utilization of common-sense—as distinct from scientifically developed—abstractions.

MORE-STRUCTURED OBSERVATIONAL TECHNIQUES

The distinction between more-structured and less-structured observational techniques is analogous to that between standardized and unstandardized interviews. Structured techniques utilize the observational situation to place data in predetermined categories, whereas the less-structured techniques develop categories which seem to be important in the particular situation. The distinction is not hard and fast, for there are degrees of structure and each method can be utilized both to develop categories and to fit data into them. The purpose of the development and utilization of categories is to obtain measurements which then may be related to one another in order to test propositions and theories.

Perhaps the best-known structured observational technique is the Bales category system.[3] The twelve categories within this system are

1. Shows solidarity.	7. Asks for orientation.
2. Shows tension release.	8. Asks for opinion.
3. Agrees.	9. Asks for suggestions.
4. Gives suggestions.	10. Disagrees.
5. Gives opinion.	11. Shows tension.
6. Gives orientation.	12. Shows antagonism.

The system was developed largely from relatively unstructured observation of a wide variety of groups, illustrating a frequent tendency of research to move from initial exploratory techniques to the employment of more-structured methods. Is is designed to aid in an analysis of the behavior of face-to-face groups concerned with a common task. The categories describe various aspects of group process: developing a group definition of the situation (Categories 6, 7), arriving at a common value system (Categories 5, 8), attempting to influence other members of the group (Categories 4, 9), coming to a final decision (Categories 3, 10), dealing with internal tensions (Categories 2, 11), and maintaining integration within the group (Categories 1, 12). With this interpretation of the categories in terms of the dynamics of a group's behavior, in which the categories operate as a system of interrelated variables, the observational system becomes a mechanism for testing a theory of group process. The fact that a theory is involved aids the observer who is attempting to

---

[3] Robert F. Bales, *Interaction Process Analysis* (Cambridge, Mass.: Addison-Wesley, 1951).

categorize both verbal and nonverbal behavior within this system. An understanding of the system as a whole and of the various relationships among the categories provides him with orientations as to how to rate behaviors that add to his knowledge of the specific definitions of each category.

Heyns' and Lippitt's review of systematic observational techniques[4] includes Chapple's procedure for the measurement of interaction,[5] a method which differs a good deal from the Bales category system. The focus here is on the temporal or durational aspects of interaction. Using a special device, the observer records when each action begins, how long it lasts, and when it terminates. On the basis of this information, Chapple and his associates have developed such measures as tempo (how often an individual starts to act), activity or energy (how much longer he talks or responds than he does not), and synchronization (the frequency with which one person interrupts or fails to respond). Although Chapple's own procedures have not taken into account the content of what is said or descriptions of what is done during the interaction, there is no reason why the two cannot be combined. One of the implications of Chapple's work is that observation which is highly detailed and accurate may be able to reveal important factors missed by less detailed and precise procedures.

LESS-STRUCTURED OBSERVATIONAL TECHNIQUES

Less-structured procedures fall into two broad types: participant and nonparticipant observation. The distinction has to do with the role of the observer within the observational situation and indicates a difference in the degree to which the observer adopts the role of member of the group.

Many of the problems and procedures of less-structured observation have been developed within the context of anthropological field work and sociological participant observation research.[6] Becker and Geer have analyzed the method of participant observation on the basis of their experiences with a study of medical students.[7] They distinguish among three types of participant observer roles: (1) the investigator may in fact be a member of the group he studies; (2) he may pose as a member although he is not; and (3) he may join the group in the role of one who is

[4] Roger W. Heyns and Ronald Lippitt, "Systematic Observational Techniques," in Lindzey, op. cit., pp. 370–406.

[5] E. D. Chapple, "The Interaction Chronograph: Its Evolution and Present Application," *Personnel*, (1949), **35** 295–307.

[6] Richard N. Adams and Jack J. Preiss (eds.), *Human Organization Research: Field Relations and Techniques* (Homewood, Ill.: Dorsey, 1960).

[7] Howard S. Becker and Blanche Geer, "Participant Observation: The Analysis of Qualitative Field Data," in ibid., pp. 267–89.

there to observe. They specify three stages through which their field work progressed: (1) selection and definition of problems, concepts, and indexes; (2) measurement of the frequency and distribution of phenomena; and (3) incorporation of the findings into a model of the organization under study. This represents within a single study an attempt both to develop important concepts and measures within the context of discovery and to construct and test propositions within the context of justification. Although their research method is initially relatively unstructured, more structured observational techniques are subsequently developed in order to provide evidence within the context of justification. With this procedure, however, the investigator must be wary of several pitfalls, which have to do with claims made within the context of justification. One of these is the possibility of circularity when hypotheses are both developed and tested on the same data. Another has to do with whether the unit of investigation is the individual or the social system as a whole. Both of these difficulties can be remedied to the extent that additional data are collected.

Although the Becker and Geer study illustrates a situation in which the researchers join the group in the role of observers, a participant observation study by Roth[8] provides an example of a study in which the investigator is in fact a member of the group. Shortly after receiving his doctorate in sociology, Roth had to be hospitalized for a tuberculosis condition. Unknown to the staff and other patients, he utilized his stay to carry on relatively unstructured observation with respect to the social structure of the hospital. Roth's observations covered a wide variety of aspects of hospital life, but the analysis and interpretation of these data (as revealed in timetables) is focused on the structuring of the passage of time within the hospital setting. "The first impression one gets of the TB patient's concern with time," Roth observes, "is that everyone is frantically trying to find out how long *he* is in for."[9] Furthermore, patients are constantly demanding to know when they will be permitted more activities, when they will get a pass, when they will get surgery, when they will be given another conference, and so on. After his analysis of the timetables or norms that structure the passage of time in the tuberculosis hospital, Roth proceeds to compare them with timetables in other settings, such as the mental hospital, the penal institution, the educational system, and the occupational career. Roth's study provides an example of research that begins at a relatively low level of abstraction and ends at a relatively high level. Although he seems to have had very little in the way of specific hypotheses to test at the initiation of the study, his conclusions with respect to the mechanism for the development of norms that structure time are sufficiently abstract to have very wide scope. They help to point

[8] Julius A. Roth, *Timetables* (Indianapolis: Bobbs-Merrill, 1963).
[9] Ibid., p. xvi.

the researcher in the direction of analyzing the dynamics of situations in general, and they provide clues as to what to look for when analyzing changes.

PARTICIPANT OBSERVATION

Although we have illustrated the methodology of participant observation, the technique is sufficiently important, especially in anthropology and sociology, to merit more extended treatment. In a classification of types of participant observation, Gold distinguishes among four categories: complete participant, participant as observer, observer as participant, and complete observer.[10] The complete participant conceals his research role and enters into the life of those he studies as thoroughly as he can. The participant as observer reveals his role as researcher, but he devotes a great deal of time and energy in participation in nonresearch roles. The observer as participant is illustrated by the one-visit interview, where the participation is kept to a minimum. The complete observer is entirely removed from social interaction with his informants; that is, he observes in unobtrusive ways.

There are major ethical problems that the participant observer must face.[11] For example, the complete observer deliberately conceals his true purposes from others; the same is true for the complete participant. As for the participant as observer and the observer as participant, they may easily find themselves in situations where their observer role conflicts with their participant role. If we recognize that the participant observer (we do not include here the complete observer) necessarily will affect the lives of those whom he is observing, the relevant ethical question shifts to *how* he should affect them as well as what will be gained, and by whom, from this observation. A complicating factor is that we know too little about human behavior to construct a balance sheet where we can neatly assess potential gains and losses and compare one with the other. Perhaps the best way to proceed in these matters is via research; the participant observer need not assume a rigid stance in anticipation of possible ethical dilemmas. Rather, he can adopt an open stance where he is assessing

[10] Raymond L. Gold, "Roles in Sociological Field Observations," *Social Forces,* **36** (1958), 217–23.

[11] See, for example, I. C. Jarvie, "The Problem of Ethical Integrity in Participant Observation," *Current Anthropology,* **10** (1969), 505–508; Peter Kloos, "Role Conflicts in Social Fieldwork," *Current Anthropology,* **10** (1969), 509–512; Ned Polsky, "Research Method, Morality, and Criminology," *Hustlers, Beats and Others* (Chicago: Aldine, 1967); George J. McCall and J. L. Simmons (eds.), *Issues in Participant Observation: A Text-Reader* (Reading, Mass.: Addison-Wesley, 1969); T. R. Williams, *Field Methods in the Study of Culture* (New York: Holt, 1967); Severyn T. Bruyn, *The Human Perspective in Sociology: The Methodology of Participant Observation* (Englewood Cliffs, N.J.: Prentice-Hall, 1966); and B. H. Junker, *Fieldwork* (Chicago: University of Chicago Press, 1960).

quite frequently the effects of his behavior on his own research (as well as nonresearch) goals and on the goals of others.

8.5 SOME DIRECTIONS

If the dynamics of interview situations are only slightly understood, then those having to do with nonverbal communication are almost a complete blank. Yet this might well be expected: language has been codified and formalized to a far greater extent than gesture. Even so, important research efforts focus on the meaning various words have for a given respondent. By analogy, we might well expect that such research is even more urgently needed for nonverbal behavior.

Some difficulties in such research are the requirement of a sharply focused framework which can suggest the specific kinds of observations needed, a methodology which can apply the framework to the multitude of possible phenomena that might be observed, and a way of assessing the effectiveness of the methodology and improving it accordingly. Here as in the case of the analysis of documents—or, indeed, any type of data collection involving complex problems of selection and analysis—recent techniques of computer simulation offer hope for reducing the complexities to manageable proportions and for devising solutions.

What such simulations might move toward, for example, is an ability to understand the meaning implied by the nonverbal behavior of a given individual or by members of a given subculture. The simulation could move back and forth between models of the production of nonverbal behavior, which would include the meanings attached to the various types of nonverbal behavior by the individual or group, and data on the actual generation of this behavior. Such models would have to become complex enough to take into account a variety of personality, social, and environmental factors in order to achieve effective results.

The promise of observational research is vast. Imagine the situation of the behavioral scientist if he had available the kind of research technology which could take into account verbal behavior as well as a wide range of nonverbal behavior (for example, gestures, body position, tone and pitch of voice, and timing of movements). If all this could be put together systematically, then we would have the basis for a much deeper, more comprehensive, and more rapid assessment of the processes producing human behavior than we now have.

EXERCISES

1. Create an observational schedule to be used by an interviewer along with the interview schedule. Focus it around a specific definition of a

problem. What kinds of questions in the interview schedule would be of aid in accomplishing your purposes?

2. Do the same for an experiment—that is, an observational schedule to be used in the context of an experiment—focused around a defined problem. What type of experiment would be helpful in achieving your goals?

3. Devise a research design in which you are a participant observer of some aspects of your own behavior; center on some definition of a problem. Take a position defending or attacking the scientific status of this type of research.

4. Develop a highly structured observational schedule for measuring one or more of the dimensions, discussed in Chapter 10, having to do with the scarcity orientation of an individual or a group.

5. Develop a relatively unstructured observational approach to measuring one of the dimensions referred to in exercise 4.

ANNOTATED REFERENCES

DENZIN, NORMAN K. (ed.). *Sociological Methods: A Sourcebook.* Chicago: Aldine Publishing Company, 1970, Part IX, "Participant Observation: Uses and Problems." This collection includes three articles: Raymond L. Gold, "Roles in Sociological Field Observations"; Virginia L. Olesen and Elvi W. Whittaker, "Role-Making in Participant Observation"; and Howard S. Becker, "Problems of Inference and Proof in Participant Observation."

POWDERMAKER, HORTENSE. *Stranger and Friend: The Way of an Anthropologist.* New York: W. W. Norton & Company, Inc., 1967. Powdermaker discusses her fieldwork experience within a humanistic context. She reveals illustrations of the role conflicts faced by the participant observer. Included are discussions of Lesu (a village on an island in the southwest Pacific), Mississippi, Hollywood, and Zambia (formerly Northern Rhodesia).

"Problems of Role Conflicts in Social Studies," *Current Anthropology,* **10** (1969), 505–26. In addition to articles by I. C. Jarvie ("The Problem of Ethical Integrity in Participant Observation") and Peter Kloos ("Role Conflicts in Social Fieldwork"), these pages include a series of comments to the articles as well as replies by the authors.

CHAPTER 9 **Simulation**

9.1 THE NATURE OF SIMULATION

Simulations are operating models or analogues of phenomena.[1] In discussing the nature of simulations we shall take up (1) the models involved and (2) the way in which the models operate over time to produce data.

The concept *model* is frequently used in a general way to denote scientific theory or ideas as expressed in a variety of ways (for example, with words, mathematical symbols, pictures, or physical objects). The use of models is standard practice in pedagogy. Addition and subtraction, for example, are often taught with the aid of concrete entities, and the student is often taught the most abstract formulations with the aid of less abstract ideas which he has previously learned and which provide him an intuitive understanding of the more difficult material.

We intend to make use of a more specialized sense of the concept, referring to systematic theory which generally (if it is sufficiently systematic) can be expressed in logical or mathematical terms.

There are two different approaches to simulation, although actually these types form a continuum rather than a rigid dichotomy: noncomputer[2] and computer[3] simulation. They differ in the degree to which their

[1] For overviews of simulation see John R. Raser, *Simulation and Society* (Boston: Allyn, 1969); Harold Guetzkow (ed.), *Simulation in Social Science: Readings* (Englewood Cliffs, N.J.: Prentice-Hall, 1962); and K. D. Tocher, *The Art of Simulation* (Princeton, N.J.: Van Nostrand, 1963).

[2] For illustrations of this type of simulation see Harold Guetzkow et al., *Simulation in International Relations: Developments for Research and Teaching* (Englewood Cliffs, N.J.: Prentice-Hall, 1963); Anatol Rapoport, *The Essential Ideas of Two-Person Game Theory* (Ann Arbor: University of Michigan Press, 1966); and Anatol Rapoport and C. J. Orwant, *Prisoner's Dilemma: A Study in Conflict and Cooperation* (Ann Arbor: University of Michigan Press, 1965).

[3] See, for example, Dimitris N. Cherafas, *Systems and Simulation* (New York: Academic Press, 1965); A. C. Hoggatt and F. E. Balderston (eds.), *Symposium on Simulation Models* (Cincinnati: South-Western, 1963); I. de Sola Pool and Samuel Popkin, *Candidates, Issues and Strategies: A Computer Simulation of the 1960 Presidential Election* (Cambridge, Mass.: M.I.T. Press, 1964); and S. S. Tomkins and S. Messick (eds.), *Computer Simulation of Personality* (New York: Wiley, 1963). For more general references on computer applications in social science that are pertinent to or include simulation procedures, see James H. Beshers (ed.), *Computer Methods in the Analysis of Large-Scale Social Systems* (Cambridge, Mass.: Joint Center for Urban Studies, 1965); Harold Borko (ed.), *Computer Applications in the Behavioral Sciences* (Santa Monica, Calif.: System Development Corp., 1962); Bert F. Green, *Digital Computers in Research* (New York: McGraw-Hill, 1963); and Dell Hymes (eds.), *Uses of Computers in Anthropology* (The Hague: Mouton, 1965).

models are systematic as well as in their emphasis on data generated by means other than a computer. Gaming, or research with noncomputer simulations, typically involves a relatively small number of individuals who are instructed to follow certain rules in order to achieve given ends (for example, to play the parts of heads of state in a game of international relations). The rules of the game are dictated by the model that the investigator has in mind. For computer simulations, the model must be sufficiently explicit that it can be used to program a computer. On the basis of this program the computer then generates data according to the rules of the game.

An operating or dynamic model is one which generates data over time. A link trainer used in training pilots is an example of this; it simulates various kinds of flight experiences, and data on the reactions to these experiences of the pilot in training are generated. The link trainer illustrates the combined man–machine or computer–noncomputer simulations; the flight experiences can be programmed in advance, and the individual reacts to them. Although a link trainer is an operating model, it has been used chiefly as a pedagogical device, rather than as a research technique.

We might illustrate an operating model that can be used for research purposes. The commercial game called Careers (Parker Brothers) may be viewed as a model of the process of occupational choice. At the beginning of the game, each player decides on the relative importance of happiness, fame, and money for himself, giving each any number he desires for a total of sixty points. These choices are kept hidden from other players, and they may not be altered during the course of the game. The object of the game is to collect the number of points originally specified of happiness, fame, and money. These points may be obtained by going through any of the eight career "paths" provided: farming, college, big business, seafaring, politics, Hollywood, uranium-prospecting in Peru, and expeditions to the moon. Each path consists of a number of squares, most of which are rewards or penalties of one type or another (for example, in the Hollywood career: "win Oscar, score 12 fame points," or "fan mail drops off slightly, cut salary by half").

Numerous choices are made by each player during the course of the game, most of which fall into one of three categories. One choice involves whether or not to enter a given career, and the entrance fees as well as the rewards and penalties that occur throughout the career path are generally among the factors taken into consideration. Another choice involves whether to move around the board by throwing the dice, by using an "opportunity card" (which permits one to move to the "entrance square" of a given occupation), or by using an "experience card" (which permits a player to move the specific number of squares printed on the card). A third type of decision occurs in the bargaining situation, which results when one player moves to a square occupied by another player. Unless the players reach a mutually satisfactory agreement, usually one in which the first player on the square pays a sum of money to the second player, the second player can "bump" the first to a penalty square (the "park bench," which represents unemployment and a resultant loss of time or money).

As a model of the choice process, the game of Careers suggests the following questions which seem to be in need of exploration:

1. In dealing with occupational choices, as well as with choice in general, what would constitute an adequate list of values? How is one to deal with the conceptual haziness of the terms representing the various values when they seem to mean different things to different players?
2. How fixed are these values in actual life? What system of propositions might be used to predict both their initial development and their subsequent transformation?
3. To what extent are individuals aware of their own values, and those of others? How does this degree of awareness affect their choice behavior?
4. How well can choices be predicted by a summation of the gaps between values and expectations as to opportunities for achieving them (that is, the formulation utilized in the medical student study)? Can the EVD formulation be improved so as to yield highly accurate predictions?
5. Even in relatively simple situations where expectations as to the opportunities for fulfilling goals are relatively clear (as in the game where these descriptions are recorded in the squares within each occupational path), to what extent are these expectations received and interpreted uniformly, and how does this affect choices?
6. To what extent do motives or transitory values developed in specific situations (such as the desire to "bump" a player simply because he is behaving obnoxiously in the bargaining situation) affect choices, and can such a process be incorporated within the theory of choice as a function of values and expectations?
7. To what extent do the objective alternatives open to the individual (the kinds of "opportunity cards" and "experience cards" he has), as well as his own awareness of them and their implications, affect choices?

As the operating model generated data, it became apparent that goals other than those of happiness, fame, and money points were involved in players' behavior. Some of these were rather subtle (for example, the desire to "bump" another player regardless of whether it helps one to win the game). Players seemed to have little awareness of such additional goals. All of this calls attention to the wide range of goals which seem to affect human behavior, and it provides clues as to techniques for measuring subtle values.

9.2 NONCOMPUTER SIMULATION AND THE EXPERIMENT

SOME DIFFERENCES

Experiments usually are undertaken when the investigator has formed very clear-cut hypotheses and when it is feasible for him to manipulate one or more independent variables in order to analyze their effects on one or more dependent variables. A high degree of control attainable in the experiment tends to make the inferences of the experimenter more definitive than those usually made in other methods of investigation. The chief advantage of such control seems to lie in the context of justification. But serious questions may be raised as to how much we do understand of what is going on even in highly controlled experiments. Although we can control for the effects of the pretest on the subjects, how much do we thereby learn about the dynamics of such effects? The same can be said with respect to the interaction effects of the pretest on the test variable or treatment. How much do we learn about human behavior when we find, for example, that a given treatment leads to a certain degree of change in the average performance of a number of individuals? Of course, it all depends on the theoretical importance or fruitfulness of the proposition under investigation. But let us assume that the proposition is potentially of great importance: How much is our understanding increased by the experimental data in nonsimulated situations?

In order to understand the basis for these questions, it is necessary to reconsider the role of scientific concepts and theory in understanding everyday phenomena. The layman often views observations as direct indicators of reality. The behavioral scientist, however, is well aware that act meaning is not action meaning, and that it is in the concepts, propositions, and theories developed by the scientist that greatest hope for understanding and predicting phenomena lies.

Let us suppose now that a scientific theory has been developed which seems to offer great promise for understanding various aspects of behavior. Even if we perform highly controlled experiments relating to any given aspect of the theory, we are neither testing the theory as a whole nor maximally using the theory itself to understand and control what is going on in the experimental situation. If the scientific theory does indeed constitute our best mechanism for understanding the reality, then it may be useful to attempt to apply it as completely as possible. Even highly controlled experiments can be further controlled by the application of theoretical knowledge within the experimental situation itself. This may lead both to improved ways of testing the theory as a whole (context of justification) and additional ideas as to what may be actually going on during the experiment.

EXPERIMENTING WITHIN THE CONTEXT OF SIMULATION

Simulation implies the introduction of methods that make use of available theoretical knowledge to control the data-collection situation. The game Careers centers on three factors: the values or goals each individual adopts within the game; the expectations for achieving the various goals each player forms as a result of reading the descriptions of the squares on the board; and the choices that have to be made by each player throughout the game. If it is indeed true that choice is primarily a function of values and expectations, then the game situation serves to sweep away the thousand-and-one extraneous factors that get in the way of the researcher when he tries to determine what actually occurred in a given experiment. The simulation makes use of available theory to structure the experimental situation and produce the very detailed data on just those relationships the investigator believes are most important for exploration and testing. If, for example, he is interested in the ways in which different kinds of expectations affect choices, then he might proceed in the following manner within the framework of a one-control-group before-and-after design:

1. Using randomization procedures, divide subjects into an experimental group and a control group.
2. Match or randomize all other conditions for these two groups.
3. Give each group the same pretest by allowing them to play with one version of Careers and record the choices made.
4. Introduce a different version of the game for the experimental group —one which incorporates certain changes in the descriptions of the squares on the board and which consequently will result in differences in expectations for achieving the various goals.
5. Record the choices made by the experimental group (posttest) and also allow the control group to play with the original version of the game once more and record their choices.

One may consequently draw inferences about the relationship between the changes in the descriptions of the squares (expectations for achieving goals) and the choices made by subtracting changes in the control group from those in the experimental group.[4]

---

[4] For some insight into the potential power of games for changing society, see Philip K. Dick, "War Game." *The Preserving Machine* (New York: Ace, 1969), pp. 18–35.

9.3 NONCOMPUTER SIMULATION AND LEVEL OF ABSTRACTION

One of the important features of simulation is that it usually entails a large gap between the surface characteristics of the simulation situation and the characteristics of the process simulated. There is, thus, a high degree of abstraction involved, that is, from the numerous characteristics of the actual process, selection of those which seem to be most crucial. The Careers game provided an example of this abstracting process.

The simulation of international relations furnishes an illustration in which this process is carried forward much further. For example, nations must be "constructed," with the complexities of their internal and external affairs somehow taken into account. The student of social research may well question the utility of such "unrealistic" simulations. Perhaps answers will emerge as a result of examining one of them.

Guetzkow has developed a simulation in which each nation is represented by one or more decision makers.[5] In one situation there are two decision makers, the internal decision maker (IDM), with final responsibility for all of the nation's policies, and the external decision maker (EDM), who conducts foreign policy and reports back to the IDM. In one series of runs of the simulation, senior and graduate students concentrating in political science were used, and it was found that some of the IDMs collaborated with their EDMs in making decisions whereas others did not. Another series showed that nations with a single decision maker tended to pay little attention to internal affairs whereas those with three frequently became bogged down in internal processes, with little time remaining for external affairs.

Goals for each nation were specified, sometimes by the researchers (for example, security, domination, cooperation, internal growth) and sometimes by the students, and each nation attempted to achieve its goals. Decision makers were also concerned with the goal of being maintained in office, with the probability of this being dependent on the degree to which the nation's goals were being fulfilled. Such calculations were made by researchers only at certain intervals, giving decision makers the opportunity to take long-range considerations into account in their efforts to fulfill the nation's goals. Nations were subsequently allowed to reformulate their goals.

At intervals, each nation received basic resources which could be used for internal or external purposes. These resources could aid in internal growth, for example, or they could be used for purposes of dominating other nations.

Nations could interact in many different ways. They could build per-

[5] Harold Guetzkow, "A Use of Simulation in the Study of Inter-Nation Relations," *Behavioral Science,* **4** (1959), 183–91.

manent forms of international cooperation or they could declare war. They could seek to establish bilateral or multilateral alliances or refrain from such efforts. Treaties could be made specifying an exchange of resources, or resources could be given by one nation to others.

As yet so little simulation in this area has been done that it is difficult to assess the utility of these efforts. However, we are able to specify some of the ways in which they might be useful (other than as training devices):

1. They may provide descriptions of international situations that have never existed but may occur in the future. For example, Kaplan discusses six distinct international systems, with only the first two having actually had historical counterparts: "(1) the 'balance of power' system, (2) the loose bipolar system, (3) the tight bipolar system, (4) the universal system, (5) the hiearchical system in its directive and nondirective forms, and (6) the unit veto system."[6] Data from simulations may aid the investigator in speculating about the range of possible systems that might occur and about the possible characteristics such systems might have. Here, simulation would offer the possibility of aid within the context of discovery.

2. They might lead to the development of specific hypotheses about the course of international events, and these may subsequently be tested by actual occurrences. Most social scientists would agree that we are still a long way from being able to make highly specific and accurate predictions, because international relations are too complex for available theories to be effective. One of the major difficulties has to do with our ability to pull together theories about the behavior of individuals and theories of group processes.

However, from the Guetzkow simulation we can see that it is possible to specify the relationships between individual and group processes in considerable detail. A given society makes its influence on the decision makers felt by means of the relationship between the degree to which national goals have been achieved and the probability that these decision makers will be maintained in office. The decision makers, in turn, can modify these goals to an extent in accordance with their own goals. They can also fail to achieve national goals in the short run and still remain in office because of the infrequency of elections. In making predictions about specific nations, it would be necessary to have accurate information about the goals of the key decision makers as well as of the nation as a whole.

It may easily be maintained that those simulations thus far investigated neglect to include any of the important complexities of international process. Nevertheless, it is possible to increase the complexity of these simulations. If predictions based on a given simulation prove to be highly inaccurate, it may be possible to discover those limitations in the simulation leading to this inaccuracy and to modify the simulation accordingly.

[6] Morton A. Kaplan, *System and Process in International Politics* (New York: Wiley, 1957).

3. A goal for social science that seems to be more easily attainable is an understanding of the ways in which the various "rules" of international relationships affect one another, and their relationship to national goals. This does not involve accurate predictions of specific events. The emphasis here is on the general requirements of a given international system, with the variation in the goals of individual decision makers not being considered.

Simulation could provide hypotheses about these relationships by setting them up as game situations with different rules and different goals. Any one game situation might then be run with different sets of individuals acting as decision makers. Although there would probably be a great deal of variation in outcomes, depending on which decision makers were playing the game, there might also be a good deal of uniformity in what occurs. This uniformity could then provide the basis for propositions about the process of international relationships.

4. It is always possible to view such simulations without attempting to draw conclusions about the process being simulated. The emphasis could, instead, be on explaining and predicting the behavior of the set of individuals who are playing the game. Success here would be no mean achievement, because it could make important contributions to general theory.

9.4   COMPUTER SIMULATION

We shall discuss one approach to the computer simulation of human behavior in order to illustrate the general procedure.[7] The following steps are involved: (1) the definition of a problem on the basis of a theoretical framework, (2) the construction of a block diagram of the processes involved, (3) the development of the equations or tables specifying the way in which the block diagram works, (4) the writing of the program, (5) the running of the computer simulation, and (6) the further development and testing of the ideas. We shall illustrate these steps with the simulation of one aspect of personality dynamics, namely, level of aspiration and achievement. Our approach will be highly oversimplified in order to keep the illustration manageable for pedagogical purposes, with a more complex computer simulation to be discussed in Section 17.4.

DEFINITION OF A PROBLEM

We are concerned with the process which produces individual achievement or lack of achievement. Our theoretical framework is related to Kurt Lewin's experimental studies of level of aspiration. Lewin and his asso-

---

[7] Our approach is based on techniques developed by Jay W. Forrester. See, for example, his *Industrial Dynamics* (Cambridge, Mass.: M.I.T. Press, 1961); *Principles of Systems* (Cambridge, Mass.: Wright-Allen Press, 1968); and *Urban Dynamics* (Cambridge, Mass.: M.I.T. Press, 1969).

ciates, in a series of experiments with children in a classroom situation, found that level of aspiration was closely related to perception of level of achievement. Children who received high grades tended to raise their level of aspiration with respect to how well they wanted to perform on the subsequent test. By contrast, low grades led to lowered levels of aspiration. This theoretical framework is supported by psychological reinforcement theory.

One approach to computer simulation is to begin with an oversimplified model and then, after it has been thoroughly explored, increase the complexity of the model. Our focus is on the way in which desired level of achievement and actual level of achievement together work to raise or lower the actual level of achievement during the next time interval. More specifically, we hypothesize that the gap between desired and actual levels of achievement works to raise or lower subsequent level of achievement. If a wide gap is maintained because of a level of aspiration which does not fall, then there will be pressure to push achievement up toward level of aspiration. However, once level of achievement approaches level of aspiration, the pressure to achieve at a great rate disappears.

This analysis is related to the theory behind the medical student study. Choice of a medical field is seen as being based on expected value deprivation. From this perspective, students avoid situations where the gap between desire and future accomplishment is expected to be great. This gap produces forces which tend to eliminate it. As for what causes aspiration to fall to level of achievement, or level of achievement to rise to level of aspiration, that is one of the problems that the simulation might clarify.

Our initial simulation will treat level of aspiration as a factor which, instead of being influenced by level of achievement, will determine level of achievement. Thus, we shall begin with aspiration fixed at a certain level; after a given time period we shall raise aspiration to a higher level and examine the implications for achievement. In addition, we shall view the rate of achievement as based not simply on the gap between aspiration and previous achievement but also on a period of time viewed as necessary to build up to a rate of achievement (Time for Action Build-up). Finally, we shall view achievements as depreciating over time, with the most recent achievements affecting subsequent achievements to the greatest extent. This rate of depreciation will be designated the accomplishment aging rate.

BLOCK DIAGRAM

The block diagram in Figure 9-1 shows the directions in which the process flows by means of arrows indicating cause-and-effect relationships.[8] There are three types of variables: level variables, represented by

---

[8] The solid arrows represent movements of quantities from place to place, whereas the broken arrows represent information take-offs which do not deplete the source of the take-off.

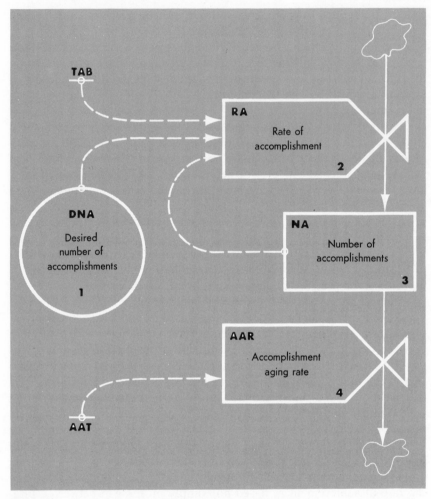

FIGURE 9-1   Block Diagram of Level of Aspiration and Achievement

rectangles (NA: number of accomplishments); rate variables, depicted as valves (RA: rate of accomplishment, and AAR: accomplishment aging rate); and auxiliary variables, represented by circles (DNA: desired number of accomplishments). In addition, there are two constants: TAB (time for action build-up) and AAT (accomplishment aging time), with the latter designating the amount of time it takes for a given accomplishment to depreciate completely.

A key idea in this approach to simulation is to capture the dynamism of ongoing behavior by distinguishing between rates, which represent instantaneous rates of change, and levels, which accumulate whatever flows in from certain rates and which are diminished by whatever flows out via other rates. Thus, the level variable NA (number of accomplishments) is determined over a period of time by RA (rate of accomplishment) less AAR (accomplishment aging rate).

The rate variables frequently are determined by a more complex process than the level variables. Thus, we have three factors involved in RA—DNA, NA, and TAB. It will be recalled that we have been viewing rate of accomplishment (RA) as based on the gap between aspiration (DNA) and previous achievement (NA), and we have referred to the necessity for this rate to develop over a period of time (TAB). As for the rate variable AAR, this is based on the number of accomplishments (because more accomplishments implies that there are more available for depreciation) and AAT.

EQUATIONS

The variables in the block diagram are numbered so as to simplify our subsequent writing of the computer program; we will take them up in order.

1. DNA (desired number of accomplishments). We will set this equal to 10 for a period of five days and then step it up to 20 for an additional twenty days. These numbers are largely but not completely arbitrary, because they have been chosen to approximate a case study of an individual's experiences. We change the value of DNA to see what effect this will have on the other variables.

2. RA (rate of accomplishment). According to our theoretical framework, RA is based on the gap between aspiration (DNA) and previous achievement (NA). Thus, we might write: RA = DNA − NA. But this is not correct because the units on one side of the equation do not match those on the other side.

$$RA = \frac{\text{number of accomplishments}}{\text{unit of time}}$$

whereas DNA − NA = desired number of accomplishments minus number of accomplishments. Thus, we are left with

$$\frac{\text{number of accomplishments}}{\text{unit of time}} = \text{number of accomplishments}$$

The situation is remedied by using the constant TAB (time for action build-up). Because we had previously thought of rate of accomplishment as determined not only by the difference between DNA and NA, but also by TAB, let us formulate the equation for RA as follows:

$$RA = \frac{DNA - NA}{TAB}$$

In this way the units on the right-hand side, a number of accomplishments divided by a unit of time, match the rate variable on the left-hand side. Thus, if DNA = 10, NA = 6, and TAB = 2 days, then

$$RA = \frac{10 - 6}{2} = 2 \text{ accomplishments per day}$$

In other words, the gap between DNA and NA (four accomplishments) builds up the rate of accomplishment over a two-day period rather than instantaneously, where each day RA is increased two units.

3. NA (number of accomplishments). Let us think of the simulation as taking place over a series of discrete time intervals where the beginning of each interval (the same as the end of the previous interval) constitutes a point in time. The number of accomplishments at any point in time (K) is based on the number at the previous point (J) incremented by the rate of accomplishment over the interval between the two points (denoted by RA.JK) less the accomplishment aging rate over this interval (AAR.JK). The equation reads

$$NA.K = NA.J + (DT)(RA.JK - AAR.JK)$$

where DT is the interval between the point J and the point K.

4. AAR (accomplishment aging rate). We assume that accomplishment aging time = five days, that is, each accomplishment has a life of five days and depreciates one fifth each day. AAR depends not only on AAT but also on NA, because the more accomplishments, the greater the rate of depreciation. If we set AAR = NA/AAT, then the units on the two sides of the equation match, that is, the rate of accomplishment on the left side is matched by a number of accomplishments per unit of time on the right side.

In order to understand computer simulation it is crucial to take the mystery out of the technique by learning how to perform all the calcula-

TABLE 9-1

Calculations for the Simulation of Level of Aspiration and Achievement

t (days)	DNA	NA	RA (DNA-NA)/2	AAR (NA/5)
0.0	10	7.14	1.43	1.43
0.5	10	7.14	1.43	1.43
1.0	10	7.14	1.43	1.43
1.5	10	7.14	1.43	1.43
2.0	10	7.14	1.43	1.43
2.5	10	7.14	1.43	1.43
3.0	10	7.14	1.43	1.43
3.5	10	7.14	1.43	1.43
4.0	10	7.14	1.43	1.43
4.5	10	7.14	1.43	1.43
5.0	20	7.14	6.43	1.43
5.5	20	9.64	5.18	1.93
6.0	20	11.26	4.37	2.25
6.5	20	12.32	3.84	2.46
7.0	20	13.01	3.50	2.60
7.5	20	13.46	3.27	2.69
8.0	20	13.77	3.12	2.75
8.5	20	13.95	3.02	2.79
9.0	20	14.07	2.96	2.81
9.5	20	14.15	2.92	2.83
10.0	20	14.19	2.90	2.84
10.5	20	14.22	2.89	2.84
11.0	20	14.24	2.88	2.85
11.5	20	14.26	2.87	2.85
12.0	20	14.27	2.86	2.85
12.5	20	14.28	2.86	2.86
13.0	20	14.28	2.86	2.86
.	.	.	.	.
.	.	.	.	.
.	.	.	.	.
25.0	20	14.28	2.86	2.86

tions by hand. This is quite easy for our simple illustration. Table 9-1 presents the results of hand calculations.

To illustrate the calculation of the first few lines, at the beginning of the twenty-five-day interval where $T = 0.0$ and DNA has been set equal to 10, NA was set equal to 5/7 DNA, that is, 7.14, in order to proceed from a point of equilibrium. Thus, when we calculate RA, we have

$$RA = \frac{DNA - NA}{2} = \frac{10 - 7.14}{2} = 1.43$$

In addition,

$$\text{AAR} = \frac{\text{NA}}{5} = \frac{7.14}{5} = 1.43$$

We can tell that this is a point of equilibrium in line 2 after the simulation has run for one-half day. DNA = 10, as it has been set at this value for a five-day period.

$$\text{NA.K} = \text{NA.J} + (DT)(\text{RA} - \text{AAR})$$

Thus,

$$\text{NA.K} = 7.14 + (0.5)(1.43 - 1.43) = 7.14$$

For the first five days the slight difference between DNA and NA is sufficient to maintain a rate of achievement (1.43/day) that is just enough to balance the achievement aging rate (1.43/day), thus maintaining a constant number of achievements.

However, at the end of five days, DNA has been set to increase from 10 to 20. At that moment ($T = 5$) it is too soon for NA to change, but RA is altered:

$$\text{RA} = \frac{\text{DNA} - \text{NA}}{2} = \frac{20 - 7.14}{2} = 6.43$$

At the end of 5.5 days this new rate of accomplishment begins to affect NA:

$$\text{NA.K} = 7.14 + (0.5)(6.43 - 1.43) = 7.64$$

In this manner, NA continues to increase, but at a decreasing rate, until $t = 12.5$, when equilibrium once again is reached, and it is maintained for the remainder of the simulation.

PROGRAM

```
1 A     DNA.K = 10 + STEP (10,5)
2 R     RA.KL = (DNA.K − NA.K)/TAB
2.1 C   TAB = 2
3 L     NA.K = NA.J + (DT)(RA.JK − AAR.JK)
3.1 N   NA = DNA*5/7
4 R     AAR.KL = NA.K/AAT
4.1 C   AAT = 5
PLOT    DNA = D, NA = A,/RA = S, AAR = R
SPEC    DT = .5/length = 25 / plt per = . 5
```

Next to the number of each line of the program is a letter which specifies the type of variable involved. Thus, A = auxiliary, R = rate, C =
constant, L = level, and N = initial value. The PLOT line specifies the
symbols which will be used in the computer print-out, and the SPEC line
indicates the computing interval (DT), the length of time the simulation
runs, and the points in time plotted on the graph which the computer
prints out.

COMPUTER SIMULATION

In Figure 9-2 we have time on the abscissa, or X axis, with the unit of
one day and points plotted at half-day intervals. The ordinate, or Y axis,
has two different sets of units, one for the two rate variables and one for
DNA and NA; the former has to do with number of accomplishments
per day whereas the latter refers to number of accomplishments.
If we refer back to Table 9-1 we may note that the computer simulation
graph depicted in Figure 9-2 reflects the values calculated in that table.
Examining the auxiliary variable DNA (desired number of accomplishments) we see this at the level of ten accomplishments for the first five
days and then stepped up to twenty for the remainder of the simulation.
The level variable NA (number of accomplishments) begins at the equilibrium level of 7.14 accomplishments, continuing at this level for five
days until DNA is stepped up to 20. Immediately afterward, NA increases until a new equilibrium point of 14.28 accomplishments is reached
after 12.5 days.
Examining the two rate variables, we note that RA begins at the equilibrium point of 1.43 accomplishments per day, remaining at this rate
until, on the fifth day, it jumps to its maximum of 6.43 accomplishments
per day. Then it falls steeply until, at day 12.5, it achieves equilibrium at
2.86 accomplishments per day. AAR begins at the same rate as does RA
and also ends at the same rate, but it goes through a different path to

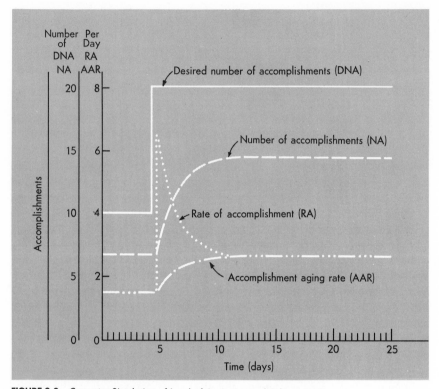

FIGURE 9-2 Computer Simulation of Level of Aspiration and Achievement

achieve this result. After the fifth day, instead of climbing steeply and then falling steeply, it gradually increases until it reaches its new rate at day 12.5.

In interpreting what is depicted by Figure 9-2, first we note a doubling of the two rate variables from their initial equilibrium rate (1.43) to their final equilibrium rate (2.86). This doubling also occurred in the case of the level variable NA, which changes from 7.14 to 14.28. All of this doubling results from the doubling of DNA from 10 to 20 on the fifth day.

We should note that when RA reaches the rate of 6.43 at the fifth day, there is no instantaneous change in NA (number of accomplishments). A change in NA begins to be manifested at day 5.5, when the increased rate of accomplishment has had some time in which to accumulate accomplishments. However, as soon as NA starts to climb, RA begins to fall, because RA is based on the difference between DNA (fixed at 20) and NA. Thus, as the gap between DNA and NA narrows, RA diminishes. This is not the case for the other rate variable, AAR, which is based on the rising NA. AAR does not rise very steeply because it is equal to one fifth of NA.

FURTHER DEVELOPMENT AND TESTING OF THE SIMULATION

A computer simulation is useful only to the extent that it suggests ideas in the context of discovery and to the extent that it can be corroborated by data in the context of justification. The present illustration is far too simplified to do very much for us in either context, especially in the context of justification. However, it does suggest several ideas in the context of discovery:

1. In the simulation, DNA (or level of aspiration) controlled what happened to all the other variables. Instead of fixing DNA at different levels, we might conceive of it as a variable that is itself determined by the other variables. This conception is corroborated by research on level of aspiration which indicates that it tends to rise on the basis of perceived level of achievement. For example, we might define DNA = 2NA, that is, the desired number of accomplishments is equal to double the number of accomplishments. In simulations run with this definition of DNA, it was found that this definition produces a continuing acceleration in the rate of accomplishment which, in turn, leads to a great increase in the number of accomplishments. For example, on the twenty-fifth day the rate of accomplishment is almost 4,000 per day.

2. One way of moving closer to a realistic model is to distinguish between NA (number of accomplishments) and a new variable, say PNA (perceived number of accomplishments). It is a trite finding of behavioral science that our information about phenomena can differ greatly from the way such phenomena would be evaluated by others.

3. We might want to insert random variation into the model at one point or another in order to represent variations in the environment over which the individual has little control. This would have an effect similar to the establishment of perceived number of accomplishments as a second-level variable; namely, greater fluctuations in the remaining variables—as distinct from smooth curves—would tend to result.

4. We might want to eliminate the accomplishment aging rate variable, with its assumption of the depreciation of accomplishments. Depreciation may be more appropriate for material than ideational phenomena.

5. We might want to bring into the model more aspects of the environment. Presently, the model can be used for a personality system or a social system; in the latter case we could speak in terms of averages for a given group (for example, average rate of accomplishment). However, it would be most useful to take into account as many situational or environmental factors as possible (for example, other social systems).

9.5 SIMULATION AND SEQUENTIAL RELATIONSHIPS

Simulation plays an important role in the analysis of sequences of phenomena or processes. Usually, whatever change is investigated in the experiment is introduced by the experimenter in the form of the test variable or treatment. In the before-and-after experiment, for example, it is the difference between the pretest and posttest situations that is under investigation. Simulation procedures, although they can be combined with such experimentation, generally involve a much more detailed concern with the analysis of change. When the attempt is made to simulate an entire process, such as that of occupational choice, a typical procedure would be to collect data having to do with many different stages in the process. Each individual might make a long series of choices, and the situations within which the choices are made may vary greatly from the beginning of the process to its conclusion. For example, the degree to which each player has fulfilled each of his goals is continually changing, and this in turn will tend to affect the degree to which he will strive for the fulfilled goals, on the one hand, and the unfulfilled goals, on the other.

The question might be raised as to whether so many changes do not lead to the kind of relatively uncontrolled situation often found in field experiments. Actually, the structuring of the situation achieved by simulation procedures, on the basis of whatever theory is available, serves as an important set of controls. Although several variables are generally allowed to change over time in the simulation as well as in the field experiment, in the simulation we know a great deal more about which crucial variables are changing and in what ways. Furthermore, the investigator can control this variation in simulation procedures, whereas in field experiments he is usually forced to vary whole sets of variables at one time without precisely knowing which ones are being varied or how much.

The importance of a knowledge of process or change must not be underestimated. Explanations attempt to describe causal relationships by filling the interstices between events or surrounding them within a more inclusive framework. A knowledge of process makes it possible to fill these interstices and provide the more inclusive framework and thus increase our understanding of what is going on. It is one thing to know that if an experimenter introduces a certain change, a given effect will follow; it is quite another thing to be able to learn about the various mechanisms that lie between the given change and the given effect and convert the change into the effect. The experiment can, of course, focus on some of these interstices, and this technique is quite valuable for arriving at an explanation. Simulation techniques, however, are especially well adapted to producing data of a more continuous nature so that long sequences of phenomena can be analyzed. Observational and interview procedures are quite valuable within the context of simulation because they provide the means for making frequent measurements.

EXERCISES

1. Design a simple noncomputer simulation focusing on a problem of interest to you. Indicate what you hope to learn from the simulation.

2. Design an experiment to be performed in the context of your simulation.

3. Develop a computer simulation without the aid of a computer, that is, go through the following steps:
   a. Define a problem around a given theoretical framework.
   b. Construct a block diagram.
   c. Develop the equations.
   d. Perform computations based on the equations over a specified time interval.
   e. Plot these computations on a graph.
   f. Interpret the results, exploring the implications for the context of discovery.

ANNOTATED REFERENCES

CLARKE, ARTHUR C. *The City and the Stars*. New York: Harcourt, Brace & World, Inc., 1956. To the extent that a writer of science fiction bases his story on some model of the universe, and to the extent that the story represents the output or extrapolation of that model, then the story is a kind of simulation; this is true for other kinds of fiction as well. Clarke's model is quite clearly defined for the reader. Further, there is an important simulation within this simulation: the technique is used as a teaching device for enabling individuals to break away from fears which have existed for a billion years.

FORRESTER, JAY W. *Principles of Systems*. Cambridge, Mass.; Wright-Allen Press, Room 516, 238 Main Street, 1968. This volume consists of a text and workbook. The technique for computer simulation expounded enables the user to develop highly dynamic formulations because it utilizes principles from calculus. At the same time no particular background in mathematics is required for the student to learn how to develop the kinds of complex models which, if the attempt were made to produce analytic mathematical solutions, would defy calculation.

RASER, JOHN R. *Simulation and Society*. Boston: Allyn and Bacon, 1969. Raser's effort is "to examine the history of simulations, discuss their theoretical and philosophical underpinnings, analyze some of their strong and weak points, deal with questions of validity and usefulness within a variety of contexts, and try to project some future directions for the field."

part three
MEASUREMENT AND SCALING

If measurement is important for testing theory, it is also true that theory is necessary for measurement. The theory may be implicit or explicit, but some idea of the nature of the world must enter into any attempt to measure a portion of that world. To the extent that the theory is effective, it will aid in obtaining accurate and precise measurement by providing explicit directions as to where or how to look for important phenomena. Yet this kind of theory generally is not available in behavioral science. Thus, a concern with precision that is not balanced by a concern for the development of fruitful theory may prove to be poor research strategy.

Chapter 10 discusses questions having to do with the strategy of measurement, validity, reliability, precision, and scales of measurement. Chapters 11 and 12 take up different types of scales as well as various procedures that may be used to construct such scales. The scales are classified into nominal, ordinal, interval, and ratio types, and their mathematical properties as well as the functions they serve are discussed.

CHAPTER 10 Principles of Measurement and Scaling

10.1 STRATEGY OF MEASUREMENT

WHY MEASURE?

One important function of measurement is that it enables the researcher to test his propositions and theories. Measures indicate when a given entity, such as John Smith's preference for pathology, is present or absent in a given situation. Measures usually also indicate degrees (for example, how important pathology is for John Smith). Scientists utilize objective measurement procedures so that each can compare his view of the world with that of other scientists. Although it is generally recognized that these procedures do not necessarily produce a picture of reality, scientists assume that this is the best way of getting as close to reality as possible.

Measurement, then, functions to tie any concept (no matter how abstract) to reality by telling the scientist what his observations imply about the phenomena to which the concept refers. Measurement thus sets the stage for testing a given proposition by allowing the investigator to make observations bearing on the various concepts involved. When this is done, a given hypothesis can be empirically tested and conclusions can be drawn, on the basis of the available evidence, with reference to its truth or falsity.

Measurement is also of help within the context of discovery. The process of constructing the measurement very often can influence the researcher to develop his ideas about the concept in question more explicitly in order to be able to build a more accurate measurement. In addition, discovery is advanced as a result of the testing of propositions, for the results indicate the next steps the investigator should take.

THE MEASUREMENT PROCESS AS DATA

For the behavioral scientist, an understanding of the measurement process may be an end in itself. For example, an understanding of the interaction between subject and experimenter can furnish ideas about the process of social interaction (context of discovery) and also provide a test of prior hypotheses about social interaction (context of justification). The same holds true for the measurement process, for we may conceive of this as a more detailed way of looking at certain aspects of the data-collection process.

Let us consider the measurement of values within the context of the medical student study. It might be hypothesized that if certain entities represent the goals of the individual, he will be able (other things being equal) to distinguish them from entities that do not represent his goals. Furthermore, it might be hypothesized that the individual will verbalize or record such distinctions in an appropriate interview or questionnaire situation. Respondents may be either unable or unwilling to indicate a given fact. This may hold true particularly for fairly abstract concepts, which are often surrounded by a variety of social pressures. The first hypothesis, however, states that the individual will be able to distinguish his own values; the second states that he will be willing to verbalize or record those values.

There is a direct, a partially direct, and an indirect way of testing these hypotheses. The direct method involves a study specifically designed to test each of them. Such a study may, of course, be incorporated within a study of other aspects of the respondent's behavior, such as the process by which he chooses a field of medicine. Using the first hypothesis, for example, one might adopt some procedure for measuring goals other than the use of questionnaires or direct questions. This might involve projective or other indirect techniques or observation of choice behavior in simulated situations. Techniques must then be devised for measuring the respondent's awareness of these goals. If we are to distinguish between the two hypotheses, it will be necessary to measure awareness by means other than a questionnaire or interview, because the second hypothesis deals specifically with the willingness of the respondent to verbalize such awareness in those situations. Thus, an independent means of getting at awareness must be found if the second hypothesis is to be tested. This might involve a prolonged observation period in a noninterview situation, or possibly the individual's indications of his awareness within the context of a simulated situation. Once the respondent's awareness of values has been measured, it can be related to his actual verbalization of such awareness in questionnaire or interview situations.

A partially direct method might simply measure the individual's goals (whether or not they are in his awareness) by indirect techniques and also measure whether or not these goals are verbalized in an interview or questionnaire situation. The variable of awareness intervenes between the existence of goals and their verbal expression, but this partially direct approach infers. that if goals exist and if they are verbalized, then they also occur in the awareness of the individual.

One indirect method actually involves no special study of the measurement situation. The investigator simply proceeds with his analysis of the relationship between the individual's values and his choice of medical fields, utilizing the interview or questionnaire measures of values. If the investigator is able to explain or predict the respondent's choice of field rather well, then this achievement indirectly implies that his procedures for measuring values are effective to an extent. According to this approach, it might be more generally stated that whenever propositions having at least a degree of support in the literature are confirmed through certain measurement techniques, the effectiveness of these techniques is to an extent demonstrated.

An examination of the measurement process itself, then, can add to the body of knowledge within the context of justification through direct or indirect tests of hypotheses. It can also aid within the context of discovery. Instead of approaching the measurement situation with a view to testing specific hypotheses, or after doing so, we might try to discover the various factors that transform the goals of the individual into the neat answers he gives in a questionnaire or interview situation. Although we may surmise that the individual's awareness of his own goals is probably biased in the direction of social desirability, there exists little in the way of research to show us the dynamics of this process. The researcher might proceed by measuring the social desirability of various values as seen by a given respondent and then try to determine, using relatively unstructured techniques, the mechanism whereby expectations about social desirability affect the individual's awareness of his own values. As for the verbalization of awareness—that is, the willingness of a respondent to present an undistorted picture of himself—the investigator might utilize some technique other than direct questions. Prolonged association with and observation of respondents might be one approach. Another might be the experimentation with a variety of different interview or questionnaire techniques in order to develop one that maximizes the willingness of the respondent to reveal his values. In such ways, the investigator might learn a good deal about those factors that increase and decrease the likelihood of distortion.

THEORY AND MEASUREMENT

It seems rather obvious that measurement and theory are integrally linked and that unless measurement furthers the development and testing of propositions and theories (whether within or outside the measurement situation itself) it has little utility. One implication of this point of view is that measurement is a tool for achieving effective theory, and that the precision of the measurement is no guarantee of its utility. We can frequently measure the age of individuals almost to the minute, and yet such precision has thus far produced nothing very remarkable with respect to scientific propositions and theories having considerable scope.

Does this mean that it is useless to try to obtain precise measurement? Not at all, for precision might substantially aid in the development of theory. Without precision, it becomes difficult to state relationships between variables in a clear-cut manner, and this hampers the development of theory. Precision alone, however, implies neither scope nor systematic import.

SOME CHOICES AND STRATEGIES

Perhaps the most important choice of the investigator is the choice of *what* to measure. Elaborate and precise measurement techniques applied to trivial concepts will be worse than useless because they represent a waste of research resources. Even very rough measurement techniques, however, may yield interesting and even important data when they are applied to important concepts, propositions, and theories. Most researchers strive to select concepts that are important with reference to existing theory or will aid in the development of theory. Thus far, however, the theoretical rewards for all the efforts that have gone into measurement have been rare, although it is true that many propositions with relatively limited scope have been, to an extent, validated.

Another choice facing the investigator is the degree to which he will focus on an analysis of the measurement process itself. Several different approaches to such analyses have been discussed, and any forthcoming results would add to our knowledge of the dynamics of human behavior within the measurement situation and aid in the development and testing of improved propositions and theory outside of the measurement situation as well.

A third choice faced by the researcher involves his selection of scaling procedure. Each procedure carries with it certain assumptions about the nature of the phenomena under investigation, and each produces a different degree of precision. The number of assumptions made and the degree of precision generally vary together, so that a greater number of assumptions tends to yield a greater degree of precision. But assumptions may be erroneous, and the researcher who seeks a great deal of precision may make assumptions that are far from correct. On the other hand, if he attains a high degree of precision on the basis of assumptions that are only partially incorrect, he may achieve a good deal of theoretical knowledge and subsequently be in a better position to improve his measurement procedures and eliminate the errors involved.

The American Psychological Association has been particularly concerned with problems of measurement within the context of the construction of psychological tests and has compiled a number of recommendations.[1] These, of course, must themselves be evaluated in terms of utility. At the very least, they alert the investigator to some rules of evi-

---

[1] An official statement of these recommendations is presented in "Technical Recommendations for Psychological Tests and Diagnostic Techniques," *Psychological Bulletin Supplement,* **51**, Pt. 2 (1954), 1–38. For a more detailed discussion of various aspects of test construction, see L. J. Cronbach, *Essentials of Psychological Testing* (New York: Harper, 1960).

dence that are widely accepted by psychologists and indicate procedures of which he might not have been aware.

10.2 MEASUREMENT VALIDITY

VALIDITY AND MEASUREMENT

In scientific usage a measurement of a given phenomenon (as designated by a given concept) is viewed as a *valid measure* if it successfully measures the phenomenon. The concept itself may or may not have a high degree of clarity. If it does, the investigator has less difficulty in locating the phenomenon to which the concept refers. He then makes the statement that his data indicate that the phenomenon he has observed constitutes a measure of the phenomenon to which the concept refers. For example, a respondent's answer to a question concerning his age constitutes data that the investigator then utilizes as a measure of the phenomenon of *chronological age.*

It should be noted that the investigator makes a *statement* that his observations constitute a measure of the phenomena referred to by the concept. Because it is a statement, it can be tested by obtaining evidence for or against it. The abstract definition of the concept is not, in itself, a statement about the nature of reality, and consequently it may not be judged in terms of truth and falsity. On the other hand, the designation of certain data and of rules for putting them together as a measurement with respect to a concept *does* constitute a statement about the nature of reality. If the answer to a question on religion were taken as a measure of age, evidence could be presented to the effect that such data do not represent the phenomena referred to by the concept *chronological age.* Some of the procedures used to collect evidence as a measurement of validity are categorized under three major headings: *face-validation procedures, criterion-validation procedures,* and *construct-validation procedures.*

FACE-VALIDATION PROCEDURES

The validation procedure that is least objective or perhaps most subject to error is *face validation*. This involves an anlysis of whether the measurement appears to get at the concept "on the face of it." Thus, for example, direct measures tend to have more face validity than measures based on projective or other indirect techniques.

Face-validation procedures are highly subjective in the sense that two researchers may easily come up with different evaluations. Perhaps even more serious is that surface similarities or differences may not be as important as less obvious ones. Thus, for example, the question "Are you maladjusted?" may, in spite of its face validity for measuring adjustment, constitute a poor measurement of this phenomenon—perhaps far less adequate than a Rorschach Test with little face validity as a measure of adjustment.

In his efforts to evaluate the face validity of a given measurement, it is often useful for the investigator to analyze carefully the meaning of the term and then trace the implications of this meaning for observable phenomena. Such an analysis can often reveal a good deal of vagueness in the meaning of the concept and lead to ideas about other variables that might be related to the concept. The term *explication* may be used to designate a reinterpretation of a given concept in this manner:

> An explication of a given set of terms, then, combines essential aspects of meaning analysis and of empirical analysis. Taking its departure from the customary meanings of the terms, explication aims at reducing the limitations, ambiguities, and inconsistencies of their ordinary usage by propounding a reinterpretation intended to enhance the clarity and precision of their meanings as well as their ability to function in hypotheses and theories with explanatory and predictive force.[2]

Thus, what might begin as an exploration of face validity might end up, through the process of explication, to be an improvement in conceptualization and lead to the emergence of new ideas for measurements and hypotheses.

Perhaps the strongest argument that can be made for face-validation procedures is that they are not very time-consuming. If the investigator is designing an interview schedule containing a large number of items, he would have to expend a considerable proportion of his limited research resources if more elaborate validation procedures were to be used on many of these items. By limiting his attention to face validation, such resources might be more fruitfully employed, for example, providing a longer training period for his staff of interviewers.

CRITERION-VALIDATION PROCEDURES

Let us now pursue the process of explication to its logical conclusion. Suppose that such a reinterpretation of a given concept or a set of concepts is effected and this results in the development of a system of hypotheses or propositions with the concept constituting an important element of this theory. A next step would involve actually testing these hypotheses, and it is with reference to such tests that *criterion-validation* and *construct-validation procedures* are concerned. They differ from face-validation procedures in that they are based on objective testing, although the resulting inference with respect to validity is still uncertain.

[2] Carl G. Hempel, *Fundamentals of Concept Formation in Empirical Science* (Chicago: University of Chicago Press, 1952).

Criterion-validation procedures involve a new measure and a well-accepted measure of a given concept. The well-accepted measure may be utilized as a criterion to aid in the assessment of the new measure. For example, let us assume that the structured-values question in the medical student study (choices: indispensable in a job, extremely important, very important, fairly important, little or no importance) is the well-accepted measure of values serving as the criterion, whereas the less-structured careers-value question constitutes the new measure being assessed. We may then proceed to investigate how close the relationship is between the criterion and the method under assessment, that is, whether individuals' values as measured by the structured-values question are very close to their values as measured by the careers-value question.

A number of questions may be raised with reference to criterion-validation procedures. One of them has to do with the procedures whereby the criterion measure itself was validated. If this validation was achieved with the aid of another criterion measure, then the question may be raised once more, and this may continue indefinitely. An additional question involves the utility of criterion-validation procedures in the first place. One may wonder why an investigator who already has a well-accepted measurement for a given concept should desire to create and attempt to validate some new measure. A third question involves the conservativeness of criterion-validation procedures. If present criterion measures are trivial and unfruitful and yet are used to judge new measures, then there is little hope for achieving a breakthrough in knowledge.

CONSTRUCT-VALIDATION PROCEDURES

The limitations of criterion-validation procedures have given impetus to a concern with the total set of propositions in which a given concept is located, and this has to do with *construct validation*. Suppose that we proceeded to test not only the relationship between the structured-values question and the careers-value question but also hypotheses about the relationship between values and preference for medical fields. Within this context, values would constitute an independent variable and preference a dependent one. We also might choose to relate values to other dependent variables. It might be convenient, in addition, to consider values as a dependent variable and test hypotheses about the origin of values. If, in addition, other investigators had done similar studies, all these data could then be utilized as evidence for or against the validity of the careers-value question.

To illustrate the way in which such evidence might be used, suppose that the hypothetical relationship between expected value deprivation and preference for a medical field is supported directly or indirectly in the literature. If this hypothesis is correct, then any valid method for measuring values should also result in its confirmation. In general, to test a measure with respect to a given concept for *construct validity,* we examine several propositions that incorporate this concept and that have already been validated to some extent. The measure in question is then utilized to test these propositions once more; if they are confirmed, we may infer that the measure has construct validity.

At this point we may examine whether or not such an approach to validation can repair some of the deficiencies involved in criterion-validation procedures. One might ask how the propositions, in which the measure being tested is inserted, were validated in the first place. If they were tested on the basis of certain specific measures of each of the concepts involved, then the general proposition is validated only to the extent that each of the measures is valid. But here we are back again to the problem of validating measures for given concepts, except that instead of having only the original measures and concepts, we now have additional ones to consider.

Thus far, it would seem that neither criterion-validation nor construct-validation procedures offer a means for definitely validating a given measurement. It is also apparent that propositions that incorporate concepts cannot be definitely validated, as such validation involves measurements that cannot themselves be definitely validated. The scientist, however, learns to live with this lack of definitive verification and settles, instead, for evidence that is not definitive but is nevertheless valuable. As this applies to criterion validation and construct validation, each time that a relationship that would indicate the validity of a given measure for a concept is tested and confirmed, additional evidence for its validity is produced. We also may obtain some degree of evidence for validity whenever a given concept is explicated.

The second question raised with respect to the adequacy of criterion-validation procedures, and which also might be posed for construct-validation procedures, concerns their utility. The investigator never possesses a perfectly valid measure of any given concept. He might do well to become dissatisfied with well-accepted measures, because they may not be as fruitful for the development of theory as new measures are. Each time some evidence is obtained as to the validity of a given measure for a concept through the confirmation of a proposition, evidence is also obtained as to the validity of the proposition as well as any theory within which it is implicated. Construct-validation procedures have an advantage over criterion-validation procedures because they alert the investigator to an entire system of propositions, rather than merely the relationship between the new measure and the criterion measure. Construct-validation procedures thus have to do with the same kind of orientation to the research process as does a concern with theory, and the development of theory that can explain and predict effectively may be an end product of both.

We should note that our initial concern over the validity of measurement has brought us to include a discussion of the validity of propositions. We might extend this discussion by distinguishing between two kinds of validity with respect to propositions, as introduced by Campbell and Stanley: "*Internal validity* is the basic minimum without which any experiment is uninterpretable: Did in fact the experimental treatments make a difference in this specific experimental instance? *External validity* asks the question of *generalizability*: To what populations, settings, treatment variables and measurement variables can this effect be generalized?"[3]

We have come full circle from a discussion of theory and propositions in Part One of this book to an analysis of measurement validity to propositions and theory once again. It appears, then, that it is not fruitful to isolate these subjects from one another; we learn more about the validity of theories and propositions as we proceed to an analysis of measurement validity, and vice versa.

10.3 RELIABILITY AND PRECISION

RELIABILITY

If a spring scale is utilized to measure the weight of an individual, and if the indicator points to the same number of pounds when the individual steps on and off the scale several times, then we have obtained evidence that the scale is a reliable measuring instrument. If, on the other hand, the indicator points to different numbers each time, then we have evidence for its unreliability. More generally, a measuring instrument is reliable if it yields the same result in repeated applications to the same phenomena. If the phenomena change (for example, if an individual becomes heavier between weighings), we would naturally expect the result obtained from the measuring instrument to change accordingly. The importance of reliability stems from the fact that it gives the investigator confidence that variations in his data are not the result of imperfections in the measuring instrument itself.

The importance of the concept of reliability also stems from the ease with which reliability may be assessed relative to validity. In determining reliability, we are not dealing with the entire system of propositions within which a given concept is involved but, rather, with the behavior of a given measuring instrument under different conditions. Although it is easier to assess the reliability of a measuring instrument, the establishment of its validity is generally more valuable. For example, a spring scale constitutes a perfectly reliable measuring instrument if it indicates

---

[3] Donald T. Campbell and Julian C. Stanley, *Experimental and Quasi-Experimental Designs for Research* (Chicago: Rand McNally, 1966), p. 5.

exactly 2 pounds each time an individual stands on it, for it is then yielding the same result in repeated applications to the same phenomena. But there would be good reason to beileve that such measurements did not constitute valid or correct indications of the true weight of the individual. Thus, a measurement of a given concept may be quite reliable and yet be quite invalid. The reverse does not hold, however, because a measuring instrument that repeatedly provided a valid index for a given concept would have to be quite reliable as well.

As with data-collection methods in general, the investigator can view the situation wherein reliability is being tested not only as a means to aid the achievement of other ends but also as an end in itself. If it is true that a given process of measurement produces a reliable measure, this can aid the researcher to develop and test propositions that explain why the measurement situation does in fact yield a reliable measure. If, for example, a reliable measure for values can be obtained, then certain factors within the measurement situations were working to produce the same result. If these factors can be identified and the relationships to the resulting data tested, a contribution may be made to our knowledge of behavioral processes. Viewing an understanding of the measurement situation as an end in itself can also lead to important knowledge even in cases where a given measuring instrument proves to be unreliable. In such cases the investigation centers around the factors that produced differing results in the two measurement situations.

Thus far reliability has been discussed with reference to the stability of measurement, that is, a consideration of variations from one time interval to another. In the example of the spring scale, we evaluated reliability by determining whether or not the same result was obtained upon successive measurements. Another way of examining the reliability of the scale is to construct another equivalent scale. If measures obtained by the two scales are the same, then we have evidence for the reliability of the measurement. Some procedures for assessing reliability focus on stability, others on equivalence, and still others on a combination of the two.[4]

Whereas techniques for assessing reliability are helpful for the various data-collection methods, these techniques have generally been developed within the context of questionnaire and interview techniques. In attempts to assess stability, the respondent may be interviewed several times in what is called a test–retest procedure, and a measure of the degree of agreement between the test and the retest may be obtained. Of course, there exists the danger that the initial test will affect the subsequent test, so that a change that occurs may be the product not of the measuring instrument itself but of its successive application. There is also the pos-

---

[4] The distinction between stability and equivalence has been developed by L. J. Cronbach in "Coefficient Alpha and the Internal Structure of Tests," *Psychometrika,* **16** (1951), 297–339.

sibility that factors other than the measuring instrument itself have resulted in an actual change in the phenomena being measured. The general procedures for dealing with such possibilities are similar to those utilized in the experiment and may involve, for example, the introduction of a control group. A less elaborate procedure is to separate the test from the retest by a period long enough to reduce substantially or eliminate the effect of the initial test and yet not so long as to change the phenomena being measured to any significant degree.

One widespread approach to the assessment of reliability by use of *equivalent* questions is the *split-half method*. If we assume that the measurement is obtained by putting together information from a number of different items, then a larger number of items may be used than might ordinarily be necessary and the items may be divided into two halves after the data have been collected.[5] The two halves are then compared to test for equivalence.

Although it may be valuable to test the reliability of a given measuring instrument before using it in investigations, is it useful for the investigator to follow this rule invariably? A similar question might be posed with respect to the validation of a given measurement: "Unless satisfactory validity or reliability has already been demonstrated, the reliability of a measuring instrument should be determined before it is used in a study, rather than after. If a research instrument is plagued by variable error, the likelihood of achieving significant results is minimized. Rather than go ahead with unreliable instruments, it may be prudent to delay the research and try to increase their reliability."[6]

The advice implies that research should proceed in stages, and that the development of valid and reliable measurement should usually precede the investigation of phenomena. But research actually seems to proceed in a back-and-forth fashion rather than in stages. Imperfect and even very rough measurements may not be easily improved until they are actually utilized in the testing of hypotheses. It may often be preferable to proceed with rough measures, because the wait for measures may be a long one, especially if the insight derived from actual research with the measures is necessary for their improvement.

One indirect but effective approach that may be used to increase the reliability of a given measurement involves the various validation techniques. The fault may lie not only in the measure but in the concept as well. For example, the concept may not be a unitary one, but may include different types of phenomena. Explication of the concept, as well as research which explored the construct validity of the measure, might

---

[5] For a discussion of the various procedures that have been developed to effect this approach, see H. Gulliksen, *Theory of Mental Tests* (New York: Wiley, 1950).

[6] Claire Selltiz et al., *Research Methods in Social Relations* (New York: Holt, 1963), p. 167.

lead to the definition of both a more unitary and improved concept. Another approach, already discussed, involves an analysis of the measurement situation itself with a view to determining what factors produced the unreliability.

An additional approach, which has been developed within the context of psychological testing, calls for adding measurement operations (for example, items in a questionnaire) of the same type as the ones used initially and utilizing the total set of items, rather than the initial set alone, to arrive at the score of a given individual. Under this procedure, very high reliabilities may readily be obtained. The rub here is that the greater the number of items included within a given measurement, the more difficult it becomes to know what the total score is getting at (that is, what concept or concepts it is measuring). Within a research context it is generally useful to avoid measures that apply to several different factors or dimensions. Thus, although an additional set of items may increase reliability, it may also result in a measurement that is too heterogeneous to be fruitful for the development of theory.

PRECISION

A given spring scale may be reliable to the pound but not to the ounce. This would occur, for example, if the weight of a given individual varied between 167 pounds, 2 ounces, and 167 pounds, 5 ounces, on the scale in question. Reliability, then, should be understood within the context of a given degree of precision, and the greater the degree of precision desired, the more difficult it is to obtain the appropriate degree of reliability. The precision of the measuring instrument is here understood to vary inversely with the width of the smallest interval it can report; very precise scales may provide measures to the nearest tenth of an ounce, whereas less precise ones may measure to the nearest pound.

It is relatively easy to obtain a high degree of reliability when little precision is needed. Thus, for example, it would be easier to develop a highly reliable measurement of a given value if only two degrees of the value were called for (for example, high and low) than if five degrees were desired.

As a science progresses, the precision of measurement tends to increase, and the scientist is able to develop more definitive tests of propositions, particularly those specifying degrees and types of relationships. Thus, for example, a distinct advance is represented by moving from a description of temperature in terms of hot and cold to a description in terms of the expansion of a column of mercury. When we deal with the mercury thermometer, we are dealing with a high degree of reliability for a high degree of precision. It is obviously useless to create multiple categories that give the appearance of a very high degree of precision unless reliability is sufficiently high. In fact, it is not only useless, but misleading as well. Within the physical sciences it is a general rule that the investigator should not include so many significant digits in any given measurement that a misleading portrayal of the reliability involved is implied. An ammeter dial fluctuating between 25 and 27 amperes should not be read as 26.000 amperes but rather as 26 amperes or 26 ± 1 amperes.

10.4 SCALES OF MEASUREMENT

THE NATURE OF SCALING

Just as there are procedures for improving the reliability of measurement, so also are there techniques for increasing its precision. A thermometer without any calibrations whatsoever may constitute a highly reliable measuring device, but the extent of this reliability could not be fully revealed until the thermometer were calibrated. Once this is done, the thermometer can then be used to determine temperature under a wide variety of conditions. These measurements may then be of great value in the development and testing of scientific theories.

Scaling procedures[7] may be viewed as techniques for producing such things as the calibrated thermometer. If the thermometer works effectively, the liquid inside it will not expand in an erratic fashion. The same holds true for effective scaling techniques. The behavior of the liquid within the thermometer may itself be the focus of investigation, but thermometers are usually conceived within a research context as providing means for the investigation of other phenomena. Similarly, an analysis may be made of the process that leads to some aspects of human behavior forming a precise scale, and this may be of interest in its own right. Research procedures in general, however, emphasize an exploration and testing of the various relationships of scaled behavior to other behavior. Furthermore, a given scaling technique may produce the kinds of measurements that may be reliable and precise, yet such measurements may be useless if they have very few relationships with other phenomena. On the other hand, a very rough categorization may be extremely valuable for the progress of knowledge if the concept involved has systematic import.

Scaling is a procedure for the assignment of numbers (or other sym-

[7] For some general treatments of scaling as well as specific illustrations of scales see S. S. Stevens, "Mathematics, Measurement, and Psychophysics," in S. S. Stevens (ed.), *Handbook of Experimental Psychology* (New York: Wiley, 1951), pp. 1–49; Charles M. Bonjean et al., *Sociological Measurement: An Inventory of Scales and Indices* (San Francisco: Chandler, 1967); Delbert C. Miller, *Handbook of Research Design and Social Measurement,* 2nd ed. (New York: David McKay, 1970); and Marvin E. Shaw and Jack M. Wright, *Scales for the Measurement of Attitudes* (New York: McGraw-Hill, 1967).

bols) to a property of objects in order to impart some of the characteristics of numbers to the property in question. The calibrations on a
thermometer indicate numbered degrees (whether Fahrenheit, centigrade, or Kelvin). When the temperature of a given entity is measured,
a conclusion is reached as to the assignment of a given number of
degrees to the temperature (a property) of that entity. Because of the
effectiveness of the thermometer as a scaling instrument, both the order
characteristics of numbers (2 is larger than 1, 3 is larger than 2, and so on)
and such characteristics as the additivity of units $(1 + 1 = 2, 2 + 1 = 3,$
and so on) are imparted to temperature (the property being measured).

Is it necessary to impart the characteristics of numbers to a given
property? Is it not true that the phenomenon already has these properties?
The answer is that phenomena are organized by human beings. Thus, it
is not the phenomena that have the characteristics of numbers ready-
made but the human beings who measure properties of phenomena in
such a way that the characteristics of numbers may be imparted to these
properties. In each case, it is a property that receives these characteristics
(for example, quantity, length, weight, temperature, and so on). In each
case, it is a specific human invention that makes it possible to impart
some of the characteristics of numbers to the properties of objects.
Reliable and precise spring scales may be used to measure weight, for
example, but the spring scale had to be invented first.

Once such a device is invented, there is no guarantee that it will actually
impart some of the characteristics of numbers to the properties being
measured. If, for example, the spring scale pointer or the fluid inside the
thermometer varied erratically, we would not be able to measure the
weight or temperature of entities in such a way that each property could
be ordered or added.

If liquids are being combined, for example, the property or variable of
volume does not necessarily have the characteristics of additivity. Two
liquids may chemically react with one another and the volume of the two
together may differ markedly from the arithmetic sum of the initial volume
of each.

An example, which is generally of greater interest to the behavioral
scientist, has to do with the measurement of values. In measuring monetary goals, for example, although we can add the quantity of money, such
additions do not generally present accurate increments of value to the
individual. To a very wealthy man, an increment of $5,000 over his present
yearly income may not be very important, whereas such an increment for
an individual with a salary of $4,000 per year would almost invariably
constitute a goal of great value. Behavioral scientists are presently en-
gaged in attempting to measure values in such a way that the characteristic of additivity is retained (see Chapter 12). If they are successful, it
will be possible to develop more accurate propositions that incorporate
the concept *value*.

SCALING PROCEDURES AND STRATEGIES

Once it is understood that the characteristics of numbers are not automatically inherent in phenomena, and once the importance of imparting such characteristics is understood, we may next inquire as to procedures for accomplishing this. Scaling procedures, as has been noted, are a means of imparting such characteristics as order and additivity to various properties of phenomena.

The number system we use was developed in such a way that the integers would have such characteristics as order and additivity. The number system is built around a set of axioms from which theorems are derived. The same is true of plane geometry. Neither number theory nor plane geometry, however, can be effectively applied to nature unless the axioms hold true for natural phenomena. Thus, plane geometry "works" on a plane surface; that is, propositions such as the Pythagorean theorem predict quite accurately, because the axioms of plane geometry seem to be true for a plane surface. The axioms of plane geometry, however, do not hold true for the surface of a sphere. In the same way, if the axioms of number theory do not hold for a given property of phenomena, we cannot expect to be able to apply its theorems to the property in question. On the other hand, if the axioms are true for the given property, then we can make use of the theorems.

It seems, then, that in order to impart various characteristics of numbers to a given property of phenomena, it is necessary that the axioms of number theory hold true for the property in question. This is not an all-or-none affair, however. Just as no proposition about nature can be validated with absolute certainty, so it is true that the validity of the axioms of number theory cannot be proved with certainty. Scaling procedures vary in the degree of attention given to testing these axioms, and this variation reflects different strategies of measurement. The differences in measurement strategy are similar to the different approaches to testing reliability, validity, or scale properties of the measure before using it in testing propositions.

Each approach involves a possible gain and a possible loss. By choosing to perfect instruments for measurement before using them, the results of the investigation may be more impressive within the context of justification. The possible loss here is the delay involved in perfecting the instruments and, in a more extreme version of this strategy, the neglect of the kinds of phenomena for which it is difficult to develop reliable, precise, and apparently valid measurements. If he proceeds before the instruments have been perfected, the investigator may get erroneous findings, but the possible gain is an immediate increase in his knowledge and the opportunity to utilize this knowledge to improve the instruments. Between these two choices, of course, there exists a whole range of alternatives. Whichever choice is made by the investigator, he would do well to take into account the possible loss involved and attempt to compensate for it as best he can. Thus, if he proceeds to use a given measurement of unknown validity, reliability, and precision, he might give priority to the further development of the measurement on the basis of his research. On the other hand, if he proceeds to develop the validity, reliability, and precision of a given measurement, he might make certain that the measurement is actually used in the development and testing of propositions as soon as possible.

EXERCISES

1. Select a measurement for a given concept which you wish to validate. Make use of (a) face-validation procedures, (b) criterion-validation procedures, and (c) construct-validation procedures. In this process of validation, did you implicitly define a problem? If yes, what is it?

2. If scaling procedures enable the researcher to use properties of numbers in dealing with phenomena, of what use are such properties in behavioral science investigations?

3. In what ways can research on the validity and reliability of measurements be helpful, and in what ways detrimental, to progress within the context of discovery?

ANNOTATED REFERENCES

CICOUREL, AARON V. *Method and Measurement in Sociology*. New York: The Free Press, 1964. Cicourel criticizes dominant approaches to measurement from the framework of ethnomethodology. The questions that he raises are basic ones, and they help him to understand the enormous limitations of existing methodology.

CRONBACH, LEE J., and PAUL E. MEEHL. "Construct Validity in Psychological Tests," *Psychological Bulletin,* **52** (1955), 281–302. The authors present a detailed rationale for construct-validation procedures and include a discussion of their relation to the philosophy of science. Their approach does not merely help to link measurement with theory, it provides the basis for a general research strategy which we shall take up in Section 12.4.

MILLER, DELBERT C. *Handbook of Research Design and Social Measurement,* 2nd ed. New York: David McKay, 1970. The author has put together the kind of book which includes a great deal of specific information about scales and sources of data. He states that "the purpose of this handbook is to assist the social science researcher in finding information he needs quickly and in brief form when he is designing and conducting research."

CHAPTER 11 Nominal and Ordinal Scales

11.1 THE DISCOVERY OF CONCEPTS

FACTOR ANALYSIS

Little is scientifically established about the process of effective conceptualization, although it seems likely that our knowledge of it will increase. One reconstructed logic of discovery that has been put forward is called *factor analysis*. This technique has been widely used in the fields of psychology and education, especially in the testing or measurement of various types of abilities and aptitudes. The theory on which this technique is based may best be stated within the context of such tests, although the technique itself is quite general and may be applied to many types of data. Fruchter states this theory as follows: "A basic assumption of factor analysis is that a battery of intercorrelated variables has common factors running through it and that the scores of an individual can be represented more economically in terms of these reference factors. An individual's score on a test is dependent upon two things: the particular abilities assessed by the test, and the amount of each of these abilities possessed by the examinee."[1]

Factor analysis is based on measures of association, the Pearsonian product–moment correlation coefficient (henceforth referred to as the correlation coefficient) being most frequently used.[2] We may view the correlation between two given variables to be a measure of the degree to which they are associated with one another, in the sense of Mill's *method of concomitant variations*. Thus, a highly positive correlation coefficient (the maximum is 1.0) would be produced if, in relating income to age, income were observed to increase with increases in age. A correlation near 0 would indicate that no relationship between income and age existed. A highly negative correlation (the minimum is −1.0) would indicate that income decreases with increases in age. In the previously

---

[1] Benjamin Fruchter, *Introduction to Factor Analysis* (Princeton, N.J.: Van Nostrand 1954), p. 44.

[2] Whereas some investigators feel that Pearsonian coefficients are the only suitable ones on which to perform a factor analysis, others have obtained interesting results using different measures of association.

quoted passage, "a battery of intercorrelated variables" means that each variable is correlated with every other variable. Measures of association are discussed in Section 15.3.

By means of rather involved mathematical techniques, this set of inter-correlations is manipulated so as to produce a number of "common factors"—usually fewer than the number of tests or variables involved in the intercorrelations. Within the context of testing, each factor represents a particular ability assessed by the set of tests. Each test is viewed as assessing this ability to a greater or lesser degree, and the index of this degree is called the *factor loading* of the test. The tests vary in their factor loadings on a given factor and in the number of factors on which they are loaded. Thus, for example, a given test may have the maximum loading of 1.0 on a given factor and loadings of 0.0 on the remaining factors. In this instance, the test provides the best possible measure of the factor in question, but constitutes a very poor measure of any of the other factors. Another test might have a factor loading of 0.5 on several factors and 0.0 on the remaining ones. This indicates that the test provides a fairly good measure of some factors and a very poor measure of the remaining ones.

An individual's score (s) on a given test is equal to the sum of various products: the test's various factor loadings ($a_1, a_2, a_3, a_4 \ldots$) and the amount of each of these abilities he possesses ($x_1, x_2, x_3, x_4 \ldots$). Mathematically, the equation is[3]

$$s = a_1x_1 + a_2x_2 + a_3x_3 + a_4x_4 \ldots$$

Like other techniques that may aid in the measurement process, factor analysis may be evaluated both in terms of the characteristics of the measures it is designed to achieve and in terms of the assumptions or theory implied as to the nature of reality. It provides an objective procedure for developing concepts that may then be scaled—one of the few procedures developed to aid the investigator in formulating concepts. Historically, factor analysis has revolutionized the field of psychological testing by empirically examining the interrelationships or correlations among the items used for a given test. Tests once thought to be made up of relatively homogeneous items with respect to the ability being tested have been found to constitute measures of a number of different factors. This has resulted in the reconceptualization of many tests, the reformulation of the items incorporated in various tests, and the development of new concepts.

---

[3] This equation is for independent (orthogonal) factors where s represents the standard score of the given individual on the given test and x_i is expressed in standard scores.

The possibilities of factor analysis in the context of discovery may be illustrated by the conceptualization of values in a recent study of value statements:[4]

> Value statements were collected from tests of values, personality tests, theoretical treatments of values, and statements made by subjects in group discussions. The resulting pool of 872 items was editorially reduced to 143, with the aim of retaining representation of all value positions. Factor analysis of the 143 items yielded . . . Factor I, *Acceptance of authority* (best item: "Obedience and respect for authority are the most important virtues children should learn"); Factor II, *Need-determined expression vs. value-determined restraint* ("Since there are no values that can be eternal, the only real values are those which meet the needs of the given moment"); Factor III, *Equalitarianism* ("Everyone should have an equal chance and an equal say"); and Factor IV, *Individualism* ("It is the man who stands alone who excites our admiration").[5]

All those items that had high loadings on Factor IV were examined in order to conceptualize this factor to find a name for and a definition or description of it (for example). These items included the following: *To be superior a man must stand alone. It is the man who stands alone who excites our admiration. The rich internal world of ideals, of sensitive feelings, of reverie, of self-knowledge, is man's true home. Whoever would be a man, must be a nonconformist. The individualist is the man who is most likely to discover the best road to a new future.* One thing all these items seem to have in common may be called *individualism,* and in this way a concept is formulated.

Factor analysis, then, provides procedures for the development of concepts, which then may be scaled.[6] Such conceptualization usually takes place before the construction of a particular type of scale, and factor analysis constitutes one of the few empirical procedures for the discovery of concepts. The procedures generally used by investigators are not so elaborate, and the different logics-in-use vary a good deal. Little research has been done on the problem of formulating effective concepts, and thus there are few reconstructed logics (such as factor analysis) available for this purpose. Some investigators, guided by whatever theory they think important, proceed from theory to concepts. Others prefer to immerse themselves in the situation under investigation, and on the basis of some process about which very little is known proceed to construct concepts.

---

[4] Robert F. Bales and Arthur S. Couch, "The Value Profile: A Factor Analysis Study of Value Statements" (mimeo), Harvard University Department of Social Relations.

[5] Ibid., p. 1.

[6] It is also possible to use factor-analysis procedures to place individuals on scales once these concepts have been developed. Each individual receives a score on a given factor which is the product of the loadings of each item or test on this factor and the individual's performance or scores on these items.

Let us now examine the assumptions or theory of factor analysis as to the nature of reality. In particular, how valid is the theory in which the test score of a given individual is seen as a function of the abilities assessed by the test and the amount of each of these abilities possessed by the individual? No definite answer is yet available.

The particular variables incorporated in such a theory would play a large part in determining its effectiveness. The factors produced by factor analysis can be no better than the items on which the analysis is based. Factor analysis may yield factors that are quite trivial for behavioral science, or it might unearth factors that, when measured, lead to the development and testing of important theory.

Alternative theories about test performance might also be put forward. For example, a good deal of social science theory suggests a conception of the personality as dynamic, with emphasis on the fluidity rather than the fixity of traits or abilities. Such theory is often tied to an emphasis on the total situation within which the individual finds himself, including his own definition or conception of it, rather than an exclusive focus on the test instrument within the research situation. Such theories, to the extent that they prove to be correct, suggest the need for changes in the assumptions on which the procedures of factor analysis are based and, consequently, the procedures as well.

Q-TECHNIQUE

One critique of the traditional approach to factor analysis or *R-technique* has been put forward by Stephenson:

> In the past, although it has been little recognized, the concrete study of behavior has depended very largely—in its systematic respects—upon assumptions about *individual differences* and upon the use of large numbers of "cases" as a basis for scientific operations and generalizations. The brilliant and penetrating analyses of famous novelists have been rejected from all scientific concern, because they deal, presumably, with particular cases or events. . . . We prefer the penetrations of the humanists [to the statistical techniques of *factor analysis*] and would like to bring them to heel, like the good hunters they have been, for our scientific purposes.[7]

Stephenson has developed what he calls *Q-technique,* which involves methods similar to those of factor analysis but which are applied to a single individual in order to discover the various factors that explain his behavior. This technique implies that the search for factors on the basis of data from large numbers of individuals tends to obscure an understanding of the dynamics of behavior as it relates to any particular individual. Stephenson's concern "is with far more than the simple opera-

---

[7] William Stephenson, *The Study of Behavior: Q-Technique and Its Methodology* (Chicago: University of Chicago Press, 1953), p. 4.

tions called Q-technique; rather, it is with a comprehensive approach to the study of behavior, where man is at issue as a total thinking and be-having being."[8]

One example of Q-technique which Stephenson provides involves a series of administrations of the Szondi Test[9] to a given individual. This projective test centers on the reactions of the subject to a series of forty-eight photographs of former mental patients—eight each for sadists, hysterics, catatonic schizophrenics, paranoids, depressives, and manics. In the first administration of the test, the subject may be asked to score each photograph, along a range of 0–8, according to how much he likes the individuals pictured. In the second administration, the subject may be asked to rate the photographs with respect to how God-fearing the individuals appear to be. Each time the subject rates the forty-eight photographs he is required to categorize a specific number of photographs within each of the possible scores from 0–8:

	Most Liked							Least Liked	
Score	8	7	6	5	4	3	2	1	0
Frequency	2	4	5	8	10	8	5	4	2 ($n = 48$)

In this manner, two sets of scores may be obtained for the forty-eight photographs. Additional sets may be obtained through the introduction of other characteristics—such as handsomeness, health, and age—in subsequent administrations of the test. The scores on each administration of the test are then correlated with the scores received on other adminis-trations of the test. In other words, instead of using the scores of a number of individuals on a series of items, *Q-technique* utilizes the scores of one individual on a series of items having to do with a number of different "conditions of instruction." Thus, the scores under each different con-dition of instruction in *Q*-technique substitute for the scores of different individuals in traditional factor analysis. Consequently, a set of correla-tions of the scores between each administration and every other adminis-tration may be produced, and common factors may be extracted in the same way as they are in traditional factor analysis. These factors, how-ever, refer to aspects of a given individual as manifested over a sequence of different conditions of instruction; they do not refer to underlying properties which a number of items may have in common.

Q-technique is subject to the same kinds of assumptions or theory as traditional factor analysis (for example, that a given score is a function of

[8] Ibid., p. 7.
[9] S. Deri, *Introduction to the Szondi Test* (New York: Grune and Stratton, 1949).

a sum of products). The derivation of factors from the scores of a number of different individuals, however, differs considerably from their derivation from the scores of one individual over a number of different occasions. The latter procedure provides a closer view of human behavior as a product of the individual's own definition of the situation. Like *R*-technique, *Q*-technique provides a reconstructed logic for the discovery of concepts, and these concepts may subsequently be scaled in various ways.

In the field of psychology there is some controversy over the status of *Q*-technique. It has been classified by some individuals as merely a variation of traditional factor analysis. Stephenson, however, maintains that this is not true, and that the differences between the two methods imply important differences in psychological, logical, and methodological principles.

LATENT-STRUCTURE ANALYSIS

Another procedure, similar to factor analysis and Stephenson's *Q*-technique in that it provides a reconstructed logic for the discovery of concepts and consequently may lead to the development of scales of various types, is *latent-structure analysis*. "The basic postulate is that there exists a set of latent classes, such that the manifest relationship between any two or more items on a questionnaire can be accounted for by the existence of these latent classes and by these alone. This implies that any item has two components—one which is associated with latent classes and one which is specific to the item."[10]

This method has not yet come into widespread use, so it is not yet possible to evaluate its utility. One feature of latent-structure analysis is its focus on probability theory as a means of inferring the relationships between "manifest" data (that is, the actual responses of individuals) and "latent" categories. According to Lazarsfeld: "The model of latent structure analysis permits us to be more precise about how these inferences are made; it brings out the assumptions implied in various measurement procedures. In developing the model, we shall find it useful to incorporate the notion of probability mechanisms into a more elaborate scheme."[11]

Latent-structure analysis may prove to be of particular value in bringing to light a systematic set of assumptions or propositions about the probabilistic relationships between manifest data and latent structures. By exposing these assumptions or propositions about the measurement

[10] S. Stouffer et al., *Measurement and Prediction* (Princeton, N.J.: Princeton University Press, 1950), p. 19.

[11] Paul F. Lazarsfeld, "A Conceptual Introduction to Latent Structure Analysis," in P. Lazarsfeld (ed.), *Mathematical Thinking in the Social Sciences* (New York: Free Press, 1954), p. 359. See also Paul F. Lazarsfeld and Neil Henry, *Latent Structure Analysis* (Boston: Houghton Mifflin, 1968).

process, it may lead to a more thorough understanding of the process itself. Lazarsfeld expresses it:

> The purpose of latent structure analysis is to provide mathematical models by which the various uses of itemized tests can be related to each other. The main purpose of the model is to bring out the assumptions which are implicit in this type of "measurement". . . . it is claimed that latent structure analysis puts practices and discussions in the measurement field into reasonable axiomatic form, and that its axioms permit algebraic operations which lead to hitherto unobserved relationships and suggest more precise meanings of the notion of measurement in the social sciences.[12]

11.2 NOMINAL SCALES

Scaling has been defined as a procedure for the assignment of words or numbers (or other symbols) to a property of objects in order to impart some of the characteristics of numbers to the property in question. One of the elementary characteristics of numbers is that each number is unique, that is, it provides a different "name" that might be used to distinguish one property of objects from other properties. This characteristic is imparted to a property of objects when the property is broken up into categories that may be used to classify the objects. Thus, if we consider human beings as having the property of sex, we may form the categories of *male* and *female* and proceed to classify human beings in this way. In this example, the words *male* and *female* provide names for the two categories, and the categories constitute a nominal scale of the property of sex. To the extent that uniqueness has been achieved, a given human being could not be ambiguously classified as *either male or female*.

The characteristics of nominal scales have been described as follows: "Two classes which are different with respect to the variable or quality being 'measured' shall not bear the same name; two individual objects which are the same with respect to this quality shall not be placed in classes bearing different names."[13] For example, individuals with the quality of maleness are not placed in the same category as individuals with the quality of femaleness, whereas two individuals with the quality of maleness (or femaleness) are not placed in categories with different names.

This is neither more nor less than the kind of classification that is quite common in ordinary language. Classifications, such as those governing colors or days of the week, for example, in which the different categories

---

[12] Lazarsfeld, "A Conceptual Introduction to Latent Structure Analysis," op. cit., p. 349.

[13] Virginia L. Senders, *Measurement and Statistics* (New York: Oxford University Press, 1958), p. 52.

or classes do not overlap, constitute a nominal scale. On the other hand, classifications with overlapping categories (for example, Protestant, Unitarian, Episcopalian) do not provide a nominal scale. Not only are nominal scales discrete, they are usually (though not necessarily) inclusive. Thus, a nominal scale for Protestantism would usually include all the Protestant denominations, whereas a nominal scale for political affiliations within the United States would generally provide categories for the minor parties as well as the major ones. Even if the minor parties were lumped together under a category called *other*, all individuals within the domain of political affiliation would still be classified. Like other scales, nominal scales are the result of a measurement process and it is well to view them in this context. The categories or classes are, to a degree, abstract, and their use in research depends on the development and use of measures or operational definitions of them. The categories and the properties or variables with which they are involved vary in scope. Thus, for example, the numerous Protestant denominations, or the different political affiliations within the United States, have considerably less scope than the categories with respect to sex. The difference in scope here pertains not only to the number of individuals each set of categories would include but also to the time dimension. Presumably, human beings have been differentiated into males and females since their origin and will continue to be differentiated in the future, but the denominations within Protestantism and the political sector of the United States have changed in the past and will probably continue to do so in the future.

It is also important to evaluate nominal scales with respect to systematic import. In the field of biology, nominal scales with respect to sex have a great deal of systematic import because there are many variables or characteristics associated with or related to sex. Each sex has many unique attributes or characteristics, and these relationships help to provide theories, explanations, and predictions for a wide variety of biological phenomena.

Although nominal scales may seem quite simple and straightforward, nevertheless difficulties are involved in such classifications. This is obvious if, first of all, we bear in mind that such scales are results of a measurement process that has all the usual difficulties with respect to the establishment of reliability, validity, scope, and systematic import. In addition, however, there are the particular problems associated with the attempt to impart the characteristic of uniqueness possessed by numbers to classes or categories of a given property or variable. Let us take, as an example, a classification of societies into *sacred* and *secular* ones, with the categories referring to differences in traditionalism. As in many nominal-scale classifications, there is the problem of what to do with the borderline cases. If these cases are assigned to one or the other of the two categories, there tends to be a certain degree of arbitrariness, for such cases might just as well be assigned to one category as to the other. The same kind of problem might arise in an interview situation in which the respondent is asked to choose the major political party he most favors. A given individual may equally favor both the Democratic and the Republican parties and he may resent being forced to make a choice he feels is not an accurate representation of his true orientation.

The problem here seems to be that the nominal scale is not sensitive enough to take into account the various gradations within a given category, and the development of scales with more of the characteristics of numbers would seem to be required. Thus, for example, sociologists generally have conceived of a continuum with the sacred society at one pole and the secular society at the other. This can also be done with respect to political orientation, with an extremely favorable view of the Democratic party at one end of the continuum and an extremely favorable view of the Republican party at the other. Such refinements do not guarantee that the resulting data will have systematic import, but they do increase the precision of the measurement and thus provide the potential for doing a great deal more with it.

11.3   ORDINAL SCALES [14]

AXIOMS FOR SIMPLE ORDER

Whereas the characteristic of numbers imparted by nominal scales to properties or variables of objects is uniqueness, ordinal scales have to do with the order relationships manifested by numbers. Thus, 1 is less than 2, 2 is less than 3, and so on, with the numbers indicating rank in this context. If individuals were lined up in such a way that their height increases from the front to the back of the line, then their height (the property in question) might be ranked by assigning a 1 to the first in line, a 2 to the second, and so on. These numbers should not be assumed to imply anything more than a rank order. For example, the difference in height between Individual 2 and Individual 1 may be much greater than that between Individual 3 and Individual 2. In addition, Individual 4 is certainly not four times as tall as Individual 1.

The assignment of ranks in terms of height is justified by the statement that the *individuals are lined up in such a way that their height increases from the front to the back of the line.* In actual research, however, no one tells the investigator that real phenomena are rank-ordered and that he is therefore justified in assigning ranks to objects in respect to a given

---

[14] Axioms for simply ordered and partially ordered collections will be taken up in this section. One additional type of ordering applied by behavioral scientists is the ordered metric scale. See C. H. Coombs, "Theory and Methods of Social Measurements," in L. Festinger and D. Katz (eds.), *Research Methods in the Behavioral Sciences* (New York: Holt, 1953), pp. 477–81.

property. The property may not, in fact, be a unitary one and thus it may not be possible to rank the objects so that they have the same characteristics as ordered numbers. The investigator is thus presented with two tasks: to order objects with respect to a given property or variable through the assignment of ranks, and to test (insofar as possible) whether the actual phenomena possess the order characteristics of numbers. The same two types of tasks are involved in the development of nominal scales. One can proceed to give names to a number of categories, but it is quite another thing to determine whether objects with the property in question actually do unequivocally fall into one category or another. If there are borderline cases that fall exactly between two categories, or cases that fit equally well into more than one category, then the actual phenomena involved do not have the nominal characteristics of numbers that the investigator hopes to impart to them.

In order to impart various characteristics of numbers to a given property of phenomena, it is necessary that the axioms of number theory hold for the property in question. Scaling procedures vary in the degree of attention given to testing this point. To understand this more fully, let us examine the axioms on which the ordinal characteristics of numbers are based:

> Let C be any collection whose elements we call *points* and which are denoted by small letters $x, y, z, a, b, \ldots$; and let there be given a "binary relation" between the points of C which we denote by $<$ and call *precedes*. Then C is called *simply ordered*, or *linearly ordered*, relative to $<$, if the following axioms [cf. E. Huntington, *The Continuum and Other Types of Serial Order* (Cambridge, Mass.: Harvard University Press, 1917)] hold:
> 1. If x and y are distinct points of C, then
> $x < y$ and/or $y < x$.
> 2. If $x < y$, then x and y are distinct.
> 3. If $x < y$ and $y < z$, then $x < z$.[15]

It should be noted that axioms are stated in very general terms, and this is the source of their great scope. We are then free to attempt to coordinate various types of phenomena with them, that is, test whether or not the axioms hold true when they are applied within a particular context. For example, C may be any collection of numbers, of individuals with different heights, or of individuals who attach different degrees of importance to a given goal or value.

Each of the four types of scales (nominal and ordinal scales are discussed in this chapter; interval and ratio scales will be taken up in Chapter 12) attempts to impart to a given property the characteristics of numbers imparted by the previous scale. Additional characteristics of numbers,

---

[15] Raymond L. Wilder, *Introduction to the Foundations of Mathematics* (New York: Wiley, 1952), pp. 45–46.

however, are involved as well. Thus, the scales form a cumulative hierarchy in terms of the characteristics which they impart. In ordinal scales, the axioms become trivial statements unless there are several "distinct points of C," for the fundamental relationship *precedes* ($<$) is defined in terms of the concept *distinct points*. This concept is quite similar to that of the uniqueness of categories, which was necessary for the development of nominal scales. Thus, ordinal scales are nominal scales as well, for they have distinct or unique points.

Various theorems can be proved by using the axioms as well as the definitions. Thus, we can prove, for example, the theorem that "If x and y are distinct points of C, then not both $x < y$ and $y < x$ hold" by utilizing Axioms 1 and 3. From Axiom 1 we know that there are three possibilities: $x < y$, $y < x$, and both $x < y$ and $y < x$. Axiom 3, however, rules out the third possibility, for if it were true, it would result in a contradiction. To prove this, let us assume that both $x < y$ and $y < x$. According to Axiom 3, if $x < y$ and $y < z$, then $x < z$. Thus, it should hold that if $x < y$ and $y < x$ (substituting x for z), then $x < x$. But this is a contradictory statement because, according to Axiom 2, if $x < y$ then x and y are distinct. But if we substitute x for y within this axiom, then $x < x$ implies that x and x are distinct, which is contradictory. Thus both $x < y$ and $y < x$ cannot be true.

This, of course, is not the only theorem that can be proved on the basis of these axioms. One important theorem has to do with the possibility of establishing a simple order among any given large number of points so that, for example, $x_1 < x_2$, $x_2 < x_3$, $x_3 < x_4$, ... What is involved here is an extension of the "transitivity" idea involved in Axiom 3 (if $x < y$ and $y < z$, then $x < z$) to any larger number of points. In attempting to determine whether these axioms actually do hold true for certain phenomena, it is very often this particular theorem that is tested. If the theorem does not hold, then (by implication) one or more of the axioms from which it was derived do not hold. Thus, for example, if we interpret *point* as *basketball team* and the binary relation *precedes* ($<$) as *invariably loses to*, we may try to establish whether the theorem holds for any given ordering of C (ranking of the set of basketball teams). If the teams are ranked so that $x_1 < x_2$, $x_2 < x_3$, $x_3 < x_4$, $x_4 < x_5$, . . . , then we might examine the data on actual wins and losses to see whether or not this theorem actually holds. Undoubtedly we would find many instances in which the theorem does not hold (for example, if Team x_1 does not lose to Team x_2 even on one occasion, or if Team x_1 does not lose to every other team in a perfectly consistent fashion).

SOME OPTIONS

There are several possible ways out of this dilemma. They seem to boil down to two general approaches: one of them involves dealing only with phenomena that satisfy a stringent set of conditions; the other involves relaxing the stringency of the conditions so that it is possible to deal with a wide range of data. The first approach is cognate to extreme operationism, in that both invoke some particular methodological goal and work toward its achievement as an end in itself rather than as a means to the achievement of theory, explanation, and prediction. This stringent approach to scaling breaks down, as did extreme operationism, because it leads to an inability to apply any scale (even a nominal one) to phenomena with certainty that the axioms will hold. Fundamentally, we do not have the ability to validate *any* proposition about the real world with certainty.

In the broad strategy of a less stringent approach, we may examine four different orientations. One of them is to be conservative about the type of scale one tries to develop for given phenomena. Because, for example, the axioms on which nominal and ordinal scales are based are more easily satisfied than those for interval or ratio scales, researchers with this orientation tend to be involved in the development of the former rather than the latter. By so doing they can be more confident that the scale they develop does in fact satisfy the relevant axioms. Another far less conservative approach focuses on the development of interval and ratio scales in spite of the added difficulties involved in the validation of a more stringent set of axioms. Thus, the less conservative approach generally results in a greater number of only partially tested assumptions about the nature of reality than the more conservative approach. In a third approach, the researcher simply makes an interpretation of terms, such as *precedes,* more in accord with actual situations. For example, rather than interpreting *precedes* as *invariably loses to,* we may interpret it as *loses more than half of the time to.* In this way, it is much easier to locate phenomena that satisfy the axioms. A fourth approach is illustrated by the orientation of Lazarsfeld with respect to latent-structure analysis. Rather than interpreting the terms of the axiom system so as to be able to satisfy the axioms more easily, one can make a point, for example, of investigating why it is that more exacting interpretations do not hold. Thus, Lazarsfeld's approach might be applied to an analysis of a "latent" classification of the teams with respect to ability, and theories incorporating probability laws might be developed to explain and predict the relationship between these latent abilities and the manifest data on wins and losses.

SUMMATED RATINGS

Many specific procedures for the construction of ordinal scales have been developed, and among these is the summated scale. Let us suppose, for example, that having unearthed the factor of individualism as one of the important values affecting behavior, we desire to rank individuals with respect to the importance of this particular value for each. One simple procedure is to give a score of 1 for each "agree" answer and a score of 0 for each "disagree" answer, as illustrated below:

	Agree	Disagree
1. To be superior a man must stand alone.	1	0
2. It is the man who stands alone who excites our admiration.	1	0
3. The rich internal world of ideals, of sensitive feelings, of reverie, of self-knowledge, is man's true home.	1	0
4. Whoever would be a man must be a nonconformist.	1	0
5. The individualist is the man who is most likely to discover the best road to a new future.	1	0

In developing an over-all score for a given individual, a logical procedure would be to sum the scores of that individual on each of the five items. Thus, an individual who agreed with all the items would have a score of 5, whereas someone who disagreed with all would have a score of 0. This procedure of summing scores over a number of different items gives rise to the term *summated scales.* It provides us with a means for ordering individuals in relation to one another. Ties will occur quite frequently in this example, however, for the only possible scores are 0, 1, 2, 3, 4, and 5, and there may be many more individuals than these six possible scores.

This is a variant of simple order, namely, a partial ordering of individuals. The definitions and axioms relating to a partially ordered collection may be stated as follows:

If C is any collection and $\leq$ a binary relation between elements of C, then C is called *partially ordered* with respect to $\leq$ if the following axioms hold:
1. For every element x of C, $x \leq x$.
2. If $x \leq y$ and $y \leq x$, then x and y denote the same element of C.
3. If $x \leq y$ and $y \leq z$, then $x \leq z$.[16]

These axioms thus allow for large numbers of ties, for the binary relation $\leq$ may be interpreted to mean *precedes* or *is tied with.* In a simple ordering, by contrast, no ties may occur, for the situation would be the following: For any two distinct points, one must precede the other. In the example cited, individuals with the same total score are tied with one another, whereas simple-order relationships are designated among individuals whose total scores differ.

As with any scale, one important question is not whether the numbers that are assigned to the different objects or individuals satisfy the axioms on which the scale is based, but whether the underlying property that is

[16] Ibid., p. 49.

scaled does so. This distinction is quite easy to overlook, for most individuals automatically tend to assign the characteristics of numbers to any items that are numbered. But how much is one quart, two pears, four planes, and seven ships? An answer of 14 has little meaning because it does not specify any specific property being totaled. In the same way, let us assume that in developing a given summated scale, we happen to utilize several items that have nothing to do with the property measured by the remaining items but, rather, some other property. This may easily occur if the concept being measured is fairly abstract, and if no prior analysis (for example, factor analysis) was utilized to discover those items that are interrelated. As a matter of fact, most summated scales developed by social scientists are ad hoc in the sense that the items involved have not been subjected to any prior analysis. There is no way of determining, on the basis of this summated rating procedure, whether items measuring different properties are incorporated into a given summated scale. The fact that the summed scores for the different individuals would constitute a partial ordering merely shows that numbers have the characteristics of numbers, and this was known before the investigation began. It is only when an ordering of the designated property has been achieved that something new has been added. Thus, an important limitation of this summated rating procedure is that it does not in itself provide evidence that the property under investigation is a unitary one and that the axioms for partial order hold for this property when it is scaled by this procedure.

Another way of looking at this deficiency is to examine the different ways in which any given score may be obtained. A score of 2, for example, may be produced in any of ten different ways: "agree" on Items 1 and 2 and "disagree" on Items 3, 4, and 5; "agree" on Items 1 and 3, and "disagree" on Items 2, 4, and 5; and so on. If as many as twenty items were involved, there would be a total of 190 different ways of obtaining a score of 2. Thus, individuals who obtain a given total score in very different ways are treated as tied in their ranking on the property in question. They may in fact be so tied, but it would seem to be quite a simple matter for the questions to vary sufficiently from one another so that different combinations of them selected by individuals imply differences among these individuals on the property in question.

LIKERT PROCEDURES

A more elaborate technique for obtaining summated ratings has been developed by Likert.[17] It may be outlined as follows:

1. It includes five categories for responses: "strongly agree," "agree," "undecided," "disagree," "strongly disagree."

[17] G. Murphy and R. Likert, *Public Opinion and the Individual* (New York: Harper, 1937).

2. Statements are classified into those which are favorable and those which are unfavorable, and approximately • the same number of statements of each type is utilized.
3. For the favorable statements, the weights given to "strongly agree," "agree," "undecided," "disagree," and "strongly disagree" are 4, 3, 2, 1, and 0, respectively. For unfavorable statements, the weights are 0, 1, 2, 3, and 4, respectively; thus, agreement with favorable statements and disagreement with unfavorable statements are treated as equivalent.
4. A large number of statements are administered to a group of respondents who are representative of those for whom the questionnaire is being constructed.
5. The responses are analyzed to determine which items discriminate best between the high-scoring individuals and the low-scoring individuals. Thus, for example, items to which high scorers and low scorers respond similarly are eliminated. This is known as an *item-analysis procedure.*

The Likert procedure for obtaining summated ratings provides some indirect evidence as to the existence of a partial order in the property itself. The item-analysis procedure increases the degree of homogeneity or internal consistency in the set of items. Although this provides no guarantee that only one property is being measured by the set of items, it seems likely that it does serve to eliminate many of those items that provide measures of different properties. It is still quite possible that the final set of items involves a number of different properties. Thus, for example, a given item may be accepted after an item analysis, but it may be either a cause or an effect of the property being measured and may not constitute a measure of the property.

CUMULATIVE SCALES

Cumulative scaling procedures focus directly on testing whether or not the axioms for simple order hold for the property under investigation. To the extent that such evidence can be obtained, the investigator can be more confident that he is dealing with a single or unitary property versus a mixture of properties. Let us return to the basketball example and assume that there are five teams: *A, B, C, D,* and *E.* If we now interpret $<$ as *invariably loses to,* then we can specify which teams must lose to which other teams in order for a given simple order among the teams to hold. We may illustrate this by setting up a matrix in which the five teams appear as both rows and columns and in which any cell represents the outcome of basketball games between the "row" team and the "column" team. Let us further specify that a plus appearing in a given cell indicates that the "column" team invariably loses to the "row" team, while a minus indicates that the "row" team invariably loses to the "column" team. Then, if one example of a simple order actually exists with respect to the property of losing or winning basketball games, the following outcomes will occur:

	A	B	C	D	E
A		+	+	+	+
B	−		+	+	+
C	−	−		+	+
D	−	−	−		+
E	−	−	−	−	

The series of pluses in the first row indicates that Teams B, C, D, and E invariably lose to Team A. In the second row we see that Teams C, D, and E invariably lose to Team B and that Team B invariably loses to Team A (the minus score). This latter piece of information is not a new statement, for the information in the first row indicated the same thing. In fact, all of the minus entries repeat the information transmitted by corresponding plus entries. In the third row, we find that Team C invariably loses to Teams A and B, while Teams D and E invariably lose to Team C, and so on. No entries appear when a team is paired against itself.

We may now examine these relationships to see whether or not the three axioms that lead to a simply ordered collection are satisfied. Axiom 1, as interpreted in this example, specifies that for any pair of teams—say, x and y—x must invariably lose to y, or y must invariably lose to x, or both. The fact that the matrix is filled up with pluses and minuses indicates that an invariable loss relationship holds for any pair of teams (except for the blank cells, which do not represent instances in which two teams are involved).

Axiom 2 specifies that if x invariably loses to y, then x and y are different teams. In looking at the matrix, we see that all of the "invariable loss relationships" involve different teams. As for the blank cells, no invariable loss relationships are involved here, so it does not matter that the teams are not separate or distinct.

Axiom 3 specifies a principle of transitivity: if x invariably loses to y and y invariably loses to z, then x invariably loses to z. Starting with the relationships among Teams A, B, and C, we note that C invariably loses to B and B invariably loses to A, and we also note that C invariably loses to A. Examining the relationships among B, D, and E, we find that E invariably loses to D, D invariably loses to B, and E invariably loses to B. Indeed, for each of the ten possible sets of three teams (ABC, ABD, ABE, ACD, ACE, ADE, BCD, BCE, BDE, CDE) this transitivity relationship holds.

Because we can show that the three axioms for a simply ordered collection hold with respect to the property of outcomes of games among Teams *A, B, C, D,* and *E,* we are able to rank these teams 1, 2, 3, 4, and 5, respectively, with respect to this property. Cumulative scaling provides the kind of data that permit the investigator to test each of the axioms that enable us to designate a given collection as a simply ordered one. In this respect it differs from summated ratings, in which, at best, the evidence for the truth of the axioms is extremely partial and indirect. It should be noted that the interpretation of the binary relation < need not be as stringent as the one adopted for illustrative purposes, that is, *invariably loses to.* If such an interpretation were adopted, we would rarely be able to find a set of basketball teams for which the axioms would be true. An interpretation of <, which would permit us to find such basketball teams more easily, might be *loses more than half of the time to.*

SCALE ANALYSIS

The major technique used to develop cumulative scales on the basis of items in questionnaires or interview schedules is called *scalogram analysis* or *scale analysis*—a procedure developed by Louis Guttman.[18] The kind of pattern that should be illustrated by items in a questionnaire in order that we may be able to rank them without violating any of the axioms for simple order is the same as the illustration provided for basketball teams. In the present example, we are dealing with a collection of items in a questionnaire, and the property involved is fear symptoms. We shall interpret the binary relation < to mean, in the context Item 1 < Item 2, that *if any individual responds positively* (for example, *yes* versus *no*) *to Item 1, he invariably responds positively to Item 2.*

In the following matrix, positive responses are indicated by a plus while negative responses are indicated by a minus. The rows represent groupings of respondents, each of which has a different pattern of responses. The columns represent the different items being tested to determine whether or not a simple order exists among them. There are nine items, and each respondent or grouping of respondents follows a pattern of pluses and minuses, depending on the response given to each item. The respondents were soldiers; the query, their physical reactions to the dangers of battle when they were under fire. The following items were tested as to the existence of a simple order.

1. Urination in pants.
2. Losing control of the bowels.

---

[18] Stouffer et al., op. cit.; for some additional developments of scale analysis, see Matilda White Riley, John W. Riley, Jr., and Jackson Toby, *Sociological Studies in Scale Analysis* (New Brunswick, N.J.: Rutgers University Press, 1954).

3. Vomiting.
4. Feeling of weakness or faintness.
5. Feeling of stiffness.
6. Feeling sick at the stomach.
7. Shaking or trembling all over.
8. Sinking feeling of the stomach.
9. Violent pounding of the heart.[19]

We may now specify that the following pattern of responses would indicate that these items are simply ordered:

Groupings of Respondents				Item Number				
	1	2	3	4	5	6	7	8	9
1	+	+	+	+	+	+	+	+	+
2	−	+	+	+	+	+	+	+	+
3	−	−	+	+	+	+	+	+	+
4	−	−	−	+	+	+	+	+	+
5	−	−	−	−	+	+	+	+	+
6	−	−	−	−	−	+	+	+	+
7	−	−	−	−	−	−	+	+	+
8	−	−	−	−	−	−	−	+	+
9	−	−	−	−	−	−	−	−	+
10	−	−	−	−	−	−	−	−	−

We may examine these patterns of responses to determine whether or not the three axioms which lead to a simply ordered collection are satisfied. Axiom 1 specifies that, for any pair of items—say x and y—either x is + and y is +, or x is − and y is +, or x is − and y is −, or x is + and y is −. Thus, any combination of + and − for any pair of items satisfies Axiom 1, and all that is required is that every cell of the matrix has either a + or a −. Axiom 2 simply requires that if, for example, Item 1 < Item 2, then Items 1 and 2 are distinct. Because all the items are distinct in this example, this axiom is satisfied.

To test the transitivity axiom, we may start by examining Items 1, 2, and 3. We may note that Item 1 < Item 2, because (1) for the first grouping of respondents, individuals who rate Item 1 positively also rate Item 2 positively; (2) one cannot maintain that Item 2 < Item 1, for the second groupings of respondents rate Item 2 positively and Item 1 negatively. We may also note that Item 2 < Item 3, because (1) the first two groupings

[19] This scale of fear symptoms is not just a hypothetical example, but was actually found to form a scale according to the various criteria of scale analysis. Originally ten items were tested and one of them ("cold sweat") did not fit into the scale. Stouffer et al., op. cit., pp. 13–14, 140–42.

of respondents rate both Items 2 and 3 positively; and (2) the third group-
ing rates Item 3 positively and Item 2 negatively, indicating that it is not
true that Item 3 < Item 2. We also find, in accordance with Axiom 3, that
Item 1 < Item 3, because (1) the first grouping of respondents rates both
Items 1 and 3 positively; and (2) it is not true that Item 3 < Item 1, for
the second and third groupings of respondents rate Item 3 positively and
Item 1 negatively. Thus the transitivity axiom holds for Items 1, 2, and 3.
There are a total of eighty-four different combinations of three items,
and it may be observed that the transitivity axiom holds for each of these.

The response patterns just discussed are those that would indicate
perfect consistency with the axioms for simple order. Even so, one would
not be able to obtain a simple order for the *respondents,* assuming that
more than ten respondents were involved, since there would be one or
more ties. However, a partial order would be obtainable. Thus, the groupings of respondents numbered from 1 through 10 may be used as a partial
ordering for the respondents. Individuals within a given grouping are
undifferentiated with respect to response pattern, but individuals from
different groupings are in an ordinal relationship with respect to one
another.

The chief contribution of *scale analysis* seems to be that it focuses
attention on a direct test of the axioms for simple order. This is important
evidence that the concept is a unitary one. Most scales that have been
developed are not perfect, although there are some examples of perfect
scales.[20] Thus, for example, it is usually the case that a certain proportion
of individuals within each grouping of respondents departs from what
may be called *the perfect scale type* for that grouping. Within scale analysis
these departures are treated as errors, and a relatively arbitrary criterion
is utilized to determine whether the proportion of errors among the total
responses is too great to maintain that the property is *scalable.* Thus, with
this scaling technique it is possible to reject the hypothesis that a series
of items can yield an ordinal scale of a given property. In Guttman's
terminology, this would indicate that the underlying property or concept
is not *unidimensional.*

Although the Guttman approach does actually test the axioms for
simple order, the question may be raised as to whether even the achievement of perfect scale patterns indicates conclusively that the underlying
property is unidimensional, that is, that not more than one property or
concept is being measured. For example, the different items may be involved in cause-and-effect relationships. In addition, one may actually
have a very poor sample of items with which to test the *unidimensionality*
of the underlying concept. When errors occur in a scale, these questions

---

[20] See, for example, the scales of Hawaiian and Eskimo kinship terminology, with coefficients
of reproducibility of 1.00, developed by Ira R. Buchler, "A Formal Account of the Hawaiian—
Eskimo—Type Kinship Terminologies," *Southwestern Journal of Anthropology,* **20** (1964),
286–318.

become even more serious. Within the context of Stephenson's work, an attempt to obtain and scale concepts that are unidimensional for a given group of respondents is less fruitful than procedures wherein the investigator explores the frame of reference or definition of the situation of a given individual. One critique sometimes made of scale analysis is that the results may vary greatly from one group of respondents to another; a series of items that scales for one group may not for another. Of course, this apparent deficiency may be turned into an advantage if it serves to direct inquiries into the factors that produce these differences.

Another important contribution provided by the technique of scale analysis is that, to the extent that the proportion of errors is small, we are able to reproduce the responses of a given individual on each of the items knowing only which grouping of respondents (or scale type) he is in. If we know, for example, that a given respondent is in the fifth grouping on the fear-symptoms scale, we can then predict with fairly good accuracy that individual's response to each of the nine items. This compares very favorably with the summated-rating techniques, in which any given score may be derived from many different combinations of items.

The procedure for testing whether a given set of items is scalable has been greatly simplified since the advent of punched-card equipment for data processing. It may be illustrated with hypothetical data for three of the items in the fear-symptoms scale: vomiting, feeling sick at the stomach, and violent pounding of the heart. We may distinguish the following steps, assuming that these data have already been punched into cards and that responses are limited to two alternatives: yes $(+)$ and no $(-)$:[21]

1. Obtain the distribution for the entire sample of $+$ and $-$ responses for each of the items and calculate the percentage of positive responses for each item.
2. Label the item with the smallest percentage of positive responses as 1; that with the next larger percentage as 2; and that with the largest as 3. Let us assume that the distribution was as follows:

	+	−	Total	Percentage +
Item 1. Vomiting	120	150	270	44
Item 2. Feeling sick at the stomach	160	110	270	59
Item 3. Violent pounding of the heart	180	90	270	67

[21] It is easier to develop scales using items that initially have more than two alternatives, for one then has the choice of dichotomizing the responses to a given item in several different ways. Of course, this introduces additional arbitrariness into the procedure, making it easier to obtain evidence for scalability and providing less opportunity for rejecting the hypothesis of scalability.

3. Start with Item 1 and sort the cards into those with positive and those with negative responses.

4. Take those cards which were positive on Item 1 and sort them into those which are positive and those which are negative on Item 2. Do the same for those cards which were negative on Item 1, sorting them into the positives and negatives on Item 2. In this way one obtains four separate piles of cards: those positive on both Items 1 and 2 $(++)$, those positive on Item 1 and negative on Item 2 $(+-)$, those negative on Item 1 and positive on Item 2 $(-+)$, and those negative on both $(--)$.

5. Continue this procedure for Item 3 for each of the four piles of cards separately. Thus, take the $++$ pile and sort it into those which are positive and those which are negative on Item 3, thus forming two piles out of the original $++$ pile: $+++$ and $++-$. Do the same for the $+-$ pile, forming $+-+$ and $+--$. Continue in this way for the original $-+$ pile and the $--$ pile separately, forming $--+$, $-+-$, $--+$, and $---$. Thus one ends up with a total of eight piles of cards, each of which has a different pattern of responses.

6. Count the number of cards in each of the piles. The following chart is of use in keeping track of the various procedures:

   The first row represents the results of Step 3; the second and third contain the results of Steps 4 and 5. The numbers in parentheses represent the number of cards in each category and are actually needed only for the third row, but recording them for the other rows provides a useful check on the sorting and counting operations. At this point, we may proceed to designate each of the response patterns as either a perfect scale type (S) or as a nonscale type (N). Results are recorded in the bottom row, depending on whether or not they are the same as one of the following perfect scale patterns:

Groupings of Respondents	Item Number		
	1	2	3
1	+	+	+
2	−	+	+
3	−	−	+
4	−	−	−

7. We now proceed to test for scalability, that is, for the existence of a satisfactory scale. One important criterion is the *coefficient of reproducibility*, which represents the degree of accuracy with which we are able to reproduce the responses of individuals if we know only

Item 1

Step	(+) (120)				(−) (150)			
Step 3 (sort on Item 1)	+ (120)				− (150)			
Step 4 (sort on Item 2)	Item 2 (+) ++ (100)		Item 2 (−) +− (20)		Item 2 (+) −+ (60)		Item 2 (−) −− (90)	
Step 5 (sort on Item 3)	Item 3 (+) +++ (90)	Item 3 (−) ++− (10)	Item 3 (+) +−+ (10)	Item 3 (−) +−− (10)	Item 3 (+) −++ (50)	Item 3 (−) −+− (10)	Item 3 (+) −−+ (30)	Item 3 (−) −−− (60)
Step 6 (determine scale and nonscale types)	S	N	N	N	S	N	S	S

in which grouping of respondents they are.[22] The formula for calculating this coefficient is

$$\text{Coefficient of reproducibility} = 1 - \frac{\text{No. of errors}}{\text{No. of questions} \times \text{No. of respondents}}$$

For this example, the number of errors is equal to the sum of the frequencies of respondents in the various nonscale types. Thus, the sum of 10, 10, 10, and 10 is equal to 40. Because there are three questions and a total of 270 respondents, we have

$$\text{Coefficient of reproducibility} = 1 - \frac{40}{3 \times 270} = 1 - .05 = .95$$

The rule widely used for determining whether or not the coefficient of reproducibility is high enough to satisfy the criterion of reproducibility is to conclude that there is evidence for scalability if this coefficient is equal to or greater than .90.[23] Thus, for the present example, we may conclude that evidence has been obtained for the scalability of the property being measured.

8. Guttman postulates other criteria for assessing the scalability of the property or, in his terms, the *universe of content*. One of them has to do with the number of categories into which answers to a given item are divided. In the present example, each of the three items was dichotomized (divided into two categories), but Guttman maintains that it would be preferable to trichotomize some of the items if there are fewer than ten. This would make it more difficult to achieve a coefficient of reproducibility of .90 or greater on the basis of chance.

Another criterion has to do with the percentage of positive responses for each item, which was calculated in Step 1. If perhaps half or more of the items result in percentages of between 40 and 60,

---

[22] The procedure ilustrated here for counting errors and thus determining the coefficient of reproducibility has been developed in a different form by W. H. Goodenough, in "A Technique for Scale Analysis," *Educational and Psychological Measurement,* **4** (1944), 179–90. This tends to be a more stringent approach than the one originally developed by Guttman and thus leads to lower coefficients of reproducibility. These coefficients, however, actually do represent the degree of accuracy with which responses to individual items can be reproduced, according to A. L. Edwards.

[23] A technique for utilizing a statistical test to take some of the arbitrariness out of this procedure is discussed by Leon Festinger, "The Treatment of Qualitative Data by 'Scale Analysis,'" *Psychological Bulletin,* **44** (1947), 149–61. This test also takes into account the number of items involved. See also Guttman's reply to Festinger in L. Guttman, "On Festinger's Evaluation of Scale Analysis," *Psychological Bulletin,* **44** (1947), 451–65.

this criterion is well satisfied. In the present example, where these percentages are 44, 59, and 67, this criterion is satisfied.

A third criterion has to do with the distribution of individuals among the various nonscale types. If any one of these nonscale types has an unusually large proportion of the total number of individuals with nonscale patterns of response, we may question the existence of scalability.

Finally, the number of items used to test for *scalability* is quite important. Guttman originally maintained that the desirable number is ten or more. In actual practice, very few scales with as many as eight items have been developed; four-item and five-item scales are quite common. One approach developed to deal with this smaller number of items so as to preserve intact the various desirable properties of the Guttman scale is known as *H-technique*.[24] It combines certain features of Latent Structure Analysis and Guttman scaling, and it seems to have been utilized successfully in a variety of investigations. Another approach is to utilize the statistical test suggested by Festinger[25] for scales with few items, in order to determine the probability that a high coefficient of reproducibility could have been obtained on the basis of chance alone.

Thus far, with respect to *scale analysis,* we have discussed the method of determining whether a given set of items satisfies the various criteria for scalability, but little has been said about the method for selecting these items in the first place. Guttman's view on this subject may be inferred from the following:

> Scale analysis as such gives no judgment on content; it presumes that the universe of content is already defined. . . . It might serve as an auxiliary argument with respect to content in this special case where there is controversy over but one or two items of a large sample of items in which the remaining items are scalable . . . [but] there must be a cogent initial argument based on content if an item is to be classified in an area. Sheer scalability is not sufficient; an item may happen to scale with an area, and yet not have the content defining the area—it may be a correlative rather than part of the definition.[26]

For Guttman, the primary tack involved in the development of an initial series of items is a conceptual one, and unless this is done any mechanical procedure for locating items cannot be expected to do the job. Edwards and Kilpatrick have developed what they call the *scale-discrimination technique,*[27] which combines some of the techniques de-

---

[24] S. Stouffer, *Social Research to Test Ideas* (New York: Free Press, 1962), pp. 274–89.

[25] Festinger, op. cit.

[26] Stouffer et al., op. cit., p. 85.

[27] A. L. Edwards and F. P. Kilpatrick, "Scale Analysis and the Measurement of Social Attitudes," *Psychometrika,* **13** (1948), 99–114.

veloped by Likert and Thurstone. (See Chapter 10 for a discussion of Thurstone's *method of equal-appearing intervals.*) The technique specifies that one start with a large number of items, selecting only those about which one can obtain agreement among a large number of judges.

A technique called *multiple-scalogram analysis*[28] has been developed which aims at producing as many unidimensional scales as are consistent with the underlying dimensions of the set of items, and providing more quantitative procedures for developing scales and testing for scalability. The procedure is designed for use in conjunction with an electronic computer and is able to handle large numbers of items with ease.

In this chapter we have discussed the two types of scales most widely used by social scientists: nominal and ordinal scales. The two types of scales to be discussed in Chapter 12 utilize more of the properties of numbers and thus more easily lend themselves to the testing of highly systematic or mathematically stated theory.

EXERCISES

1. Compare and contrast factor analysis with inferences from general theory as techniques for the discovery of fruitful concepts.

2. If ordinal scales are definitely superior to nominal scales in the kinds of mathematical properties they enable us to employ in dealing with phenomena, are there any reasons for employing nominal scales at all?

3. For a given concept construct a series of items which could be the basis for a Likert summated-ratings scale, and construct an additional series of items having to do with the same concept as the basis for scale analysis. What are the similarities and differences between your approaches to these two procedures?

4. Discuss the conceptual task of selecting a series of items as the basis for scale analysis. What guidelines can you suggest for the development of scales that are fruitful for the advancement of knowledge?

ANNOTATED REFERENCES

LAZARSFELD, PAUL F., and NEIL W. HENRY. *Latent Structure Analysis.* Boston: Houghton Miffllin Company, 1968. The authors present here the method of latent-structure analysis in sufficient detail and with sufficient examples to guide the student in developing facility with this relatively complex measurement technique. They comment that scale analysis rules out "certain combinations of possible

---

[28] J. C. Lingoes, *Multiple-Scalogram Analysis: A Generalization of Guttman's Scale Analysis.* Unpublished doctoral dissertation, Michigan State University, 1960. See also the brief description presented by E. L. Kelly and J. C. Lingoes in Harold Borko (ed.), *Computer Applications in the Behavioral Sciences* (Englewood Cliffs, N.J.: Prentice-Hall, 1962), pp. 193–95.

response patterns" and thus eliminates "the possibility of gaining a great deal of additional knowledge." It is to this variety of response patterns that they address themselves.

MCKINNEY, JOHN C. *Constructive Typology and Social Theory.* New York:Appleton-Century-Crofts, Inc., 1966. In his introduction, Paul F. Lazarsfeld defines the constructed type as "a purposive, planned selection, abstraction, combination, and (sometimes) accentuation of a set of criteria with empirical referents that serves as a basis for comparison of empirical cases." The volume is replete with theoretical illustrations of constructed types and is suggestive for the context of discovery of nominal scales.

WILDER, RAYMOND L. *Introduction to the Foundations of Mathematics.* New York: John Wiley & Sons, Inc., 1952. The foundations of modern mathematics are presented in a way which is intelligible to any student with an ability for abstract thinking. The topics include the axiomatic method, set theory, the real number system, mathematical logic, intuitionism, formalism, and the cultural setting of mathematics. For a more recent treatment of similar topics see Abraham S. Luchins and Edith H. Luchins, *Logical Foundations of Mathematics for Behavioral Scientists* (New York: Holt, 1965).

CHAPTER 12 Interval and Ratio Scales

12.1 INTERVAL SCALES

INTRODUCTION

The distinction between ordinal and interval scales is that the latter have a constant unit. Consequently, it is possible to perform the operations of additions and substractions on interval scales and come up with meaningful results. If IQ's were characterized by a constant unit, the difference between an IQ of 40 and 80 would be the same as that between 80 and 120. However, this does not in fact seem to be the case. The latter difference lies within the "normal" range, whereas the former distinguishes between an ability to cope with the tasks presented to most individuals and a general inability to do so. This illustrates the difficulties involved in the development of interval scales, even in areas where a great deal of research has been done.

Approaches to scaling vary in the degree of attention given to testing whether the axioms of number theory hold for the phenomena under study. By choosing to improve instruments for measurement before using them in testing propositions, one might be able to gain by an increase in the probability of correct conclusions. The losses might include the delay involved, and the possibility that a less cautious approach might produce the kind of information that could aid in the improvement of the scaling procedure.

The medical student study provides an example of a formulation that is meaningful to the extent that interval scales of the key variables are available. This is because (1) the difference is taken between value scores and scores representing expectations for achieving the corresponding values, and (2) all of these difference scores are then summed. Thus, we have the operations of subtraction and addition involved in the calculation of expected-value deprivation. In that study the primary evidence advanced for the presence of interval scales was indirect. The operations of subtraction and addition were performed, and the meaningfulness of the resultant (EVD) was partially tested by determining its relationship to specialty preferences. Because close relationships were found, as hypothesized, this was taken as partial evidence for the meaningfulness of the mathematical operations and, consequently, the interval properties of the scales. The procedure here is similar to construct validation procedures, where the untried measurement achieves validity to the extent that it yields data that support well-accepted propositions.

PROPERTIES OF INTERVAL SCALES

For a fuller understanding of interval scales, it is necessary to discuss their mathematical properties. If we return to the terminology used in the discussion of ordinal scales, then we let C represent any collection whose elements we call *points*. One set of properties which must be possessed by an interval scale is that represented by the axioms for simple order. Interval scales must meet other requirements as well, but they do constitute ordinal scales as well. The positive integers in the real number system, for example, constitute an interval scale, but they also possess ordinal properties—for example, 1, 2, 3, 4 . . . (1 precedes 2, 2 precedes 3, 3 precedes 4 . . .).

Interval scales also possess certain properties associated with the equivalence relationship, which may be symbolized by $=$. These are the properties possessed by nominal scales, and interval scales constitute nominal as well as ordinal scales. They were discussed informally in Section 11.2, and we may now list these defining properties or axioms of nominal scales, using mathematical notation:

1. If x is an element of S, then $x = x$ (reflexiveness).
2. If $x = y$, then $y = x$ (symmetry).
3. If $x = y$ and $y = z$, then $x = z$ (transitivity).[1]

These axioms have to do with the decomposition of the collection C into nonoverlapping classes. If, for example, classes do overlap, then the equivalence relationship is not transitive (that is, property 3 does not hold). To illustrate, let us categorize illness into the categories *mental* and *physical,* and let us interpret the relationship $=$ to mean *is in the same category of illness as* and let us assume a situation where the categories of illness overlap, as illustrated on the following page.

Assume that individual x is in E (mental illness); y is in F (mental and physical illness); and z is in G (physical illness). Then it is true that $x = y$ (the two are in the same category of mental illness), and it is also true that $y = z$ (they are both physically ill). But it is not true that $x = z$ (x is mentally ill but not physically ill, whereas z is physically ill but not men-

[1] Raymond L. Wilder, *Introduction to the Foundations of Mathematics* (New York: Wiley, 1952), p. 47.

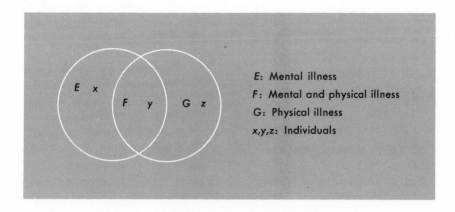

tally ill). Of course, if we have nonoverlapping categories, such as *male* and *female,* the transitivity property holds, as illustrated:

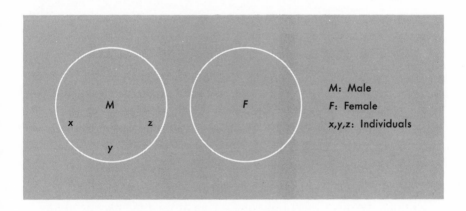

Thus, the fact that x and y are of the same sex, and y and z are of the same sex, implies that x and z are of the same sex.

An additional set of properties for interval scales may be stated as follows:

1. If $x = y$, it is not true that $x < y$, and it is not true that $y < x$.
2. If $x = y$, then if $x < z$, it also must hold that $y < z$.
3. If $x = y$, then if it is not true that $x < z$, it is also not true that $y < z$.

These properties interrelate the properties of simple order with those of equivalence, and they serve to define further the relationship of equivalence. If we substitute appropriate positive integers for x, y, and z, it is easily seen that positive integers possess the above properties.

One additional set of properties which serves to define the property of addition is as follows:[2]

1. If $x + y = z$, then $y + x = z$. This is known as a commutative property—that is, the order in which elements are added does not affect the sum.
2. If $x = x'$ and $0 < y$, then $x' < x + y$. Here 0 precedes y and thus y is more than 0. Consequently, when y is added to one of two equivalent quantities, the result is that the quantities are no longer equivalent.
3. If $x = x'$ and $y = y'$ then $x + y = x' + y'$. This statement, that when equals are added to equals, the results are equal, is known as the axiom of equals.
4. $x + (y + x) = (x + y) + z$. What is involved here is an associative property. The order in which the operations of addition take place has no effect on the results.

Properties 2 and 3 may be illustrated by an example from tennis. With respect to Axiom 2, let x represent the playing ability of Player X, and let x' represent the ability of Player X'. According to the equation $x = x'$, the abilities of the two players are evenly matched. Now we may introduce Player Y to the scene. His playing ability y is better than no ability whatsoever, for he does manage to hit back the ball occasionally, but it is much inferior to that of Player X or Player X'. Now, according to Property 2, the playing ability of Player X' is inferior to the combined abilities of Players X and Y. This, however, probably would not hold true in an actual match, for Player Y would not add anything to Player X's game and would in all likelihood detract from it. We can see here that Property 2 is fundamental if we are to be able to perform the operation of addition. Without this property, we cannot treat the playing ability of tennis players on an interval scale.

To assess Property 3, let X, X', Y, and Y' be four tennis players, and let their corresponding abilities be x, x', y, and y'. Also, let us assume that playing abilities are matched in accordance with Property 3, so that $x = x'$ and $y = y'$. Now if we arrange a doubles match so that X and Y are paired against X' and Y', it does not follow that the two teams will be evenly matched. Each player interacts with his partner in certain ways, and one team may be far more mutually compatible than the other. Our conclusion, thus, is that the playing ability of tennis players does not seem to constitute an interval scale.

One scale possessing interval properties is the centigrade temperature

---

[2] For this listing of properties, as well as some of the examples subsequently used for illustrative purposes, see Virginia Senders, *Measurement and Statistics* (New York: Oxford University Press, 1958), pp. 60–62.

scale. The difference between 1°C and 2°C is equivalent to the difference between 85°C and 86°C. The equivalence may be established with reference to the number of calories of heat required to change the temperature of a standard substance. Thus, it takes one calorie to raise the temperature of water from 1° to 2°, and it also takes one calorie to raise its temperature from 85° to 86°. Consequently, through the simple calculation of temperature changes by means of subtraction, we have a meaningful statement about the number of calories required to produce the change in temperature. Furthermore, we will find that all the preceding properties of interval scales hold for the centigrade scale. For example, let us assume that we have four jars of equal size: X, X', Y, and Y'. Let each jar be half full of water, and let the temperature of the water in the jars be 10°, 10°, 90°, and 90°C, respectively. These temperatures may be designated as x, x', y, and y', and we thus have the equalities specified by Property 3: $x = x'$ and $y = y'$. We now pour the water from Jar X into Jar Y, and that from Jar X' into Jar Y'. According to Property 3, $x + y = x' + y'$—that is, the temperature of the water in the two jars (now full) should be equivalent. This would in fact be the case, thus partially corroborating the statement that the centigrade scale of temperature possesses interval properties.

THE METHOD OF EQUAL-APPEARING INTERVALS

Perhaps the method best known in behavioral science for developing scales with interval properties is the *method of equal-appearing intervals*.[3] Let us assume that we would like to develop an interval scale for the value of *individualism*. This is one of the values that emerged from factor analysis[4] (see Section 11.1). The general procedures involved in the method of equal-appearing intervals may be summarized as follows:

1. The researcher chooses the concept or variable he would like to measure, in this case, the value of *individualism*.
2. On the basis of his ideas about the concept, he constructs (or gathers) many statements which seem to be closely related to the concept. In the original description of the method, for example, 130

[3] L. L. Thurstone and E. J. Chave, *The Measurement of Attitude* (Chicago: University of Chicago Press, 1929).

[4] Robert F. Bales and Arthur S. Couch, "The Value Profile: A Factor Analytic Study of Value Statements," Department of Social Relations, Harvard University (mimeo). Once a factor analysis is performed and several factors are isolated, it is usually necessary to develop measures for these factors if use is to be made of this knowledge. In particular, it may be important to develop an interval scale of the various values emerging from the factor analysis. It should be noted that the method of equal-appearing intervals is not necessarily tied to that of factor analysis. As a matter of fact, very few of those interval scales developed by this procedure were based on the initial results of a factor analysis.

statements were used in developing a scale for measuring attitude toward the church.

3. The individuals selected as judges[5] rate each statement with reference to its degree of "favorableness" or "unfavorableness." This was accomplished in the original study by giving each judge a large number of cards, each of which contained a separate statement. In addition, each judge was given a set of eleven cards containing the letters *A* to *K* and arranged in the following order:

Unfavorable					*Neutral*					*Favorable*
A	B	C	D	E	F	G	H	I	J	K

Each judge is asked to sort the cards containing the statements into the eleven piles represented by the lettered cards. Under Card *A* are to be placed the statements expressing the most unfavorable feelings about the concept being measured. Under Card *F* (the middle card) are to be placed the neutral statements, while under Card *K* are to be placed the most favorable statements. Under the other lettered cards are to be placed the statements representing varying degrees of favorableness or unfavorableness.

4. The judgments obtained from those judges who are believed to have performed their task carelessly are eliminated, together with those statements which receive widely different ratings from different judges.

5. Each of the remaining statements is given a scale value corresponding to the median or middle position to which it is assigned by the judges. Here, Pile *A* is designated as having a score of 1; Pile *B*, a score of 2, and the scores of the remaining piles increasing to a score of 11 for Pile *K*.

6. A final selection of about twenty to twenty-two items is made with the aim of obtaining a set of statements spread out evenly along the scale from one extreme position to the other. Where a choice exists among a number of statements with approximately the same scale values, preference is given to the one obtaining the highest degree of agreement among the judges. Thus, for example, an item placed into Piles *D*, *E*, *F*, *G*, and *H* by equal numbers of judges would be rejected in favor of one placed only into Piles *E*, *F*, and *G* by groups of equal size. At this time the investigator often constructs a duplicate form of the scale, utilizing the same criteria of equal spacing and giving preference to items with the least dispersion among judges. This provides the investigator with the means for testing the

---

[5] Although the original study was based on 300 judges, subsequent research has shown that data from as few as fifteen judges may correlate highly with data obtained from large numbers of judges.

scale for reliability by correlating respondents' scores on one scale with their scores on the duplicate form.

7. A hypothetical example of how some of these items might look, together with hypothetical scale values, follows this paragraph. These items are then used in research studies as a way of measuring the value of *individualism* for a given sample of individuals. Thus, a scale value for a given respondent is obtained by summing the scale values of all the items to which he agrees, and then calculating his average or median scale value. Ideally, individuals will agree only with items which are similar to one another. If an individual agrees with statements that vary widely in scale value, he may have quite ambiguous feelings with respect to the concept being measured.

Scale
Value

1.1   The suppression of one's own individual will in order to adopt the will of society is the way for man to achieve his noblest purposes.

2.8   Man's true nature is best served when he follows the will of the majority.

4.5   Disagreement with one's friends is often foolish because it tends to cause arguments.

6.1   Self-expression is valuable, but it should not be unchecked if man is to enjoy the benefits of living in society.

7.5   Man's development of his own capacities should be an important goal for him.

8.9   Frequent conformity to the wishes of others constitutes a betrayal of man's own identity.

10.4 Man's own individual self-development to the limit of his capacities is the major purpose of his existence.

EQUAL-APPEARING INTERVALS, GUTTMAN SCALING, AND SUMMATED RATINGS: A COMPARISON

In evaluating the *method of equal-appearing intervals,* it is useful to compare it with other scaling procedures.[6] One of the most important criteria for evaluation involves the ordinal or interval properties of the scale produced. It will be recalled that scaling was defined as a procedure that imparts some of the characteristics of numbers to a given property of objects. This allows the investigator to make use of these characteristics in developing and testing his theory. With respect to the three procedures under consideration, it seems that only the Guttman procedure provides definite criteria for deciding whether or not a given scale has certain characteristics of numbers.

[6] For a comparison of different varieties of scales see Charles R. Tittle and Richard J. Hill, "Attitude Measurement and Prediction of Behavior: An Evaluation of Conditions and Measurement Teachniques," *Sociometry,* **30** (1967), 199–213; and Harry S. Upshaw, "Attitude Measurement," in Hubert M. Blalock and Ann B. Blalock (eds.), *Methodology in Social Research* (New York: McGraw-Hill, 1968), Chap. 3.

One might also say that the Guttman procedure is located mainly within the context of justification whereas the others are primarily within the context of discovery. The Guttman procedure describes how data may be assessed in order to determine whether or not a scale exists, but it gives little direction for the development of a set of items to test for scalability beyond emphasizing the importance of conceptualizing or defining the *universe of content*. The Likert and Thurstone procedures involve a set of directions that take the researcher from the construction of items to their final selection for the scale, but they provide no test within the context of justification for ordinal or interval properties.

Because no provision is made for testing within the context of justification, a given scale produced by the Likert or Thurstone method may or may not have ordinal or interval properties. One would have to devise additional procedures in order to test for these properties. We might, for example, start by specifying that 90 per cent of all respondents must agree only to those items that are adjacent to one another in the method of equal-appearing intervals. In this way, if we know the scale value for a given respondent, we can predict fairly accurately those items with which he will agree. Thus, we shall be able to reject those scales that have somewhat ambiguous items. Such a procedure would be analogous to the rejection, in the Guttman scaling method, of any set of items for which a coefficient of reproducibility of .90 is not obtained.

We might proceed in a manner similar to that described for the four half-full jars of water in order to test for the following property of interval scales: if $x = x'$ and $y = y'$, then $x + y = x' + y'$. Let X and X' be two individuals whose scale values, x and x', are equivalent, and the same for Y, Y', y, and y'. We might define the operation of addition within this context as a jointly agreed upon response of the individuals involved. Thus, $x + y$ would represent the scale value of these joint responses. Then, assuming that each individual within a pair has an equal influence on the joint decision,[7] we could determine whether or not it is in fact true that $x + y = x' + y'$.

Closely related to the evaluation of scales in terms of the presence or absence of interval and ordinal properties is what Guttman calls the *unidimensionality* of the universe of content. If a series of items actually measured several dimensions or properties at the same time, it usually would not be possible to develop a Guttman scale indicating a partial order among respondents, let alone develop an interval scale. Of the three procedures under consideration, none provides a definitive test for unidimensionality, although the Guttman technique goes farthest toward providing the possible items that constitute indexes of the property in question. Thus, any set of items selected by a given investigator may not represent a fair sample from this universe of content. Given this situation,

---

[7] If this were actually undertaken, it would be desirable to match subjects on the degree to which they make their influence felt in this kind of interpersonal situation.

the best that we can do is to devise criteria that will enable us to tell whether the "unfair" sample of items under consideration seems to be unitary. Evidence to this effect is obtained in the Guttman scaling procedure whenever a high coefficient of reproducibility occurs, indicating a simple order among the items. Such a simple order would generally not appear if several dimensions were involved in the items. The Likert and Thurstone procedures do not provide such a test, although the latter might be modified so that a criterion, that a very high proportion of respondents must agree only to items contiguous in scale value, might be utilized to accept or reject a given scale. In this way, evidence would be provided as to the interval characteristics of the items in a manner similar to that involved in the Guttman scaling procedure.

The three procedures might also be evaluated with reference to the individuals to whom a given scale applies. In the Guttman and Likert procedures, no separate group of judges is involved. Consequently, these methods are not subject to the criticism that judges may see things differently from the actual respondents. Of course, a scale developed for a given set of respondents by any of the three procedures may not have the same properties for another set of respondents. For example, a set of items scalable according to Guttman criteria for one sample may not be so for another sample. As a matter of fact, it may be true that each person's idea of a given concept differs to some extent from everyone else's. Thus, it may be necessary to shift to the kind of approach illustrated by Stephenson's Q-technique, where the responses of each individual are analyzed separately.

12.2 RATIO SCALES

Ratio scales have all of the properties of nominal, ordinal, and interval scales. In addition, however, a ratio scale possesses an absolute zero point, so that multiplication and division become meaningful operations. One example of a ratio scale is the Kelvin scale of temperature. The zero point for both the centigrade scale (the temperature at which water freezes) and the Fahrenheit scale (the lowest temperature Fahrenheit could produce—that of a mixture of snow and salt) is an arbitrary one. In the Kelvin scale, however, temperature has a direct interpretation in terms of the motion of molecules, and $0°K$ is that point at which there is no motion whatsoever. Only with this type of scale is it meaningful to multiply or divide a given temperature. We cannot say that $30°C$, for example, is three times as warm as $10°C$, even though this scale does have interval properties. In the Kelvin scale, however, $30°$ and $10°$ are directly translatable into the motion of molecules, which is three times more rapid at the former temperature than at the latter. Other examples of ratio scales are measures of length, weight, and time intervals.

Ratio scales enable the investigator to state relationships among variables as products or ratios. (Of course, this is of no use unless it is theoretically important to state relationships in this way.) For example, we might state that an individual's preference for a given event is a product of its utility for him and his expectations as to its likelihood. Thus, an individual may be asked his preference between being given $1 if the sun rises tomorrow or $50 if a penny turns up heads. Here the financial rewards are related to the utilities of the alternatives, whereas the likelihood expectations involve the individual's subjective feelings as to the probabilities of each. (This formulation will be developed in some detail in Section 17.3.)

The proposition that one chooses between two events in this manner is quite similar to the expected-value-deprivation hypothesis in the medical student study. There individuals were seen to make those choices that seemed to lead to a minimizing of expected-value deprivation.

THE MEASUREMENT OF UTILITY

How are scales which possess ratio properties to be constructed? Galanter[8] provides an illustration of this procedure for the measurement of both utility and subjective probability. His procedure for the measurement of utility is to determine the relationship between utility and its monetary equivalent. The strategy here is based on the view that money already constitutes a unidimensional ratio scale. Thus, a determination of the number of *utiles* that correspond to a unit of money might also give a utility scale ratio properties. The technique involves giving a group of subjects these instructions:

> Suppose I were to give you, as an outright gift, $10.00. This $10.00 does not come from me, but comes from a foundation whose resources are limitless. You will be taking nothing away from me when I give you this $10.00. Presumably, this will make you happy to a certain degree. Now, I want you to think about how much money you would want in order to feel twice as happy as the $10.00 would make you feel.[9]

Responses ranged from $20 to $100, with a median of $45. Thus, for almost all the respondents, a doubling of "utility" involves more than a mere doubling of the amount of money. The same procedure was repeated for two other groups of subjects, except that the base amount of money was set at $100 for the second group and $1,000 for the third. The median amount of money associated with a doubling of utility for these two groups was $350 and $500, respectively. On the basis of these results, a

---

[8] Eugene Galanter, "The Direct Measurement of Utility and Subjective Probability," *American Journal of Psychology*, **75** (1962), 208–20.

[9] Galanter, op. cit., p. 211.

function describing the relationship between utility and its monetary equivalent was calculated.[10]

THE MEASUREMENT OF SUBJECTIVE PROBABILITY

The measurement of subjective probability was accomplished in several different ways. In one, subjects rated the likelihood of ten events (for example, *You would survive an airplane crash; You can break a raw egg with a hammer*). One procedure required subjects to rate each event on a 100-point rating scale from 0 to 100. Subjects were to assign a 0 to those events they were absolutely certain would not occur, whereas 100 was to be assigned to events they were absolutely certain would occur.

A similar rating procedure was utilized for another group of subjects, each of whom was asked to assign a number to each of a series of events. No limitation was placed on the size of the numbers, but subjects were asked to represent the less likely events with smaller numbers and the more likely events with large ones. In addition, subjects were told to "assign the numbers to the events so that the numbers are proportional to the likelihood." Thus, an event which is twice as likely to occur as another event is to be given a number twice as large. This is the method of *magnitude estimation.*

The likelihood ratings obtained from these two procedures were generally quite similar, once the ratings obtained from the method of magnitude estimation were standardized so as to make their range comparable to that involved in the 100-point rating scale. The difference between these procedures and the method of equal-appearing intervals is substantial; in the former, no intervening group of judges decides on the weights given to each item; the respondents themselves determine these weights. In addition, the scales are not limited to a range of eleven units; they have a much wider range. This feature is especially important where items occur which, in the subject's view, are very much different from other items. The magnitude-estimation technique in particular allows the subject as great a range as he desires. An additional difference between the magnitude-estimation technique and that of equal-appearing intervals is that in the former, subjects are directly encouraged to think in terms of ratios.

ASSESSMENT OF RATIO PROPERTIES

Galanter used an indirect procedure for testing his degree of success in the construction of scales of utility and subjective probability. It is an example of a construct-validation procedure. His basic proposition is that the probability of choice depends only on the difference in the expected

---

[10] The function is $U = 3.71M^{0.43}$, with U expressed in utiles and M in dollars.

utilities of the alternatives. Subjective expected utility may be calculated by taking the product of the likelihood of the event and its utility, the two scales which have been developed. Assuming that this proposition is correct, we would be able to predict the probability of choice of any given event. The predicted probability of choice could then be compared with the actual probability of choice of the event. Agreement between the two would provide indirect evidence as to the successful achievement of ratio properties within the scales.

In order to carry through this test, it is necessary to devise a procedure for measuring the actual probability of choice of a given event. The method devised had to do with a set of paired events, between which subjects were asked to choose (for example, being given $1 if the sun rises tomorrow or $50 if a penny turns up heads). The actual probability of choice of a given event was then computed as the proportion of times that it was chosen over the alternative choice within the sample. This was then compared with the predicted probability of choice of the event, based on the product of the likelihood of the event and its utility. Results indicated a close relationship between the actual and predicted probabilities for the set of events under consideration. Two things are thus achieved simultaneously: (1) evidence is obtained as to the achievement of ratio properties for the scales of utility and subjective probability and (2) additional confirmation is provided for the proposition that the probability of choice depends on the difference between the expected utility of the alternatives.

The magnitude-estimation procedure for the construction of ratio scales has recently been used to construct a scale of the relative gravity or seriousness of delinquent acts. Subjects were asked to rate the seriousness of a number of violations of the law. Some of the results of the study are the following:

> The most strongly supported conclusion on the basis of the data at hand is that all the raters, although constrained in their use of the magnitude-scale assignments, tended to so assign the magnitude estimations that the seriousness of the crimes is evaluated in a similar way, without significant differences, by all the groups. . . . Because of the inherent ratio quality of the magnitude judgments, the particular numbers used by the raters are not especially relevant; rather, it is the ratios of offense seriousness that are presented intact.[11]

12.3 SOME SELECTED MEASUREMENT PROCEDURES

SINGLE-ITEM MEASUREMENT

Most of the measures used by behavioral scientists are based on single items. For example, single items were utilized in the *structured-values*

---

[11] Thorsten Sellin and Marvin E. Wolfgang, *The Measurement of Delinquency* (New York: Wiley, 1964), p. 268.

question for measuring occupational values in the medical student study. The following constitute some examples of these items, each of which was utilized to measure a separate value:

What Importance Would Each of the Following Things Have in Your Ideal Job?	Indis- pensable in a Job	Extremely Important	Very Im- portant	Fairly Impor- tant	Little or No Impor- tance
a. Developing warm per- sonal relationships with patients	____	____	____	____	____
f. Having prestige among my colleagues in the medical profession	____	____	____	____	____
k. Having the chance to help people	____	____	____	____	____
l. Having the chance to increase continually my understanding of basic processes	____	____	____	____	____

One advantage of single-item measurement is the speed with which it enables research to proceed. Rather than focus attention on the development of multiple-item scales, the investigator is free to concentrate on the development and testing of a variety of propositions. The popularity of single-item measurement is thus readily understandable, for most investigators prefer to get through with the business of measurement as quickly as possible. One justification for this procedure is that, as a result of developing and testing propositions, the investigator may glean new ideas about the concept being measured and these may lead to substantial improvements in the measuring instrument. In addition, the investigator is free to measure a wider variety of concepts during a given interview or questionnaire session. A Thurstone equal-appearing interval scale, for example, would require a total of twenty to twenty-two items for each concept scaled in this manner. The investigator must also take into account the factor of the boredom of the respondent; this was a frequent reaction by respondents to those parts of one interview schedule designed to furnish the raw materials for a number of Guttman-scale analyses.[12]

A final argument which may be put forward in defense of single-item measurement is that it may not be inferior to multiple-item measurement for many research situations. For example, in the medical student study,

[12] Bernard S. Phillips, *Technical Materials for an Interview Survey of the Aging* (Urbana, Ill.: Small Homes Council—Building Research Council, 1962).

single items from the structured-values question were used to measure the occupational values of respondents. An additional procedure for measuring these values used responses to the careers-value question. Each value was measured by three separate items, and a Guttman-type scale was developed for each set of items.[13] It was then found that the Guttman-type scales led to almost exactly the same results as the single-item measures when it came to predicting the respondents' preferences among medical fields. This does not mean that the scaling procedure was completely useless in this instance, for it provided some evidence for the unidimensionality of the different values that formed scales.

The disadvantages that may be attached to the use of single-item measurement are numerous, although they are not unique to this type of measurement. Every item in a questionnaire must measure something, but it may also get at several things at the same time. A given item may mean quite different things to different respondents, or one thing to one grouping of respondents and something else to another. Also, the different response categories may vary in meaning among respondents. One person's notion of what is *indispensable* in a job may be equivalent to another person's conception of what is *extremely important* in a job.

Some of these difficulties may be at least partially resolved by certain multiple-item techniques. Thus, for example, Guttman scaling provides some evidence for the unidimensionality of the concept for the respondents. One generally would not be able to obtain a coefficient of reproducibility of .90 or higher unless a fairly high degree of uniformity existed among the respondents as to the meaning of each item, as well as to the different response categories for each item.

In addition, multiple-item measurements are generally more reliable than single-item techniques. The question of validity, however, is somewhat more complex. On the one hand, the magnitude-estimation procedure used by Galanter seems to have resulted in some validation of a multiple-item scale as a measure of subjective probability. The greater the number of items in a given scale, however, the greater is their potential for measuring more than one factor for a set of respondents.

SEMANTIC DIFFERENTIAL

A method that attempts to get at the underlying meaning which a given concept has for an individual or group has recently been developed by Osgood, Suci, and Tannenbaum.[14] Subjects are asked to rate a given concept (for example, *surgeon*) by locating it between two polar ad-

---

[13] Bernard S. Phillips, "Expected Value-Deprivation and Occupational Preference," *Sociometry*, **27** (1964), 151–60.

[14] Charles E. Osgood, George J. Suci, and Percy H. Tannenbaum, *The Measurement of Meaning* (Urbana, Ill.: University of Illinois Press, 1957).

jectives. The space between the adjectives is divided into seven units, indicating closeness of meaning to each of the adjectives. One of the questions utilizing the *semantic-differential* approach in the medical study was the following:

			Surgeon				
Colorful	:	:	:	:	:	:	Colorless
Feminine	:	:	:	:	:	:	Masculine
Outgoing	:	:	:	:	:	:	Self-centered
Awful	:	:	:	:	:	:	Nice
Hard	:	:	:	:	:	:	Soft
Ordinary	:	:	:	:	:	:	Individualistic
Introverted	:	:	:	:	:	:	Extroverted
Pleasant	:	:	:	:	:	:	Unpleasant

This technique may be used to compare the meanings the different medical fields have for respondents. For example, it might provide clues as to why some individuals rated general practice favorably in spite of a high degree of expected-value deprivation for that field. The analytic procedures involved in such comparisons are quite simple. In this instance one might compare those medical students favorable to general practice and high on expected-value deprivation for the field with students who are unfavorable to general practice and are also high on expected-value deprivation for that field. A difference between two individuals on a given pair of polar objectives is measured by the number of categories by which their ratings differ. The maximum difference is 6 (because there are only seven categories) and the minimum difference is 0. One group's ratings may be compared with that of another by comparing the medians of the two.

Osgood and his co-workers, on the basis of a series of factor analyses, have emphasized that the meaning of concepts for respondents seems to involve evaluation, potency, and activity. Individuals tend to judge or evaluate concepts according to such polar adjectives as *good–bad, nice–*

awful, and *beautiful–ugly.* Potency may be indicated by *strong–weak, large–small,* and *heavy–light,* whereas activity may be indicated by *fast–slow, active–passive,* and *sharp–dull.* In the question utilizing the semantic differential, the adjectives *awful–nice* and *pleasant–unpleasant* reflect evaluation; *feminine–masculine* and *hard–soft* reflect potency. Factors other than evaluation, potency, and activity were isolated by Osgood and his associates, and one of these is receptivity, measured by *colorful–colorless,* or (in other cases) *sensitive–insensitive, savory–tasteless,* and *interesting–boring.* The remaining pairs utilized in the example (*outgoing–self-centered, ordinary–individualistic,* and *introverted–extroverted*) were thought to be of special interest in the problem under investigation. All of them concern sociability, a variable that seemed to be of some importance in trying to understand why students might or might not be interested in various medical fields.

The semantic differential seems to provide a path toward a better understanding both of the measurement situation within the research process and of the individual's fundamental expectations as to the meanings of concepts. Within the research process, subjects or respondents are often bombarded by a variety of verbal stimuli, and it is often assumed that the meanings attached to these stimuli are relatively uniform. Such an assumption can be tested by the semantic-differential approach, and the meanings assigned by a given individual may be differentiated from those assigned by any other. The medical student study provides an example of the use of this method as a means of getting at the individual's fundamental expectations. The method itself is more general than the specific factors isolated in the initial studies. It promises a far more thorough and detailed understanding of the symbolic aspects of human behavior than has yet been attempted or attained.

SOCIAL RELATIONSHIPS

Some specialized techniques bear on concepts of crucial importance to behavioral science: social relationships and expectations. One of these techniques, the *sociometric test,*[15] is concerned with social interaction and social relationships. An example of this approach is provided by the medical student study. Some of the questions administered to the students were

1. Whom do you like best?
2. Who knows most about medicine?

[15] For a discussion of the origin of this technique, see J. Moreno, *Who Shall Survive?* (Washington, D.C.: Nervous and Mental Disease Publishing Co., 1934). For a more recent discussion see Gardner Lindzey and Edgar F. Borgatta, "Sociometric Measurement," in Gardner Lindzey (ed.), *Handbook of Social Psychology,* Vol. I (Cambridge Mass.: Addison-Wesley, 1954), pp. 405–48.

3. Whom would you like most to represent medical students (at some meeting)?
4. To whom do you talk most about your plans for the future?
5. Who knows best where he is going?
6. Who has the widest range of interests?
7. To whom would you go for advice on a personal problem?
8. Who will make the best doctor?

These questions were designed to aid in the assessment of medical students' influences on one another with respect to preferences for the various medical fields. One of the first steps was to find out whether the preference patterns of more popular students differed from those of students who were less popular.

Students were divided into popularity groups on the basis of how often their names were mentioned by other students in response to Questions 1, 4, and 7 above, the items that seemed to provide the best indications of actual social relationships among students. Results indicated that within the high-popularity group the preference patterns of freshmen, sophomores, juniors, and seniors were similar. Among the low-popularity group, however, an important change in preference patterns occurred between freshman and junior years; freshmen tended to agree very little on their preferences for the medical fields, but this degree of agreement increased during the sophomore and junior years. The inference was drawn that these low-popularity students are exposed to less peer-group influence than the more popular ones, and consequently are slower to reach a common standard of agreement on their preferences.

This analysis represents only a fragment of the vast amount of data provided by this one medical school on student interrelationships. For example, the patterns of social relationships of a given student have yet to be related to his values and expectations. Such analyses may yield a greater understanding of the dynamics involved in choice of medical field.

An approach that may be utilized in conjunction with an analysis of social relationships is *agreement analysis*,[16] a technique that requires an electronic computer. It is possible to determine with which persons a given individual is in agreement on a series of items. For example, the voting patterns of United States senators may be analyzed in this way. The result will be a number of partially overlapping groupings of senators who voted similarly on a large number of issues. Each grouping constitutes a *type,* and research may then proceed as to the origin and impact of such types. Many senators will appear in a number of types, but each type will be based on a different set of votes. The set of votes corresponding to a given type may be called the *pattern*. This kind of basic data on

[16] L. L. McQuitty, "Agreement Analysis: Classifying Persons by Predominant Patterns of Responses," *British Journal of Statistical Psychology,* **9** (1956), 5–16.

types and patterns can then be combined with an analysis of the patterns of social interaction among senators for a more complete understanding of the dynamics of social interaction.

EXPECTATIONS

A theoretical analysis of the relationship among expectations, norms, and roles provided by Rommetveit[17] is based on the idea that expectations are both "sent" and "received" by individuals. Thus, ego expects alter to do X (sent expectation), and alter understands what ego expects (received expectations). Most expectations are supported by direct or indirect rewards or punishments. A given individual may or may not "receive" whatever was "sent." In any case, he acts on the basis of whatever it is that he "receives." His behavior or choices may or may not conform to these expectations, depending on the strength of the attendant rewards and punishments. When expectations are recurrent, we may speak of a *social norm,* and a *social role* may be thought of as a system of norms directed at a given category of individuals.

Within this theoretical framework, it would be desirable to obtain three pieces of information: the expectations a given individual sends out, those he receives, and his behavior in the context of whatever expectations he receives. An example of how these different kinds of data are obtainable is provided by the structured-values question in the medical student study. Within this context, the expectations we are dealing with involve the fundamental occupational goals or values which a medical student should or should not have. The three pieces of data may be obtained in the following ways:

1. *Expectations received.* The student can be asked directly about the way other medical students would expect him to answer the series of questions on occupational values. But because in our society, with its emphasis on individualism and free choice, many individuals might not want to admit being subject to such expectations, a more effective device is simply to inquire about a given respondent's conception of the importance attached by other medical students in his class to each of the values. Whichever approach is used, it is often quite difficult to assess exactly what kinds of sanctions are employed to back up these expectations, for they may be quite subtle.
2. *Expectations sent.* A direct method might involve questions on how the respondent would expect other medical students in his class to rate the importance of the various values. The expectations sent by

[17] Ragnar Rommetveit, *Social Norms and Roles* (Minneapolis: University of Minnesota Press, 1955).

a given medical student class could then be calculated by taking into account those sent by each member of the class. An indirect approach would involve obtaining each student's rating of the importance he himself attaches to each value, and then to use these data for all students to infer the expectations sent out by the medical student class as a whole.

3. *Actual behavior.* The actual behavior or choice of a given student with respect to the importance of a set of occupational values would be simply his own ratings of the importance of these values. This can then be analyzed in relation to the expectations sent and those received.

The entire indirect approach can be managed in a single question with several parts. The following is a format developed for the medical student study which can be used to obtain all three types of data:

Most people have some idea of what they would want in an ideal position—i.e., they could dream up a job that had all the things they like. What importance would each of the following things have in your ideal job? Put a check in Column A, B, C, D, or E.

Aside from referring to things that may or may not be important to you *personally*, these statements may refer to things that are important to other students in medical school. What importance do you think these things generally have to other students in your class? Put a check in Column F, G, or H.

You will work better on this question if you work first on Column A through E on all questions and then come back to work on questions F through H.

In My Ideal Job I Would Like an Opportunity for:

	Yourself				
	A	B	C	D	E
	Indis-pensable in a Job	Extremely Important	Very Impor-tant	Fairly Impor-tant	Little or No Impor-tance (or would rather not have)
1. Developing warm personal relationships with patients	___	___	___	___	___
2. Having a practice which is not exceedingly demanding physi-cally	___	___	___	___	___

	Other Medical Students in Your Class		
	F	G	H
	Indis-pensable in a Job	Some Impor-tance	Little or No Impor-tance (or would rather not have)
1. Developing warm personal relationships with patients	_____	_____	_____
2. Having a practice which is not exceedingly demanding physically	_____	_____	_____

It should be noted that in this approach the investigator may select any grouping he believes to have an influence on the behavior of the individuals under investigation. In this case, the medical school class was used as the relevant grouping, but research might equally well proceed with respect to the student's friends within medical school. These may be determined on the basis of sociometric analysis, and their response might then be utilized to measure the expectations sent.

12.4 CRITERION VALIDATION AND CONSTRUCT VALIDATION AS ALTERNATIVE RESEARCH STRATEGIES

At the close of Chapter 10 we contrasted two strategies for scaling, one involving the perfection of scales prior to their utilization and the other proceeding to test propositions with imperfect scales. These two types of approaches also were contrasted in previous chapters (for example, in the quantitative versus the qualitative orientation and in the field experiment versus the laboratory experiment). In our discussion of criterion and construct validity in Section 10.2, and again in our analysis of options in Section 11.3, a similar contrast was put forward. In the former case, criterion-validation procedures reflect a concern with the perfection of measurement instruments prior to utilizing them, whereas construct-validation procedures imply a concern for the utilization of imperfect measuring instruments so as to get on with the business of testing hypotheses. In the latter case, one of the options for the development of scales involved dealing only with phenomena that satisfy a stringent set of conditions, whereas the other involved relaxing the stringency of the conditions so as to be able to deal with a wide range of data.

We are now in a position to clarify the nature of these two contrasting approaches, conceived of as general strategies, by relating them to various aspects of the scientific method. We begin with our definition of the scientific method as a triple synthesis of ideas with ideas, ideas with experiences, and experiences with experiences. Implicit in this conception is the idea that, other things being equal, the wider the synthesis, the further science has proceeded. However, the integration of knowledge must not be at a superficial level; it is just such superficiality which has been the chief source of criticism directed at broad formulations. Let us, then, add to our concern for synthesis an equal concern for analysis: the conceptual splitting apart of phenomena in order to probe as deeply as possible. Indeed, effective syntheses are based on effective analyses of the relevant phenomena into the kinds of elements which can be put together easily.

The key difference between the criterion- and construct-validation strategies is that the former emphasizes the importance of analysis and the latter that of synthesis. Yet what we must understand, despite this apparent difference, is that every synthesis implies a certain kind of analysis and every analysis implies a given synthesis. Thus, the important question for the scientist is not *whether* one should develop a synthesis or an analysis but rather *what kinds* of syntheses and analyses are most fruitful for scientific progress?

We can leave the question quite open, just as science itself is open. A synthetic approach can easily degenerate into one which fails genuinely to integrate ideas, because of insufficient analysis; and an analytic approach can become one which erects barriers to important ideas outside of its defined boundaries. Equally, a synthetic approach can increasingly widen the scope of knowledge, and an analytic approach can continue to increase its depth. By leaving the question open, we are in a sense answering it; it is for the progress of science itself to point the direction for the kinds of methodologies that are best for fostering such progress, an idea in keeping with the pragmatic basis of the scientific method. This "answer" is consistent with the idea of construct validation, which looks to the testing of theories as a basis for validating the methodology behind the construction of theories. It is also consistent with criterion validation in that a genuine synthesis should at least take into account available knowledge about tools of measurement that have been developed in the past, with these tools used to help direct attention toward the development of improved tools.

Although these alternative strategies may sound harmonious, failures of each to make progress in the contexts of discovery and justification, coupled with lack of recognition of these failures, can produce divergence and lack of mutual support. Thus, for example, criterion-validation procedures have too often been a stumbling block within the context of discovery by holding up relatively minute victories within the context of justification as models of virtue for all to follow. There is a tendency in modern behavioral science to equate the finding of statistically significant relationships with an end point rather than a beginning of an investigation, and there may even be widespread fear of departing from this well-established mode of thinking and plunging thereby into unknown territory. By failing to hold up higher criteria of success, such as prediction, such victories can become Pyrrhic, leading to a lack of impetus to search for ideas much better than those presently available.

Equally, a vague and amorphous synthesis which strives for relevance may achieve little more than a way of translating a variety of disparate languages into a common tongue without any gain beyond what could have been said in any one of the component languages. Such an approach could be used to rule out attempts at hard analytic measurement procedures and the quantitative analysis of data on the grounds of lack of relevance to the issues of the day. Such an approach, however, would not constitute a genuine synthesis which builds up something that is more than its separate parts. The problem here is not an emphasis on synthesis but rather a failure in achieving the kind of synthesis which represents a genuine advance within the context of discovery and which can give evidence of this within the context of justification.

EXERCISES

1. Under what conditions would you tend to use the method of (a) equal-appearing intervals, (b) scale analysis, and (c) summated ratings?

2. What evidence, direct or indirect, does the method of equal-appearing intervals provide to the effect that a given scale it produces has the properties of interval scales?

3. How would you defend the method of magnitude estimation as one which produces ratio scales?

4. Because ratio scales have more of the properties of numbers than interval, ordinal, and nominal scales, are there any reasons why all the scales of the behavioral scientist should not be ratio scales?

5. Use the semantic-differential technique to investigate the meaning of a concept from behavioral science among several behavioral science students. Attempt to infer underlying orientations about behavioral science from the responses you obtain, and check these out in semistructured interviews.

ANNOTATED REFERENCES

OSGOOD, CHARLES E., GEORGE J. SUCI, and PERCY H. TANNENBAUM. *The Measurement of Meaning.* Urbana, Ill.: University of Illinois Press, 1957. This book is the result of an attempt to develop improved measures of the meanings which words have for individuals and groups. The semantic-differential technique, the outcome of these efforts, is discussed in terms of the general theory on which it is based, the specific procedures involved, and a variety of problems to which it has been applied.

SELLIN, THORSTEN, and MARVIN E. WOLFGANG. *The Measurement of Delinquency*. New York: John Wiley & Sons, Inc., 1964. The research reported here represents one of the first, and also one of the few, applications of the technique of magnitude estimation to sociological problems in the construction of ratio scales. There is discussion of the general rationale for this technique, although most of the volume deals with the specific problem at hand.

TITTLE, CHARLES R., and RICHARD J. HILL. "Attitude Measurement and Prediction of Behavior: An Evaluation of Conditions and Measurement Techniques," *Sociometry*, **30** (1967), 199–213. Reprinted in Norman K. Denzin (ed.), *Sociological Methods: A Sourcebook* (Chicago: Aldine, 1970), pp. 151–66. In a study of the degree of correspondence between measured attitude (taking into account a number of different scaling procedures) and other behavior, the authors conclude that "the degree of correspondence observed is at least a function of (1) the measurement techniques employed, (2) the degree to which the criterion behavior constitutes action within the individuals' common range of experience, and (3) the degree to which the criterion behavior represents a repetitive behavioral configuration.

part four ANALYSIS
OF DATA

The consensus of the scientific community in a given instance may be wrong. One of the most important safeguards against a tyranny of the majority is found in the presentation of scientific evidence. Good analytic procedures require that the scientist make clear the decision-making process through which evidence is weighed and conclusions drawn. In this way other scientists can look at the results of any particular investigation and attempt to separate the data from the conclusions drawn by the investigator. The scientist is free to decide for himself how to weight evidence and what conclusions to draw, but he is also responsible for clarifying as much as he can the process by which he assigns such weights and draws conclusions. How well he can do this depends on his understanding of this process and, in particular, on his knowledge of the implicit assumptions he makes.

In Chapter 13 we discuss some of the procedures which have been developed for the nonstatistical analysis and presentation of data about one and two variables. Chapters 14 and 15 contain some of the basic principles of statistical decision making, along with illustrations of statistical procedures. Chapter 16 deals with the analysis of more than two variables within the context of the search for cause-and-effect relationships.

CHAPTER 13 **One and Two Variables**

13.1 ONE VARIABLE

DESCRIPTIVE AND CAUSE–EFFECT ANALYSES

One-variable analysis is descriptive of a given entity by taking into account only one variable at a time. Thus, a number of variables may be involved so long as the investigator does not interrelate one with another. What is achieved in this way is an initial description of the characteristics of the entity under consideration. For example, let us assume that a sample of individuals is drawn from a given community. Some of the facts resulting from an initial one-variable or descriptive analysis might be the following:

1. Sex: 55 per cent, females; 45 per cent, males.
2. Race: 87 per cent, white; 13 per cent, Negro.
3. Age: 40 per cent, 0–20; 31 per cent, 21–40; 29 per cent, 41 or over.
4. Religion: 35 per cent, Protestant; 44 per cent, Catholic; 21 per cent, Jewish.
5. Income: 33 per cent, under $4,000; 28 per cent, $4,000–$6999; 26 per cent, $7,000–$9,999; 13 per cent, $10,000 or over.
6. Education: 88 per cent, high school or less; 12 per cent, beyond high school.

Although six variables are described above, none is interrelated or cross-tabulated with any other by the researcher. Thus, a description of the sample with respect to sex, race, age, religion, income, and education is provided, but we do not know, for example, what proportion of males are white or what proportion of females are high school graduates. Such descriptive analyses are valuable in the social sciences chiefly as a prelude to two-variable and multivariate analysis. This emphasis, in part, explains why the term *hypothesis* is used primarily in the context of statements about the relationship between two or more variables. It is conceivable to use the term *hypothesis* in the context of one variable, but such usage is rare. Thus, for example, we might have hypothesized that Nixon would win over Humphrey in the 1968 presidential election. The single variable here is the vote for president, which is categorized under the different candidates. But the social scientist is generally not interested in doing research on hypotheses unless they show promise of leading to an understanding of the mechanisms of human behavior. What will happen in a particular place at a particular time may have intrinsic interest to many individuals, but the social scientist centers his interest on hypotheses with far wider scope.

This does not mean that social scientists are uninterested in what happens in American presidential elections. Such interest is frequently found, for example, among political scientists, sociologists, and psychologists. Nevertheless, interest centers more on the question of *why* a given event has happened, is happening, or will happen than *what* occurs. Answers to these *why* questions constitute explanations that may shed considerable light on the dynamics of behavior. In studying a given presidential election, for example, we may learn a great deal about the general mechanisms that are effective in changing the political expectations and values of human beings. Such information might follow in the wake of such questions as "Why did the individuals who voted for Humphrey do so?" The mere fact that a certain proportion of Americans voted for a given candidate in a given election does not go very far toward explaining human behavior in general.

Of course, we have to start somewhere, and description is usually viewed as an important beginning. We cannot proceed to study why a given individual voted for Humphrey unless we know whether or not he actually *did* vote for Humphrey. Descriptive data constitute an important prelude to cause-and-effect analyses. If we are ignorant of the characteristics of a given population, we may have considerable difficulty in formulating hypotheses about their behavior. A knowledge of its characteristics with respect to sex, race, age, religion, income, and education, for example, may be highly suggestive.

In a survey, a choice usually does not have to be made between a descriptive analysis and a cause-and-effect analysis. A typical procedure in survey analysis involves obtaining the "marginals" or frequency distribution of the respondents on each question and then proceeding to two-variable and multivariate analyses. Thus, for example, the number of individuals of each sex, religion, and so on, would be tabulated. This would usually be followed by a percentage breakdown for each of the questions (to determine the proportions of male and female, and so on). Once this is accomplished, the results would be used as an aid to the development of a cause-and-effect analysis.

With the advent of electronic data processing, such descriptive analyses take very little time. The most time-consuming task is not the processing of data by machines, but the planning procedures of the investigator as well as his analysis and interpretation of the processed data. Thus, all the frequencies, as well as the percentages, in response to each of the questions in a detailed survey of a large sample can be calculated and printed by an electronic computer in an hour or so.

HISTORICAL STUDIES

The distinction between descriptive one-variable analyses and cause-and-effect analyses may also be illustrated in a historical context. Weber's *Protestant Ethic and the Spirit of Capitalism*[1] is concerned with a historical fact, the origin of capitalism. His focus is not, however, on a description of the various pieces of evidence for the existence of capitalism at different periods in different countries; rather it is the identification of those factors or variables which seemed to be associated with the existence of capitalism. What is involved here is the relationship among two or more variables, one of which has to do with evidence for the existence of capitalism [for example, a relationship is established between one variable (the Protestant ethic) and another (the accumulation of capital)]. A descriptive analysis would deal with each of these variables separately. It is quite different, however, to interrelate the two variables, to compare individuals who believe in the Protestant ethic with those who do not in terms of their degree of accumulation of capital.

The question might be raised whether a historical fact such as the rise of capitalism should be of interest to the scientist. Is it not true that such an occurrence was relatively unique and is not likely to be repeated? If so, of what possible utility can an understanding of this occurrence be to the scientist who is interested in understandings that are not very limited in time and space? In answering this question, it is important to understand that in one sense every event is unique to some extent; none will ever be repeated in exactly the same way or in the same context. But there is also similarity or correspondence among events, and one of the tasks of the scientist is to explore these similarities. In particular, although capitalism may never rise again in the same way, certain similar values will in all probability continue to affect the personal decisions of individuals as well as the economy of nations in every era.

13.2 QUALITATIVE ANALYSIS: CONCEPTUALIZATION OF VARIABLES

MIGRATION TO SKOPJE: AN EXAMPLE OF CODING

Whereas factor analysis constitutes a technique for developing concepts, a technique fairly involved mathematically, coding procedures for open-ended questions are qualitative in nature and have the same pur-

---

[1] Max Weber, *Protestant Ethic and the Spirit of Capitalism,* translated by Talcott Parsons (London: George Allen and Unwin, 1930).

pose. The present illustration is taken from an interview-survey conducted in Skopje, Yugoslavia, during the summer of 1963. The study examined the impact of migration from a rural to an urban area.[2] The specific survey question to be used for illustrative purposes is: "What do you think was the biggest change in your life as a result of your moving to Skopje?" The 284 individuals who were interviewed had all come to Skopje since World War II as part of an enormous migration that tripled the population of the city.

Respondents tended to be quite vocal in answering the question, and their answers, needless to say, varied a good deal. A primary task for the investigators was to organize or systematize the answers in such a way that maximum use could be made of this information.

The open-ended question was conceived of as functioning primarily in the context of discovery rather than in the context of justification. In this situation one does not start with a fixed set of concepts; rather, one examines the responses to develop concepts that seem to be fruitful. The situation here is similar to that portion of the medical student study where the students were asked to indicate what they liked most and least about working in a number of medical fields. Their responses seemed to fall naturally into a number of categories, and these were subsequently utilized in the formulation of closed questions on the basic goals or values taken into account by medical students when choosing a field of medicine.

A first step in the coding of responses to open-ended questions, then, is the formation of a number of nonoverlapping categories into which all of the responses may be placed. Alternatively, we may say that the investigator develops a nominal scale for the responses, because nominal scales are sets of nonoverlapping categories. The subsequent step in the medical student study was the attempt to develop a series of interval scales, each one based on a given category of the nominal scale. As we shall see, in the Skopje study the nominal scale provided the basis for the development of a single new concept which utilized aspects from all of the categories within the nominal scale.

The categories of response that emerged from the answers to the question "What do you think was the biggest change in your life as a result of your moving to Skopje?" were (1) standard of living, (2) social, (3) cultural, (4) intellectual, (5) occupational, (6) activities, (7) urban atmosphere, (8) no special changes, (9) negative changes, and (10) personality changes. Some of these are illustrated below.

1. *Standard of living.* Many of the responses were general with respect to improvement in the standard of living (for example, "Life is better here"; "There is a higher standard of living and better salary"; "Better-

[2] Collaborating with the author in the Skopje study were D. Miljovska and V. Taneski of the University of Skopje, and Irwin Sanders. The study is described in "The Urban Personality and the Rural Personality," Department of Sociology, Boston University (mimeo).

ment of my material conditions"; "Comfortable life"). Increased income was sometimes cited, but response tended to focus on actual changes in consumption patterns. Housing constitutes the item most frequently cited (for example, "A larger flat and better housing conditions"; "I bought a house of my own, and now there is enough room for the whole family"). A variety of other goods and services was mentioned (for example, "I have more access to hospitals, medicines, doctors"; "I bought a refrigerator and an electric stove"; "We eat better"; "I started to dress better"; "I started to devote myself to luxurious things").

2. *Cultural.* A marked change for the better in cultural life is noted by many of the respondents, with particular emphasis on variety ("I found myself in an atmosphere I was fond of and wanted to live in. Now I go more often to exhibitions, concerts, to the theater, cinema. I have a more heterogeneous life"; "We stay at home more. I had the opportunity to read books and to reach a higher cultural level"; "Now I again have the chance to go to concerts, exhibitions, theaters"; "I have widened my cultural and entertainment life"; "I simply have a considerably more beautiful and better life here than in a smaller place").

3. *Occupational.* The relief from hard physical labor and long hours, with the consequent opportunity for increased leisure-time activities, was often noted ("There is relief from hard manual work we had at Radoish"; "I need not walk 15 kilometers to my house now"; "I never have to use the hoe again"; "The work here is easier than in the village"; "I do not go to the field now"; "When I have time to spare I go to the cinema"; "I have more leisure time"). A number of them mentioned being no longer unemployed. Other comments emphasized the more challenging nature of the new jobs and increased interest in work ("I found a job that corresponds to my ability"; "I am improving the quality of my craft"; "I work with great enthusiasm because it suits me"; "I advanced in rank and received a higher function"; "My exemplary work was orally acknowledged by the enterprise"). Even the job of the housewife was affected by similar changes ("As a housewife I started to cook the specialties"; "I keep the household a little tidier"; "Here I can do the home duties better because we have a better dwelling").

4. *Urban atmosphere.* Responses were not always phrased in specific terms; a number referred to the over-all character or atmosphere of Skopje ("The atmosphere itself is different, from a village into a town"; "Now I live in a bigger and much livelier town"; "The way of living is more positive than the previous one"; "There are more possibilities for everything because the town is bigger"; "The thought that I am a citizen of Skopje has made me feel prouder"; "There is another atmosphere here, other customs"; "I expected and found vividness in the cultural and community life").

5. *Negative changes.* A very few individuals indicated a type of change which was undesirable ("I am dissatisfied with my job, with myself"; "As

far as young people are concerned, I do not know, but for the old people, the entertainment life is very poor"; "I work very hard and I have limited spare time"; "There is disorder here").

In 1938 Louis Wirth wrote, with respect to urban populations in the United States: "The personal traits, the occupations, the cultural life, and the ideas of the members of an urban community may . . . be expected to range between more widely separated poles than those of rural in-habitants."[3] On the basis of the changes indicated by the respondents in this study, the community of Skopje in 1963 seemed to illustrate the same characteristics referred to by Wirth. The special characteristics of the urbanized community can be brought into focus quite sharply when seen through the eyes of newcomers from rural areas or small towns. The urban way of life, as described by the migrants, represents far more than an improvement in income, housing, general living standards, opportunities for employment, and formal education for children; it represents a whole new world of people, ideas, activities, and culture. It provides far more challenging occupational opportunities and the type of atmosphere which stimulates the individual to grow intellectually and learn about a new way of life. It generally provides more leisure so that the individual can take advantage of these opportunities.

SOME FUNCTIONS OF QUALITATIVE ANALYSES

One function of such an analysis is that it makes the investigator feel so close to the phenomena under investigation that he has little difficulty in formulating hypotheses and theories about the processes involved. This is akin to what is accomplished by a good novelist or playwright; his characterizations come alive for his audience, and his audience feels as if it understands the behavior of the fictional individuals. For the scientist such a feeling for the subject constitutes an important source of ideas within the context of discovery. Whether or not these ideas subsequently bear fruit cannot be assured, of course, for hypotheses must still survive examination in the context of justification.

The analysis just described was instrumental in helping to develop several ideas about the urbanization process. One of them is the concept of *heterogeneous personality* and of *homogeneous personality*. The heterogeneous personality is conceived of as tending to have a highly differentiated set of goals or values and to see many different alternative courses of action in a given situation. As a result, it tends to exhibit a wide range of behavior in social and nonsocial situations and to bring to bear these wide-ranging values and expectations on any given decision. The homogeneous personality, on the other hand, tends to perceive fewer alter-

---

[3] Louis Wirth, "Urbanism as a Way of Life," *The American Journal of Sociology*, **44** (1938), 11.

native courses of action in a given situation, brings to bear fewer goals or values on any given decision, and consequently behaves in a less differentiated way.

The concepts of heterogeneous and homogeneous personality may be thought of as constituting a new nominal scale which selects from the preceding ten-category nominal scale certain aspects, that is, differentiation of goals and awareness of alternative courses of action. Here we may speak of the single variable of personality type with two categories, heterogeneous and homogeneous personality. This variable may also be conceived of as referring to a single dimension or continuum rather than simply two discrete points or categories. In this view the completely heterogeneous personality would represent one polar type, whereas the totally homogeneous personality would represent the other, and individuals would be located somewhere along this continuum. With this conception it would be appropriate to attempt to develop ordinal, interval, or ratio scales measuring *degree of personality heterogeneity.*

It is difficult to describe the exact process whereby the descriptive analysis contributed to the development of the conception of degree of personality heterogeneity. Many of the responses revealed in one way or another a widening of horizons, and the degree to which horizons are widened seems to constitute the essence of the variable of personality heterogeneity.

One of the advantages of the survey as a research technique is that it is often possible to develop and test ideas within a single survey, although it is always desirable to have additional confirmation from other studies. When, for example, the data reveal a relationship between social class and type of mental illness, it is misleading to pretend that this hypothesis was formulated before the data were processed and that the data therefore validate the hypothesis. Ideas can be legitimately developed and tested within the same survey only when different kinds of data are used for each task. In this way, the process is not circular. This can often be done quite easily because a good survey tends to be comprehensive and yields a wide variety of data.

From the investigator's interest in the variable of personality heterogeneity (an interest which was in good measure developed out of the descriptive analysis), two hypotheses were formulated and these were initially tested in other portions of the Skopje data. One hypothesis dealt with the factors leading to the development of the heterogeneous personality, whereas the other has to do with its impact on the adjustment of the individual to his life in Skopje. These hypotheses themselves owed much to the descriptive analysis, which indicated that the origins of the heterogeneous personality lay in the exposure provided by the urban environment to a wide variety of experiences in many different aspects of life. This suggested a number of specific hypotheses about the degree of such exposure. Factors that seemed to determine the degree of exposure to a variety of experiences included the number of years in Skopje, the size of the community of previous residence, the frequency of previous moves, the degree of education, the kind of occupation, and the level of income. Each of these hypotheses received confirmation; that is, relationships were shown to exist between the various indexes of degree of exposure to a wide variety of experiences and the degree of heterogeneity of the personalities involved.

Some American studies of urbanization imply that personality differentiation is indicative of schizoid tendencies and maladjustment. A reading of the responses of migrants to Skopje seems to provide no evidence for this. As a matter of fact, the responses to the open-ended question seemed to indicate that the individuals who are experiencing personality differentiation are quite pleased with the process and seem to be well adjusted to the urban environment. As a result, it was hypothesized that a high degree of personality heterogeneity is related to various indexes of satisfactory adjustment. This hypothesis received confirmation when the relevant data were analyzed.

It seems, then, that the descriptive analysis of open-ended questions can serve the following functions: (1) provide a "feel" for the phenomena under investigation, which might prove to be suggestive within the context of discovery; (2) suggest the formulation of particular concepts or variables; and (3) suggest the formulation of particular hypotheses. Often such descriptive data suggest not only the general outlines of concepts and hypotheses, but also very specific ideas for measurement. For example, the measurement of degree of personality heterogeneity involved differentiation of goals or values. One implication of this definition is that the number of goals or values important to a given individual might provide an index of degree of heterogeneity. This index could be utilized, for respondents had been presented with a series of twenty-one fixed-alternative questions concerning the importance (to them) of different possible goals.

13.3 TWO-VARIABLE ANALYSIS OF "REASONS"

AN ILLUSTRATION: REASON ANALYSIS

Reason analysis (see Section 6.4) is a series of procedures for analyzing the range of possible "reasons" that might be given in response to a particular Why? question. In the present context, reason analysis may be used to illustrate two things: a two-variable analysis technique (in the tradition of John Stuart Mill's method of difference), and a relatively structured approach to the analysis of open-ended questions.

The example used will be an interview survey of 192 women in Cambridge, Massachusetts, which focused on their reactions to illness. Some of the questions asked set up hypothetical choice situations. One of them is the following:

> 11. Your father, who has arthritis, now lives alone at the age of seventy-three. He has a tendency to neglect his diet, mainly because he can't get around to shop easily and cooking is difficult for him. Also, his home is quite a mess. One person has suggested that someone be obtained who could shop, cook and clean for him, while another feels that he might be better off in a home for the aged. Which do you think is best?
>   Someone to shop, cook and clean (homemaker).
>   Home for the aged.
> 11a. What are the reasons for your choice?

Unlike the Skopje study, this analysis was preceded by the formulation of a definite set of hypotheses. As a result, the answers to the open-ended question could be used as preliminary evidence for or against the hypotheses. The three hypotheses involved were the following:

> 1. Choices (decisions) of human beings result in part from their values or goals.
> 2. Choices (decisions) of human beings result in part from their expectations as to the values that might be involved in each of the options under consideration.
> 3. Choices (decisions) of human beings result in part from their perceptions of social pressures for the various options.

These hypotheses will be recognized as being similar to those involved in the medical student study.

The data in response to this open-ended question are presented in Table 13-1, which is the product of procedures for categorizing the answers. Table 13-1 shows the relationship among responses pertaining to goals, value expectations, and social pressures on the open-ended question (11a), and the choice made in the fixed-alternative question (11). For example, twenty-four individuals who chose a homemaker in Question 11 also mentioned the goal of individuality in Question 11a. On the other hand, only one individual who chose a home for the aged in Question 11 also mentioned the goal of individuality. On the basis of these data, we may conclude that there is a relationship between two variables (the goal of individuality and the choice of a homemaker for the aged).

Another relationship which appears to exist within the table has to do with the value expectation for good personal adjustment in the father's own home. A total of forty-nine individuals who chose a homemaker also mentioned this value expectation, while only one individual who chose a home for the aged mentioned it. Other variables which appear to be related to the variable of choice of homemaker or a home are (1) a value expectation of safety for the patient, (2) a value expectation that homes for the aged are unsatisfactory, (3) a perceived social pressure

from the father, and (4) a perceived social pressure about the responsibility of the family.

In only one of these relationships are there more individuals choosing a
home for the aged who mention the item in question. Only eight individuals who chose homemaker mentioned safety for the patient, as compared with twenty-five who chose a home for the aged. Thus, we speak of
the *direction* of this relationship as being opposite to that of the others,

TABLE 13–1

Reason Analysis for Respondents Choosing "Homemaker" and
"Home for Aged"*

Reasons	Examples	Home-maker N	Home for Aged N
Goals			
Individuality	"He can go and come as he wants"	24	1
Sociability	"He has his friends"	6	5
Value Expectations			
Financial: negative on home for aged	"Not enough money for a home"	4	0
Financial: positive	"In the long run it will be cheaper"	4	0
Personal adjustment: posi-tive on his own	"He would be happer at home"	49	1
Personal adjustment: posi-tive on home for aged	"There he would have contact with people of his own age"	0	1
Safety for the patient	"There is somebody to take care of him twenty-four hours a day"	8	25
Homes for the aged are generally unsatisfactory	"I worked in homes. They are not good"	23	0
Social Pressures			
Expectations of the father	"He would expect us to keep him home"	15	1
Family responsibility in general	"Family should look out for its own"	20	1

* A total of 140 of the respondents (73 per cent of the total sample) chose "homemaker," with forty-two
respondents (22 per cent) choosing "home for the aged," and ten respondents (5 per cent) not answering.
Some respondents mentioned several reasons for their choice.

for the other items related to the choice of a homemaker whereas this one is related to the choice of a home for the aged.

There exist statistical procedures which the investigator can utilize to make his decisions as to which items are related to the choice of home-maker or a home and which are not (see Chapters 14 and 15). One ad-vantage of such procedures is that they make explicit the criteria for such decisions. In this way, other investigators are free to examine these criteria as well as the ultimate decision. In the analysis described, by contrast, the explicit criteria used to make these decisions have not been presented. Consequently, it is more difficult to obtain agreement that the interpretation made by the investigator is a wise one. The reader may suspect, for example, that the investigator had a particular ax to grind. Once the criteria are outlined, however, the decisions of the investigator are placed on a more objective basis, and it is consequently easier to arrive at consensus within the scientific community.

REASON ANALYSIS AND MILL'S METHOD OF DIFFERENCE

The analysis illustrates Mills *method of difference.* We start with an initial difference among individuals with respect to whether or not their choice in Question 11 was a homemaker or a home for the aged. Now we examine the data to see whether any differences in the items men-tioned in Question 11a occur. Any difference that occurs between the homemaker and home-for-the-aged groupings will be regarded as partial evidence for the existence of a cause-and-effect relationship between the two variables involved.

We may infer, on the basis of the data in Table 13-1, that there is some evidence for a causal relationship between choice of homemaker or home and the goal of individuality. This is because twenty-four of the 140 respondents choosing "homemaker" (or 17 per cent) also mentioned the goal of individuality whereas only one of the forty-one respondents choosing "home for the aged" (2 per cent) referred to this goal. More generally, we may infer that there is evidence for the validity of the hypothesis: *choices of human beings result in part from their values or goals.* We may also infer that there is some evidence for the hypotheses con-cerning value expectations and social pressures.[4]

It is obvious to the present-day scientist that such inferences are un-certain. For example, there is a close relationship between changes in the salaries of Presbyterian ministers in Massachusetts and changes in the

---

[4] Of course, the investigator does not stop at this point in his investigation of cause and ef-fect. The evidence in this table is not very great, and there may be many reasons why the reasons given in Question 11a may not in fact constitute causes of the answer to Question 11. As indicated in Chapter 6, respondents may either be unable or unwilling to tell the truth. For example, respondents may attempt to give a reason in Question 11a that is perfectly consistent with their choice in Question 11, even though it does not represent their true feelings.

price of rum in Havana,[5] but it would be ridiculous to assume that a cause-and-effect relationship therefore exists between the two. Similarly, we cannot be sure that the three hypotheses tested, each of which states a cause-and-effect relationship, are true. It should be noted that the inference drawn from the data was that there is "some evidence" for the hypotheses, which is not the same as stating that the hypotheses are true.

REASON ANALYSIS AND MILL'S METHOD OF AGREEMENT

Mill's *method of agreement* may also be illustrated by utilizing the data from Table 13-1. To do this, let us examine the column under "Homemaker." The numbers in this column may be viewed as representing the amount of "agreement" among individuals between the homemaker choice and the particular item under consideration. For example, twenty-four individuals who chose the homemaker also mentioned the goal of individuality; forty-nine felt that the father's personal adjustment would be better in his own home; twenty-three felt that homes for the aged are generally unsatisfactory, and so on. The degree of agreement indicated by each of these items provides limited evidence for the existence of a cause-and-effect relationship. The same is true for the column under "Home for the Aged," where the item on safety for the patient is quite frequently mentioned by those individuals who made this choice. One might say, for example, that there is some evidence to the effect that an expectation that the personal safety of an aged individual will be very great in a home for the aged constitutes one reason for the choice of a home for the aged.

Of course, such an inference is much more soundly based when the *method of difference* is brought to bear on the data. Thus, the inference is more plausible when we can say that twenty-five of the forty-two individuals (60 per cent) who chose "home for the aged" also mentioned safety, whereas only eight of the 140 individuals (6 per cent) among those who chose "homemaker" also mentioned safety. Had these percentages been identical, a concern with safety would have been no more related to the choice of a home for the aged than to the choice of a homemaker. Using the *method of agreement* it is not possible to detect such an equivalence, since this method focuses on either those individuals choosing "homemaker" or those choosing "home for the aged," but not on a comparison between these groups. Thus, the method of agreement would have implied a conclusion contradicted by the method of difference. A more thorough picture is provided by the method of difference, for the method of agreement presents only partial data. This is why scientists tend to depend on and utilize the former far more than the latter.

[5] This bit of information comes from Darrell Huff, *How to Lie with Statistics* (New York: Norton, 1954).

ONE-VARIABLE AND TWO-VARIABLE ANALYSIS COMPARED

This two-variable analysis of reasons may be compared with the foregoing one-variable analysis of the Skopje data with reference to the contexts of discovery and justification. In the present analysis, the investigator started with a set of hypotheses and utilized the data to provide partial tests for them. The results of such testing tend to suggest that additional studies might be developed (for example, the collection of data for testing the theory as a whole, rather than just the separate hypotheses). Thus, it might be said that the study had an initial function within the context of justification and a subsequent one within the context of discovery. With respect to the Skopje analysis, hypotheses were not fully formulated prior to the analysis, but the analysis itself suggested the formulation of a variable as well as that of several hypotheses. These hypotheses were then partially tested on additional data which happened to be available from the same survey. Thus, the one-variable analysis functioned initially within the context of discovery, but it led to a testing of these ideas within the context of justification. The similarity between these two studies is obvious: both enable the researcher to move back and forth between the context of discovery and the context of justification. This movement is the essence of the research process, with its never-ending cycle of developing and testing ideas, of striving to achieve explanations that are ever more comprehensive and detailed, of seeking to achieve predictions that are more and more accurate, of developing theories of ever-widening scope.

13.4 TWO-VARIABLE ANALYSIS OF STRUCTURED DATA

AN ILLUSTRATION: STUDENT GRADES

A special type of two-variable analysis was involved in the study of choice of a homemaker or a home for the aged. Respondents were asked for their own definitions of the situation with respect to their reasons for making one choice or another. As was pointed out in previous discussions of the interview situation, respondents may be unable or unwilling to convey their reasons. On the other hand, it is entirely possible that the reasons they do give are perfectly valid. Finally, whether or not the reasons are valid, the responses given illustrate human behavior in a particular interaction situation, and thus constitute data that may lead to important understandings of the dynamics of behavior.

Such a two-variable analysis differs from one that does not call upon respondents to examine the causes of a given effect. The latter approach does not depend on the ability of the respondent to perceive such relationships and his willingness to convey them. Of course, no assumption is being made here that the approach that depends on the introspection of the respondent is in any sense inferior to one that does not; as a matter of fact, it is very often useful to supplement one type of analysis with the other. The nonintrospective approach involves simply the cross tabulation or relationship of any given variable with any other variable in order to carry forward the understanding of a given process. These variables may aid the investigator to arrive at the action meaning (that is, the respondent's own conceptions of the processes involved) of the respondent without directly ascertaining his act meaning.

The two-variable analysis of data which do not involve the act meanings of respondents may be illustrated by an exercise conducted in an introductory sociology class. One of the requirements of the course was that each student analyze questionnaire data and submit a research report based on this analysis. The assignment involved a considerable amount of work, including the use of IBM data-processing equipment and the performance of several statistical tests. At an early stage in the assignment, students were asked whether or not they were interested in it. Results are shown in Table 13-2.

TABLE 13-2

Degree of Interest in a Class Assignment

Interested (%)	Not Interested (%)	Total (%)
44	56	100 (N = 43)

SOME CONVENTIONS FOR TABULAR PRESENTATION: ONE VARIABLE

Several facts about single-variable data should be emphasized. First, it should be noted that Table 13-2 includes a reference both to the variable involved ("degree of interest") and to its different categories ("interested," "not interested"). In addition, the table indicates the percentage of students who were interested and not interested. Percentage analysis is utilized extensively in the behavioral sciences because of the clarity with which it conveys information and the ease with which it allows comparisons to be made. This will become apparent in Tables 13-3 and 13-4, which present data on two variables. One additional fact about Table 13-2 is that the total number (or frequency) of students in the class is listed in parentheses. This is done because percentages can be quite misleading when we do not know what frequencies are involved. For example, the statement that *67 per cent of students are interested and 33 per cent are not* may mean that two students are interested and one is not, or it may mean that 200 students are interested and 100 students are not. When the total numbers of students is included in the table, a reader may calculate the frequency of students who are interested and those who are not by multiplying the decimal equivalent of each percentage by the total number of students:

Interested	$0.44 \times 43 = 19$
Not interested	$0.56 \times 43 = 24$

The question might be raised as to why the frequency was not presented along with the percentage for each category in Table 3-2. Actually, this might well have been done. There are no standard rules for the construction of tables other than one widely accepted general goal: clear and unambiguous communication. Because only one variable is involved in Table 13-2, it would not be particularly confusing to include frequencies along with the percentages. When two or more variables are included in a given table, however, an inclusion of all of the frequencies as well as the percentages tends to make it somewhat more difficult to obtain a clear picture of the data. Clarity is especially important if we take into account the fact that the scientific literature in any given field is voluminous, and that the amount of time which may be devoted to a given research report is necessarily quite limited.

One final point about Table 13-2 has to do with something that is omitted rather than included, the way in which the variable "degree of interest" fits into the researcher's theory. In particular, does the investigator have in mind any concept represented by this variable which constitutes an element of theory and which is perhaps more abstract than the variable under consideration? In the analysis of data, it is all too tempting to stay at the concrete and specific level of the wording of the question (in a survey) and neglect the development of more abstract concepts, but the scope of the study is thereby reduced. In Table 13-2, "degrees of interest" is conceived of as getting at a particular goal or value, namely, the performance of the class assignment. The substitution of the word *goal* for *interest* does not by itself increase the scope of the study, but the concept of goal or value is already conceived of by the investigator as an important element of propositions and theory.

SOME CONVENTIONS FOR TABULAR PRESENTATION: TWO VARIABLES

After the introductory students completed their assignment, the research reports were graded. The investigator at that point focused his efforts on the attempt to discover the factors that affected the grades on these reports. One hypothesis tested was that the degree of interest in the paper affected the grade obtained. (The data that test this hypothesis are presented in Table 13-3.)

Although Table 13-3 may look simple enough, several of the proce-

TABLE 13–3
Grades Obtained by Students with Different Degrees of
Interest in a Class Assignment

| | Degree of Interest | |
| | Interested | Not Interested |
Grade	(%)	(%)
B— or higher	58	25
C + or lower	42	75
Total	100	100
	(19)	(24)

dures involved require explanation. First, the general format is quite similar to that of Table 13-2. Both specify the variable(s) involved as well as the particular categories of each. Also, both tables deal with percentages and present the frequencies in parentheses. Table 13-3, an with each percentage were included. Unlike Table 13-2, in which the percentages could be calculated only in one direction, Table 13-3 presents example of a fourfold table because it is composed of four major cells or entries, would be a good deal more cluttered if the frequency associated a choice of directions. Let us designate *degree of interest* as the independent or causal variable and *grade* as the dependent or effect variable in this table. Then the totals used to calculate the percentages may represent summations of the frequencies in each of the categories of the independent variable or the dependent variable. If they are calculated for the independent variable, as they are in Table 13-3, we say that the percentages are computed "in the direction of the independent variable."

Table 13-4 is identical to Table 13-3 except that its percentages are computed in the direction of the dependent variable; that is, the totals on which the percentages are based are summations of the frequencies in each of the categories of the dependent variable.

TABLE 13–4
Grades Obtained by Students with Different Degrees of
Interest in a Class Assignment

| | Degree of Interest | | |
| | Interested | Not Interested | Total |
Grade	(%)	(%)	(%)
B— or higher	65	35	100 (17)
C + or lower	31	69	100 (26)

It is generally easier to communicate information when percentages are computed in the direction of the independent variable (as in Table 13-3). This can be understood when we attempt to state the results derived from each of the two tables. Table 13-3 indicates that 58 per cent of those students who were interested in the class assignment received a grade of B— or higher, whereas only 25 per cent of those students who were not interested received a grade of B— or higher. Thus, the percentage of high grades is substantially higher among those students showing interest in the assignment than among students who did not. It would of course constitute an equivalent statement to say that the percentage of low grades is substantially lower among those students showing interest in the assignment than among those students who did not.

Table 13-4 indicates that the percentage of students showing interest in the assignment is substantially higher among those students who received high grades than among those who received low grades. Thus, the reasoning is from the dependent variable or effect (those receiving high grades and those receiving low grades) to the independent variable or cause. By contrast, Table 13-3 compares percentages between the two categories of the independent variable (degree of interest) and reasons from the independent variable to the dependent variable. Because it is easier to reason from cause to effect rather than from effect to cause, it is conventional to compute percentages in the direction of the independent variable, as in Table 13-3.

Another consideration is the degree of accuracy to which percentages should be computed. In Tables 13-3 and 13-4 they were computed to the nearest whole per cent. This degree of accuracy should suffice for most purposes. The great advantage of not computing percentages to the nearest tenth or one hundredth of 1 per cent is the clarity achieved. The situation would be different, however, if, for example, this rounding procedure obliterated very slight differences between individuals in the two categories of the independent variable. Let us suppose, for example, that 10,000 students were interested in the assignment and 10,000 more were not. Let us also assume that 42.4 per cent of the interested students obtained high grades while 41.6 per cent of the uninterested students obtained high grades. This difference may be statistically significant, but it would be lost if both figures were rounded to the nearest whole percentage point. Of course, such a situation happens rarely. A more usual reason for calculating percentages to the nearest tenth of 1 per cent is to conduct more exact statistical tests. Even in such cases, however, it is not essential to present figures that are accurate to the nearest tenth of 1 per cent in the research report.

If we grant that a relationship has been established between degree of interest in the class assignment and grade received, what general implications does such a finding have? Here we must look to those concepts and propositions that represent a higher level of abstraction. Degree of interest in the class assignment may be viewed as an indicator of the value of the class assignment to the individual, whereas the grade on the research report is a reflection of a large number of choices or decisions the student made during the preparation of his report. Thus, one proposition representing a higher level of abstraction than that which relates interest to grades is the same as one of those previously discussed in the context of the study of reactions to illness in Cambridge, Massachusetts: *Choices (decisions) of human beings result in part from their values or goals.* At this level of abstraction, the data constitute partial evidence for a proposition of much wider scope.

ADDITIONAL INDEPENDENT VARIABLES

Thus far in the search for factors which affected the students' grades, only one factor has been considered, interest in the assignment. Another factor that was tested had to do with the seating arrangement of the students. It was noted by the instructor that about half the students tended to bunch up in the first three rows of the large lecture room and that most of the remaining students were packed in the rear of the room; few students occupied seats in the center. This pattern suggested that the seating arrangement might constitute an indicator of the degree to which the student valued the class lectures and discussions. Table 13-5 contains the data used to test the hypothesis that seating arrangement affected grades on the research reports.

TABLE 13-5
Grades Obtained by Students with Different Seating Positions

	Seating Position	
Grade	Rows 1–3 (%)	Rows 4–15 (%)
B — or higher	55	24
C + or lower	45	76
Total	100	100
	(22)	(21)

The relationship emerging from these results seems to be about as substantial as the one between interest in the assignment and grade. If we considered these data in relation to a proposition at a higher level of abstraction, we might say that partial evidence is also provided here for the proposition that *choices of human beings result in part from their values or goals.* It should be noted that Table 13-5 utilizes data collected by means of observation as well as through paper-and-pencil tests. Although most of the examples of analytic procedures presented here are based on questions put to respondents, procedures for analyzing other types of data are generally no different from these.

When these results were presented to the students in the class, they seemed generally to be quite surprised. Few of them seem to have suspected that the factors of interest in the class assignment and seating position would be closely related to grade on the assignment. This points up the importance to the investigator of cross tabulations that are not based solely on the respondent's definition of the situation. This is not to deny that the respondent's definition of the situation may be quite suggestive in its own right. In this case, the students were asked what other factors they thought might have affected the grades; some of the answers are analyzed in Tables 13-6 and 13-7.

The data in Table 13-6 do not indicate any relationship between social science background and grade. Although it might be argued that 41 per

TABLE 13-6

Grades Obtained by Students with Different Social Science Backgrounds

Grade	One or More Courses in Sociology, Psychology, or Anthropology (%)	No Previous Courses in Sociology, Psychology, or Anthropology (%)
B — or higher	41	38
C + or lower	59	62
Total	100	100
	(22)	(21)

TABLE 13-7

Grades Obtained by Students from Different College Classes

Grade	Freshman or Sophomore (%)	Junior or Senior (%)
B— or higher	27	59
C + or lower	73	41
Total	100	100
	(26)	(17)

cent of students among those with the greatest social science background received high grades as compared with only 38 per cent of those with the least background, such a percentage difference is insignificant when the actual frequencies are taken into account. As a matter of fact, of the twenty-two individuals with the greater background nine of them obtained a B— or higher, whereas eight out of the twenty-one individuals with the lesser background obtained a B— or higher. If the frequencies were very much higher, however, the difference between 41 per cent and 38 per cent might have some significance.

Table 13-7 indicates a definite relationship between college class and grade received. We may infer that the insights of professional social scientists are not the only ones effective in explaining human behavior: the definition of the situation by those individuals whose behavior is to be explained constitutes another important source of ideas. Once this relationship between college class and grade on the class assignment is shown, however, there remains to seek an explanation on a more abstract and theoretical level. Table 13-6 indicates that it is probably not the additional courses upper classmen have taken that give them an advantage over lower classmen. One possible explanation might have to do with study habits (for example, upper classmen may have learned to receive or perceive more accurately than lower classmen the expectations sent by the instructor as to what is required). Such an interpretation would have to be checked by the collection of additional data. For example, the instructor might give the class instructions that are then to be summarized by the students, and the different classes might then be compared on the accuracy of their interpretations. Other interpretations of the data in Table 13-7 are also possible.

From the tables presented, it can perhaps be seen that research is a cumulative process. In the search for factors affecting grades on the class assignment, many different hypotheses are possible. For any hypothesis that is verified, it remains to obtain a theoretical interpretation. At that point, additional data most probably will be needed to check the alternative interpretations.

EXERCISES

1. Discuss the pros and cons of the idea that any so-called descriptive study in fact contains numerous implicit hypotheses.

2. Discuss the pros and cons of the idea that there is no such thing as a qualitative study which cannot be transformed into a quantitative study.

3. On the basis of any one of the five categories of response discussed in the Skopje example of Section 13.2, develop a series of six items that you would expect to form a Guttman-type scale.

4. Discuss some of the implicit assumptions behind the technique of reason analysis.

5. Define a problem for which you can obtain evidence from a group of students. Collect data through questionnaire procedures and perform a series of two-variable analyses analogous to those in Section 13.4.

ANNOTATED REFERENCES

BATTEN, THELMA. *Reasoning and Research: Guide for the Beginning Social Science Researcher.* Boston: Little, Brown and Company, 1970. The author weaves in a good deal of logic along with her explanations of research procedures, making interesting use of an analogy between games and the research process. The result is a synthesis of important aspects of the philosophy of science, along with specific research procedures. Nevertheless the book is quite down to earth and contains material that is generally learned only through actual participation in research.

BROWN, ROBERT. *Explanation in Social Science.* Chicago: Aldine Publishing Company, 1963. Brown's thesis is that all description is in part explanation, and that the degree to which it includes explanation varies. Thus, even one-variable analysis is guided by the researcher's theory, whether consciously or (more often) unconsciously.

LAZARSFELD, PAUL F., and MORRIS ROSENBERG (eds.). *The Language of Social Research.* New York: The Free Press, 1955. This reader consists of sixty-four articles about a variety of studies. Its major parts deal with concepts and indexes, multivariate analysis, analysis of change through time, formal aspects of research on human groups, empirical analysis of action, and general problems in the philosophy of social science.

CHAPTER 14 Principles of Statistical Decision Making

14.1 THE NATURE OF STATISTICS

FUNCTIONS OF STATISTICS

A fairly recent conception of statistics is "a body of methods for making wise decisions in the face of uncertainty."[1] This differs from many widely held conceptions of statistics. For example, statistics is often thought of as a collection of facts stated in numerical terms. This is partly in agreement with the first definition, for it is desirable to utilize whatever facts are relevant if one is to come up with wise decisions. Moreover, the properties of numbers have been found to be most useful when attempts have been made to apply them to phenomena under study and use them as a basis for decisions.

One important distinction between a conception of statistics as *a collection of facts* and as *a body of methods for making wise decisions* is that the former makes no reference to any human agent whereas the latter indirectly brings in the decision maker by referring to *decisions.* But who are the decision makers to whom reference is made? What kinds of decisions are they involved in making? And by what criteria may we judge whether or not a decision is wise?

According to one point of view, "the purposes for which statistical data are collected can be grouped into two broad categories, which may be described loosely as practical action and scientific knowledge."[2] The practical actions may include anything from the decision by a university administrator on whether or not to raise tuition to the decision of a secretary on whether or not to carry her umbrella. Scientists, however, are concerned with decisions that lead to the furthering of knowledge

---

[1] W. Allen Wallis and Harry V. Roberts, *Statistics: A New Approach* (New York: Free Press, 1956), p. 3. More recent books on statistics designed for the social scientist include John H. Mueller et al., *Statistical Reasoning in Sociology,* 2nd ed. (Boston: Houghton Mifflin, 1970); Albert Pierce, *Fundamentals of Nonparametric Statistics* (Belmont, Calif.: Dickenson, 1970); Ralph H. Kolstoe, *Introduction to Statistics for the Behavioral Sciences* (Homewood, Ill.: Dorsey, 1969); John T. Roscoe, *Fundamental Research Statistics for the Behavioral Sciences* (New York: Holt, 1969); and Robert S. Weiss, *Statistics in Social Research* (New York: Wiley, 1968).

[2] Wallis and Roberts, op. cit., p. 4.

about reality. They, as well as the university administrator and the secretary, probably evaluate the wisdom of a given decision on the basis of the effect of its outcome on their values. If, for example, the secretary decides to carry her umbrella and it actually does rain, her goal of avoiding being drenched is achieved and she evaluates the decision as an intelligent one. A scientist may decide, on the basis of available evidence, that a particular hypothesis is valid and is therefore worth exploring. If this leads to important discoveries, he too will probably decide that his decision was a wise one.

The decision-making procedures of the layman and the scientist may be quite similar. For example, the university administrator, in making his decision about a tuition increase, probably takes into account a number of factors or goals. For example, additional funds may be desired in order to make faculty salaries more competitive, to pay for increased maintenance costs, or to finance the expansion of the physical plant. On the other hand, he may be concerned about the possible loss of high-quality applicants to the university. His action may constitute an attempt to make the kind of decision that maximizes gains and minimizes losses. But how does the administrator know, for example, what the actual effect of a tuition raise will be on high-quality applicants to the university? The chances are that he knows very little about this, but he must make his decision even in the face of uncertainty. The wise administrator gathers whatever facts on the situation he can and then makes his decision in such a way as to maximize the probability of achieving his goals.

The scientist too has numerous decisions to make, such as the decision as to which of several theories to attempt to develop and test further. The selection of the most promising theory may lead to a substantial increase in scientific knowledge, whereas the selection of a sterile or invalid theory may not. The scientist, like the administrator, must make his decision in the face of uncertainty. Although data on each theory are available, results are never certain in any science. In the behavioral sciences in particular, results thus far have tended to be quite limited and tentative. The wise scientist carefully examines whatever data are available and then makes his decision in such a way as to maximize the probability of achieving his goals.

Statistical procedures may aid in the decision-making process of both the administrator and the scientist. They may aid in the collection of additional data by specifying, for example, probability sampling procedures. They may aid in the analysis of the data by providing quantitative rules for inferring the nature of reality from these data. They may aid in the decision-making process by replacing an intuitive method with a highly objective and quantified process that makes maximum use of the data available.

STATISTICS AND SCIENTIFIC COMMUNICATION

If statistics is conceived of as "a body of methods for making wise decisions in the face of uncertainty," how is it to be distinguished from the research procedures discussed in earlier chapters? Is it not true that all research strategy attempts to accomplish the same end? The key distinction between statistics and other research methods is that statistics provides a *quantified* approach to research. Statistical procedures rely heavily on mathematics and, in particular, on the concept of probability and the rules for combining probabilities that have been developed by mathematicians.

Somewhat more insight into the nature of statistics may be gained if we examine what this approach achieves in the context of justification. Statistics, like any other research strategy, is not a disembodied set of rules that is "right" for a certain class of situations; rather, it is a set of procedures utilized by scientists in their search for the nature of reality. As such, statistics may well be evaluated with respect to its impact on the communication process that binds together the scientific community.

Statistical procedures may serve to make quite clear the exact basis on which the scientist collects, analyzes, and interprets his data. Knowing this, other scientists are in a position to understand more thoroughly what has been done and to make use of this information in furthering their own efforts. It may be decided, for example, to repeat or replicate the research conducted by another scientist, or to introduce certain modifications in theory or method in order to examine the impact of these changes. Other scientists may be dissatisfied with the analysis and interpretation of data collected by a given scientist. If that scientist utilized statistical procedures, however, they are in a position to understand better the basis for his conclusions.

Statistical procedures provide more than the possibility of effective communication within the scientific community. Scientists largely agree on what a lawyer would call *rules of evidence*. That is to say, there is considerable agreement on what kinds of data are admissible as evidence and what conventions may be followed for assessing the implications, for a particular hypothesis, of a given set of data. It is in this area that statistical decision procedures play an important role. The conventions or rules for assessing the implications of such data are often based on explicit statistical formulations which predict the probability that the scientist is correct or is in error in his decision on whether to accept or reject a given hypothesis. Statistical procedures also play a role in the collection of data which is "admissible" as evidence. The role of statistics in probability sampling procedures has already been referred to. Another example is that of randomization procedures in the context of the experiment. These rules or conventions for the acceptance of evidence also aid in the communication process among scientists. For example, even if a given scientist does not subscribe to the generally accepted conventions, at least it will be perfectly clear to him which procedures have been utilized, and he is thus in a position to make maximum use of whatever has been accomplished.

THE CONTEXT OF DISCOVERY

There are at least four ways in which statistical decision procedures may aid the scientific community in the context of discovery. One of these is indirect, namely, through what they accomplish within the context of justification. For example, a conclusion, made on the basis of statistical calculations, that there is substantial evidence for the validity of a given hypothesis serves to point the scientist in a certain direction. Through the acceptance of a given hypothesis, the scientist learns that further work in the development and testing of that hypothesis and related hypotheses might be fruitful. On the other hand, if the evidence obtained does not support the hypothesis, the scientist will be led to alter it or look to other hypotheses.

A second way in which statistics might be of aid seems to be more of a program than a reality. At present, although rules of evidence in the context of justification may be widely accepted, no corresponding set of rules have been tested and widely accepted in the context of discovery. Each scientist selects the methods and theory he believes will be most fruitful. For example, the process whereby a given scientist is exposed to the results of various research studies tends to be very unorganized. He may or may not subscribe to a particular journal or book, and may decide to adopt a research procedure or theory simply because it is familiar. Or he may be impressed by the prestige of the originator of the method or theory.

These decision procedures are a far cry indeed from statistical decision procedures. If certain goals for the scientific enterprise are widely accepted, then it may be possible to utilize statistical decision procedures to aid in the evaluation of the various methods of discovery. For example, evidence may be gathered about the degree of utility which each of the various data-collection methods has had for the explanation of human behavior, or the kinds of situations in which each seems to have been most effective. On the basis of such evidence, rules might be developed for selecting some procedures over others in certain situations, and these rules might even be extended to the selection of hypotheses or theories.

This does not mean that complete consensus is possible among scientists as to which method or theory is most appropriate for a given research situation. The degree of agreement will depend on the weight of evidence for a particular method or theory in a given situation. The determination of this weight would, in turn, depend on rules for the acceptance of evidence. And again, although any given scientist may not agree with his colleagues on the rules for accepting data as evidence or those for weighing it, he will at least be able to understand more completely the basis on which his colleagues arrived at their decisions. He may even be encouraged to collect the kind of data which might indicate to his colleagues that other rules of evidence and decision making are more effective for moving toward the goals of science.

A third way in which statistics may be of aid in the context of discovery is also more of a program than a reality. Here we may utilize an analogue from the context of justification. Within the context of any given statistical test of hypotheses, the investigator has a number of options. For example, he has to decide whether his finding of a relationship that actually does not exist is more disastrous than his not finding a relationship that does exist. Statistical decision procedures provide a mechanism for numerically weighting these two results so that the investigator may make his choice. Thus, a degree of consensus has been achieved on the choice of tactics for deciding exactly how a given statistical test may be applied. An increase in this degree of consensus awaits further proof that some tactics are more effective than others in a given situation.

Within the context of discovery, the investigator generally does not consider an entire range of methods or theories from which a choice is to be made; rather, he centers on one particular method or theory, and the choice he makes is among the several options that exist for the collection of data within the context of this method or theory. For example, in the use of interviewing procedures there are choices to be made on the relative proportions of open-ended and fixed-alternative questions, on the degree to which an interview is to be standardized, on the use of projective techniques and indirect methods, on the way in which data are to be recorded, on the various ways in which the social-desirability variable is to be handled, and on many other points as well. At present only very limited data are available on the relative effectiveness of the different choices, and the data are even more limited on their relative effectiveness in the context of the special characteristics of a particular research situation. Thus, the investigator is generally constrained to make intuitive decisions, and the basis for these decisions is rarely communicated to the scientific community.

It would be possible to rationalize these procedures so as to achieve a degree of consensus on a strategy for making these decisions within any given research context. This would result in a breakdown of the various less-pragmatic bases for making these choices. Thus, for example, the parochial attachment of a given investigator to the exclusive use of open-ended questions in all research situations might give way to a degree of consensus on the value of a certain proportion of open-ended questions for a given research situation. Naturally, each investigator would still be free to reject the generally accepted strategy, but at least he would be able to understand more thoroughly what other scientists have done, and he might be challenged to conduct investigations designed to improve on the generally accepted strategy.

It is perhaps superfluous to add that in order for consensus to be reached on any given strategy, a good deal of evidence for its effectiveness must be presented. Such evidence, in turn, depends on the existence of the kind of theory that can provide thorough explanations and accurate predictions for the various types of research situations. For example, theory must be able to predict what the reactions of individuals of various types will be to open-ended and fixed-alternative questions on a given topic.

A fourth use of statistics in the context of discovery stems from the fact that statistical decision procedure is itself a theory that might be fruitfully applied to the choices of human beings. Thus far, statistical decision theory has been used largely in the choices scientists face in the collection and analysis of data. Thus, the choices scientists *might or should* make have been stressed, rather than the choices they *actually* do make. It is possible, however, to use statistical decision theory to focus on what choices human beings (including scientists) actually do make in a given situation. Here, no assumption needs to be made that human beings are incredibly rational and always make optimal choices; indeed, the situation is very similar to that in the medical student study, where *rationality* was defined in such a way that each individual was conceived of as acting on the basis of his own particular expectations and his own set of values. Furthermore, as in the medical student study, no prior assumption is made that the theory has already been proved in the context of justification.

The question might be raised as to whether or not there is any utility in employing statistical procedures on any given aspect of investigation. As a matter of fact, this question has been quite pointedly asked by several sociologists with respect to the testing of hypotheses in survey research.[3] The answer lies in the contributions statistical procedures can make in the contexts of justification and discovery. Thus, the question is always a legitimate one, as is any question on the utility of a given method or theory. When the available evidence indicates that a particular method or theory is less fruitful than another, it seems wise for the scientist to select the approach that appears to be more effective. At the present time it seems that statistical procedures may be of great value both in the context of justification and in the context of discovery.[4]

[3] See, for example, Hanan Selvin, "A Critique of Tests of Significance in Survey Research," *American Sociological Review*, **22** (1957), 519–27.

[4] For a reply to Selvin, see Robert McGinnis, "Randomization and Inference in Sociological Research," *American Sociological Review*, **23** (1958), 408–14. For more recent contributions to this controversy see Denton E. Morrison and Ramon E. Henkel, "Significance Tests Reconsidered," *The American Sociologist*, **4** (1969), 131–40; and Robert F. Winch and Donald T. Campbell, "Proof? No. Evidence? Yes. The Significance of Tests of Significance," *The American Sociologist*, **4** (1969), 140–43.

14.2 THE NATURE OF PROBABILITY

An understanding of the concept of probability as conceived mathematically is essential for learning the nature of statistics. This term is a common one in ordinary usage and conveys the idea of the likelihood of a
given event or occurrence. Thus, a highly probable event is one which
will most likely occur, whereas an event with a low probability is not
likely to occur. The mathematics of probability may be viewed as providing the basis for this kind of interpretation of probability.

From a mathematical point of view, the probability of an event is a
number that lies between 0 and 1, inclusive. More subjectively, the probability of a tossed coin's coming up heads will be 0 when we are certain
that heads cannot occur, .5 when the chance of heads occurring appears
to be as great as the chance for tails, and 1 when we are certain that
heads will occur. Furthermore, if we consider a number of alternative or
mutually exclusive events, and if one among these events must occur, then
the sum of the probabilities of the separate events is equal to 1. This may
be illustrated by tossing a coin twice and considering the alternative
events: two heads (HH), one heads and one tails (HT or TH), and two
tails (TT). If we assume that the probability of a heads on a single toss
is .5, then the probability of HH is equal to .5 $\times$ .5, or .25. Similarly, the
probability of TT will be .5 $\times$ .5, or 25. The probability of HT (heads on
the first toss and tails on the second) is .5 $\times$ .5, or .25. The probability of
TH is the same, i.e., .5 $\times$ .5, or .25. Thus, the probability of HT or TH
is .50. These probabilities are listed below:

Probability of two heads $= p(HH) = .50 \times .50 = .25$
Probability of two tails $= p(TT) = .50 \times .50 = .25$
Probability of one heads and one tails $= p(HT) + p(TH) = (.50 \times .50) + (.50 \times .50) =$
$.25 + .25 = .50$
Probability of two heads, or two tails, or one heads one tails $= p(HH) + p(TT) + [p(HT) +$
$p(TH)] = .25 + .25 + .50 = 1$

MULTIPLICATION AND ADDITION RULES

The above example illustrates several principles or laws of combining
probabilities which are fundamental to the mathematical formulation of
probability. One of them is the *multiplication rule*, which states that *if A
and B are two events, independent of one another, the probability of getting
both A and B is the product of the probability of Event A and the probability
of Event B.* For purposes of illustration let us define Event A as *heads on
first toss* and Event B as *heads on second toss*. These two events are in-

dependent of one another because obtaining heads with the first toss cannot affect whether or not heads is obtained with the second toss. According to the multiplication rule, the probability of heads turning up on both the first and second tosses is equal to the product of the probability of a heads on the first toss and the probability of a heads on the second toss. Stating this in mathematical terms, we have

Probability of two heads = $p(HH) = p(H) \times p(H) = .50 \times .50 = .25$

This multiplication rule was used in the above example for the calculation of $p(HH)$, $p(TT)$, $p(HT)$, and $p(TH)$, although it was not stated explicitly.

Another principle illustrated above is the addition rule, which states that if *A, B, C, . . . J are all mutually exclusive events, then the probability of getting either A or B or C . . . or J is equal to the sum of the probabilities of the separate events A, B, C, . . . and J*. Let us consider the following as the three mutually exclusive events:

Event A = Occurrence of two heads = (HH)
Event B = Occurrence of two tails = (TT)
Event C = Occurrence of one heads and tails = (HT) or (TH)

These events are mutually exclusive because, for example, it is not possible for both two heads and two tails to occur in two tosses of a coin. According to the addition rule, $p(A$ or B or $C) = p(A) + p(B) + p(C) = .25 + .25 + .50 = 1$. Thus, like the multiplication rule, the addition rule was used in the above example although it was not explicitly stated.

The addition rule was also used in another part of the example, the calculation of the probability of Event C (the occurrence of one heads and one tails). Here there are two ways in which this event may take place: if the first toss comes up heads and the second one comes up tails, or if the first toss comes up tails and the second comes up heads. We may consider these occurrences to be Events A and B, respectively. The two events are also mutually exclusive. It was necessary in the example to calculate the probability of one heads and one tails, which may be stated as $p(HT$ or $TH)$, or $p(A$ or $B)$. This is a situation in which the addition rule may be applied, and we have the following:

$p(A$ or $B) = p(HT$ or $TH) = p(HT) + p(TH) = .25 + .25 = .50$

INTERPRETATIONS, AXIOMS, AND THEOREMS

Having outlined and illustrated some of the mathematics of probability, it will be useful to explore its relationship to interpretations of probability, which are useful to the scientist. The discussion here will be similar to that having to do with the mathematical properties of the various scales of measurement. There, it will be recalled, interpretations were made within the context of such illustrations as the play of a basketball team, and it was determined whether the axioms that stated the properties of a given scale were found to hold for the illustration.

A more complete presentation of the interpretation of axiomatic systems involves definitions and theorems in addition to axioms and interpretations. Although it is beyond the scope of this volume to present a rigorous discussion of the mathematics of probability, an informal treatment of the derivation and function of a probability theorem will follow. The aim here is to show how the mathematical definition of probability, as well as the addition and multiplication rules, are incorporated in a probability theorem. The theorem itself will be interpreted so that it will be seen to be useful to the scientist in the decision-making process.

Probability is an uninterpreted term within the mathematical field of probability theory just as the terms *point* and *line* are uninterpreted in plane geometry. In order to make use of the mathematics of plane geometry, it is necessary to interpret these terms or coordinate them with entities in the physical world. In addition, the axioms of plane geometry must hold true for the phenomena under investigation. When the interpretation is made and we have evidence that the axioms hold, the multitude of theorems in plane geometry may be effectively applied to predict phenomena. On the other hand, if one or more axioms do not hold, then the theorems may be incorrect. Thus, for example, one of the axioms of plane geometry is that one and only one line can be drawn through a given point so that it is parallel to a given line that does not contain the point. On the surface of a sphere, however, it is possible to draw many lines through a given point that are parallel to (that is, do not intersect with) the original line. Consequently, this axiom does not hold for the surface of a sphere, although it does hold for the surface of a plane; the same is also true for the other axioms of plane geometry. We would thus expect the theorems of plane geometry to hold true for plane surfaces, but not for spherical surfaces.

There is a parallel between the nature of probability theory and that of plane geometry which might help to explain the relationships between the mathematics of probability and its applications in the area of statistical decision making. First, the mathematically uninterpreted term *probability* may be interpreted in several ways. One of them is known as the *frequency interpretation of probability*. For example, the probability of heads coming up on a single toss of a coin is the relative frequency of heads occurring in an infinite number of tosses. Thus, if a coin were tossed an infinite number of times and heads came up 50 per cent of the time, then we would state that $p(H) = .50$. On the other hand if heads came up 41 per cent of the time, we would state that $p(H) = .41$. Such an interpretation allows us to form a tie between the uninterpreted term *probability* and something that can be observed.

Of course, it is not possible for the scientist or anyone else to toss a coin an infinite number of times, and thus he must be satisfied with a finite series of tosses. Consequently, it is not possible for him to know for certain what the probability of any event is. This lack of certainty about the nature of reality is, of course, characteristic of scientific investigation and is inherent in the human situation. The best that the scientist can do is to estimate the "true probability" on the basis of limited data.

We may now view the addition rule and the multiplication rule as constituting axioms of probability theory. We may check whether or not these hold in the coin-tossing situation by using the frequency interpretation of probability. Thus, for example, we might toss each of two coins a very large number of times and, on the basis of the results, estimate $p(H)$ for each. Let us assume that it is .50 for each coin. Then we might toss the two coins jointly a very large number of times in order to determine whether or not $p(HH) = .25, p(TT) = .25$, and $p(HT \text{ or } TH) = .50$. If such relative frequencies (or relative frequencies very close to them) are in fact obtained, then we may conclude that there is evidence for these axioms when the frequency interpretation of probability is made.

A theorem that would be of particular value for the example at hand is one which would provide us with the probability of a given number of heads in tossing a coin not only twice but any number of times. (We shall not always be dealing with oversimplified situations, and it will be important to utilize larger samples.) Such a theorem would, then, enable us to calculate the probability of getting exactly r heads in N tosses of a coin, where N refers to the number of tosses and r is any number from 0 to N, inclusive. This theorem (the binomial theorem) does exist, and it may be stated in the following form, which has been especially adapted to our example:

BINOMIAL DISTRIBUTION

$$p(r) = \frac{N!}{r!(N-r)!} \times p(H)^r p(T)^{N-r}$$

or	probability of exactly r heads	=	number of ways of getting r heads	$\times$	probability of one of the ways of getting r heads

$N!$ should be read *factorial N*, and it is defined as $(N)(N - 1)(N - 2)$ ... $(2)(1)$.

Similarly, $r!$ is equal to $(r)(r - 1)(r - 2)$ ... $(2)(1)$, and the same holds true for $(N - r)!$ Also, it should be noted that $0!$ is defined as 1.

Let us first test this theorem on the calculations previously made for the probability of two heads, one head, and no heads in two tosses of a coin, taking the calculation of $p(2\ heads)$ first. Here $N = 2$, and $r = 2$. Then, substituting in the formula, we have the following for the number of ways of getting two heads:

$$\frac{N!}{r!(N - r)!} = \frac{2!}{2!(2 - 2)!} = \frac{(2)(1)}{(2)(1)0!} = \frac{2}{(2)(1)} = \frac{1}{1} = 1$$

Thus, according to the calculation, there is only one way in which two heads may be obtained in two tosses of a given coin (and this checks out with our previous example): *HH* or heads on the first toss and heads on the second. (Of course, all of this may seem exceedingly trivial, but the results will not be as obvious when we move on to a more complicated example.) The probability of this one way of getting two heads is calculated as follows:

$$p(H)^r p(T)^{N-r} = (.50)^2 (.50)^{2-2} = .25 (.50)^0$$

Because any number taken to the power of 0 is equal to 1, we have $.25(.50)^0 = .25(1) = .25$. Thus, substituting these calculated values in the equation:

$$p(2\ heads) = \frac{N!}{r!(N - r)!} p(H)^r p(T)^{N-r} = 1\,(.25) = .25$$

This is the same value as that obtained previously, and thus the theorem works in this instance.

The theorem may also be tested on the calculation of the probability of one heads in two tosses. Substituting in the formula, we have

$$p(1\ heads) = \frac{2!}{1!(2 - 1)!} \times (.50)^1(.50)^{2-1} = \frac{2}{1(1)} \times (.50)(.50)$$

It should be noted that for this calculation there were two ways of getting one heads: heads on the first toss and tails on the second, or tails on the first toss and heads on the second. Because the result is the same as that previously arrived at on the basis of the rules of multiplication and addition, the theorem checks out correctly once more.

Finally, the calculation for the probability of no heads in two tosses is

$$p(0 \text{ heads}) = \frac{2!}{0!(2-0)!} \times (.50)^0 (.50)^{2-0} = \frac{2}{1(2)} \times 1 (.25)$$

$$= 1(.25) = .25$$

Here once more the result provided by the theorem is the same as previously calculated.

The theorem is based directly on the axioms, although a formal proof of it would require several other theorems from permutation and combination theory. The term $N! / r! (N - r)!$ represents the number of ways of getting r heads, and this is multiplied by the probability of one of the ways of getting r heads. Each way of getting r heads, however, has the same probability as any other way of getting r heads, because differences in the order of occurrence of a given number of heads do not change the probability of that sequence. Thus, for example, $p(HT) = p(TH) = (.50)$ $(.50) = .25$. This would be true even if the probability of a heads was equal to .10. Thus, $p(HT) = (.10) (.90) = .09$; also, $p(TH) = (.90)(.10)$ $= .09$. Consequently, when we multiply the probability of one of the ways of getting r heads by the number of such ways, we are in reality doing the equivalent of *summing* or adding all the separate probabilities of getting r heads, and this is a utilization of the axiom for the addition of probabilities. The axiom for multiplication is utilized within the term $p(H)^r$ $p(T)^{N-r}$, which represents the probability of one of the ways of getting r heads. Here the exponents simply provide a shorthand for the successive multiplication of each of the probabilities by itself a given number of times.

This presentation of some of the rules of probability in the form of axioms and a theorem (and utilizing the mathematical definition of probability) illustrates the way in which the mathematics of probability is related to data about the real world. Thus far, one interpretation of the concept of probability has been presented, and two axioms and one theorem have been illustrated. To complete the picture, it is necessary to show how the theorem may be valuable for the scientific process, just as the theorems of plane geometry are valuable for the calculation of spatial relationships. This theorem is of great aid to the scientist in the decision-making context. The scientist must continually make decisions about the nature of reality, and these decisions are based on a limited amount of data. Theorems such as this, by quantifying various aspects of the decision process, enable the scientist to make maximum use of his data and, at the same time, to communicate effectively to other scientists the basis for his decision.

14.3   STATISTICS AND THE DECISIONS OF THE SCIENTIST

DECISIONS, STATES OF NATURE, AND TYPES OF ERROR

In order to illustrate the way in which theorems of probability or mathematical statistics can aid the scientist in his decision-making process, it is useful to begin with a very simple example, the tossing of a coin. And it is in this context that the basic principles of statistical decision making will be presented. (More realistic examples are provided in Chapter 15.)

The problem with which we begin is one in which a decision is to be made on the basis of a number of tosses as to whether or not a given coin is a "fair" one [*fair* being defined to be the situation where $p(H) = .50$]. There are thus two possible states of nature or reality under consideration: the coin is fair, and the coin is not fair [the latter designated as $p(H) \neq .50$]. Also, there are two alternative decisions from which a choice is to be made: the coin is fair, and the coin is not fair. We may schematize this decision situation as follows:

TABLE 14–1

Alternative Decisions and Alternative States of Nature

	Decisions	
States of Nature	Coin Is Fair	Coin Is Not Fair
	$p(H) = .50$	$p(H) \neq .50$
Coin is fair	Correct decision	Type I error
Coin is not fair	Type II error	Correct decision

As in the case of a great deal of scientific research, it is useful in the process of statistical decision making to specify particular hypotheses. In this way the nature of the decision to be made is clarified through an exact statement of the alternatives. Let us assume that the investigator starts with the hypothesis that the coin is fair [that is, that $p(H) = .50$]. This starting hypothesis, which is set up for purposes of testing, is called the *null hypothesis* and is symbolized as H_0. An alternative is the hypothesis that the coin is not fair. This is called the *alternative hypothesis* and is symbolized as H_1. This terminology is used as follows to state the two alternatives involved:

$$H_0 : p(H) = .50$$
$$H_1 : p(H) \neq .50$$

The investigator has two alternatives. He may decide that the coin is fair [that is, *accept H_0 (the null hypothesis)*] or he may decide that the coin is not fair [that is, *reject H_0 (the null hypothesis)*]. His decision may be correct or incorrect as to the actual state of nature. Thus, as may be seen in Table 14–1, the two correct decisions are (1) that the coin is fair in the situation where the coin is actually fair, and (2) that the coin is not fair in the situation where the coin actually is not fair. These may be stated in other language as (1) accepting a true null hypothesis, and (2) rejecting a false null hypothesis. In either event, a decision is made in favor of either the null hypothesis or the alternative hypothesis. Acceptance of the null hypothesis constitutes a direct decision in favor of this hypothesis; rejection implies a decision in favor of the alternative hypothesis, for the only logical alternative to a decision that the coin is fair is the decision that the coin is not fair.[5]

Any given decision made by the scientist may not be a wise one, for he is always uncertain as to the true state of nature. For example, even if the coin were tossed a million times and it came up heads on every occasion, there is still a finite probability that the coin is a fair one. This probability can be calculated by extending the multiplication rule to more than two independent events:

$$p(1,000,000 \text{ heads}) = (.50)(.50)(.50)(.50) \ldots = .50^{1,000,000}$$

Naturally, this probability is very close to 0, but it is not equal to 0. Thus, even in the face of overwhelming evidence to indicate that the decision to accept H_0 is correct, an investigator may in fact be erroneous in coming to this decision. Acceptance of a null hypothesis that is in reality false is designated as *Type II error*. Rejection of a null hypothesis that is in fact correct is designated as *Type I error*.

Thus, the two possible correct decisions are (1) acceptance of a true null hypothesis, and (2) rejection of a false null hypothesis, whereas the possible incorrect decisions are (1) rejection of a true hypothesis (Type I error), and (2) acceptance of a false null hypothesis (Type II error).

[5] It is conventional for researchers to avoid directly stating that they accept the alternative hypothesis (for example, "the coin is fair"). Rather, the convention in such an event is to state that "the null hypothesis is not rejected" or that we "fail to reject H_0." Such statements are more conservative than the statement "H_1 is accepted" and are in accord with the scientist's general lack of certainty as to the truth of his conclusions.

Rejection of a null hypothesis constitutes either a Type I error or a valid decision, whereas acceptance of a null hypothesis constitutes either a Type II error or a valid decision. In either case, the investigator is never in a position to determine for certain whether or not he is in error.

PROBABILITY DISTRIBUTION UNDER THE NULL HYPOTHESIS

Having outlined the relationship between the decisions of the scientist and the states of nature, we may turn to the data which the scientist utilizes for making his decision. It is here that statistics plays a vital role, for it helps the scientist "to make wise decisions in the face of uncertainty." We shall focus in particular on the binomial theorem discussed in Section 14.2, and attempt to show how it enables the scientist to utilize his data through the application of the mathematical formulations in probability theory. In other words, we assume (and this can be checked) that the axioms of probability hold for the coin-tossing situation, and we also interpret the concept of *probability* according to the frequency interpretation. Then this theorem may be used to make certain predictions on the basis of the limited data at hand, and these predictions are utilized to make the fundamental scientific decision.

Let us assume that the data on which the investigator must base his decision as to whether or not the given coin is fair consist only of the results of six tosses of the coin. An important aspect of these data is the number of times heads comes up in the six tosses; the particular order of occurrence is irrelevant to the purposes at hand. Before considering the actual data that emerge from a given series of six tosses, let us analyze each of the different possibilities. There are seven possible occurrences or events: the number of heads might be zero, one, two, three, four, five, or six. Because the null hypothesis, or the hypothesis actually tested, is that $p(H) = .50$, or $\frac{1}{2}$, we begin with the assumption that this is the true state of nature. We may subsequently make the decision that the initial assumption was correct, or we may decide that it was incorrect. In either case, our decision may either be correct or incorrect with respect to the actual state of nature.

Having assumed that $p(H) = .50$, or $\frac{1}{2}$, we may proceed to calculate the probability of each of the possible events by means of the binomial theorem. For example, the calculation for $p(0 \text{ heads})$ is

$$\frac{6!}{0!(6-0)!}\frac{1}{2}^0\,\frac{1}{2}^{6-0} = \frac{6!}{1(6!)}1(\tfrac{1}{2})^6 = \frac{1}{1}(\tfrac{1}{2})^6 =$$

$$(\tfrac{1}{2})(\tfrac{1}{2})(\tfrac{1}{2})(\tfrac{1}{2})(\tfrac{1}{2})(\tfrac{1}{2}) = 1/64, \text{ or } .0156$$

Similarly, the probabilities of one, two, three, four, five, and six heads may be calculated under the assumption that the coin is fair (that is, under the null hypothesis that $p(H) = .50$). The results of these calculations are listed in Table 14-2.[6]

TABLE 14-2

Probability Distribution of Number of Heads for Six Tosses of a Coin Under the Assumption That $p(H) = .50$

Number of Heads	Probability
0	1/64 or .0156
1	6/64 or .0937
2	15/64 or .2344
3	20/64 or .3125
4	15/64 or .2344
5	6/64 or .0937
6	1/64 or .0156
Total	64/64 or 1.000

LEVEL OF SIGNIFICANCE AND REGION OF REJECTION

These probabilities for each of the possible events, on the assumption that the null hypothesis is correct (the coin is fair), constitute valuable information for the investigator in making a wise decision on the basis of limited data. In particular, these probabilities help the investigator to set up rules for deciding whether or not the coin is fair for each of the possible events or occurrences. Let us suppose, for example, that the investigator would like there to be no more than a probability of .05 that he will decide that the coin is biased when it is in reality fair. In such a situation he would be rejecting a true null hypothesis, or making a Type I error. The probability of making a Type I error is called the *level of significance* of the testing or decision procedure and is symbolized by α. In this situation, then, one possible rule for decision making is to set α, or the probability of making a Type I error, to be no more than .05.

Once this rule is set up, we may follow through its implications as to which events or occurrences should lead the investigator to decide that the coin is unfair and thus reject the null hypothesis. After all, the purpose of such rules for decision making is that they can provide direction for the investigator for any given set of results. Consequently, the next step in this decision-making procedure is to establish a *region of rejection,* that is, a set of events which would lead the investigator to decide that the

[6] I am indebted to Elizabeth Shuhaney of the Mathematics Department of Boston University for many of the techniques of presentation utilized in the remainder of this chapter.

coin is biased. Of course, such a region of rejection could have arbitrarily been established in the first place without the benefit of any statistical manipulations. Thus, a given investigator might set up a rule that if zero, one, five, or six heads occur, he will decide that the coin is biased. Without the statistics, however, he will have only a vague idea about the probability that the decision will be incorrect. Statistics would aid him in making an accurate estimate of the probability of Type I error (α), and this knowledge might lead to his constructing a region of rejection that is more effective for his purposes. In addition, it would aid anyone else to interpret and weight properly the results of the experiment.

ONE-SIDED AND TWO-SIDED TESTS

With a rule specifying the probability of Type I error as no more than .05 (the level of significance), then the rejection region in this example would be zero or six heads. This conclusion is reached by first making a determination as to whether the null hypothesis may be rejected only by events at one extreme of the probability distribution or whether it may be rejected at both extremes. A *two-sided test* or decision procedure might specify, for example, a rejection region of 0 or 6 heads. If the alternative hypothesis is $p(H) \neq .50$, this automatically implies a two-sided test, for such an inequality may result in either of two ways: if $p(H)$ is greater than .50, and if $p(H)$ is less than .50.

With a two-sided test we examine Table 14-2 for a region of rejection that includes both a small and a large number of heads, the total probability for which does not exceed .05. The only region of rejection that satisfies these criteria is one which consists of zero and six heads. By the rule of addition, the probability of either zero or six heads, on the assumption that the coin is fair, is .0156 + .0156, or .0312. With a rejection region consisting of zero and six heads, the probability that the investigator will reject the null hypotheses and decide that the coin is biased when it is really a fair coin is .0312. This satisfies the initial criterion that the probability of Type I error be no more than .05. It also gives the investigator a rule for decision making specifically constructed on the basis of his desire to limit the probability of Type I error to a certain level. With such a rule the investigator can make a decision as to whether or not the coin is fair for any possible occurrence or event with the knowledge that only a very small chance exists that he will committ a Type I error.

In a variation of this example, the investigator might be concerned only about whether or not the coin is biased in a particular way (for example, in favor of heads over tails). In such a situation it would be most appropriate for him to set up a *one-sided test* or decision procedure. If we retain the desire of the investigator to limit the probability of a Type I error to .05, then the appropriate rejection region consists of six heads. Here, $\alpha = .0156$. The rejection region does not include zero heads because, in this one-sided test, the investigator is interested only in whether or not $p(H)$ is greater than .50. It is of no concern for him to distinguish the situation where $p(H) = .50$ from the situation where $p(H)$ is less than .50.

TIMING OF THE DECISION

It should be noted that in order to perform a statistical test, it is conventional to decide on a one-sided or two-sided test as well as on the level of significance *in advance*. By proceeding in this manner, the investigator leaves his hypothesis open to acceptance or rejection. If, on the other hand, the investigator examined the data before setting the level of significance, he might be tempted to adjust the level so as to reach the conclusions that he is interested in reaching.

There is a perfectly legitimate way to avoid setting up levels of significance in advance, and this involves viewing the analysis as exploratory, rather than as a test of an hypothesis. In this way the investigator may freely proceed to examine the relationships among the variables in his study. He may calculate for any given null hypothesis which might have been set up the exact probability of rejecting it if it were actually true (α).

For example, let us suppose that 0 heads occur in six tosses of a coin and that the null hypothesis, which might have been set up in advance (but was not), is that the coin is fair [that is, $p(H) = .50$]. Then we might simply indicate that the probability of obtaining nine heads in six tosses of a fair coin is .0156 without using this information either to accept or to reject definitely the null hypothesis. Utilizing this procedure, the investigator might proceed to make such calculations for all those relationships that seemed, on examining the data, to be significant.

14.4 RELATIONSHIP BETWEEN TYPE I AND TYPE II ERRORS

In his use of statistical procedures for testing hypotheses, we have seen the investigator make certain decisions before he can perform such tests. One of these is his setting of the *level of significance,* or the probability of making a Type I error. However, such a decision is generally affected by his evaluation of the loss or disadvantage incurred by making a Type I error as opposed to a Type II error (accepting a false null hypothesis). This is because, for a given size sample the probability of a Type I error varies inversely with the probability of a Type II error. In this section the interrelationship between these two types of error will be further explored. The aim is to provide the student not with a detailed manual of statistical procedures, but rather with a more thorough understanding of the role of statistics in the social scientist's decision-making process.

THE "LAW OF THE CONSERVATION OF UNCERTAINTY"

Thus far we have illustrated a situation in which the investigator sets a limit to the probability of Type I error. There is, however, an additional type of error with which the investigator should be concerned: Type II error, the decision that the coin is fair when it is really biased. The probability of Type II error is designated by β.

Let us continue with the coin-tossing example in which the investigator sets up a null hypothesis that the coin is fair and then decides to limit the probability of Type I error to .05. Let us assume also a two-sided test, with the null hypothesis being $p(H) = .50$ and the alternative hypothesis being $p(H) \neq .50$, and let the data consist of the number of heads resulting from six tosses, as before. One question that might be considered is the effect on the probability of Type II error (β) of setting the probability of Type I error (α) at a given level. Intuitively, it would seem that the investigator must pay a price, in terms of β, for setting up an α which is very small (in other words, that α and β vary inversely). Let us compare the rejection region of 0, 6 with that of 0, 1, 5, 6. With the smaller rejection region, $\alpha = .0312$, whereas with the larger one, $\alpha = .2186$. With the smaller α, the investigator is more conservative and will be very cautious in rejecting the null hypothesis. The only results in the rejection region for this α are zero and six heads, but the null hypothesis that the coin is fair will be accepted for any other result. In other words, even if as many as five heads or as few as one heads result, the investigator would accept the null hypothesis that the coin is fair.

But could it not occur very easily that the coin is really biased in favor of heads and come up heads five times in six tosses? Of course it could, and yet in the case of the smaller α the investigator would make the decision to accept the null hypothesis that the coin is fair in this case. That is because the event *five heads* does not lie in the rejection region. By making such a decision, the investigator is making a Type II error, that is, accepting a false null hypothesis by deciding that the coin is fair when it is actually biased. Also, in the case of the smaller α, if the coin were actually biased against heads, and heads came up once in six tosses, the investigator would decide that the coin is fair when it is actually biased and thus commit a Type II error here as well.

The point being made here is that the investigator who is conservative with respect to Type I error pays a price in terms of Type II error. By wanting to avoid a decision that the coin is biased when it is really fair, he increases the probability of his deciding that the coin is fair when it is actually biased. This can be further illustrated if we consider the decision situation relating to the larger α, where the rejection region includes zero, one, five, and six heads. Here, the probability of Type I error (α) is .2186, which is much greater than the situation where $\alpha = .0312$ as in the previous example. If an inverse relationship between α and β exists, we would expect to find a much smaller β with $\alpha = .2186$ than with $\alpha = .0312$.

This is in fact the case. With $\alpha = .2186$, the rejection region includes zero, one, five, and six heads. If the coin were biased in favor of heads, we would be far more likely to detect this if our decision procedure is to decide that the coin is biased if as many as five heads occur than if we were more conservative. In the conservative case, five heads were in the region for *accepting* the null hypothesis that the coin is fair. The same would hold for the situation where the coin is actually biased against heads coming up. For $\alpha = .2186$ the event *one heads* is in the rejection region, whereas it is not for $\alpha = .0312$.

We have tried to show on an intuitive basis that α and β vary inversely. We might think of this as a kind of "law of the conservation of uncertainty" analogous to the physical law having to do with the conservation of energy. What it refers to is that, for a given set of data and a given rule for calculating the probabilities of events, an increase in the probability of Type I error (α) serves to decrease the probability of Type II error, and vice versa. Thus, if an investigator decides to shift from a .05 level of significance to the .01 level, he pays a price for this reduction in the probability of Type I error (α): the price is that the probability of Type II error (β) will be increased.

THE CALCULATION OF TYPE II ERROR

We may now illustrate this relationship between α and β through actual calculations by comparing the decision situation where $\alpha = .0312$ with that where $\alpha = .2186$. In order to calculate β for each of these situation, it is necessary to make the assumption that $p(H) \neq .50$. If we are to calculate β, the probability of accepting a false null hypothesis, we must have a situation where the null hypothesis is in fact false, that is, where $p(H) \neq .50$. Once this assumption is made, we may proceed to list the probabilities of each of the possible number of heads that might occur under this assumption, as was done with the previous assumption that $p(H) = .50$.

But we cannot calculate these probabilities unless we have more specific information. To say that $p(H) \neq .50$ leaves almost completely open the question of what $p(H)$ actually equals. It may be equal to .10, .20, .80, .90, or just about any other decimal figure. In our previous calculations of the probability distribution for the various numbers of heads, we had the specific information that $p(H) = .50$. Without that, we could not have utilized the theorem for calculating probabilities, for $p(H)$ is one of the terms in the formula. Consequently, we must make a specific assumption as to the value of $p(H)$ in the present instance. It can be any decimal so long as it differs from .50, that is, any probability for which the null hypothesis $[p(H) = .50]$ is actually false. Let us assume that $p(H) = .10$. We may now proceed to illustrate one of the calculations that will be utilized to provide the data for a table of the probability distribution for numbers of heads for six tosses of a coin, under the assumption that $p(H) = .10$.

$$p(0 \text{ heads}) = \frac{N!}{r!(N-r)!} \, p(H)^r p(T)^{N-r} = \frac{6!}{0!(6-0)!} \, .10^0 (.90)^{6-0} =$$

$$\frac{6!}{1(6!)} \, 1(.90)^6 = \frac{1}{1}(.90)(.90)(.90)(.90)(.90)(.90) = .5314$$

The entire table follows:

TABLE 14-3

Probability Distribution of Number of Heads for Six Tosses of a Coin Under the Assumption That $p(H) = .10$

Number of Heads	Probability
0	.5314
1	.3543
2	.0984
3	.0146
4	.0012
5	.0001
6	.0000
Total	1.0000

Let us assume that we still have the same null hypothesis that the coin is fair. We may begin with the calculation of β for the $\alpha = .0312$ situation. Here the rejection region consists of 0 and 6, and the acceptance region consists of 1, 2, 3, 4, and 5. It is the acceptance and not the rejection region which is of interest here because we are concerned with β, or the probability of *accepting* a false null hypothesis.

If the state of nature is that $p(H) = .10$, then the probabilities for the occurrence of 1, 2, 3, 4, and 5 are (from Table 14-3) .3543, .0984, .0146, .0012, and .0001, respectively. The probability of accepting the null hypothesis is the probability of either one, two, three, four, or five heads. Thus, the addition rule holds, and the sum of these probabilities is .4686. In other words, $\beta = .4686$.

Now we may calculate β for the $\alpha = .2186$ situation and compare it with the β just calculated. For $\alpha = .2186$, the rejection region consists of 0, 1, 5, and 6, and the acceptance region consists of 2, 3, and 4. The probabilities corresponding to the events in the acceptance region are .0984,

.0146, and .0012 (from Table 14-3). Because the probability of accepting the null hypothesis (β) is equal to the sum of these probabilities, β = .1142.

In comparing the α = .0312 and the α = .2186 decision situations, we find that the β's which correspond to them are .4686 and .1142, respectively. These calculations show that a shift from a smaller α to a larger α leads to a shift from a larger β to a smaller β, and vice versa. Thus, we have an illustration of what may be facetiously called the *law of the conservation of uncertainty*. It should be noted that the "law" does *not* state that the total probability of error ($\alpha + \beta$) remains constant. In the illustration where α = .0312, $\alpha + \beta$ = .4998. In the situation where α = .2186, $\alpha + \beta$ = .3328. Actually, what happens to β when α is changed depends on what value we assume for $p(H)$. In other words, the null hypothesis may be wrong in many different ways because a biased coin may have various degrees of bias. Thus, no general formula has been developed for calculating β on the basis of α. The calculation is different for each different assumption we make as to $p(H)$.

SETTING THE LEVEL OF SIGNIFICANCE

Thus far we have discussed the way in which a specific decision procedure can be developed on the basis of limiting α to a certain probability, as well as the way in which α and β are related to one another. Nothing, however, has been said about another, more general decision procedure, the decision as to which level to set for α and, consequently, β. The crucial question for the investigator in setting α has to do with the relative importance he attaches to making a Type I and a Type II error. Let us assume, for example, that his decision as to whether or not the coin is fair will be the basis for his entering or not entering a gambling game with another individual where he will bet $1 on each throw of the coin and where he will win or lose depending on whether the other individual guesses correctly which face of the coin turns up. In such a situation, unless the investigator happens to be quite wealthy, it will be very important for him to avoid making a Type II error—i.e., deciding that the coin is fair when it is actually biased. If he makes a Type II error and decides that the coin is fair, he will enter the gambling game and will probably lose his shirt. It may be less important for the investigator to avoid making a Type I error (that is, deciding that the coin is biased when it is really fair). In such a situation, setting α equal to .2186 would seem to be a wiser strategy than setting α equal to .0312. This is because, on the assumption that $p(H)$ = .10, for example, β = .1142 in the former case whereas β = .4686 in the latter. Thus, the chance that the investigator will decide to enter the gambling game when the coin is heavily biased against heads is much greater for α = .0312 than for α = .2186.

For another type of individual, however, such a strategy may be un-desirable. Suppose, for example, that we have a wealthy individual who enjoys coin-tossing games and who would be afraid of offending the other player by refusing to enter the game. In such a situation, the selection of $\alpha = .0312$ makes more sense than $\alpha = .2186$, because the individual would be more concerned about making a Type I error (deciding that the coin is biased when it is actually fair) than a Type II error. The latter would lead to his deciding to enter the game with a biased coin and thus risk losing money, but this would constitute a relatively small loss for a wealthy individual. Thus, the $\alpha = .0312$ strategy would be a better choice for an individual who cares more about making Type I error than Type II error.

Other considerations are involved in statistical decision making. For example, the investigator would do well to take into account not only the β associated with one particular assumption about the state of nature $[p(H) = .10]$ but the β's that would correspond to many other states of nature as well. In addition, there are generally many ways of estimating the probability distribution for a given research situation. In addition, there is the whole question as to whether or not additional data should be collected before making any decisions. Each of the choices affects every other one, and the investigator must somehow take all of them into account. The difficulty of handling so complex a set of factors is obvious, but statistical procedures provide the means of making decisions that are pragmatically oriented to the achievement of these goals.

EXERCISES

1. Discuss the question of whether statistical tests of significance in the behavioral sciences do more harm than good.

2. If statistical procedures are valuable partly because they make clear the basis on which the scientist processes data, how can this kind of clarity be extended to other aspects of the research process?

3. Of what value is the mathematical formulation of the concept of probability to the behavioral scientist in ways other than as a basis for statistical decision making?

4. Draw an analogy between the statistical decision making of the scientist and the everyday decision making of the individual. What are the similarities and the differences?

5. What is the relationship between the relative probabilities of Type I and II errors, on the one hand, and the contexts of discovery and jus-tification, on the other?

ANNOTATED REFERENCES

BONDURANT, JOAN V. *Conquest of Violence: The Gandhian Philosophy of Conflict.* Berkeley: University of California Press, 1965. No, this reference is not in the wrong place, though some might think it farfetched to include it here. Statistics constitutes one language for communication within the community of scientists. When we understand that it is communication we want to achieve and that statistics is simply a tool toward this end, then we shall find it easier to place statistics in proper perspective. This reference is placed here to serve as a reminder of this view. Bondurant presents the Gandhian approach in such a way that we come to see it as the application of principles of communication among individuals and groups, principles that might well be applied to the two cultures of quantitative and qualitative researchers.

BROSS, IRWIN D. J. *Design for Decision.* New York: The Free Press, 1965. This book is quite elementary in the sense that no special mathematical or statistical background is required. Yet it is quite advanced in the sense that it communicates the flavor of statistical decision theory. Furthermore, its implications go beyond statistics as a tool for testing hypotheses to decision theory as a model for understanding human behavior.

GOLDBERG, SAMUEL. *Probability: An Introduction.* Englewood Cliffs, N.J.: Prentice-Hall, Inc., 1960. As the title suggests, the emphasis is on elementary probability theory. This can be used as a foundation both for statistics and mathematical models. If the student has a smattering of calculus, he will be able to move to Goldberg's *Introduction to Difference Equations* (New York: Science Editions, 1961), which has illustrative examples of mathematical models from economics, psychology, and sociology.

CHAPTER 15 Sampling, Statistical Testing, and Degree of Association

15.1 PROBABILITY SAMPLING

THE NATURE OF PROBABILITY SAMPLING

Certain aspects of sampling procedures[1] were taken up within the context of the collection of data (see Section 4.3). Probability sampling was referred to as a method for selecting a subset of units from a larger set of these units (population) so that each unit or subset of units of the population has a known probability of being included in the subset or sample. The method may be illustrated in the context of the coin-tossing example.

We may designate as the unit to be sampled the number of heads resulting from six tosses of a given coin. The population may be designated as an infinite number of such units, with these data being derived from an infinite number of sets of six tosses of the coin. Let us consider whether the number of heads resulting from one set of six tosses may be considered to be a probability sample. The criterion here has to do with whether or not each possible event—that is, each number of heads from zero to six—has a known probability of occurring. Table 14-2 lists these known probabilities on the assumption that the coin is a fair one. As explained in Chapter 14, they were calculated by means of a theorem based on the multiplication and addition rules or axioms. Also, $p(H)$ was interpreted as the relative frequency of heads in an infinite number of tosses. On the assumption that these axioms actually apply to the coin-tossing situation, each number of heads has a known probability of occurring.

But how do we know whether or not the multiplication and addition rules or axioms actually apply in the coin-tossing situation? This can be indirectly tested by a very large number of sets of six tosses. For example, the calculated probability of zero heads resulting from six tosses, using the multiplication and addition rules, is .0156 (from Table 14-2). In 1,000 sets of six tosses let us suppose that we actually obtain fourteen situations

---

[1] For a detailed discussion of sampling see Bernard Lazerwitz, "Sampling Theory and Procedures," in Hubert M. Blalock and Ann B. Blalock (eds.), *Methodology in Social Research* (New York: McGraw-Hill, 1968), Chap. 8; and Freda Conway, *Sampling: An Introduction for Social Scientists* (New York: Humanities Press, 1967).

where all six tosses in a given set come up tails. This would constitute a relative frequency for the zero heads in six tosses situation of 14/1,000, or .0140. Let us now suppose that we toss the coin 9,000 additional sets of six tosses, or a total of 10,000 such sets, and end up with a total of 162 situations where zero heads occur in the six tosses; here the relative frequency would be 162/10,000, or .0162. Finally, let us suppose that we obtained a relative frequency of .0157 in 20,000 sets of six tosses.

These hypothetical relative frequencies tend to converge on the calculated value of the probability of zero heads in six tosses (.0156) as the number of sets of six tosses increases:

Number of sets of six tosses	1,000	10,000	20,000	
Relative frequency of zero heads in a set	.0140	.0162	.0157	(.0156 = calculated probability)

If, indeed, data indicated that the larger the sample, the closer the actual relative frequencies were to the calculated probability, this would constitute evidence in support of the idea that the multiplication and addition rules or axioms actually apply to the coin-tossing situation. In other words, there would be evidence for interpreting the mathematical conception of probability as corresponding to the relative frequency of the occurrence of heads in a coin-tossing situation.

Although the coin-tossing situation can aid in portraying the nature of probability sampling, it is difficult to understand its importance to the social scientist unless we talk about the sampling of human populations. For the social scientist engaging in surveys, for example, probability sampling techniques enable him to select a sample in such a way that it will in all likelihood be highly representative of the larger population in which he is interested, with the degree of representativeness depending on the size of the sample. If he desires to predict, for example, the vote in a given municipal election, such techniques will aid him to do this and still interview only a limited number of respondents constituting only a small proportion of the electorate.[2]

To illustrate this let us assume that the electorate consists of a total of 1 million individuals, and that 530,000 (or 53 per cent) plan to vote for the Republican candidate and 470,000 (or 47 per cent) for the Democratic candidate. By using probability sampling techniques the investigator will

---

[2] The prediction of election returns is not a simple task, because of such factors as a substantial proportion of undecided voters and changes in voting preference subsequent to the survey. Some of the dynamics involved are outlined in Paul F. Lazarsfeld, Bernard Berelson, and Hazel Gaudet, *The People's Choice* (New York: Columbia University Press, 1948).

generally be able to avoid the selection of a sample that is overrepresented by Republican voters or by Democratic voters. Also, the larger the sample, the greater will be the likelihood that the percentage of Republican voters in the sample will be the same as this percentage for the entire municipality. For example, data for different sizes of samples might look like this:

Size of sample	100	1,000	2,000	
Relative frequency of Republicans in the sample	.49	.545	.5380	(.5300 = actual proportion of Republicans)

Here, as in the coin-tossing situation, successively larger probability samples yield relative frequencies that are closer and closer to a given probability. For the coin-tossing situation this was the calculated probability of zero heads in six tosses, whereas in this example it is the actual proportion of Republicans in the electorate.

These hypothetical data also illustrate the efficiency of probability sampling techniques. A sample of 2,000 from a total electorate of 1 million constitutes only two tenths of 1 per cent. Yet such a small proportion of the population can provide data which very closely approximate what would be discovered if a census of the entire electorate were taken.

The general utility of probability sampling techniques for the social scientist stems from his desire to provide evidence for propositions that have wide scope on the basis of limited numbers of individuals. He would like to establish propositions that hold for all human beings. Given this situation, probability sampling techniques enable him to stretch his research resources enormously. He is able to draw conclusions about the behavior of very large populations (for example, the electorate of 1 million individuals) on the basis of data obtained from relatively small samples (for example, the sample of 2,000 individuals).

SOME TYPES OF PROBABILITY SAMPLES

Simple Random Samples

The simple random sample may be illustrated using the example of a lottery. Let us imagine that each individual in the population from which the sample is to be drawn is represented by a slip of paper and that all slips have been very thoroughly mixed in a bin. Then if successive slips are drawn from the bin, with thorough mixing taking place between each draw, a simple random sample of individuals (represented by the slips) may be drawn from the population.

Social scientists do not, of course, actually obtain simple random samples in this manner. A typical technique is to construct a list of all individuals in the population and to assign a unique number to each individual. Then they select as many individuals as they desire for their sample by obtaining numbers from a table of random numbers and using these numbers to designate the individuals in their sample. These random numbers are generally presented in a format such as that on p. 311.[3]

Suppose, for example, that we wish to obtain a simple random sample of ten students from a total class of ninety-four students. We could proceed by first listing all of the students and assigning to each a number from 1 to 95. Those students assigned one-digit numbers (1, 2, 3, 4, 5, 6, 7, 8, or 9) would have their numbers recorded with a 0 preceding them (01, 02, 03, 04, 05, 06, 07, 08, or 09) so as to utilize the table of random numbers more easily. The table could then be entered at any point (for example, the sixth column of row 1) and the researcher could proceed horizontally from left to right (82854 55846 18076 12415) to the end of the row. He could then start row 2 and proceed from left to right (61078 52433 . . .), and so on. The numbers could be recorded in pairs (that is, 82, 85, 45, 58, 46, 18, 07, 61, 24, 15. These ten numbers could then be used to designate the desired sample of ten individuals.

The student may well wonder how such tables of random numbers are constructed. The general procedure is to locate a natural or man-made process that can be used to generate numbers in such a way that (1) each of the ten numerals has the same probability of appearing, and (2) each subset of numerals (for example, each pair) has the same probability of appearing. The numerals generated are then tested, using their relative frequencies of occurrence as an interpretation of these probabilities, and the decision is made as to whether or not they constitute a set of random numbers.

Each of the preceding random digits, for example, was produced by summing ten digits, each of which had to do with a different type of information (for example, shipment weight, revenue, serial number of the car). Only the units digit of the resulting sum was retained, and this constituted the digit used for the table of random numbers. The resulting table was then subjected to various tests for randomness. In one test, for example, the frequency of each digit's occurrence was listed, whereas in another test adjacent pairs of digits were examined. Results of these tests indicated that the table did in fact constitute a table of random numbers.

Stratified Probability Samples

Stratified probability samples are probability samples selected by dividing the population into strata and then selecting, for example, a

---

[3] Interstate Commerce Commission, *Table of 105,000 Random Decimal Digits* (Washington: 1949, Statement No. 4914. File No. 261–A–1, p. 10). Tables of random numbers may be found in most standard textbooks on statistics.

Columns

Rows	1	2	3	4	5	6	7	8	9	10	11	12	13	14	15	16	17	18	19	20	21	22	23	24	25
1	3	5	3	4	8	8	2	8	5	4	5	5	8	4	6	1	8	0	7	6	1	2	4	1	5
2	6	1	0	7	8	5	2	4	3	3	2	2	1	8	4	3	3	9	9	8	8	7	4	3	6
3	6	6	6	8	2	2	5	4	4	2	8	3	6	6	8	6	6	2	3	6	7	9	6	5	5
4	7	3	7	7	8	6	3	4	6	9	5	0	0	8	3	7	0	6	9	6	1	3	5	5	8
5	7	4	1	5	7	4	6	0	1	2	9	7	7	6	5	2	7	5	5	2	4	9	6	1	7
6	8	2	4	5	3	1	9	5	3	2	4	9	9	8	8	1	3	1	7	6	9	4	2	1	9
7	0	1	1	3	7	8	6	1	6	8	7	8	2	5	7	8	6	2	4	9	4	6	1	3	4
8	7	3	1	6	1	4	6	0	6	1	3	0	9	4	6	2	2	2	1	0	7	9	3	0	2
9	1	8	6	0	8	1	8	1	9	8	1	9	4	6	8	7	6	3	5	8	6	9	2	0	3
10	2	5	6	2	7	6	3	1	0	7	3	0	8	0	6	8	0	8	5	7	8	4	3	8	3

simple random sample from each stratum. Using the preceding example in which ten students are to be selected from a class ninety-four, let us suppose that they are to be interviewed about their conceptions of the desirability of having female candidates for president. Presumably, male students would vary to some extent from female students on these opinions. If the researcher desired to obtain a sample of ten which was genuinely representative of the entire class, he might do well to make sure that males were neither overrepresented nor underrepresented in his sample.

The actual sampling procedure might involve, first of all, an assessment of the ratio of males to females in the class as a whole. Let us assume that this ratio is 1:1, that is, there are forty-seven males and forty-seven females. The researcher might then choose his sample of ten individuals in such a way that this ratio is retained; that is, he might choose five males and five females.[4] This might be accomplished, for example, by assigning a unique two-digit number to each male and then choosing five males with the aid of a table of random numbers. The same process could then be repeated for the females, and the result would be a probability sample of the entire class which is stratified on the basis of sex.

Clustered Probability Samples

Clustered probability samples are probability samples in which groupings or clusters of the units to be sampled are first selected by means of a probability sample. Let us use for illustrative purposes here the example in which the political preferences of an electorate of 1 million individuals within a given municipality are being investigated. One clustering technique would be to utilize the census tracts within the city as the clusters or groupings of individuals, and first to take a simple random sample of census tracts. Then, within each of the census tracts thus selected, the investigator might proceed to take a simple random sample of the individuals residing there. A less expensive approach would be to select a simple random sample of city blocks (constituting smaller clusters), and finally to select every *n*th household (for example, every third one) within those blocks selected.[5]

---

[4] This is an example of proportional stratified sampling. If the investigator feels that more information is needed from one stratum than from others, he may use disproportional stratified sampling techniques. For example, suppose that the attitudes of the females were relatively homogeneous while those of the males varied greatly. In this situation the investigator might select seven males and three females, and in the final analysis weight each female's opinions more than that of each male so as to secure a representative picture of the class as a whole.

[5] The last stage of this multistage sampling procedure, wherein each *n*th unit is selected, illustrates *systematic sampling* techniques. With this procedure we start with a random starting point among the first *n* units and then take every *n*th unit. This technique is much more convenient than simple random sampling. One disadvantage of it is that every set of elements does not have the same probability of being chosen.

The advantage of clustered samples is the savings in costs and time. The investigator in this example saves greatly in interviewer travel costs, because all interviews are concentrated within a number of specific areas. Also, the survey can be done much more rapidly through this exclusion of other areas of the city. A disadvantage is that there is a greater danger of overrepresenting or underrepresenting a particular group than in the case of simple random sampling.

15.2   TESTS OF SIGNIFICANCE

TESTS OF SIGNIFICANCE ON NONPROBABILITY SAMPLES

Statistical tests of significance refer to decision procedures for accepting or rejecting a given null hypothesis. The principles of such procedures were discussed in Chapter 14, in the context of a coin-tossing situation. (For a more comprehensive discussion of statistical tests as well as measures of association, see the standard textbooks on the subject.)

Using a probability sample, each event has a known probability of occurrence. Thus, in the coin-tossing situation, we are able to calculate the probability of any given number of heads and, consequently, are able to test a null hypothesis at a given level of significance.

Although the magnitudes of α and β are clear in the case of a probability sample, we are unsure about the probabilities of Types I and II error for a nonprobability sample. Granting that nonprobability samples have a very important place in data-collection procedures, one question which arises has to do with the appropriateness and the interpretation of statistical tests used on such samples. It might be argued that any procedure might well be utilized if it aids in the context of discovery or justification. With a nonprobability sample we would be unsure about α and β, or, more accurately, we would be less sure about α and β than if we had a probability sample. The statistical test, however, can provide a means for distinguishing those hypotheses that seem to be more valid than others, and thus it might be of aid both in the context of discovery and in the context of justification. Of course, we should keep in mind that the α, which provides the criteria for a given set of decision procedures through its determination of the rejection region, may vary a good deal from the α which is actually correct. But this uncertainty about α and β constitutes only one of the many uncertainties involved in the research process.

From a strict point of view, of course, any generalization to a larger population on the basis of a nonprobability sample is not possible because it is not possible to calculate the probability of Type I error (α), because the sample itself has no known probability of occurrence when compared with other possible samples. It is possible to adhere to this point of view and, at the same time, utilize the advantages of statistical testing within the context of discovery. The approach that might be taken was outlined in Section 14.4 and has to do with the use of statistical calculations for exploratory but not for testing purposes. Thus, the investigator would not use the results of his calculations to decide that a given hypothesis was or was not true for the larger population from which the sample was drawn. However, he could proceed to calculate the probabilities of rejecting them if they were actually true (α). He would realize that the accuracy of such calculations is based on the assumption of probability sampling, but he nevertheless might use them to locate those hypotheses which seemed to be worth following up in future studies.

THE BINOMIAL TEST: AN EXAMPLE OF A STATISTICAL TEST

Numerous statistical tests have been developed to fulfill a variety of the decision-making purposes of researchers. The binomial test has been selected for detailed illustration here because of its simplicity. In addition, it has already been utilized in Chapter 14 within the context of the coin-tossing example. The aim here is to show how a statistical test is used within the context of a more realistic example. Although the example is more realistic than that of coin tossing, the degree of realism is still limited for the sake of simplicity.

Table 13-1 was based on a study of the health decisions of a nonprobability sample of 192 women from Cambridge, Massachusetts. The data from the table deal with the relationship between a choice of a homemaker or a home for the aged and the appearance of certain responses on an open-ended question as to the reasons for the choice. We may proceed by setting up a null hypothesis to the effect that there is no relationship between the choice and the various reasons for the choice. Such a procedure constitutes a *reductio ad absurdum*, for the null hypothesis is set up so that its consequences may be examined, and if the probability is small that the data which actually did occur can occur under this assumption of the null hypothesis, we shall decide to reject the null hypothesis.

Let us examine one of the value expectations given in the reasons for the choice of a homemaker or a home. The data on this point are

Value Expectations	Example	Choice of Homemaker N	Choice of Home for Aged N
Financial: negative on home for aged	"Not enough money for a home."	4	0

The number of individuals who were negative on the financial aspects of a home for the aged, out of the original sample of 192, is only four.

Nevertheless, it is still possible (although unusual) to conduct statistical tests with samples of this size. On the assumption that there is no relationship between the choice of homemaker or home for the aged and whether or not the respondent was negative on the financial aspects of a home for the aged, the probability that any given respondent who mentioned this also chose the homemaker should be equal to the probability that any given respondent who mentioned this also chose the home for the aged. Thus, the null hypothesis is that the probability that a person who is negative on the financial aspects of a home for the aged chose the homemaker, which may be designated as $p(K)$, is equal to .50.

We may next decide as to whether the test is to be one-sided or two-sided. A two-sided test would be appropriate if we had no more reason to suspect that $p(K)$ is greater than .50 than to suspect that it is less than .50. Actually, however, we have reason to suspect that $p(K)$ is greater than .50, because it is eminently reasonable to hypothesize that persons who are dissatisfied with the financial aspects of a home for the aged are individuals who are more likely to choose the homemaker rather than a home for the aged. Thus, a one-sided test would be most appropriate in this situation. Our hypotheses are

$$H_0:p(K) = .50$$
$$H_1:p(K) > .50$$

The investigator must also determine the level of significance. He must set α, or the probability of a Type I error, at a certain level, thereby determining the probability of Type II error (β). What is usually involved here is a balancing of the relative harm resulting from each type of error while taking into account the size of the sample involved. According to Bernoulli's theorem, the larger the sample, the closer its characteristics to those of the population from which it was drawn. Thus, even if a given null hypothesis is correct for a given population, the characteristics of a small sample may depart a good deal from the general pattern. In other words, the total probability of making an incorrect decision tends to be greater for a small sample than for a large one. Thus, if we set α at a low level, we will find that, for a small sample, β will be very high. If we hold α constant and increase the sample size, β will be correspondingly reduced. In the present situation it might be well to set α fairly high so as to reduce the very large β which would otherwise result. Because $\alpha = .05$ is conventional for many situations, let us then set $\alpha = .10$. By adopting such a procedure, we reduce the probability of Type II error, that is, acceptance of the null hypothesis when it is actually false. Consequently, we reduce the probability of coming up with a finding that there is no relationship between the two variables in the population when one does actually exist. Thus, while setting α fairly high increases the probability of finding relationships that actually exist, it also increases the probability of finding relationships that actually do not exist.

Before proceeding with the calculations, some attention might be given to the fact that we are dealing with a nonprobability sample. Even if the sample of 192 women were a probability sample drawn from all women in Cambridge, the four women who happened to mention the negative financial aspects of homes for the aged would not constitute a probability sample of any particular population. Because we are using a statistical test, although we have no probability sample, it is well to remember that there is no population to which we can generalize our results. Nevertheless, statistical analyses may legitimately be performed in an exploratory vein.

We may now calculate the probability distribution of the number of homemaker choices by four respondents under the assumption that $p(K)$ = .50. Table 15-1 is directly analogous to Table 14-2. Because the test being made is a one-sided one, and in particular, H_1 specifies that $p(K)$ > .50, the rejection region includes only the event *four homemaker choices*. This is, first of all, the side of the distribution of homemaker choices which corresponds to H_1. Furthermore, this is the only event for which the probability of Type I error is less than or equal to the predetermined limit of .10. If the events *three or four homemaker choices* were placed in the rejection region, then α would be equal to .0625 + .2500, or .3125, which would greatly exceed the limit of .10.

TABLE 15-1

Probability Distribution of Number of Homemaker Choices for Four Respondents Under the Assumption That $p(K)$ = .50

Number of Homemaker Choices	Probability
0	1/16 or .0625
1	4/16 or .2500
2	6/16 or .3750
3	4/16 or .2500
4	1/16 or .0625
Total	16/16 or 1.000

In the actual data, where all four of the individuals who were negative on the financial aspects of a home for the aged made the homemaker choice, the number of homemaker choices falls within the rejection region, and we are thus able to reject the null hypothesis. What can we now do with this result? Certainly we cannot state that a relationship between dissatisfaction with the financial aspects of homes for the aged and the homemaker choice exists for women in the city of Cambridge. But, after all, such a statement does not seem particularly earth-shaking, nor does it, in that form at least, seem to give promise for the advancement of science. If the relationship is restated in its more abstract form, however, its implications will become more clear. At a higher level of abstraction what has been examined is the relationship between values and choices. In particular, the finding provides an illustration of the general proposition that the individual's choice is related to his expectations concerning the goals involved.

Of what use is this finding? This depends, of course, on what is done with it. In the context of justification we can do very little with it. Although it bears on a proposition relating to choice behavior, the nonprobability nature of the sample permits us, from a strict point of view, to talk only about the four individuals for which we have relevant data. Within the context of discovery it provides the investigator with encouragement to pursue a line of inquiry in which choices are conceived of as a product of expectations concerning goals.

The foregoing illustration indicates one of many possible procedures for performing a quantitative analysis on qualitative data. A given piece of research need not be polarized into *either* a nonstatistical study *or* a statistical study. Unfortunately, much research in the social sciences reflects such a polarization as well as a lack of appreciation for the utility of the other approach. For example, participant-observation studies rarely incorporate any statistical analyses. The latter are, of course, not necessarily important. The crucial question is whether any given method of data collection or analysis is rejected because of its lack of utility, or whether it is rejected out of hand.

The illustration may be used for other purposes as well. Our choice of a sample of size four was not only for convenience of calculations, but for illustration of the idea that statistical testing may be performed with quite small samples, contradicting a myth to the effect that large samples are required for statistical analysis.[6]

In the preceding chapter we discussed the relationship between the probability of Type I and Type II errors. Within the present context of the sampling of human populations, we might note that with a small sample, assuming that we hold constant the probability of Type I error (the level of significance), the probability of Type II error increases over that for a large sample. In other words, there is no greater probability of finding a statistically significant relationship in the sample when no

---

[6] There is a lively controversy over this matter in the *American Anthropologist*, Vols. 70 and 71; see Robert A. Benfer, "The Desirability of Small Samples for Anthropological Inference," *American Anthropologist*, **70** (1968), 949–51; and Richard P. Chaney and R. Ruiz Revilla, "Sampling Methods and Interpretation of Correlation: A Comparative Analysis of Seven Cross-Cultural Samples," *American Anthropologist*, **71** (1969), 597–633. I am indebted to Pertti J. Pelto for bringing the matter to my attention.

relationship exists in the population (rejecting a true null hypothesis), but there is a greater probability of not finding a statistically significant relationship in the sample when a relationship does in fact exist in the population (accepting a false null hypothesis). Thus, one is less likely to uncover relationships in the population using small samples, but one is no less likely (assuming that level of significance is held constant) to come up with relationships that are incorrect.

15.3 MEASURES OF ASSOCIATION

The behavioral scientist is interested in more than determining whether or not a relationship exists between a given independent variable and a given dependent variable. For example, knowledge of falling bodies would not be greatly advanced by the information that a relationship existed between the time a body is in free fall and its velocity. It is important to know whether this independent variable (amount of time in free fall) is a very important factor in predicting distance fallen or if it is merely a relatively trivial factor among other more important ones. When the scientist is able to determine which among many possible independent variables are most important for explaining and predicting a given dependent variable, he has made a considerable advance in his investigation of the nature of the types of relationships involved. Thus, for example, he would be able to specify the relative importance of age, sex, religion, social class, group affiliations, level of aspiration, and many other factors in explaining the development of delinquent behavior patterns.

It might seem that degree of relationship can be determined by a test of significance. For example, could we not set α equal to a very small value, for example, .001? Then would it not be true that, if the null hypothesis is so decisively rejected, a close relationship between the variables exists? The answer is no, because the size of the sample greatly affects the ease of rejecting the null hypothesis at a given level of significance. Two given variables might have the same degree of relationship in two different samples, but we might be able to reject the null hypothesis at $\alpha = .0001$ if the sample is very large, although we might not even be able to reject the null hypothesis at $\alpha = .10$ if the sample is very small. There is no necessary relationship between the degree to which two variables are interrelated and the level of significance at which it is possible to reject the null hypothesis.

It should be recognized that the finding of a high degree of relationship between two variables does not automatically guarantee that the relationship is therefore an important one. For example, Variables A and B may be closely related because some third variable C causes both. In such a situation, A does not cause B nor does B cause A, and this is an illustration of the well-known saying that "correlation is not causation."

One of the simplest measures of association is the percentage difference. Table 13-3 showed that the percentage of students receiving B— or higher is substantially higher among those students who showed interest in the assignment than among those students who did not show interest. By subtracting the smaller percentage (the percentage with B— or higher among those now showing interest) from the larger one (the percentage with B— or higher among those now showing no interest), we are able to obtain a measure of the degree of relationship between the two variables. In this example, we have 58 per cent — 25 per cent = 33 per cent. This finding may be compared with others such as that in Table 13-6. There the degree of social science background was related to grade, with 41 per cent of those with social science courses obtaining B— or higher and 38 per cent of those without social science courses obtaining B— or higher. The percentage difference here is 41 per cent — 38 per cent = 3 per cent. In this way we can show that the relationship seems to be much closer in Table 13-3 than in Table 13-6.

Perhaps the most widely used measure of degree of association is the Pearsonian product-moment correlation coefficient r (usually simply designated the correlation coefficient). We may illustrate this with data from the medical student study. Let us designate the degree of interest in close relationships with patients as Variable X; also, let us designate degree of interest in research as Variable Y. The scores for three of the medical students in the study were

	X	Y
Student A	1	3
Student B	3	1
Student C	2	2

The correlation coefficient provides a measure of the degree to which the two variables vary together, where the relationship between the two is conceived of as a directly proportional or linear one. If they vary in opposite directions in a perfectly consistent linear fashion, as in the preceding illustration, $r = -1$. If they vary together in the same direction in a perfectly consistent linear fashion, $r = 1$. If there is no linear relationship between them, then $r = 0$. Thus, r can take any value between -1 and $+1$, inclusive. The closer it is to $+1$, the greater the degree of linear relationship between the two variables in the same direction. The closer it is to -1, the greater the degree of linear relationship in the opposite direction. The closer it is to 0, the smaller is the degree of linear relationship between the two variables. The computing formula for r is

$$r = \frac{N\Sigma XY - (\Sigma X)(\Sigma Y)}{\sqrt{[N\Sigma X^2 - (\Sigma X)^2][N\Sigma Y^2 - (\Sigma Y)^2]}}$$

Here, N corresponds to the number of instances—in the present illustration, 3 (students). In addition to N, there are five quantities needed in order to calculate r: ΣX, ΣY, ΣXY, ΣX^2, and ΣY^2. It should be noted that ΣXY is calculated by summing each of the products of X and Y. Thus, $\Sigma XY = (1 \times 3) + (3 \times 1) + (2 \times 2) = 3 + 3 + 4 = 10$. Also ΣX^2 and ΣY^2 are calculated by summing the squares of the variable in question. Thus, $\Sigma X^2 = 1^2 + 3^2 + 2^2 = 1 + 9 + 4 = 14$. All the calculations for these five quantities are presented in Table 15-2.

TABLE 15–2

Calculation of r, the Product-Moment Correlation Coefficient

X	Y	XY	X^2	Y^2
1	3	3	1	9
3	1	3	9	1
2	2	4	4	4
$\Sigma X = 6$	$\Sigma Y = 6$	$\Sigma XY = 10$	$\Sigma X^2 = 14$	$\Sigma Y^2 = 14$

$$r = \frac{3(10) - 6(6)}{\sqrt{[3(14) - 6^2][3(14) - 6^2]}} = \frac{30 - 36}{\sqrt{(42 - 36)(42 - 36)}} = \frac{-6}{\sqrt{(6)(6)}} = -1$$

Thus, $r = -1$, indicating a maximum degree of linear relationship between the two variables, although in opposite directions. Thus, among the three medical students, a high degree of interest in research is associated with a low degree of interest in close relationships with patients, and vice versa.

We might also calculate r for the following situation, where X and Y are the same variables as in the previous illustration, but three different students are involved:

X	Y	XY
2	1	2
3	1	3
1	1	1
$\Sigma X = 6$	$\Sigma Y = 3$	$\Sigma XY = 6$

For this illustration, it is not necessary to calculate ΣX^2 and ΣY^2, for the numerator is equal to 0 and consequently $r = 0$. In the numerator we have $N\Sigma XY - (\Sigma x)(\Sigma Y) = (3)(6) - (6)(3) = 18 - 18 = 0$. Thus, $r = 0$, and there is no relationship among these medical students between an interest in research and an interest in close patient relationships.

In Chapter 11 correlations were referred to within the context of factor analysis, a technique which is applied to a set of correlation coefficients for purposes of concept formation and measurement. They are more generally used in the analysis of cause-and-effect relationships where linear or directly proportional relationships are involved. In the medical student study, for example, the correlation coefficient can provide a measure of the degree of relationship betwen expected value deprivation and the probability of an unfavorable rating of a given specialty. If a linear relationship exists between any two variables (for example, age and income), the correlation coefficient can be used to evaluate how close the relationship is.

The correlation coefficient, a measure of *degree* of relationship, also has implications for the prediction of one variable by means of the other, and there the *type* of relationship is involved. The closer the correlation coefficient is to 1 or -1, the more accurately we can predict one variable by means of the other. The type of relationship used in making this prediction is a linear one, or one of direct proportionality. As the correlation coefficient approaches 0, the accuracy of any linear prediction of one variable by means of the other decreases.

It should be noted that the relationship between two variables need not be a linear one. The relationship may not be one of direct proportionality (for example, the relationship between s and t in $s = \frac{1}{2}gt^2$). Here, s varies with the square of t and is not directly proportional to t; this is a curvilinear rather than a linear relationship. In these situations, nonlinear measures for assessing degree of relationship, as well as nonlinear mathematical functions for purposes of prediction, are called for.

As a matter of fact, it may be argued that just about all the relationships that behavioral scientists are interested in are nonlinear. Whenever feedback relationships occur among a given set of variables, the likelihood of nonlinearity is great. This is especially true when we begin to increase the number of variables involved in a given situation. If we assume that human systems are open systems, then we had best take to heart the limitations of correlational analysis. In the following section we shall expand our discussion of limitations to statistical testing.

15.4   SOME LIMITATIONS OF STATISTICAL TESTING

In addition to the ways in which statistical analysis facilitates social research, there are serious problems associated with it. These problems stem from a lack of understanding of the limitations of statistical tools, and it is to such limitations that we address ourselves here, to be discussed under the headings of analysis, mathematical approach, static orientation, context of justification, scientific orientation, group emphasis, unrealistic assumptions, and conservative bias.

ANALYSIS

Behavioral scientists utilize statistics primarily in order to perform tests of significance between pairs of variables. What this approach can easily degenerate into is analysis without synthesis, that is, a narrow interest in minute aspects of a complex system of factors while losing sight of the larger context. When we find two factors related statistically, such a finding frequently leads us to ignore the problem of interrelating a large number of factors. The difficulty is not that analysis is of no importance but rather that analysis without synthesis is not cumulative. It is one thing to establish statistical significance among a number of pairs of variables, but it is quite another to relate all these variables to one another.

At its worst, a focus on analysis leads to a kind of compartmentalization of the mind—analogous to a specialization among disciplines which erects barriers to communication—which leads it to locate statistical significance but miss genuine significance. We assume here that to attain genuine significance we must not only analyze but also integrate enough factors that an important portion of a given phenomenon is taken into account. Analysis without synthesis is closely related to the age-old quest for certainty. The researcher manifests a powerful desire to achieve great depths of knowledge by narrowing his field of vision. By so doing, however, he loses sight of the total context within which his observations are embedded: phenomena outside of his range of vision, intangible phenomena which cannot be seen, his own relationship to the research process. Thus, what he may end up with is, instead of depth, a very superficial understanding of the phenomena observed, one which ignores the way in which it affects and is affected by its context.

MATHEMATICAL APPROACH

Let us distinguish between two broad types of usages of mathematics in social research, as a tool for constructing scales for measurement purposes and as a tool for describing relationships among variables. In the former case the trend has been toward devising scales with more and more of the mathematical properties that characterize numbers, that is, growing interest in moving away from nominal scales and toward ratio scales. As for the latter case, a similar trend may be observed. Tests of significance are analogous to a nominal-scale approach. For example, an important question is whether two or more samples come from the same or different populations, analogous to the fundamental question about nominal scales: to what degree are they overlapping or nonoverlapping? By contrast, builders of mathematical models of human behavior tend to develop the kinds of models within which the variables involved are assumed to have ratio properties.

The foregoing implies that statistical testing tends to employ very little of the analytic and synthetic power of mathematics. It is analogous to working with nominal scales in the field of measurement. The implication we draw is not that statistical testing or nominal scales are useless, but rather that these approaches are quite limited. If we assume that mathematics offers us powerful tools for scientific research, then these approaches make use of very few of these.

STATIC ORIENTATION

For almost all the statistical tests that behavioral scientists perform, the order of occurrence of the variables in question is immaterial. Thus, for example, the same kinds of tests tend to be used for the analysis of survey data, where order of occurrence frequently is a mystery, and experimental data, where order generally is known. By implication it is difficult to tell very much about order of occurrence on the basis of statistical tests. Yet such knowledge appears to us to be absolutely crucial to attaining even the barest beginnings of an understanding of behavioral phenomena, let alone a knowledgeable view of complex processes.

If statistical testing tells us very little about time order, it tells us even less about such complexities as rates of change and acceleration of phenomena, about time constants, about the ways in which rates lead to cumulation of levels, about factors producing exponential growth and decay as distinct from constant-rate equilibria, about time delays in the relationships among rates and levels which tend to produce oscillation, and about how to infer the behavior resulting from a complex system of variables representing a set of rates and levels.

If statistical testing requires little or no knowledge of time order or, indeed, more complex knowledge of dynamics, and if it tells us little or nothing about these same topics, then it does not motivate the behavioral scientist to become interested in dynamic relationships. Worse, it motivates him to ignore such problems.

CONTEXT OF JUSTIFICATION

When testing for significance, the problem for the investigator is whether certain relationships among variables are of such a nature as to hold at given levels of significance; or, more in the argot of the statistician, the problem is whether several samples can or cannot be said to come from the same population. Such testing, thus, is not concerned with the problem of how to construct hypotheses and theories which promise to be of genuine importance. For a relationship to be statistically significant it does not matter whether the relationship is completely trivial or of great importance. And if the major need of the behavioral sciences is one of *constructing* important new hypotheses and theories as distinct from testing available ones, then the statistical testing procedure has little utility.

It might also be maintained that a concern with statistical testing is diversionary; it focuses attention away from the context of discovery. If such testing were utilized in proper perspective it would not divert attention in this manner. However, the problem is that such testing frequently becomes an end in itself. It is much safer to make use of known and prestigeful techniques than to use unknown ones of dubious prestige.

SCIENTIFIC ORIENTATION

Statistical testing seems to have taken on a kind of aura within behavioral science which very nearly equates it, for many individuals, with an infallible criterion of scientific truth. The basic problem is that behavioral scientists do not generally apply criteria to the testing procedure itself so as to be able to evaluate it properly. For example, we know very little about the net effects of such procedures on the progress of behavioral science in the last twenty-five years. Without such research, we tend to take testing procedures for granted.

Related to this is the aura of prestige which mathematics has for science and which, consequently, statistics carries within behavioral science. However, in the preceding paragraphs on the mathematical approaches taken in behavioral science we distinguished between the relatively elementary approach taken within statistics and the more powerful tools associated with mathematical models. What is needed is not the worship of mathematics but an understanding of why it has been effective. If its effectiveness has been based on its ability to synthesize vast amounts of information as a result of incorporating elements (numbers) with ratio properties, enabling us to relate concepts in numerical ways, then statistical testing is almost beside the point. Although it is helpful, it does not harness the power of mathematics.

GROUP EMPHASIS

Although tests of significance leave open the question of what the unit of analysis should be (for example, whether we should study a sample of groups, a sample of individuals, or a sample of the behavior of a given individual), it has become traditional to avoid sampling the behavior of a given individual and designating a set of his behaviors as the population. Behind this tradition is the general emphasis of sociology on the group as well as a possible confusion of the statistician's concept of population with its ordinary meaning. The statistician wishes to generalize from a *sample* to a *population,* with these terms referring to a *subset of elements* and a *set of elements.* Yet the experimental psychologist may come to believe that if his study is to have widespread implications, he must do research on a number of subjects (with the individual as the element) in order to generalize to a large population, with *population* carrying the everyday meaning of the word.

But no research can be generalized to large numbers of individuals simply on the basis of some statistical manipulations. The theory and measurements involved must take into account a sufficient proportion of the dynamics of whatever processes are involved if understanding and ability to predict are to emerge. By the traditional focus of statistical testing away from exploring the complex interrelationships among elements of the personality system, a great deal of the context of any human situation may be lost, and with it, much of our ability to achieve comprehensive understanding or accurate prediction.

UNREALISTIC ASSUMPTIONS

Related to the analytic emphasis of statistical testing is its general focus on a set of factors that are assumed to be acting independently of one another. Of course, such an assumption is not made because investigators really believe that these factors operate independently; rather, it is made in order to be able to reject the assumption. The reason for this indirect approach has to do, in all probability, with the nature of mathematics. The mathematics required to handle such a situation is quite manageable, whereas the case of dependence becomes quite complex mathematically.

This assumption is empirically unrealistic if we assume that almost all hypotheses being tested have some support in the literature, for this implies that we already have rejected the assumption of independence and have found some relationship among the variables in question. Thus, by making the assumption of independence in order to make use of statistical tests we in effect set up a straw man.

Of course, it can easily be argued that by such a process we obtain ever more evidence for the existence of a relationship, because each research context represents a different situation. Although this is true, it may be a poor strategy for research. We should make the kinds of assumptions which carry us as far as existing knowledge can take us in order to go beyond existing knowledge. The strategy implied here is to assume dependence and attempt to explore the ways in which variables are interrelated. This moves us beyond determinations as to whether there *exist* relationships that are not independent and into the study of the *types* of relationships that are manifested.

PASSIVE ORIENTATION

Because statistical tests have come to be used, traditionally, to investigate relationships among a small number of factors, they have given impetus to the kinds of experiments which deal with few factors. Thus, it is the laboratory experiment rather than the field experiment which tends to be the most appropriate setting for their use. Another reason for this is the supposed relative ease of measurement in the laboratory as distinct from the field situation. As a result, the behavioral science experimenter tends to stay inside of his own world and not attempt to experiment with or change the outside world.

It may be argued, partly on the basis of the growing literature on experimenter effect, that the world of the laboratory is also a complex one. Thus, if the statistical testing approach previously was deemed inadequate to handle the complexities of field studies, why should it now be adequate to deal with the complexities of laboratory studies? We can learn little about the complex processes inside and outside of the laboratory unless we go beyond statistical testing. If we do so, we will learn to develop the kind of information which may indeed enable us to effect decisive changes both inside and outside of the laboratory.

EXERCISES

1. Define the kind of problem about which you can obtain evidence from statistical tests dealing with data from a single individual.

2. Referring to Exercise 1, make up the kind of data that can be tested by the binomial test and use the probability distribution in Table 15-1.

3. Referring to Exercise 1, make up the kind of data which can be the basis for calculating the Pearsonian product-moment correlation coefficient, and proceed to calculate r.

4. Using the same subtopics employed in Section 15.3, develop a series of arguments on the limitations of a nonstatistical approach to behavioral science research.

5. Develop a discussion on the limitations of statistical testing centering on a topic not covered in Section 15.3.

ANNOTATED REFERENCES

CAMILLERI, SANTO F. "Theory, Probability, and Induction in Social Research," *American Sociological Review,* **27** (1962), 170–78. Camilleri views the process of verification as one designed to advance a system of propositions, with each hypothesis constituting only one element of such a system. The testing of a hypothesis should advance the process of theory construction, helping the researcher to decide on a constructive course of action as a result of the test.

LAZERWITZ, BERNARD. "Sampling Theory and Procedures," in Hubert M. Blalock and Ann B. Blalock (eds.), *Methodology in Social Research*. New York: McGraw-Hill Book Company, 1968, Chap. 8. In this fully packed chapter, Lazerwitz treats simple random sampling, systematic selection, cluster sampling, sampling with probability proportional to a measure of size, the sampling equation, a simplified model for the sampling errors of cluster samples, and specific sample design techniques. For more extensive treatment of sampling, reference may be made to Leslie Kish, *Survey Sampling*. New York: John Wiley & Sons, Inc., 1965.

MORRISON, DENTON E., and RAMON E. HENKEL (eds.). *The Significance Test Controversy: A Reader*. Chicago: Aldine Publishing Company, 1970. This controversy reflects existing polarization, notably that between the quantitative and the qualitative approach, between an emphasis on theory and an emphasis on method, and between an interest in statistical significance and an interest in significance. An understanding of the nature of the controversy can help us to overcome the polarization.

CHAPTER 16 Multivariate Analysis

In his analysis of data the general aim of the researcher is to provide the kind of evidence which can lead to an understanding of causal processes. The chapter begins with a discussion of some of the complexities involved in such processes and goes on to consider the way in which theory can contribute to an understanding of cause-and-effect relationships. Attention is then shifted to the analysis of relationships among three variables (one-variable and two-variable analysis techniques were discussed in Chapter 13). Given an initial situation in which there is a relationship between two variables, several different things can occur when the investigator controls on a third variable, and a number of examples are used to illustrate these various possible occurrences. We conclude with a discussion of the limitations of multivariate analysis.

16.1 THE CAUSAL PROCESS

It was once generally thought that for every effect there existed one and only one cause and that if several causes are discovered then the effect must really be more than one. For example, Émile Durkheim uncovered what he decided were three causes of suicide.[1] He therefore concluded that suicide is not a unitary concept, and that actually there are three different types of suicide, that is, three different effects. The contemporary approach involves allowing for and expecting a number of different causes for a single effect. Physicians, for example, distinguish between *predisposing causes* and *precipitating causes* of death. This assumes not only multiple causation but also sequential occurrence (to some extent); one set of causes is predisposing and thus occurs prior to another set of causes, which is precipitating.

A PHYSICAL SCIENCE EXAMPLE

The complexity of the causal process may be illustrated by the kinds of answers given to a child's query as to why, for example, the lamp turns on (Event Z) in his room when the wall switch is flipped (Event F). When

[1] Émile Durkheim, *The Rules of Sociological Method* (translated by Sarah A. Solovay and John H. Mueller), edited by George E. G. Cattin (New York: Free Press, 1950).

the child is very young, we might simply answer that a wire (Event *G*) connects the wall switch to the lamp. When he is older we might introduce the idea of an electric current (Event *H*), which flows through the wire and heats up a bit of metal inside the light bulb (Event *I*), and that some objects (such as this piece of metal) become very bright when they are heated. A more thorough explanation would refer to the latest scientific theory bearing on the situation. For example, we might introduce the idea that a difference in electrical potential exists between the two ends of the wire attached to the energy source (Event *K*) and that flipping the switch completes the circuit (Event *L*) and thereby allows electrons to move freely from the higher level to the lower one (Event *M*).

We might diagram the relationships involved here by letting an arrow between two events designate a cause-and-effect relationship. Thus, *A* → *B* signifies that Event *A* causes Event *B*. Also we may designate a situation in which Events *A* and *B* jointly operate to cause *C*:

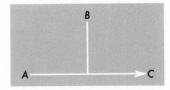

The following diagram summarizes this discussion:

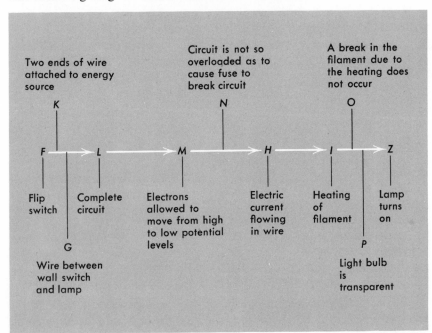

Note that three additional events have been added: *N, O,* and *P*. We might examine these three events together with Events *K* and *G,* comparing them to the other events, all of which are listed along the same line. The distinction is not in terms of relative importance, for the omission of any one of the ten events leading to Z would prevent the lamp from turning on. Also, multiple causation exists not only in the process as a whole, but also in certain portions of the process. For example, Events F, G, and K all contribute to Event L (the completion of the circuit). In order to complete the circuit, the switch must be flipped, a wire must connect the switch to the lamp, and both ends of the wire must be attached to an energy source. The distinction between Events G, K, N, O, P and Events F, L, M, H, I, and Z seems to be that the former represent the initial characteristics of the situation and the static characteristics at a given point in time, whereas the latter seem to be closely related to dynamic changes in the situation.

PHYSICAL AND BEHAVIORAL SCIENCE COMBINED

The causal process does not begin with Event F and end with Event Z. The following provides an illustration of what might occur prior to F:

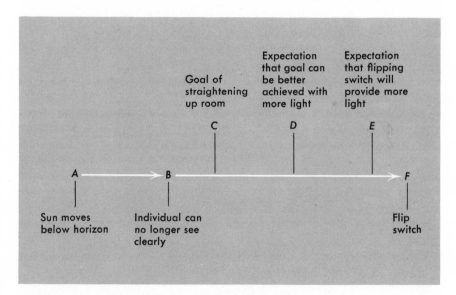

This example of the reasons why a given person might flip the light switch ends where the previous analysis begins, thus providing an explanation that covers a wider span of time. In this manner, the comprehensiveness of the causal analysis is increased. One might also, of course, continue with the causal process by examining the impact of turning on the lamp on subsequent events, thus increasing the comprehensiveness of the total explanation. It should be noted that the total explanation includes aspects of physical and behavioral science, perhaps indicating a certain unity of science.

In addition to evaluating the explanation of a given causal process with respect to comprehensiveness, one can also look to the degree of detail provided. For example, the first diagram distinguishes nine events which occur between flipping the switch (F) and the lamp turning on (Z), though only a split second actually elapses between F and Z. It would be possible to distinguish many more initial conditions (for example, the filament is made of a substance that becomes very bright when it is heated; the two wires are well insulated from one another). It is also possible to specify additional changes in the situation which lead to the lamp turning on (for example, electrons move from the source of energy to the wire in the household). One could go on and on adding both comprehensiveness and detail, and this constitutes a never-ending aspect of the scientific process.

This attempt to explain certain causal processes involved fundamental theory both in physics and behavioral science. The function of theory in this context is to select from among the myriad initial conditions and dynamic factors those most directly relevant to the causal process under investigation. With respect to the behavioral science part of the explanation, one could conceivably refer to the many different experiences which occur throughout the life of the individual and which lead to his flipping the switch in this particular situation. A given theory of choice, however, may postulate that it will be enough to focus on a few goals and a few expectations in the present situation.

A BEHAVIORAL SCIENCE EXAMPLE

Another example of a causal sequence may be diagrammed as follows:

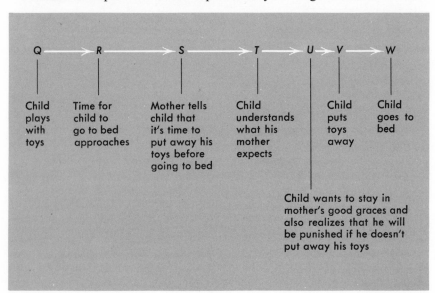

The theory involved here is that one goal is developed on the basis of other goals. The other goals in this situation are the desire to stay in the mother's good graces and the desire to avoid punishment. In this way the child gradually learns that the goal of putting away one's things is a desirable one to have. The theory here is simply an extension of that involved in the medical student study. In this case, choice among alternatives leads to the development of goals.

THEORY AND CAUSATION

Thus far in our discussion of the causal process we have talked about causes and effects as if we had a special kind of insight into the nature of reality. The actual situation in which the scientist finds himself contains a multitude of variables and a complex network of interrelationships among them. Some of the relationships have to do with only two variables, whereas others are concerned with a larger number. The relationships vary in degree of closeness as well as in kind. If the preceding examples of causal processes seemed somewhat complex, when we deal with merely statistical relationships among variables the complexity is compounded many fold.

Theory, which enabled us to find a path through the complexities of the causal process, is also our best tool for finding our way through the maze of relationships among variables. Earlier sections of this volume outlined the role of theory in the definition of a research problem, in the collection of data, and in measurement; its role in the analysis of data is no less important.

In Chapter 13, "One and Two Variables," attention was called to the two-variable situation and hypotheses that relate two variables at a time. The emphasis was on testing a particular hypothesis more or less in isolation from other hypotheses. But the history of science seems to indicate that advances are made when the scientist attempts to develop and test systems of hypotheses, or theories. We could think of the scientific process as a vast search for tiny pieces of a very complicated puzzle in the situation where many of the objects found are not pieces of the puzzle but merely look like them. The finding of such a deceptive piece would correspond to a Type I error (rejection of a true null hypothesis and, thus, acceptance of the alternative hypothesis), whereas the failure to find a piece in a location where it actually was buried corresponds to a Type II error (accepting a false null hypothesis that, for example, no relationship exists between two variables). It would seem that one of the best ways of proceeding in such a situation is to try to put the pieces of the puzzle together and to make maximum use of those sets of pieces that have already been put together successfully. The analogy might be between trying to put together pieces and testing scientific theory within the context of justification. Also, we might draw an analogy between using sets of put-together pieces to find other pieces and the further development of theory within the context of discovery. Theory would constitute the best tool for determining whether any isolated piece is a deceptive piece or not by testing whether or not the isolated piece fits into the set of pieces.

The importance of integrated sets of hypotheses, or theory, for the analysis of data is commented on by Camilleri:

> In the development of systematic theory, the purpose of research is not primarily to determine the empirical adequacy of a particular hypothesis. Its purpose is to test the coordinated formal system that produced the hypothesis as a theorem. The question of testing a hypothesis thus would not occur until that hypothesis had been set in an explicit deductive context. . . . The empirical truth of the particular hypotheses the researcher checks upon is valuable chiefly for its instrumental use in determining what he should do with the deductive system by which he produced the hypothesis. It is this conceptual relevance that we refer to as the systematic import of an empirical result.[2]

Camilleri emphasizes the importance of testing systems of hypotheses as well as the limitations of testing a given hypothesis that is isolated from such a system (that is, from theory). In this context he discusses the limitations of statistical tests of hypotheses, for these have thus far been primarily designed for testing a given hypothesis in isolation from others. Very little in the way of statistical techniques seems to have been produced for the testing of theory.

16.2 THREE VARIABLES: AN ILLUSTRATION OF A SPURIOUS RELATIONSHIP

We now shift our attention to the process whereby the researcher makes decisions about the nature of the causal process on the basis of data on the interrelationships among variables. We shall consider, primarily, the three-variable case, for the complexities of the tabular analysis of four and more variables are beyond the scope of this book. When inferring causal processes on the basis of relationships among variables, we are making decisions in the face of uncertainty. The problem here is the general one which faces the scientist. The process of statistical decision making is only one example of the scientist's efforts to develop strategies for making wise decisions about the nature of reality. The causal process represents the reality, and the relationships among variables are utilized to make decisions about this reality.

[2] Santo F. Camilleri, "Theory, Probability, and Induction in Social Research," *American Sociological Review,* **27** (1962), 177.

We shall begin with a situation that occurs quite frequently, one in which the researcher has found evidence for the existence of a relationship between two variables and is seeking to carry forward the investigation. In particular, he is interested in obtaining additional evidence as to whether or not the two variables stand in a cause-and-effect relationship to one another.

One important guide for obtaining such evidence is Mill's method of difference, which deals with two situations that differ in one respect and have every other circumstance in common but one (the second respect in which the two situations differ). In this event, according to Mill's method, we may interpret one of the respects in which the situations differ as the cause, and the other as the effect. Of course, the present-day research framework that most scientists have adopted no longer permits the statement with certainty that any given cause-and-effect relationship exists. But the method of difference may nevertheless be used to provide evidence for or against a given cause-and-effect relationship even if the evidence is not viewed as adding up to certainty.

A TWO-VARIABLE RELATIONSHIP

To illustrate the procedure, let us assume that the effect we are investigating is the amount of property damage caused by any given fire in communities within the United States. We shall designate the variable *amount of damage* as y, the dependent variable. Let us now consider, as one of the possible causes of the amount of damage, the *number of fire engines present at the fire,* and let us designate this as variable x. Of course, this is a ridiculous hypothesis in terms of our knowledge of such things, but it will be to our advantage to set up a situation in which we know no actual causal relationship is likely. If we know what the nature of reality is, we can better understand the strategies designed to make correct decisions about it on the basis of relationships among variables.

Table 16-1 presents hypothetical data on the relationship between x and y.

TABLE 16-1

$[xy]$: The Relationship Between Number of Fire Engines (x) and Amount of Damage (y)

Amount of Damage	Number of Fire Engines	
	0 or 1 (%)	2 or more (%)
$10,000 or more	30	59
Under $10,000	70	41
Total	100	100
	(1,500)	(700)

The data indicate the percentage of fires producing property damage of $10,000 or more among those fires at which two or more fire engines were present is substantially greater than that among those fires at which one or no fire engine was present.

A STATISTICAL TEST

A statistical test on the data will determine whether or not the relationship between x and y is statistically significant. Because the binomial test (discussed in Chapter 15) does not apply to a situation in which two variables are cross-tabulated or interrelated as shown in Table 16-1, the t-test for the significance of differences between proportions will be employed.[3]

We might specify the null and alternative hypotheses as follows:

$$H_0: P_1 = P_2$$
$$H_1: P_1 > P_2$$

A one-sided test is indicated in this situation, for we would ordinarily suspect that the number of fire engines would be greater in a situation where the amount of damage is great. P_1 and P_2 refer to the proportions

---

[3] The t-test makes use of a sample statistic already discussed in the context of measures of association: the difference between the proportions in the table. From Table 16-1 it can be calculated that $p_1 - p_2 = .59 - .30 = .29$. In Table 16-1, p_1 refers to the proportion of fires with damages of $10,000 or more among those fires at which two or more fire engines were present, whereas p_2 refers to the proportion of fires with damage over $10,000 among those fires where one or no fire engine was present. In this test, we assume that an infinite number of samples of size $700 + 1,500 = 2,200$ had been drawn from the same population. If a suitable transformation of the sample statistic $(p_1 - p_2)$ is made, we can assume that this sampling distribution will be a *t-distribution*. By setting up a level of significance and a region of rejection, we will then be able to decide whether to accept or reject the null hypothesis.

The formula for this transformation, which is the basis for the t-test for the significance of a difference in proportions, is

$$t = \frac{p_1 - p_2}{\sqrt{\left(\dfrac{n_1 p_1 + n_2 p_2}{n_1 + n_2}\right)\left(1 - \dfrac{n_1 p_1 + n_2 p_2}{n_1 + n_2}\right)\left(\dfrac{n_1 + n_2}{n_1 n_2}\right)}}$$

Here p_1 and p_2 refer to the two sample proportions (for example, .59 and .30); n_1 and n_2 refer to the column totals on the basis of which the proportions are calculated (for example, 700 and 1,500). Tables containing the calculated values of the transformation are available for the convenience of the researcher. See Vernon Davies, "A Rapid Method for Determining the Significance of the Difference Between Two Percentages," Stations Circular 151, Washington Agricultural Experiment Stations, Washington State University, Pullman, Wash.

of fires where the amount of damage is $10,000 or more in the popula-
tions from which the sample was drawn (where two or more fire engines,
or one or none, respectively, are involved). We might conceive of each
population as consisting of a large number of fires from which the sample
was drawn by means of probability sampling. It remains now to specify
the level of significance. Let us here set $\alpha = .05$. Thus, if H_0 is rejected
at this level, the probability that a difference in the appropriate direction
does not exist in the population will be no greater than .05.

Calculations indicate that a sample difference between p_1 and p_2 of .29
is in fact statistically significant at the .05 level. Thus, we reject the null
hypothesis that P_1 equals P_2 and accept the alternative hypothesis, $P_1 >
P_2$. In other words, we find the relationship between the number of fire
engines and the amount of damage statistically significant at the .05 level.

This example provides another illustration of the fact that statistical
relationships and cause-and-effect relationships may be two quite different things. In this case, because of the nature of the data, it is quite
obvious that no cause-and-effect relationship actually exists, although
there is a statistically significant relationship. But the investigator is usually not so fortunate as to know that a given independent variable could
not possibly be the cause of a given dependent variable. Are there any
further tests that will provide additional evidence as to whether or not
the relationship is a causal one?

Following Mill's method of difference, we shall begin by comparing
two groupings of fires—those with one or no fire engine, and those with
two or more—with respect to the amount of damage *after* the groupings
have been equated on certain other factors. Mill's method actually calls
for equating the two groupings in all respects, but this is not possible. If,
after the groupings have been equated on a number of factors, we still
observe a relationship between the number of fire engines and the amount
of damage, then this may be taken as evidence for a causal relationship
between these two variables. The rationale here is the same as that utilized
in the before-and-after experiment with one control group. The experimental and control group are subjected to different treatments, but are
equated insofar as possible in all other respects. If a difference then
emerges between the two groups on the "after" test, we attribute this to
the difference in treatments or the independent variable. On the other
hand, if no difference emerges on the "after" test, we have evidence to
the effect that no causal relationship exists between the independent
variable and the dependent variable.

CONTROLLING ON A THIRD VARIABLE

The way in which we will to some extent equate the two groupings of
fires will illustrate nonexperimental procedures of analysis in general
and survey analysis in particular. The analysis of data in the context of

the experiment has already been taken up in Chapter 5. A widely used technique of survey analysis is to set up a series of three-variable tables, with a different third variable used to equate the two original groupings in each of the tables. These third variables are called *control variables.* The third variable introduced in Table 16-2 is the type of fire engine sent to the fires, that is, new or old ones. (Let us assume for purposes of this illustration that no combinations of both old and new fire engines appeared at a given fire.)

Table 16-2 is just like two fourfold tables joined together. A one-sided *t*-test for the significance of the difference between proportions indicates that both are significant at the .05 level. This table illustrates a situation in which the control variable is irrelevant to the relationship between the independent variable and the dependent variable. (We could just as well introduce hundreds of other irrelevant variables and still come up with the same statistically significant relationship between number of fire engines and amount of damage.) It is typical of situations in which the control variable (*z*) does not result in a change in the initial relationship between the independent variable (*x*) and the dependent variable (*y*). As can readily be seen in Table 16-2, the relationship between number of fire engines and amount of damage is the same regardless of whether new or old fire engines are involved.

TABLE 16-2

[*xy; z*]: The Relationship Between Number of Fire Engines (*x*) and Amount of Damage (*y*) Controlling on Type of Fire Engine (*z*)

	New Fire Engines			Old Fire Engines	
	0–1 Fire Engines (%)	2 or More Fire Engines (%)		0–1 Fire Engines (%)	2 or More Fire Engines (%)
$10,000 or more	30	59	$10,000 or more	30	59
Under $10,000	70	41	Under $10,000	70	41
Total	100	100		100	100
	(1,350)	(630)		(150)	(70)

Having illustrated a situation in which the control variable is not related to either the independent variable or the dependent variable, we shall now illustrate a situation in which it is related to both. Let us assume that an analysis was made the aim of which was to relate the number of alarms (*t*) sent out after each fire was discovered by the fire department and variables *x* and *y* (number of fire engines and amount of damage, respectively). Tables 16-3 and 16-4 present the relationships between *t* and *x* and between *t* and *y*, respectively.

Table 16-3 shows the relationship between the number of alarms (*t*) and the number of fire engines (*x*), and this relationship is statistically significant at the .05 level. A statistically significant relationship at the .05 level is also found for the data in Table 16-4, where number of alarms (*t*) is related to amount of damage (*y*). If a relationship between two variables is indicated by a line of dashes, then the following diagram summarizes the relationships among *x*, *t*, and *y*:

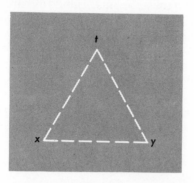

It remains to investigate the interrelationships among the three variables when taken together. In particular it would be useful to determine

TABLE 16-3

[*tx*]: The Relationship Between Number of Alarms (*t*) and Number of Fire Engines (*x*)

Number of Fire Engines	0–1-Alarm Fire (%)	2–3-Alarm Fire (%)
2 or more	17	50
0 or 1	83	50
Total	100	100
	(1,200)	(1,000)

TABLE 16-4

[*ty*]: The Relationship Between Number of Alarms (*t*) and Amount of Damage (*y*)

Amount of Damage	0–1-Alarm Fire (%)	2–3-Alarm Fire (%)
$10,000 or more	5	80
Under $10,000	95	20
Total	100	100
	(1,200)	(1,000)

whether controlling on Variable t alters the relationship between x and y. The relationship between x and y remained the same when we controlled on z, a variable which was related neither to x nor to y, and consequently additional support was found for a causal relationship between x and y. If in the present situation we have a disappearance of the relationship between x and y, evidence will be presented against the existence of such a causal relationship according to the method of difference. This is because, when the 0–1 engine fire is equated with the 2-or-more engine fire with respect to the number of alarms, no corresponding difference with respect to amount of damage results. Table 16-5 presents the relationship between number of fire engines (x) and amount of damage (y) with a control on the number of alarms (t).

TABLE 16-5

[xy; t]: The Relationship Between Number of Fire Engines (x) and Amount of Damage (y) Controlling on Number of Alarms (t)

	Number of Alarms					
	0–1-Alarm Fire			2–3-Alarm Fire		
	2 or More Fire Engines (%)	0–1 Fire Engines (%)		2 or More Fire Engines (%)	0–1 Fire Engines (%)	
$10,000 or more	5	5	$10,000 or more	80	80	
Under $10,000	95	95	Under $10,000	20	20	
Total	100	100		100	100	
	(200)	(1,000)		(500)	(500)	

Table 16-5 may be viewed as a combination of two fourfold tables, as was Table 16-2. Each of the two fourfold tables in Table 16-5 deals with the relationship between the number of fire engines and the amount of damage. The difference between them is that in the left-hand table only 0–1-alarm fires are involved, whereas in the right-hand table only 2–3-alarm fires are included. Thus, the number of alarms is controlled in each of the two fourfold tables. The result is that the relationship we found earlier between the number of fire engines and the amount of damage completely disappears.

In accordance with Mill's method of difference, evidence has here been presented against the existence of a cause-and-effect relationship between the number of fire engines and the amount of damage. Of course, we knew this all along, but most realistic research situations will not be so obvious. We might now attempt to diagram the causal relationships we suspect might exist among x, y, and t. Solid lines with arrowheads will be used to indicate a suspected causal relationship.

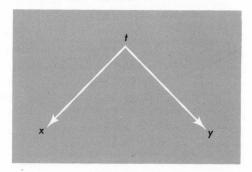

There is no causal arrow between x and y because the statistical relationship between these variables disappears when we control on t. Of course, we have no assurance that there is a causal relationship between t and y, because some other variable m might cause both the number of alarms and the amount of damage:

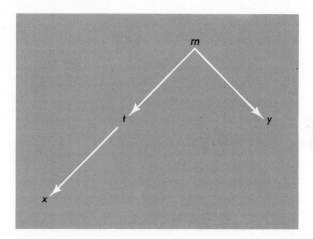

As a matter of fact, this is the actual situation, as most of us would not accept the idea that the number of alarms (t) actually causes the degree of damage (y). If we conceive of m as the initial seriousness (intensity, spread, and type) of the fire, then a serious fire will affect both the number of alarms and the degree of damage. Thus, any given causal diagram may become quite complex. There is always the possibility that some additional variable causes a suspected cause or a suspected effect. In this situation illustrated by m, t, and y, we designate the initial suspected causal relationship as a *spurious relationship*. Another illustration of a spurious relationship is that between the number of fire engines (x) and the amount of damage (y). Although it appeared on the basis of Table

16-1 that there might be a causal relationship between x and y, when we controlled on the number of alarms the initial relationship was found to be a spurious one.

The relationship between the initial seriousness of the fire (m), the number of alarms (t), and the number of fire engines (x) illustrates a different kind of interrelationship among three variables. Here we designate the number of alarms (t) as the *intervening variable,* for it occurs between event m (initial seriousness of the fire) and event x (number of fire engines). As we saw in Section 16.1, one characteristic of the scientific process is the search for variables which intervene between any two given variables. Thus, with respect to the electric-light example, a whole series of variables intervened between F (flipping the wall switch) and Z (the lamp turning on).

We might question the direction of the arrows which have been drawn in the diagrams shown. The arrows were drawn between the events from the one occurring earlier in time to the one occurring subsequently. Our general knowledge tells us that m (initial seriousness) occurs before y (degree of damage), and that m would precede t (number of alarms), which would, in turn, precede x (number of fire engines).

Although it is possible to take into account the sequence of events on the basis of general knowledge, nothing in the tables indicates which event actually comes first. In Table 16-5, for example, we present the relationship between the number of fire engines (x) and the amount of damage (y), controlling on the number of alarms (t). Part of our resulting interpretation is that t causes x, and that x does not cause y, because both x and y result from some other factor. These conclusions are based not only on the data presented in the tables, but also on our general knowledge about the time order in which the events occur. As a matter of fact, we would come to completely different conclusions on the basis of similar data if we had other ideas about this time order.

16.3 THREE VARIABLES: AN ILLUSTRATION OF AN INTERVENING VARIABLE

This point might be illustrated by reference to other hypothetical data. Let us designate x as race, y as IQ score, and t as degree of education. We will now present in Tables 16-6, 16-7, and 16-8 the same data as are presented in Tables 16-1, 16-3, and 16-4. The difference is that we shall be thinking in terms of variables for which a different time order exists.

There is no need to carry through the statistical analysis of these tables, for the same data were analyzed for Tables 16-1, 16-3, and 16-4. Here as in those tables we have the situation where x is related to y, t is related to x, and t is related to y. Diagrammatically it might be summarized in

TABLE 16–6

[xy]: The Relationship Between Race (x) and IQ Score (y) in an American City

IQ Score	Negro (%)	White (%)
100 or more	30	59
Under 100	70	41
Total	100	100
	(1,500)	(700)

TABLE 16–7

[tx]: The Relationship Between Degree of Education (t) and Race (x)

Race	Not a High School Graduate (%)	High School Graduate or More (%)
White	17	50
Negro	83	50
Total	100	100
	(1,200)	(1,000)

TABLE 16–8

[ty]: The Relationship Between Degree of Education (t) and IQ Score (y)

IQ Score	Not a High School Graduate (%)	High School Graduate or More (%)
100 or more	5	80
Under 100	95	20
Total	100	100
	(1,200)	(1,000)

the same way as previously:

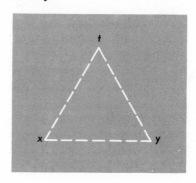

We have found that race (*x*) is related to IQ score (*y*), degree of education (*t*) is related to race (*x*), and degree of education (*t*) is related to IQ
score (*y*). It remains now to examine a table relating the three variables
with one another to shed additional light on the causal process involved.
Table 16-9 includes the same numerical data as is contained in Table
16-5.

TABLE 16-9

[xy; t]: The Relationship Between Race (x) and IQ Score (y) Controlling on Degree of
Education (t)

IQ Score	Not a High School Graduate		High School Graduate or More	
	White (%)	Negro (%)	White (%)	Negro (%)
100 or more	5	5	80	80
Under 100	95	95	20	20
Total	100	100	100	100
	(200)	(1,000)	(500)	(500)

As with Table 16-5, there is no relationship between *x* and *y* when we
control on *t*. The causal process might be symbolized in the following
way:

$$x \rightarrow t \rightarrow y$$

In words, race (*x*) affects opportunities for education, and degree of education (*t*) affects IQ (*y*). Thus, poorly educated whites and Negroes both
tend to have low IQ scores, and highly educated whites and Negroes do
equally well in obtaining high IQ scores. The reason Negroes tended
to have lower IQ scores than whites in Table 16-6 is that among Negroes
a much smaller proportion had had a formal education than among
whites. When we control on education we see that, when Negroes are
equated with whites in terms of formal education, they do just as well
on their IQ scores.

It should be noted that the interpretation of the same numerical data
can vary greatly, depending on our general knowledge of the time sequence involved. In the case of the fire engine example we concluded that
the number of alarms (*t*) causes the number of fire engines (*x*) (that is,
t → *x*). In the present example, however, we conclude that race (*x*) causes
degree of education (*t*)[4] (that is, *x* → *t*). Also, we previously concluded

that the number of fire engines (x) does not cause the amount of damage (y), and that this idea of a causal relationship between the two is spurious. In the present example, however, we do not find that the relationship between x and y is spurious; rather, we find that x and y are causally interrelated through an intervening variable (t). Specifically, race (x) affects degree of education (t), and degree of education affects IQ score (z). We might conclude that, in the analysis of survey data, it is necessary to use whatever knowledge one has about the phenomena under investigation to make assumptions about the time order of the events involved.

Thus far we have distinguished two types of results that might occur when we have an initial relationship between x and y and then control on a third variable (t):

1. As in the case of Table 16-2, where the third variable was the type of fire engine, the initial relationship between x and y is maintained within each of the categories of the control variable.
2. The initial relationship between x and y disappears or diminishes within each of the categories of the control variable. This might be interpreted in two different ways, on the basis of one's knowledge of the time order of the events:
   a. Interpret t as an intervening variable: $x \rightarrow t \rightarrow y$.
   b. Interpret the initial relationship between x and y as spurious:

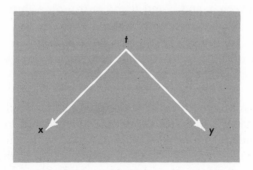

As we saw in the fire engine example, such an explanation itself might be incorrect, for the number of alarms (t) in all probability does not cause the amount of damage (y). We thus had to resort to the introduction of a fourth variable, the initial seriousness of the fire (m), which was conceived of as causing both t and y:

---

[4] Actually, of course, a very long sequence of events intervenes between race and education. This causal process seems to be more complex than the causal process which linked the flipping of a light switch and a lamp turning on.

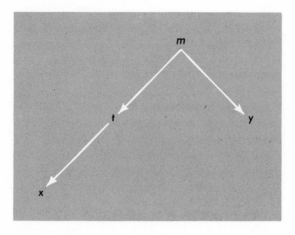

Such additional complexities are quite likely in the analysis of the causal relationships among any set of three variables.

16.4   THREE VARIABLES: AN ILLUSTRATION OF A THIRD POSSIBILITY

TABULAR ANALYSIS

There is a third type of result that can occur when we have an initial relationship between x and y and then control on a third variable (t):

3. The initial relationship between x and y disappears or diminishes within one of the categories of the control variable but is maintained or intensified within the other category.

This third possibility will be illustrated by means of actual rather than hypothetical data. We shall utilize the example presented in Section 13.4, dealing with student grades on a class assignment. Let us designate the students' degree of interest in the class assignment as x, their grades as y, and their seating position as t. According to Tables 13-3 and 13-5 the relationship between x and y and between t and y seems to be quite definite. We might proceed to utilize the t-test for the significance of a difference between proportions on each of these tables, with H_1 being one-sided and $\alpha = .10$. In each of the tables, the relationship proves to be statistically significant. Thus, the relationship between interest and grade, and between seating position and grade, is statistically significant. We might now test for the relationship between interest in the assignment (x) and seating position (t). The relevant data are presented in Table 16-10.

There is no statistically significant relationship between the two variables, in spite of the percentage difference of 50 per cent − 38 per cent = 12 per cent. A more exact statement is that a 12 per cent difference could

TABLE 16-10

[tx]: Relationship Between Seating Position and Degree of
Interest in a Class Assignment

Degree of Interest	Seating Position	
	Rows 1–3 (%)	Rows 4–15 (%)
Interested	50	38
Not interested	50	62
Total	100	100
	(22)	(21)

have occurred with a probability greater than .10 from a population where the true difference in proportions $(P_1 - P_2)$ is equal to 0. Schematically, the following relationships have been established thus far:

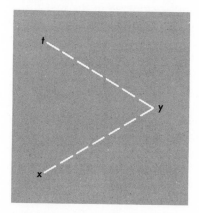

Let us now proceed to investigate further the causal process involved by looking at the interrelationship within a three-variable table. In Table 16-11, we control on seating position (t) and examine the relationship between interest and grade within each of the categories of t.

This table differs from the preceding ones in that the entries are frequencies and not percentages. Percentages would be entirely too misleading for frequencies as small as these. We shall perform separate tests of significance on the left-hand fourfold table and on the right-hand fourfold table. The tests will be one-sided because our alternative hypothesis specifies that the proportion of high grades is greater among the interested than among the uninterested students. In addition we shall specify that $\alpha = .10$.

The left-hand table results indicate a statistically significant relationship at the .10 level.[5] As for the right-hand side, the relationship is not

[5] For this table, the sample is too small to utilize the *t*-test tables used earlier. The test used was the chi-square test, corrected for continuity. For details on this test see, for example, Sidney Siegel, *Nonparametric Statistics for the Behavioral Sciences* (New York: McGraw-Hill, 1956), pp. 104–11.

TABLE 16-11

[xy; t]: The Relationship Between Degree of Interest in Assignment (x) and
Grade (y) Controlling on Seating Position (t)

	Rows 1–3			Rows 4–15	
	Interested N	Not Interested N		Interested N	Not Interested N
B— or higher	8	4	B— or higher	3	2
C+ or lower	3	7	C+ or lower	5	11
Total	11	11	Total	8	13

statistically significant at this level.[6] Thus, we find a relationship between interest and grade among students in the first three rows but not among students in the fourth to fifteenth rows. This illustrates the third possible result when we have an initial relationship between x and y and then control on a third variable t. In the present example, a statistically significant relationship between x and y no longer exists within one category of the control variable, whereas it is retained in the other.

Such mixed situations are difficult to interpret. Often they force the investigator to reconsider his original ideas and come up with an improved formulation. In the present situation, the frequencies are so small that it is difficult to make a definitive interpretation. Over-all, however, there seems to be limited evidence to the effect that degree of interest (x) and seating position (t) operate independently of one another at least to some extent.

In further exploring the data, let us first examine the percentage of individuals with high grades who are both interested and seated in the first three rows—the two factors most conducive to high grades. Among these eleven students we have eight (or $8/11 = 73$ per cent) with high grades. Of the thirteen students who are not interested and are seated in the fourth to fifteenth rows, two, or 15 per cent, have high grades. Finally, among the nineteen students who have only one factor favorable for high grades, we have 38 per cent with high grades. This great increase in the percentage of high grades, as one factor is combined with another, provides evidence for the independent operation of t and x on y.

In evaluating the technique of three-variable analysis within the context of nonexperimental research, it is apparent that it is possible to apply the idea behind Mill's method of difference by controlling on a series of third variables. Results may be quite useful in understanding the nature

---

[6] The frequencies here make it inappropriate to use the chi-square test. Consequently, the Fisher exact probability test was utilized. For details, see ibid., pp. 96–104.

of the causal process involved. The survey techniques of analysis are analogous to those used in the before-and-after experiment with one control group.

SOME LIMITATIONS OF SURVEY DATA

But there are also important limitations in these survey procedures:

1. In the experiment with randomization, we can effectively equate the experimental and control groups on a large number of variables simultaneously. Within the three-variable analysis procedure for nonexperimental data, however, we only equate the groupings within the two categories of the independent variable on one variable at a time. Thus, it is the experiment that comes much closer to the specification of Mill's method of difference, that the groupings be equivalent on all other factors, than the survey.
2. Within the experiment, events are directly manipulated by the investigator, whereas no such manipulation generally occurs in the survey. Without such manipulation, the survey researcher has little to go on in his attempt to determine the time order of events within a given causal process.

SOME STRATEGIES OF SURVEY ANALYSIS

There are also strategies of research available for easing the impact of these fundamental limitations. Some of these are as follows:

1. Certain statistical procedures too technical for this book, such as multiple and partial correlation and the analysis of covariance, aid the researcher in dealing effectively with more than three variables at a time. If the analysis becomes complicated in this way, however, an incisive theory becomes very important for guiding the researcher within the maze of resulting data.
2. With large samples, it is possible to control on several variables simultaneously, as was illustrated in the case of one control variable. Here, as above, effective theory is needed to interpret the complex results. It seems to be desirable at least to have completed a series of three-variable analyses before moving on to a four-variable analysis.
3. By retrospective questions, or by interviewing respondents over a series of points in time (called the *panel study*), the researcher can learn a good deal about the order in which events occur.
4. In dealing with the limitations noted in (2) and (3) above, perhaps the tool most essential for the scientist is his willingness to make

assumptions about uncontrolled variables and the sequence of events, in the face of his lack of adequate knowledge about them. Without this willingness, he could not make any decisions about the nature of the causal process. For example, it is usually possible, when survey data are involved, that a variable which is treated as an effect of some other variable may actually be a cause of it, or that the two variables might cause one another. Also, many other variables may play important roles in the causal process. They may be involved as intervening variables, or they may lead to the interpretation that the relationships among other variables are spurious. If the investigator is willing to make certain assumptions about the time sequence involved (making use of his general knowledge insofar as possible) and about the lack of influence of other variables that are not taken into account, he can get on with the investigation.[7] In this way he may subsequently find out a great deal more about the time sequence involved, as well as about the role of other variables. If the investigator is unwilling to make such assumptions, if he is overly concerned with the limitations of his study, then he may fail to make any progress whatsoever.

In recent years the above strategies (especially 1, 2, and 4) have been gathering momentum.[7] At this juncture it is difficult to predict where they will lead. They are at the very least getting across a point of view in support of a concern with the interrelationships among propositions as distinct from series of isolated propositions.[8] However, if this point of view is to have an important impact on the conduct of research, it must be applied in conjunction with important or fruitful theories of human behavior. Unfortunately, the methodology involved tends to be somewhat technical, and this militates against widespread usage.

16.5 SOME LIMITATIONS OF MULTIVARIATE ANALYSIS

In Section 15.3 we discussed some limitations of statistical testing; we centered our attention there on tests of significance for relationships be-

---

[7] Some of the econometrics literature having to do with causal models, as well as a development in the literature of mathematical statistics known as "path analysis," provide a basis for these strategies. A few illustrations of this recent work are Herbert A. Simon, "Spurious Correlation: A Causal Interpretation," *Journal of the American Statistical Association,* **49** (1954) 467–79; Hubert M. Blalock, *Causal Inference in Nonexperimental Research* (Chapel Hill: University of North Carolina Press, 1961); Otis Dudley Duncan, "Path Analysis, Some Sociological Examples," *American Journal of Sociology,* **72** (1966), 1–16; and Hubert M. Blalock, "Theory Building and Causal Inferences," in Hubert M. Blalock and Ann B. Blalock (eds.), *Methodology in Social Research* (New York: McGraw-Hill, 1968), Chap. 5.

[8] This supports Camilleri's (op. cit.) emphasis on systematic theory and systematic import.

tween two variables. This section represents an extension of that discussion, where our focus of attention will be on multivariate analysis involving three or more variables. Such analyses are most frequently done in the context of survey data. Sometimes they involve complex technologies beyond the scope of this book, such as multiple and partial correlation, regression analysis, and path analysis. We shall repeat six of the eight subtopics considered in Section 15.3: analysis, mathematical approach, static orientation, scientific orientation, unrealistic assumptions, and passive orientation. As for the other two, context of justification and group emphasis, the ideas presented in Section 15.3 within the context of tests of significance appear to apply equally in the multivariate case.

ANALYSIS

Industrial societies tend to emphasize the material at the expense of the nonmaterial, and we would thus tend to slip into the assumption that the sheer increase in the *number* of variables taken into consideration also represents an increase in the *quality* of the investigation. Yet this is not necessarily the case. By taking more variables into account, we are making a step in the direction of synthesis beyond that of two-variable tests of significance. But the size of the step generally is quite small. In addition to uncovering the existence of relationships between pairs of variables, we are also discovering whether relationships exist among larger numbers of variables. But we still learn nothing about the types of relationships involved. Thus, we are not yet in a position to see how all the variables work together to produce a given result.

MATHEMATICAL APPROACH

Whereas our remarks on the mathematical approach associated with statistical testing would also apply to most kinds of multivariate analysis, regression analysis constitutes an exception. Although the topic of regression is beyond the scope of this book, we can obtain a general idea of the approach involved in order to see what kinds of mathematics are involved.

Most applications of regression analysis have to do with linear regression. On the basis of the available data, a linear equation which can be used to predict the dependent variable from the independent variable(s) is constructed. This equation takes a form we have already discussed within the topic of factor analysis (Section 11.1). The equation from factor analysis reads

$$s = a_1 x_1 + a_2 x_2 + a_3 x_3 + a_4 x_4 \ldots$$

Instead of thinking of the *s* as an individual's test score, the *a*'s as the test's various factor loadings, and the *x*'s as the amounts of various kinds of abilities that he possesses, let us think of this as a multiple-regression equation. Now the *s* becomes the dependent variable, the *x*'s become independent variables, and the *a*'s become a series of weights that are applied to the independent variables in an attempt to achieve accurate prediction of the dependent variable.

Unfortunately, linear equations such as the preceding appear to be far too simple to account for the complexities of human behavior. For example, they are not equal to the task of dealing with simple feedback relationships. They do treat variables as if they had ratio properties, thus representing an advance in utilizing the tools of mathematics, but the approach appears to be overly simple.

STATIC ORIENTATION

Our remarks in Section 15.3 also apply here: multivariate analysis tells us little about the dynamics of relationships. But multivariate analysis, because it represents in some ways an advance over two-variable analysis, by this token may also have greater deficiencies. While representing the kind of technical advances which improve the effectiveness of survey work, multivariate analysis serves at the same time to perpetuate the survey as a key form of data collection and tends to hinder the search for more effective methods.

SCIENTIFIC ORIENTATON

If two-variable statistical tests carry an aura of scientific prestige because of the mathematics involved, then multivariate analysis represents an escalation of this phenomenon. However, as we have indicated in Section 15.3, mathematics is not used in a way which generally can cope with the complexities of human behavior.

UNREALISTIC ASSUMPTIONS

The assumption that, among a set of independent variables, each operates independent of the others is the basis for almost all uses of multiple-regression analysis; there is the additional idea that the separate effects of these independent variables are additive, as illustrated by the equation from factor analysis. This assumption is not made, as it is in the case of statistical testing, simply in order to be able to reject it. The assumption becomes the basis for a formula (the multiple-regression equation) used to predict the dependent variable from a set of independent variables. Our ability to predict accurately from such a formula generally is not very good in the behavioral sciences; part of the reason for this may be that this assumption of independence is not in accord with reality. In order to do better, however, we must learn about the complex ways in which the independent variables are related to one another and to the dependent variable, ways that are less simple than those assumed within multiple-regression analysis.

PASSIVE ORIENTATION

Our view here is similar to that expressed in the preceding paragraph on static orientation: multivariate analysis, by functioning so as to improve the effectiveness of the survey as an instrument for data collection, may also be functioning to divert attention from other modes of data collection, such as field experiments. The problem is one of balance. Multivariate analysis represents a set of specialized techniques that are more effective than their predecessors in improving the benefits to be derived from survey research techniques. However, if we asume that survey techniques, in contrast to other modes of data collection such as the field or natural experiment, already are overemphasized, then ways of improving these techniques can lead to a still greater imbalance.

EXERCISES

1. Make up data to illustrate three kinds of three-variable relationships: (1) a spurious relationship, (2) an intervening variable, and (3) a third possibility. Present your data in tabular form, following the format of the tables in the text.

2. Conceive of a complex set of relationships among five variables, one which seems to be in accord with actual experience (whether personal experiences or research data), and construct a diagram with cause–effect arrows to represent the situation. To what extent can three-variable analysis succeed in uncovering the situation?

3. With respect to Exercise 4, to what extent do you conceive of the different variables as acting independently of one another? To what extent do you see interaction effects, that is, situations where the joint action of several of the variables is more (or less) than the sum of the separate effects of each variable?

ANNOTATED REFERENCES

BLALOCK, HUBERT M. "Theory Building and Causal Inferences," in Hubert M. Blalock and Ann B. Blalock (eds.), *Methodology in Social Research*. New York: McGraw-Hill Book Company, 1968, Chap. 5. The techniques of causal analysis for survey data involving a correlational approach are presented here, including some of the more recent developments. In general, the aims of this mode of analysis parallel those for this chapter, including such goals as the testing for spurious relationships, but Blalock's emphasis is more on the analysis of multiple variables. His focus on causal models is closer to the material in Chapter 17.

HAMPDEN-TURNER, CHARLES. *Radical Man: The Process of Psycho-Social Development.* Cambridge, Mass.: Schenkman, 1970. In Chapter 1, "The Borrowed Toolbox and Conservative Man," Hampden-Turner takes to task eight cornerstones of scientific tradition and method: science and power; prediction, control, and experimentation; the null hypothesis, detachment and technique; science, pure and applied; precesion and invariability; empiricism and physicalism; mathematics and reductive analysis; and value-free science. In later chapters he outlines "an alternative method designed to avoid the injurious aspects" of the tools borrowed from physical science.

ROSENBERG, MORRIS. *The Logic of Survey Analysis.* New York: Basic Books, Inc., 1968. Rosenberg focuses on three-variable analysis, presenting a detailed treatment of the subject. He includes a large number of illustrations throughout the book. This approach is not a correlational one, by contrast with that of Blalock, and thus it complements the latter.

part five
APPLICATIONS OF LOGIC AND MATHEMATICS

More than anything else, Part Five represents an attempt to look to the social science of the future. What emerges may appear to be crystal-ball gazing. Our rationale for this kind of activity is not that our own forecasts are correct; rather, circumstances are such, in social science and outside of it, that it is highly inefficient and impractical not to develop visions of the future.

CHAPTER 17 Some Applications of Logic and Mathematics

17.1 LANGUAGE

THE LANGUAGE OF MATHEMATICS

The language of mathematics is similar in some respects to everyday speech. Two characteristics which seem to be associated with any language are its facilitation of communication and its aid in coping with reality. The language of everyday speech and writing depends on a degree of agreement among its users as to the meanings of words, and in this way the communication of abstract ideas becomes possible. Through its selection of certain concepts as distinct from others, language provides fundamental tools for its users which aid in their dealings with the world. Thus, for example, words are developed which provide labels for those objects that must be dealt with in one way or another by the users of the language. The same holds for the development of labels for the abstract ideas which the users of the language desire to manipulate.

It is within this realm of abstract ideas that the language of mathematics functions. The concept *seven things,* for example, is abstract in the sense that it can be used to designate objects that appear to be completely different. The objects being counted may be countries or mice, yet the one concept *seven things* has sufficient scope so as to apply to both. As with nonmathematical concepts, there is a degree of agreement among the users of this concept and the concept aids in communication between them. Words for numbers as "high" as seven have been developed in some languages but not in others. In the latter it is probable that such concepts would, in the view of the societies involved, have little utility for the styles of life found there. This illustrates the idea that mathematical concepts are similar to nonmathematical concepts in aiding the user to cope with reality. Each language defines those aspects of reality which appear significant to its users, and these decisions vary from one culture to the next.[1]

[1] This idea might be carried further through an exploration of the complex ways in which the values of a given society affect the development of its language. The idea is not limited to the societal level. For example, we can also investigate the development of scientific language in the community of scientists. We can even examine the idea that each individual selects from the available concepts a "private language" which he sees as best serving his own purposes. Such a private language might involve a further specification of the meanings of words than is provided in the vague, generally accepted meanings implied by ordinary usage.

Although mathematical concepts may be quite useful to the non-mathematician, our primary concern here is with the role such concepts play in the community of scientists. The language of mathematics possesses certain special advantages over everyday speech. There is less than total agreement about meanings of words among the users of ordinary language. Words tend to have a wide variety of connotations which vary among different users of the language; thus, the uniformity of usage is limited. Among scientists who communicate in the language of mathematics, however, this difficulty of communication almost completely disappears: mathematics constitutes an international language that is neither vague nor ambiguous.

One reason for the effectiveness of mathematics in the communication process is that it is relatively divorced from the labels or symbols used in everyday speech. This poses the difficulty for the scientist of learning a new language. Actually, this is no small difficulty, and it serves to limit the number of individuals who can effectively communicate in the language of mathematics. But along with this difficulty comes the tremendous advantage of uniformity of usage. Because everyday speech is not involved, the vagueness and ambiguity associated with it are not present either. It is this vagueness and ambiguity which presently plague teachers of the behavioral sciences in their efforts to get across concepts phrased in ordinary language.

Even more harmful for the scientific process is that this vagueness and ambiguity are conveyed among scientists as well. Although a given word may be assigned a specific definition by a given investigator, the definition itself consists of words, each of which has a degree of vagueness and ambiguity. In this way the investigator may unwittingly skirt the central issues as to possible alternative definitions. Ordinary language permits him to avoid making such decisions by hiding in what has been called the *penumbra of vagueness* attached to a given word.

This might be illustrated by a leading textbook's definition of *role* (sometimes called *social role*): "... *a pattern of behavior associated with a distinctive social position*—e.g., that of father, teacher, employer, or patient. Most roles specify the rights and duties belonging to a social position; they tell the individual what he ought to do in his role as father, or teacher, to whom he has obligations, and upon whom he has a rightful claim."[2]

It seems that there is an ambiguity in this definition and that the different meanings implied represent quite different approaches to the research process. In the first sentence the reference seems to be to the uniformity in the behavior displayed by the many different occupants of a given position (for example, the actions which all or most fathers have

[2] Leonard Broom and Philip Selznick, *Sociology* (New York: Harper, 1963), p. 16.

in common). The second sentence, however, refers to the "rights and duties" involved or, in other words, the expectations as to how an individual *should* act or behave as compared with how he actually *does* act. A definition along the lines of the first sentence of the quotation would lead to circular reasoning if we attempted to explain uniformities in behavior by means of a concept of *role* defined in terms of uniformities of behavior. Thus, in attempting to explain the behavior of students in coming to class on time by saying that this is part of the role of students, we would in effect be saying that *students come to class on time because they come to class on time.*

A definition of *role* in terms of rights and duties or expectations does not, on the other hand, lead to such circularity. The expectations of students with respect to the utility of coming to class on time are not the same as their overt behavior, as is indicated by the fact that many students do not conform to this expectation.

Mathematical language forces the scientist to eliminate such ambiguities. The verbal languages are desperately needed for their specific "content" with respect to the explanation of phenomena, but mathematics might well be used to restate nonmathematical propositions and theories. If the original nonmathematical theory is any good, an appropriate mathematical reformulation of it may remove various ambiguities and reveal crucial issues.

This brings us to the second characteristic of the language. The special potential of mathematics for the advancement of science seems to be a function of its high level of abstraction as well as of its utter clarity. We have seen, in discussing propositions and theory, that a high level of abstraction is generally associated with wide scope. Because the concepts of mathematics are so very abstract, we might very well expect them to have considerable scope. As a matter of fact, the scope of mathematics is so great that very often the same kinds of formulations are useful for different sciences. This is the case with respect to probability theory, and we shall see in Section 17.3 an illustration of its use in the reformulation of the theory of choice behavior used in the medical student study.

The clarity of mathematical language, so valuable for purposes of scientific communication, also enables the scientist to deal with complexity. *Theory* has been defined as a system of propositions, and mathematics is particularly well adapted to stating complex relationships among a number of variables in a clear-cut fashion. More important, the use of mathematics encourages the scientist to think in a more systematic way than he ordinarily might. If it is true that theory is the scientist's best tool for the development and testing of explanations and predictions, and that the language of mathematics is a highly appropriate one for stating theory, then mathematics becomes extremely useful for the scientific process.

SOME LIMITATIONS OF MATHEMATICAL FORMULATIONS

Mathematics is not, of course, the only language for stating theory. Statements of theory in ordinary language are not *ipso facto* old-fashioned. The language of mathematics constitutes a tool for further developing a given theory, but if the theory itself is not promising no amount of mathematics can improve it. Mathematics is sometimes mistakenly conceived of as an automatic means for the explanation of phenomena. Sometimes the very complexity and sophistication of the type of mathematics utilized is seen as self-justifying. Yet such complexity can be a disadvantage, for difficulties may emerge in attempts to test a highly complex formulation. Furthermore, although a more mathematically sophisticated formulation might be of interest to a mathematician, this is certainly not a useful criterion for evaluating theory. Mathematical complexity is only a means to the end of formulating statements of the systematic interrelationships among propositions. If this end is as easily served by very simple formulations, so much the better.

THE LANGUAGE OF LOGIC

The language of logic is very similar to that of mathematics. Like mathematics, logic is highly abstract and has no "content" rooted in any particular kind of phenomena. For example, the principle of the excluded middle is that *any proposition must be either true or false.* The statement does not refer to any particular types of propositions, but to propositions in general. Its utility may be judged by giving it specific interpretations and attempting to apply it, as is quite frequently done in many different aspects of the scientific process. For example, it is common scientific procedure to set up a null hypothesis and an alternative hypothesis. A decision to reject the null hypothesis entails a decision to accept the alternative hypothesis. This is an example of the utilization of the principle of the excluded middle, in which the null hypothesis is viewed as being *either* true *or* false. Our assumption, in keeping with the principle of the excluded middle, is that the null hypothesis is either true or untrue, and that if it is untrue then the alternative hypothesis must be true.

But is the proposition that *light illustrates the behavior of particles* true or false? In some situations it is true; in others, false (for example, the phenomenon of the diffraction of light where light illustrates the behavior of waves as opposed to particles). When the principle of the excluded middle is interpreted so that it may be applied to such propositions, it does not seem to hold. Similarly, in mathematics, many of the theorems of Euclidean plane geometry prove false when interpreted so as to apply to the surface of a sphere.

Both logic and mathematics have been used by the sciences in statements of theories. Both are also useful for the methods of science (that is, the methods of determining the nature of reality), where they function primarily within the context of justification rather than that of discovery. According to Cohen and Nagel, "Logic may be said to be concerned with the question of the adequacy or probative value of different kinds of evidence. Traditionally, however, it has devoted itself in the main to the study of what constitutes proof, that is, complete or conclusive evidence."[3] Mathematics, too, has had similar applications in the context of statistical decision making as it applies to the assessment of evidence.

Of course, there is no reason why both logic and mathematics cannot be applied to the context of discovery. Some of the possibilities for this use of mathematics were presented in Section 14.1, in the discussion of statistical decision making. And Kaplan presents one argument for a logic of discovery: "The point is, however, that 'invention' *can* be cultivated. Though the scientific enterprise has a significant element of luck in it, it is not wholly a game of chance, and scientific training surely enhances in some degree the skill of the players. The 'logic of discovery' is, so to say, the strategy of playing the game."[4]

At present there is considerable ferment within the community of behavioral scientists for the utilization of the languages of mathematics and logic in the statement of propositions and theories. This has resulted, in part, from the impact of the electronic computer, which facilitates the possibilities for the development and testing of such formulations. The recent literature in this area is vast, with the emphasis on mathematical formulations.[5] A few illustrations, selected for presentation in Sections

---

[3] Morris R. Cohen and Ernest Nagel, *An Introduction to Logic and Scientific Method* (New York: Harcourt, 1934), p. 5.

[4] Abraham Kaplan, *The Conduct of Inquiry* (San Francisco: Chandler, 1964), p. 16.

[5] Recent publications include Hubert M. Blalock, *Theory Construction: From Verbal to Mathematical Formulations* (Englewood Cliffs, N.J.: Prentice-Hall, 1969); Scientific American, *Mathematical Thinking in the Behavioral Sciences* (San Francisco: Freeman, 1968); David J. Bartholomew, *Stochastic Models for Social Processes* (New York: Wiley, 1968); Otomar J. Bartos, *Simple Models of Group Behavior* (New York: Columbia University Press, 1967); William R. Catton, *From Animistic to Naturalistic Sociology* (New York: McGraw-Hill, 1966); Frank Harary et al., *An Introduction to the Theory of Directed Graphs* (New York: Wiley, 1965); Fred Massarik and Philburn Ratoosh (eds.), *Mathematical Explorations in Behavioral Science* (Homewood, Ill.: Richard D. Irwin and Dorsey, 1965); and S. Sternberg et al. (eds.), *Mathematics and Social Sciences* (The Hague: Mouton, 1965). For the reader who requires a background for dealing with these formal treatments, see, for example, A. D. Aleksandrov et al. (eds.), *Mathematics: Its Content, Methods, and Meaning*, Vols. 1–3 (Cambridge, Mass.: M.I.T. Press, 1969); Martin Gardner, *Logic Machines and Diagrams* (New York: McGraw-Hill, 1958); Samuel Goldberg, *Introduction to Difference Equations* (New York: Science Editions, 1961); M. J. Holt and A. J. McIntosh, *The Scope of Mathematics* (New York: Oxford University Press, 1966); Morris Kline, *Mathematics: A Cultural Approach* (Reading, Mass.: Addison-Wesley, 1962); Abraham S. Luchins and Edith H. Luchins, *Logical Foundations of Mathematics for Behavioral Scientists* (New York: Holt, 1965); Robert McGinnis, *Mathematical Foundations for Social Analysis* (Indianapolis: Bobbs-Merrill, 1965); Scientific American, *Mathematics in the Modern World* (San Francisco: Freeman, 1968); and Chris A. Theodore, *Applied Mathematics: An Introduction* (Homewood, Ill.: Irwin, 1965).

17.2 and 17.3, bear on a theory of choice behavior, and we may look for the degree to which formal statements (logical or mathematical) may aid in its development.

17.2 THE LOGIC OF CHOICE

A DESCRIPTION OF AN EXPERIMENT

Let us examine an experiment on a single individual, which took place under highly controlled conditions.[6] The subject was asked to predict whether a plus symbol or a check symbol would occur on each of 200 trials, and he was instructed to make as many correct predictions as possible. After he made each prediction, he was told which event actually did occur. The selection of each event was determined by a random process, but the subject was not aware of this.

The aim of the experiment was to investigate the cognitive process which led to the subject's predictions of the set of events. The specific technique for collecting data is called the *thinking aloud procedure.* The subject is simply instructed to verbalize as he is performing the task, and the protocols which emerge deal directly with the task.

The cognitive processes involved in the subject's choices proved to be quite complex. The decision-making process seemed to include two major stages: the explanation of the event which had most recently occurred, and the prediction of the next event on the basis of this explanation as well as other factors. Because the subject was not informed that the symbols presented to him were generated by a random process, he assumed that it was in fact possible to "explain" the occurrence of a given symbol. In particular, his cognitive process represented an attempt to understand and predict the behavior of the experimenter, who he believed to be making the decision as to which symbol should appear on a given trial.

AN EXPLANATION OF THE BINARY CHOICE PROCESS IN THE EXPERIMENT

Analysis of the protocol indicated that the subject treated each event as an element in one or another of a set of possible patterns (for example,

---

[6] Julian Feldman, "Computer Simulation of Cognitive Processes," in Harold Borko (ed.), *Computer Applications in the Behavioral Sciences* (Englewood Cliffs, N.J.: Prentice-Hall, 1962), pp. 336–59. For additional work in this area see E. A. Feigenbaum and J. Feldman, *Computers and Thought* (New York: McGraw-Hill, 1963); Kenneth M. Sayre and F. J. Crosson (eds.), *The Modeling of the Mind: Computers and Intelligence* (Notre Dame, Ind.: University of Notre Dame Press, 1963); and W. R. Reitman, *Cognition and Thought: An Information Processing Approach* (New York: Wiley, 1965).

$+ \lor + \lor + \lor \cdots \lor \lor \lor \lor \cdots + + + + \cdots \lor \lor + + \lor \lor + + \lor \lor + +$
. . .). In the first stage of the decision-making process, the subject
selects one of these patterns as the basis for explaining what happened with respect to the event that most recently occurred. Let us
call this the event at trial t, and preceding events will be designated the
events at trials $t - 1, t - 2, t - 3$, and so on. We may diagram the process
whereby the subject arrives at an explanation of the event at trial t as a
series of choices, each of which implies its own set of options or alternatives for future choices. The following is a diagram, adapted from Feldman,[7] of these choices:

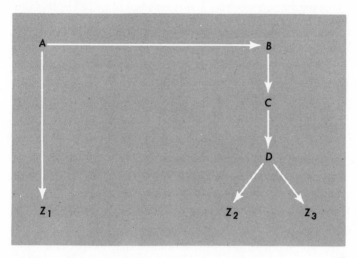

The diagram shows that the subject can arrive at three possible explanations for a given event at trial t: Z_1, Z_2, and Z_3. With respect to
each of these explanations of the most recent event, the subject then
proceeds to determine whether or not he should "guess opposite" to this
explanation during the next trial.[8] This choice process is somewhat more
complex than the explanation process for trial t and will not be discussed
here.

The subject's initial choice (see diagram) occurs at A, where he evaluates the pattern he used in predicting the event for trial t. If the pattern
itself could have successfully predicted the event for trial t, then he
chooses explanation Z_1 (which is simply the explanation that the event
at trial t was an instance of this pattern). For example, if the pattern

[7] Feldman, "Computer Simulation of Cognitive Processes," op. cit., p. 343.

[8] To be more precise, there are three alternatives which are programmed for the subject in
the guess-opposite process: (1) in trial $t + 1$ "guess opposite" to the explanation of the event
at trial t; (2) in trial $t + 1$ "guess opposite" to the pattern which was used as the basis of the
explanation at trial t (here, note that the pattern is not the same as the explanation, for the
latter might be a "throw me off" explanation); (3) use the explanation of the event at trial t to
predict the event at trial $t + 1$.

he used was a progression of $\sqrt{}$'s, and if the event was a $\sqrt{}$, then he retains this explanation. If, however, the pattern could not have successfully predicted the event for trial t, then the subject moves to B, where he evokes those patterns that could have predicted the event successfully, and he focuses on patterns that could have predicted the event at $t - 1$ as well as the event at t.[9]

Having evoked a set of patterns, the subject then moves to C, where he makes a choice among them. He selects that pattern which he selected most often on all the preceding trials, moving to situation D. At D the subject decides whether or not the pattern selected was utilized in his unsuccessful prediction for trial t. If it was not involved in this unsuccessful prediction, then he chooses explanation Z_3 (which is the explanation that the event at trial t is an instance of this pattern). If, however, the pattern selected had just been utilized in the unsuccessful prediction at trial t, then the subject chooses explanation Z_2 (this explanation of what occurred at trial t is that the experimenter tried to "throw me off").

After arriving at an explanation for the event or occurrence at trial t, the subject then goes through a complex series of choices on the basis of which he decides whether or not to "guess opposite" to this explanation. Finally, he arrives at a prediction of a $+$ or a $\sqrt{}$ for the event at trial $t + 1$.

The foregoing explanation of the process through which the subject chooses a $+$ or a $\sqrt{}$ for a given trial was developed by the experimenter on the basis of the "think-aloud" protocols as well as the subject's actual choice of symbols in a series of trials. Whether or not this explanation is correct is not known, but some evidence may be provided by the extent to which it explains the entire series of choices made by the subject. Although in common usage the concept *prediction* refers to events that have not yet occurred, the behavioral scientist sometimes uses it in a different sense, that is, an explanation which reproduces the choices actually made. Thus, successful "prediction," in this respect, is analogous to a high *coefficient of reproducibility* in the context of Guttman scaling.

Although it would have been possible for the experimenter himself to make "predictions" on the basis of the explanation given, together with the "guess-opposite" explanation for each of the 195 trials run (after a preliminary set of five trials), this would have been quite laborious. To make the experiment feasible, an electronic computer was programmed so as to use these explanations in predicting the subject's choice on each trial. Here the computer functioned as a kind of "logic machine," simulating the logical operations of the subject in making his choices.

One potential difficulty in this process arises when a given prediction by the experimenter (or by the computer program) is erroneous. If the

---

[9] It should be noted that the same pattern which led to the unsuccessful prediction at trial t is also evoked if it could have predicted correctly the events of trials $t - 1$, $t - 2$, and $t - 3$.

program's erroneous prediction is assumed by the computer to be the actual choice of the subject, then the original error would be compounded, for the computer would be operating on the basis of incorrect information. The greater the number of errors made, the greater would be the compounding of those errors, and the result would be a highly inaccurate series of predictions.

This difficulty may be avoided by introducing the idea of *conditional prediction*. Whenever the computer's prediction differed from the subject's, the subject's prediction was substituted for that of the computer. Of course, this was still counted as an error for the experimenter's explanation (or the computer program). By this technique, however, no given error was allowed to be compounded into other errors. As a result, when 195 of the conditional predictions of the computer program were evaluated accurately, 193 were correct and only two were incorrect.

It is not only the experimenter's explanation of the subject's final choice of a symbol for a given trial which may be tested, but intermediate explanations as well. For example, one of the three possible explanations that the subject may develop for the most recent event is that Z_1 (that is, the pattern that was the basis for his previous predictions at trial t) actually was the correct pattern. Actual data are available from the subject (based on his "think-aloud" protocol), which indicate whether he in fact came to this conclusion when it was warranted. In 117 out of 120 trials where the pattern previously used would have in fact been the basis for a correct prediction, the subject retains this pattern as the appropriate explanation. This constitutes an intermediate check on the experimenter's analysis.

THE IMPORT OF THE EXPERIMENT

This binary-choice experiment illustrates a number of different points with respect to the language of logic in particular, and the research process and behavioral science theory in general.

1. A rather obvious difference between this logical formulation and a mathematical one is that the former involves very little use of mathematical symbols or mathematical operations. There is one mathematical operation involved in the subject's attempt to explain what occurred at trial t, and this occurs in situation C (see diagram). Here the subject selects one from among a set of possible patterns, and the basis of his choice involves a numerical comparison. In particular, he selects the pattern he had selected most often on all of the preceding trials.

2. The experimenter's explanation of the process by which the subject explained the event at trial t, as illustrated by the above diagram, is very similar to the diagrams of causal processes presented in Section 16.1. The difference has to do with the fact that the present situation does not focus on the process leading to one possible occurrence but, rather, includes

three. In the electric-light example, we were concerned with the process leading to the lamp turning on, and no alternatives were taken into account. Here, however, three different alternatives may occur, as designated by Z_1, Z_2, and Z_3. In the following diagram, we will show only the process leading to the choice of Z_3 so as to demonstrate the relationship between the two types of diagrams:

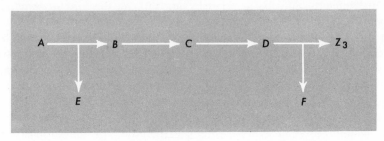

Here *A, B, C, D,* and Z_3 are the same as the situations previously designated by these letters in the Feldman experiment. However, *E* replaces Z_1 and *F* replaces Z_2. Thus, *E* refers to the subject's decision that the pattern which was the basis for his prediction of the event at trial *t was* the correct one to take into account. In order for the subject to move to situation *B,* he must avoid this choice; otherwise, he will come up with explanation Z_1. Also, in moving from *D* to Z_3 a necessary condition is that *F* must not occur. Event *F* refers to the subject's decision that the pattern he selected was just utilized in his unsuccessful prediction of the event at trial *t.*

3. Computer simulation in this example involves moving back and forth between the researcher's explanations and predictions and the data he is attempting to explain and predict. Thus, the fundamentals of this research procedure, in which hypotheses and theories are subjected to test, are no different from those involved in other types of research.

4. This experiment illustrates the testing of a system of propositions, or a theory, rather than one or a series of isolated propositions. The theory involved is quite similar to the theory of choice behavior utilized in this book. This may be understood if the research situation is analyzed for correspondences between the two.

First, the subject is instructed to attempt to maximize his number of correct predictions. Thus, if we assume that this instruction is followed, only one goal on the part of the subject guides his choices. He then makes a series of choices, and each choice would seem to be based on his expectations as to how he might best achieve this goal. In situation *A,* for example, the subject is deciding between two alternatives: Z_1 and *B.* Z_1 is chosen if the pattern he previously chose to be the basis for his choice of a symbol at trial *t* actually proves to have been an accurate basis for his choice. Thus, this pattern was instrumental to the subject's being able to achieve his goal of correct prediction at trial *t,* and the subject seems to make the assumption that it will continue to be effective for trial $t + 1$. On the other hand, if the pattern proves to have been an inaccurate basis for his choice at trial t, he will then move into situation B and proceed to look for other patterns.

It should be noted that the important expectations of the subject seem to have to do with two types of phenomena: (1) his expectations as to which one among several alternatives provides the best chances for achieving his goal of accurate prediction, and (2) his expectations as to what alternatives or options exist in a given situation. We may thus classify the subject's sequence of behavior at each point along the road to final choice of a symbol: (1) his expectations as to the alternatives or options (in situation A, for example, the alternatives are B and Z_1), (2) his expectations as to which among the alternatives will provide the best chances for achieving his goal of accurate prediction (these expectations will depend on the specific criteria he has set up for evaluating the probability that each alternative will lead to an accurate prediction), and (3) his choice among the alternatives which he has set up (with respect to situation A, for example, the subject chooses between B and Z_1).

5. Unlike investigations such as the medical student study, this experiment has special advantages for the uncovering of the time order of events. By means of the "think-aloud" protocol, intermediate states leading up to each choice may be investigated. For example, it is possible to determine whether the subject actually arrives at the explanation which the theory predicts for him. On the basis of such determinations, the theory that applies to different aspects of the causal process may be checked out, and we are not limited to an all-or-none decision as to whether the theory is correct or incorrect.

6. This experiment provides an opportunity to test the theory on a large number of choices by a single individual. In contrast, the medical student study focused on one choice that was made by a large number of respondents. It is rather unusual to test a theory utilizing data from only one individual, but it is possible. The results would, of course, be more impressive if the same computer program were able to predict successfully, in a subsequent series of 195 trials, 193 of them. Nevertheless, the unit of investigation is not the individual but the choice he makes, and the relevant number of units is not 1 but 195. There are both advantages and disadvantages associated with focusing an investigation on one individual. For example, it is entirely possible that the sequence of events may have been relatively unique to that particular individual. Thus, the same program might not work well for many other individuals. The theory, however, is more general than the program. Thus, quite different programs developed for various individuals might have in common the same general theory. For example, individuals may set up different alternatives for themselves and have different expectations as to the impact of choosing a given alternative on the success of predicting the symbol of

trial $t + 1$. Yet, even with such differences, these individuals all might be attempting to maximize expected utility in each of their decisions.

A possible advantage of focusing on the behavior of the individual is that there may be no substitute for getting at the individual's own "definition of the situation,"[10] if we are to explain and predict his behavior. In his presidential address, "Bringing Men Back In," George Homans takes a similar position: "If a serious effort is made to construct theories that will even begin to explain social phenomena, it turns out that their general propositions are not about the equilibrium of societies but about the behavior of men."[11]

7. By conducting the experiment under highly controlled and simplified conditions, the investigator was able to achieve a great deal of closure. A standard argument is that the experimental situation is so "unrealistic" that the results cannot possibly have wide scope. The fallacy in this argument is the assumption that the degree of realism of a situation is determined by its appearance. The scientist's best tool for perceiving reality is comprehensive theory. Thus, when an experimental situation is structured along the lines of such theory, the results may prove to have much wider scope than those stemming from research in everyday settings. The closure that may be achieved in such experimental situations can serve to eliminate those factors that would otherwise confuse the data. Of course, once the conclusions are drawn, they must be tested in everyday settings as well.

8. The degree of success of the experiment with respect to the proportion of the subject's choices that were successfully predicted cannot be ignored. Although the predictions were conditional ones and "backward predictions," the achievement of 193 correct predictions in 195 trials is impressive. Within the context of a pragmatic approach to methods and theory, it is this kind of result that serves to lend weight to the ideas involved in the investigation. If the student of behavioral science is bewildered by the task of locating those researches which are most significant, he might do well to pay close attention to the magnitude of correlations and, in this case, the accuracy of predictions. Although high correlations and accurate predictions may have very little scope and thus be quite trivial, when they are attached to propositions and theories of considerable scope they may be extremely significant.

9. There is an interesting analogy between the experimenter's explanations and predictions, and the subject's explanations and predictions, with the former dependent on the latter. The subject did not, however, verbalize his *general* procedure for arriving at explanations and predic-

[10] The concept "definition of the situation" was introduced by W. I. Thomas in *The Unadjusted Girl* (Boston: Little, Brown, 1923), pp. 41–44.

[11] George C. Homans, "Bringing Men Back In," *American Sociological Review,* **29** (1964), 818.

tions, perhaps because he was not aware of it. The experimenter's theory represents a statement of this general procedure, as checked against the actual behavior of the subject.

17.3   A MATHEMATICAL FORMULATION OF A THEORY OF CHOICE BEHAVIOR

THE GALANTER STUDY AND THE MEDICAL STUDENT STUDY COMPARED

Underlying the approach taken through much of this book is a theory of choice behavior in which the choice among alternatives is viewed as a function of their relative expected deprivations. The formulation of the concept *expected value deprivation* represented an attempt to provide a mathematical statement of the theory within a specific context. Section 12.2 presented some of the work of Galanter on a mathematical statement of the choice process which suggests a different mathematical formulation that might be applied to the medical student data. In this section we shall first summarize the relevant work of Galanter and then proceed to develop its implications for a new approach to the medical student study. In the process, it is hoped that the process of developing a mathematical formulation, as well as the functions of such formulations, will be clarified. Galanter summarizes the purposes of his study as follows:

> The present study was designed, therefore, to discover whether direct measurements of utility and likelihood are possible. The study divides itself into three parts: (1) the measurement of utility; (2) the measurement of likelihood by three methods; and (3) the prediction of choices made by people when we have knowledge of the likelihood and the utility of the alternatives.[12]

His basic proposition is that the probability of choice of a given alternative depends only on the difference in the expected utilities of the alternatives. Thus, for example, Galanter attempts to predict the choices of his subjects as between being given $1 if the sun rises tomorrow and $50 if a penny turns up heads. He measures both the subjective utility of the various amounts of money and the expectations of his subjects as to the likelihood of each of the two events. He then calculates the subjective expected utility of each of the events by taking the product of its likelihood and utility. This product constitutes his estimate of the probability of the choice of each event, and this prediction may then be compared with the actual choice behavior of the subjects.

There are three basic differences between the Galanter approach and that used in the medical student study:

[12] Eugene Galanter, "The Direct Measurement of Utility and Subjective Probability," *American Journal of Psychology,* **75** (1962), 210.

1. The measures adopted by Galanter are based on scores averaged for the group as a whole. Also, he does not attempt to predict the choice of any given individual; rather, he focuses on the *probability of choice* within the group as a whole. For example, the actual probability of choice of a given event is computed as the proportion of times that it was chosen over the alternative choice among all of the subjects. Averaging techniques for the group were also used in the calculation of the utility and the subjective probability of each event. In the medical student study, on the other hand, the values and expectations of each student were computed separately, and predictions of preferences among the medical fields also were made separately for each student.

2. The mathematical formulation of choice as a product of subjective probability and utility differs from the mathematical formulation within the medical student study. There, it will be recalled, the mathematics involved the difference between a given value (utility) and an expectation rating as to the opportunities for fulfilling the value.

3. In the medical student study, a set of ten values was involved in a single decision, that is, preference for the various medical fields. The Galanter study, however, dealt with a number of different types of choices. More important, the Galanter study took into account only the utility of each event as a whole, rather than that of a number of different components. In the medical student study, the differences between value scores and expectations for achieving the corresponding values in a given medical field were summed over the set of ten values. This summed difference score for a given medical field was calculated for each medical student for the medical field in question.

It would seem that each approach has it own special advantages. The medical student study took into account the individual's own definition of the situation, and the measurement of utility was based on a number of values. The Galanter study, on the other hand, employs the concept of subjective probability, which is a possible interpretation of the concept of probability. This interpretation differs from the frequency interpretation, which has resulted in many useful applications in the statistical decision-making process. Whether the axioms of probability will hold for this interpretation, and whether the theorems which follow from them will have useful applications for the study of human behavior, remains to be seen.

A COMBINED FORMULATION

It is possible to utilize an approach which combines the advantages of both of the above orientations. Such an approach could retain the emphasis of the medical student study on performing a separate analysis for each individual while at the same time shifting to a substitution of subjective probability for expectation. It could also be designed to take into account both deprivation and fulfillment, and not merely deprivation alone, as in the case for the medical student formulation. This might be designated as an expected utility formulation, as distinct from calculations of expected value deprivation (EVD).

One expected utility formulation which takes into account both fulfillment and deprivation derives from the concept of "mathematical expectation," an idea which has long been in use by mathematicians and statisticians. We will first illustrate it within the simple context of a gambling game before applying it to the medical student study. Suppose that an individual is trying to decide whether or not to play a shell game where he would be required to guess which of three shells a pea is under. Suppose that if he guesses correctly he receives $10, whereas if he guesses incorrectly he is required to pay $4. The question he might pose is whether he stands to gain or lose in the long run if the game is an honest one and if he makes his choices on a random basis.

For a given choice of a shell under these conditions, the probability that the choice will be correct is one third ($p = \frac{1}{3}$), whereas the probability of an incorrect choice will be two thirds ($1 - p = \frac{2}{3}$). He then has a one-third chance of gaining $10 ($V_1 = \$10$) and a two-thirds chance of losing $4 ($V_2 = -\$4$) on each guess that he makes. One might say, consequently, that his average expected gain for each choice he makes is one third times $10 plus two thirds times $4, or $pV_1 + (1 - p)V_2$. This comes to $\frac{1}{3} \cdot \$10 + \frac{2}{3} \cdot (-\$4)$, or $3.33 - \$2.67$, or $0.66. Each guess then is worth $0.66 to him, and he could expect to gain somewhere in the neighborhood of $66 by making 100 guesses.

The same idea might be illustrated within the context of the medical student study by calculating the mathematical expectation for a given student where only one medical field and one value are concerned. Let us assume that a given student is very interested in research ($V = 3$) and, correspondingly, he is negatively oriented to an equivalent extent to being deprived of research activities ($-V = -3$). Let us also assume that he feels there is a zero probability ($p = 0$) of being able to do research in general practice and, conversely, he is certain ($1 - p = 1$) of being deprived of research activities in this field. Then the expected utility of entering general practice, taking only the value of research into consideration, is

$$pV + (1 - p)(-V) = pV - (1 - p)V = (0)(3) - (1)(3) = 0 - 3 = -3$$

Of course, a calculation of the expected utility of entering general practice would involve repeating this procedure for each of the values which are relevant and then taking the grand total. This might be expressed symbolically as

$$\text{Expected utility} = \Sigma \, [p_i V_i - (1 - p_i) V_i]$$

We may now inquire as to how the expected utility formulation compares with the EVD approach utilized in the medical student study. Although the expected utility formulation has not yet been applied to the medical student data, we may nevertheless evaluate it in a preliminary fashion on the basis of a few examples. Two questions in particular seem most immediate: Is the expected utility approach sensitive to deprivation, as was the EVD formulation? Is it sensitive to fulfillment, a capacity which was not inherent in the EVD model?

The answer to the first question is already implied in the preceding illustration of the procedure for calculating expected utility. There the situation involved an individual with great interest in research and no hope of being able to do research in general practice. The expected utility calculated was -3, with the fact that this quantity is negative indicating deprivation. In addition, the model can differentiate between different degrees of deprivation. Thus, the expected utility model seems to retain the advantages of the EVD formulation in that it is sensitive to deprivation.

As for the second question, let us consider the same individual's reaction to the field of pathology taking only this value of research into consideration. Let us assume that he is certain ($p = 1$) of being able to do research as a pathologist and, conversely, that he feels there is no chance ($p = 0$) of being deprived of research activities in this field. Then his expected utility of entering pathology where only the value of research is involved is

$$pV - (1 - p)V = (1)\,(3) - (0)\,(3) = 3$$

By yielding a positive score of 3 in a situation where only fulfillment (vs. deprivation) is involved, this model seems to be sensitive to fulfillment. A further check on this sensitivity would be to note whether the model distinguishes between differential degrees of fulfillment. Let us assume that the same student has a medium degree of interest in continued learning while practicing ($V = 2$) and is certain that opportunities for learning would be available to him as a pathologist ($p = 1$). Then the expected utility pathology has for him with respect to this one value is

$$pV - (1 - p)V = (1)(2) - (0)(2) = 2$$

Thus, the model does seem to differentiate between different degrees of fulfillment by yielding the scores of 3 and 2 for situations of fulfillment of a strong interest and fulfillment of an interest of medium intensity.

This sensitivity to degrees of fulfillment was not possessed by the EVD model. In the case of a student who is very interested in research ($V = 3$) and who is certain of being able to do research as a pathologist ($E = 3$), the expected value deprivation involved would be $V - E = 3 - 3 = 0$. If the student had medium interest in continued learning ($V = 2$) and certainty that opportunities for learning would be available in pathology ($E = 3$), the expected value deprivation would be zero also. This is because only those situations where V is greater than E enter into the calculation of EVD.

The idea of mathematical expectation, which is the basis for the expected utility formulation, is one of a class of mathematical models of decision making which has been designed for situations where "risk" or probabilities are involved. Luce and Raiffa distinguish between models having to do with decision making under conditions of certainty, conditions of risk, conditions of uncertainty (where the probabilities cannot be estimated), and conditions where there is a mixture of risk and uncertainty.[13] Although numerous mathematical models have been developed for each of these types of situations, they generally involve procedures for maximizing fulfillment and/or minimizing deprivation.

It is extremely easy to find many flaws in any one of these formulations. The EVD formulation, for example, completely omitted taking fulfillment into account. In addition, the value and expectation measurements were limited to a three-point scale, whereas some degrees of interest or degrees of expectation may have been many times as great as others. Furthermore, measurements were based on the written statements of respondents, and these may have differed from the actual situation. In spite of these and other deficiencies, however, the EVD formulation yielded an index which proved to be very closely related to the probability that students would rate a given field unfavorably. This seems to indicate that there are some advantages involved in testing what appears to be an extremely rough model rather than abandoning the test altogether for want of superior data.

The expected utility model might be tested in the same way as was the

---

[13] R. Duncan Luce and Howard Raiffa, *Games and Decisions* (New York: Wiley, 1957). Game theory generally has to do with situations where there is a mixture of risk and uncertainty, linear programming provides an example of decision making under certainty, whereas statistical decision making has to do with situations where there is uncertainty as to the state of nature.

expected-value-deprivation model. Here the procedure would be analogous to that described for the EVD formulation in Chapter 1. A determination could thus be made as to whether students with low expected utility for a given field tend to rate it unfavorably, and whether students with high expected utility for a given field tend to rate it favorably.

It should be noted that the expected utility formulation involves a sum of products. In the discussion of ratio scales in Chapter 12, it was stated that ratio scales are quite useful in that they enable the investigator to formulate product relationships among variables. Thus, the development of ratio scales of subjective probability and utility would be quite valuable in testing this formulation.

One important limitation of this formulation is that it is essentially static, that is, it does not take into account sequences of preliminary choices which result in a given choice. Its advantage is that it does present a theoretical formulation of the mechanism of any given choice. The logical formulation within the binary-choice experiment illustrates a great concern with such sequences. There, however, although rules are presented whereby a given choice is made, the development of these rules themselves must be placed within the framework of a general theory in order to achieve a more comprehensive explanation. To the extent that such static and dynamic formulations are put together effectively, the behavioral scientist will be able to explain processes occurring over a period of time.

IMPLICATIONS FOR MEASUREMENT

If a given mathematical formulation of a theory proves to be effective, it may provide considerable aid in the measurement process itself, for effective theory can provide us with an understanding of the measurement situation. For example, let us assume that the expected utility formulation is effective in predicting an individual's choice if we know the initial conditions involved (that is, his relevant goals or values and his subjective probability as to opportunities for achieving them within each of the available alternatives). Then it would be possible to measure indirectly the individual's values if we knew both his subjective probabilities and his actual choices.

More specifically, there are three classes of variables: values, subjective probabilities, and choices. Ordinarily we might be interested in using the first two to explain and predict the third, but we can also use the second and third in order to predict or measure the first. This might be done so as to provide an indirect method of measuring those values about which considerable social desirability or social undesirability exists. This procedure is an example of a construct-validation procedure (see Section 10.2). The approach need not be circular, for we need not turn right around and use the values thus measured to "predict" the same choices that were used to infer the values. We can use these measures of values to predict other choices which are made by the individual. As in the general case of construct-validation procedures, the efficiency of such measurements is evaluated on the basis of the accuracy of such predictions.

17.4 A PARADIGM FOR THE CONSTRUCTION OF OPEN SYSTEMS

INTRODUCTION

Although poetic license does not traditionally extend to the scientific community, perhaps the tradition can be changed. In this last section I (note the stylistic change from *we*) would like to speculate with as much freedom as possible about what the approach taken in this book seems to point toward.

A recurrent theme is an open-systems orientation which stresses the interrelatedness among all phenomena as well as their dynamic qualities. Applying this idea to the research process, we may note that any research procedure employed by the scientist implies, directly or indirectly, the entire universe in which the scientist is immersed. Most probably he is aware of only a minute portion of the universe surrounding him. His many taken-for-granted and implicit assumptions prevent him from examining and questioning the nature of this universe. And because he knows very little about where he is, he is unable to find a direction which will take him where he would like to go.

Research procedures are types of human behavior and, as such, employ the heart, the head, and the hand. In my effort to explore the implications of the open-systems approach, I shall wander into three areas, correspondingly: the fictional world of Null-A, a nonfiction world in which the paradigm implicit in the world of Null-A can be analyzed via such devices as Model AN-A, and the Yarlan Zey construction of reality, which employs the Berger and Luckmann approach to the construction of reality.

THE WORLD OF NULL-A[14]

Gilbert Gosseyn, thirty-four; residence, Cress Village, Florida; height 6 feet, 1 inch; weight, 185 pounds; no special distinguishing marks; alive in A.D. 2560; potentially immortal; possessor of an extra brain which has yet to be developed; participant in the games which determine position

---

[14] *The World of Null-A* (New York: Berkley Medallion, 1970), was constructed by A. E. Van Vogt in 1948. In these few pages I have attempted to enter into the spirit of that world, employing key ideas contained in Van Vogt's classic. The footnotes these pages contain illustrate my belief that art and science should be joined.

and wealth in the A world of Earth or even, for those who win top honors, the opportunity to move to the Null-A world of Venus. . . .

Who is Gosseyn? How can he harness the potentially infinite power in his brain? How much time does he have left before he and his world are destroyed? How does his personal struggle relate to the dynamic of evolution in the universe as a whole? What is the role of the Semantics Institute on Korzybski Square?[15] If Gosseyn is a pawn about to be queened, who are the players of the game. . . .

Gilbert Gosseyn, you are everyman. Your extra brain exists in every normal human brain. Your search for your identity, like your search for the nature of the universe, will be a never-ending one. You will have to find out for yourself how much time is left. You can be infinite if you so choose. You are the leading edge of the universe You have the potential power to control the evolutionary process. You must not depend on others for solutions. You must not depend on some future situation. You must act NOW AND FOREVER-MORE to structure development in yourself and in your environment.

I can give you some pieces of the puzzle to help you get started, but the puzzle is continually expanding and your knowledge of the known relative to the unknown will continually decrease unless you keep moving. And you had best move at an accelerating pace, because the puzzle is expanding exponentially. The most important piece for you in the present situation, Gilbert Gosseyn, is for you to understand the nature of the A or Aristotelian elements within yourself. This is why Marcuse's emphasis on negation[16] is so vital. Gosseyn, your every action reveals that, however much you believe otherwise, you live almost completely in the Aristotelian world. It is a world of scarcity,[17] spurious culture,[18] and nonsituational ethics.[19]

You endlessly search outside of yourself for the levers of power, but these are only mirages. Whenever your wheels do spin, and that is seldom enough, they hardly ever touch the ground. You are alive only intermittently, and for very brief periods, just as the "brilliant" scientist or "innovative" artist whose creative work encompasses only a minute portion of his existence. You are

---

[15] See Alfred Korzybski, *Science and Sanity: An Introduction to Non-Aristotelian Systems and General Semantics* (Lancaster, Pa.: Science Press, 1933).

[16] Herbert Marcuse, *Negations: Essays in Critical Theory* (Boston: Beacon, 1969).

[17] The centrality of scarcity for an understanding of human societies as they are, and a view toward a different kind of society, is sketched in Manfred Stanley, "Nature, Culture and Scarcity: Foreword to a Theoretical Synthesis," *American Sociological Review,* **33** (1968), 855–70. For some other views relating to scarcity see Richard Kostelanetz (ed.), *Beyond Left and Right: Radical Thought for Our Times* (New York: Morrow, 1968); R. Buckminster Fuller, *Ideas and Integrities* (New York: Phaedra, 1963); Charles Hampden-Turner, *Radical Man* (Cambridge, Mass.: Schenkman, 1970); and B. F. Skinner, *Walden Two* (New York: Macmillan, 1948).

[18] Edward Sapir, "Culture, Genuine and Spurious," *Culture, Language and Personality* (Berkeley: University of California Press, 1962), pp. 78–119.

[19] Joseph Fletcher, *Situation Ethics: The New Morality* (Philadelphia: Westminster, 1966).

a divided self[20] *living in a divided world.*[21] *You separate mind from body, science and art from one another, and both from life,*[22] *self from other, past from present, and both from future. You fear death, change, life, others. You hate youself. Most damaging of all, you are convinced that you can do no better. You are sure that you are right.*[23]

As you move into the world of Null-A, Gilbert Gosseyn, you will learn to convert failure into success, achieve altruism through selfishness,[24] *expand your consciousness to include more of the universe and the infinity of time. You will learn to construct yourself and your environment in accordance with your situational needs.*[25] *You will continually accelerate your expansion of subjective time. You will become a living example of the renaissance of Renaissance man.*

MODEL AN-A

One way in which the scientist can take a body of ideas seriously is to formalize them via some logically complete system of axioms and theorems, or at least to outline the character of such a formalization. In the present context, I shall attempt a formalization of the combined worlds of A and Null-A in which we live. However, because I am interested in a paradigm for the construction of *open* systems, my paradigm will be open as well. There will be no attempt made to move toward a logically complete system of ideas. Indeed, some evidence from work in the foundations of mathematics indicates that it would be impossible to attain a logically complete paradigm of the degree of complexity to be discussed.[26] I can start with a series of axioms without any attempt to be formal with respect to definitions and without any attempt to derive theorems from these axioms:

1. All systems and elements of systems are causally interrelated.

[20] In addition to the vast literature on alienation, reference is made to R. D. Laing, *The Divided Self* (New York: Pantheon, 1969).

[21] See the literature on bureaucratic organizations, for example, Harold L. Wilensky, *Organizational Intelligence* (New York: Basic Books, 1967).

[22] See Rudolf Steiner, *Goethe as Scientist,* trans. by O. D. Wanamaker (New York: Anthroposophic Press, 1950); Maurice Stein and Larry Miller, *Blueprint for Counter Education* (Garden City, N. Y.: Doubleday, 1970); and W. T. Jones, *The Sciences and the Humanities: Conflict and Reconciliation* (Berkeley: University of California Press, 1967).

[23] See T. W. Adorno et al., *The Authoritarian Personality* (New York: Harper, 1950); and M. Rokeach, *The Open and Closed Mind* (New York: Basic Books, 1960).

[24] Erich Fromm, *Man for Himself* (New York: Holt, 1947).

[25] Peter L. Berger and Thomas Luckmann, *The Social Construction of Reality* (New York: Doubleday, 1967).

[26] See Ernest Nagel and James R. Newman, "Gödel's Proof." *Scientific American* (June, 1956), 221–30.

2. New elements are at specified time intervals being formed.
3. All systems undergo transformation at specified time intervals.
4. All systems are capable of incrementing (or decrementing) the goal fulfillment they are able to attain over any specified time interval.
5. A system's ability to achieve its goals depends on (a) its ability to integrate information relevant to its own goals, (b) its ability to integrate information relevant to the goals of its environment, (c) its environment's ability to integrate information relevant to the environment's goals, and (d) its environment's ability to integrate information relevant to the system's goals.
6. Ability to integrate information relevant to given goals is dependent on ability to integrate information about how to integrate information.
7. Ability to integrate information about how to integrate information relevant to given goals is dependent on ability to integrate information about how to integrate information about how to integrate information relevant to these goals.
8. And so on.

The infinite sequence of axioms illustrated here has many parallels. For example, in the language of science we speak of theory as encompassing statements about phenomena, but we also speak of methodology as encompassing statements about how to discover and obtain evidence for statements about phenomena. By going one step further, we can discuss metamethodology, which has to do with statements about how to discover and obtain evidence for statements about how to discover and obtain evidence for statements about phenomena, and we can continue to meta-metamethodology, metametametamethodology, and so on *ad infinitum.*

Another example comes from the calculus. The first derivative of a function at a particular point in time refers to its slope at that point, or the rate of change of the function at that instant. If we plotted the distance traveled by an auto against elapsed time, then the derivative at any instant would be the auto's velocity at that instant. Moving to the second derivative, here we are concerned about the rate of change of the rate of change, or, with reference to our auto, its rate of acceleration at any given instant. We may speak of an infinite number of derivatives and, correspondingly, rate of change of acceleration, rate of acceleration of acceleration, rate of change of rate of acceleration of acceleration, and so on.

A third example is analogous to the first and has to do with computer programs. We can devise computer programs for accomplishing given objectives, and we can also construct programs which themselves generate programs for accomplishing objectives. Similarly, we can conceive of the construction of programs for the construction of programs for the construction of programs for accomplishing given objectives, and so on.

The final illustration will be somewhat more extended; it is related to the third example in that it has to do with computers. In Section 9.4 a detailed illustration of computer simulation was presented, with the illustration kept extremely simple to enable a thorough mathematical treatment. In the present context what is called for is a model which can manage incrementally greater complexity, and consequently I shall simply sketch out a block diagram and avoid any mathematical treatment.[27]

Figure 17-1 presents a block diagram of AN-A. Beginning with the rate and level variables (valves and rectangles), let us examine them in the context of Axiom 4. There are four basic loops here: the system's inter-

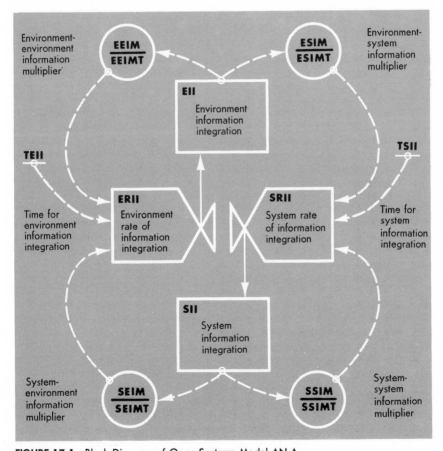

FIGURE 17-1   Block Diagram of Open-Systems Model AN-A

[27] The approach here, as in Chapter 9, is based on techniques developed by Jay W. Forrester in his *Industrial Dynamics* (Cambridge, Mass.: M.I.T. Press, 1961), *Principles of Systems* (Cambridge, Mass.: Wright-Allen, 1968), and *Urban Dynamics* (Cambridge, Mass.: M.I.T. Press, 1969). For some perspective on the various approaches to simulation see Geoffrey Gordon, *Systems Simulation* (Englewood Cliffs, N.J.: Prentice-Hall, 1969).

action with itself (lower right), its interaction with its environment (lower left), the environment's interaction with itself (upper left), and the environment's interaction with the system (upper right). These four loops correspond to the four components of Axiom 5. If we interpret the kind of information in AN-A as relevant to goal fulfillment, then we can use this computer simulation to help us draw out the logical implications of Axiom 5 in particular situations. Thus, the simulation brings us closer to an assessment of how well this axiom applies to a given situation.

As for the block diagram's relation to Axiom 1, the interrelations among all systems and system elements are structured in the diagram. Concerning Axiom 4, the diagram is set up in such a way that increments or decrements occur over the time intervals specified by the two constants, Time for System Integration of Information (TSII) and Time for Environment Integration of Information (TEII). With respect to Axiom 3, the system and environment are transformed at intervals which depend on TSII and TEII, and continual transformation can be approached as a limit provided that the time intervals become progressively shorter.

Thus far we have not dealt with Axiom 2, the formation of new elements, or with Axioms 6 and beyond. These are of special importance because they are the basis for the open-ended character of the model. To understand their relation to the block diagram we must examine the four auxiliary variables or multipliers which appear on the corners of the diagram. Within the present context, it is not important for the reader to know the technical way in which these multipliers work so long as he understands that they function as residual categories. Let us assume that there is always more to learn about any given phenomenon, and that at any given time the researcher is able to conceptualize only a limited number of factors operating within the system and within its environment. The multiplier auxiliary variables are set up to summarize all unspecified factors involved in each of the four loops.

By using these auxiliaries appropriately, the block diagram can provide an adequate interpretation for Model AN-A. Suppose that, during the research process, we learn more about the system as well as the environment and, as a result, are able to pull out and specify factors which formerly were lumped into the residual auxiliaries. Then Axiom 2, which specifies the formation of new elements, is satisfied. Axioms 6 and beyond specify the nature of additional information that is required. The situation is analogous to that for Axiom 2: information about how to integrate information can be gathered in successive investigations, and the same is true for information about how to integrate information about how to integrate information, and so on.

Thus far the discussion of Model AN-A has been a relatively formal one. In a less formal vein, the model defines the universe in such a way that infinite development is possible for any system, whether that system be Gilbert Gosseyn in the year 2560 A.D., an individual alive today, a social system, a biological system, or even a physical system. The way it works is analogous to that for any deviation-amplifying system,[28] such as the accumulation of capital in industry, the evolution of living organisms, processes producing mental illness, or other vicious circles like that relating to the culture of poverty or the escalation of international or marital conflict. A more mundane example is a snowball rolling down a hill: the more snow it picks up, the faster it rolls; and the faster it rolls, the more snow it picks up.

With respect to the block diagram for Model AN-A, the higher the level of system information integration (other things being equal), the greater is the system's rate of information integration, and vice versa (other things being equal). To the degree that Gilbert Gosseyn, or everyman, defines himself as infinite, he will be accepting the paradigm for infinite development defined by the block diagram. Of course, it is as yet an open question as to how well such acceptance by a human system, whether an individual or a group, will actually produce incremental development. Model AN-A, and the block diagram providing a particular interpretation for it, has yet to be tested experimentally. The statements in italics in the preceding discussion of the world of Null-A are based on the assumption that this model is in fact a valid one, and they proceed from that point. *If* the model is correct, *then* we can expect Gosseyn, as a result of the incremental process which could be produced by the model (other things being equal), to become "the leading edge of the universe," to "learn to convert failure into success," to "continually accelerate" his "expansion of subjective time," and many other things as well.

We might note the importance of the time constants in distinguishing among different kinds of systems. For example, a physical system such as the solar system can take billions of years before information feedback can be produced via the evolution of living things; a human being can develop information feedbacks, and change on the basis of this experience, far more rapidly. But, as in the advice given to Gosseyn, he might open himself to changing for only minute portions of his existence, or he might learn to structure himself as an open system "now and forevermore."

THE YARLAN ZEY CONSTRUCTION OF REALITY

We can talk about the integration of information, or even about the integration of information about the integration of information, but such a discussion is too abstract for an understanding of how to test Model AN-A. For a more concrete understanding, let us turn to another science fiction story, Arthur C. Clarke's *The City and the Stars*.[29] Diaspar

---

[28]Magoroh Maruyama, "The Second Cybernetics: Deviation-Amplifying Mutual Causal Processes," *American Scientist,* **51** (1963), 164–79.

[29](New York: Harcourt, 1956).

and Lys are the last cities on earth, a billion years in the future. Diaspar is a domed city, controlled by a vast computer which structures a static way of life for its inhabitants. They have a deep fear of the unknown, of leaving the city, of change; in other words, they are like everyman.

The inhabitants amuse themselves with dreamlike adventures which have total realism for them. They are presented with dream stimuli which feed directly into their nervous systems and produce the same sensations as actual experiences would. In this way, the people of Diaspar undergo an enormous variety of experiences without any risk to themselves. This and a great many other comforts were provided by Yarlan Zey and others when the city was founded.

A psychologist from Lys devises a technique which he hopes will conquer the fear of leaving the city of Diaspar, and he puts it to work on Jeserac, the individual from Diaspar who has come closest to conquering this fear:

> Obediently, Jeserac followed Yarlan Zey into the building, his mind a receptive, uncritical sponge. Some memory, or echo of a memory, warned him of what was going to happen next, and he knew that once he would have shrunk from it in horror. Now, however, he felt no fear. Not only did he feel protected by the knowledge that this experience was not real, but the presence of Yarlan Zey seemed a talisman against any dangers that might confront him.[30]

Jeserac was under the impression that he was going through a dream adventure, and that he was accompanied by a rather powerful protector. Actually, it was no dream that he experienced. When he awoke he found himself outside of Diaspar, and his fear was conquered.

The cities of Lys and Diaspar constitute quite different cultures: the former emphasizes the humanistic, individualistic tradition, and the latter is oriented toward the positivistic, analytic tradition. In the former, man developed the power of mind to an extremely high degree, even to the point of being able to communicate by mental telepathy. In the latter we see the development of a computer culture with fantastically sophisticated computer aids in every aspect of life, yet the individual remains to a great extent conformist and passive. Jeserac's ability to depart from Diaspar is symbolic of the joining of these two cultures, or, in language closer to some of the concerns expressed in this book, the cultures of theory and research or qualitative and quantitative orientations or synthesis and analysis or the field experiment and the laboratory experiment. It is the separation of such cultures which appears to be a key obstacle to development, whether it be research development or development of other types.

The Yarlan Zey technique takes a step beyond the uncovering of the

[30] Ibid., p. 267.

individual's fundamental assumptions or paradigms. It takes these into account, but at the same time it gives him a choice which enables him to go beyond his limitations. Movement out of Diaspar is "not real," and the presence of Yarlan Zey is "a talisman against any dangers." In this way the balance is shifted so that Jeserac is able to make a choice leading to his development while at the same time his fears are taken into account. Once this choice is made, a displacement of goals can result. The new goal, leaving the city and learning about the civilization of Lys or about other aspects of the universe, can come to represent an important fulfillment for many other goals of the individual. Moreover, negative consequences formerly associated with leaving the city may fail to materialize. This process of goal displacement can be illustrated by many findings from social science:[31] for example, the rigidification of bureaucracies,[32] the secular shift from early Calvinism to later Calvinism,[33] the change from interest in salvation to interest in achievement,[34] the shift from achievement to success,[35] the iron law of oligarchy,[36] the shift from sect to church,[37] the displacement of the goal of community development in favor of the accomplishment of some immediate task,[38] and the displacement of concepts.[39]

Almost all of the preceding displacements involve a certain narrowing of the perspective of the individual or group, a movement away from the city of Lys and toward the city of Diaspar. None of them involves a definite movement toward an open-systems orientation, toward building bridges between the cultures of Lys and Diaspar. It is the latter with which I am concerned here. I believe that the process necessary for this kind of goal displacement works in the same way as the previously cited displacement. What is required to accomplish this is, first of all, the uncovering of a system's fundamental paradigms which reveal its basic goals and, second, a restructuring of the system's choices so that it has more to gain by moving toward an open-systems orientation than by moving away from it.

[31] For a discussion of the literature on goal displacement see Bernard S. Phillips, *Sociology: Social Structure and Change* (New York: Macmillan, 1969), pp. 133–37, 287–98, 372.

[32] Robert K. Merton, "Bureaucratic Structure and Personality," *Social Theory and Social Structure* (New York: Free Press, 1949), Chap. 5.

[33] Richard H. Tawney, *Religion and the Rise of Capitalism* (New York: Harcourt, 1926).

[34] Max Weber, *The Protestant Ethic and the Spirit of Capitalism* (New York: Scribner, 1958).

[35] Leo Lowenthal, "Biographies in Popular Magazines," in William Petersen (ed.), *American Social Patterns* (Garden City, N.Y.: Doubleday, 1956).

[36] Robert Michels, *Political Parties* (New York: Free Press, 1949).

[37] David O. Moberg, *The Church as a Social Institution* (Englewood Cliffs, N.J.: Prentice-Hall, 1962).

[38] Roland L. Warren, *The Community in America* (Chicago: Rand McNally, 1963), pp. 330–31.

[39] Donald A. Schon, *Invention and the Evolution of Ideas* (London: Social Science Paperbacks, 1967). (Formerly published as *Displacement of Concepts*.)

This final section of the book itself constitutes an illustration of the Yarlan Zey technique for the construction of reality. In the opening paragraph I asked the reader to grant me poetic license and help me "to speculate with as much freedom as possible." This is analogous to the structuring of a situation for Jeserac where he believed he was merely engaging in a dream adventure. The adventure in this section also has to do with a journey between the culture of the computer and the humanistic cultural tradition. I might now reveal explicitly, as I already have implicitly, that I believe this kind of speculation to constitute a more important reality than a nonspeculative approach to the research process, at least in the context of the present state of social science and of the universe. I believe that a serious imbalance exists in social science, and in human affairs generally, which overemphasizes the analytic at the expense of the synthetic, the material at the expense of the ideational, the group norm at the expense of the individual's creative development. If such an imbalance does indeed exist, then the kind of information we need—the kind of reality that is most important for us—is that which will enable us to build bridges between Diaspar and Lys.

EXERCISES

1. What can we learn from the language of mathematics and logic to aid us in the process of scientific communication generally, that is, communication with words as well as numbers?

2. Perform the binary-choice experiment on a subject who has not read about it and, on the basis of a series of trials, construct a model that you think might be able to predict his pattern of choices.

3. Test your predictions in an additional series of trials. Interview the subject in an attempt to learn about the sources of your errors, and reconstruct the model on the basis of this interview.

4. Write a short science fiction story within which you portray an open-systems view of some aspect of the scientific process.

5. Develop a block diagram of a closed-systems model which would contrast with Figure 17-1.

ANNOTATED REFERENCES

SCIENTIFIC AMERICAN. *Mathematics in the Modern World.* San Francisco: W. H. Freeman, 1968. This collection of articles from the *Scientific American* includes pieces on "Innovation in Mathematics," "Probability," "Geometry and Intuition," "The Foundations of Mathematics," "Paradox," "Symbolic Logic," "Gödel's Proof," "The Evolution of the Physicist's Picture of Nature," "Mathematics in the Social Sciences," "The Theory of Games," "The Mathematics of Communication,"

"Computer Logic and Memory," "The Uses of Computers in Science," "System Analysis and Programming," "Cybernetics," and "Man Viewed as a Machine."

STEIN, MAURICE, and LARRY MILLER. *Blueprint for Counter Education*. Garden City, N.Y.: Doubleday & Company, Inc., 1970. The authors' general aim is a new approach to education. Going through their material—which includes three very large wall charts, many tables of contents from interesting books and magazines, and an emphasis on the ideas of Marcuse and McLuhan—is the kind of experience which can easily broaden one's perspectives.

VAN VOGT, A. E. *The World of Null-A*. New York: Berkley Medallion, 1970. This edition includes a new introduction by the author describing reactions to his book over the years and summarizing his philosophy in part as follows: "In *World*, we have the Null-A (non-Aristotelian) man, who thinks gradational scale, not black and white—without, however, becoming a rebel or a cynic, or a conspirator, in any current meaning of the term. A little bit of this in the Communist hierarchies, Asia and Africa in general, and our own Wall Street and Deep South, and in other either-or thinking areas . . . and we'd soon have a more progressive planet."

Index of Names

Adams, Richard N., 166n.
Adorno, T. W., 377n.
Aleksandrov, A. D., 361n.
Angell, Robert, 148n.
Aristotle, 14n., 98
Ashby, Ross W., 5n.

Back, Kurt W., 12n.
Balderston, F. E., 171n.
Bales, Robert R., 165, 165n., 166, 211n., 239n.
Bartholomew, David J., 361n.
Bartos, Otomar J., 361n.
Batten, Thelma, 281
Bauer, Raymond A., 16n.
Beals, Ralph L., 83n.
Becker, Ernest, 37
Becker, Howard S., 166, 166n., 167
Benfer, Robert A., 317n.
Berelson, Bernard, 64n., 308n.
Berger, Peter L., 10n., 37, 377n.
Beshers, James H., 171n.
Black, Max, 72n.
Blalock, Ann B., 97n., 124, 307n., 350n., 353
Blalock, Hubert M., 97n., 124, 307n., 350n., 353, 354, 361n.
Blau, Peter M., 5n.
Blumer, Herbert, 8n.
Boguslaw, Robert, 85
Bondurant, Joan V., 306
Bonjean, Charles M., 205n.

Borgatta, Edgar F., 50, 50n., 250n.
Borko, Harold, 171n., 233, 362n.
Braybrooke, David, 39n.
Brodbeck, May, 39n.
Bronowski, J., 14n., 85
Broom, Leonard, 358n.
Bross, Irwin D. J., 306
Brown, Robert, 281
Bruyn, Severyn T., 8n., 168n.
Buchler, Ira R., 227n.
Buckley, Walter, 4n., 44n.
Burtt, E. A., 12n.

Camilleri, Santo F., 326, 334, 334n., 350n.
Campbell, Donald T., 144n., 145n., 201n., 288n.
Cattin, George E. G., 329n., 361n.
Chaney, Richard P., 317n.
Chapple, E. D., 166, 166n.
Chardin, Pierre Teilhard de, 6n.
Chave, E. J., 239n.
Cherafas, Dimitris N., 171n.
Cicourel, Aaron V., 12n., 208
Clarke, Arthur C., 189, 381
Cohen, Morris R., 103n., 104n., 361, 361n.
Comte, Auguste, 14n.
Conway, Freda, 307n.
Coombs, C. H., 217n.
Couch, Arthur S. 211n., 239n.
Crittenden, Kathleen S., 11n.

Index of Subjects